21ST CENTURY
GAME DESIGN

21ST CENTURY GAME DESIGN

CHRIS BATEMAN

RICHARD BOON

CHARLES RIVER MEDIA, INC.
Hingham, Massachusetts

Publisher: Jenifer Niles
Cover Design: Tyler Creative
Cover Image: © 1989 Suzanne Treister

CHARLES RIVER MEDIA, INC.
10 Downer Avenue
Hingham, Massachusetts 02043
781-740-0400
781-740-8816 (FAX)
info@charlesriver.com
www.charlesriver.com

This book is printed on acid-free paper.

Chris Bateman and Richard Boon. *21st Century Game Design*.
ISBN: 1-58450-429-3

Library of Congress Cataloging-in-Publication Data
Bateman, Chris Mark.
  21st century game design / Chris Bateman and Richard Boon.
    p. cm.
  title: Twenty-first century game design.
  Includes bibliographical references and index.
  ISBN 1-58450-429-3 (pbk. : alk. paper)
  1. Games—Design and construction. 2. Video games—Design and construction.
  3. Computer games—Design and construction. I. Title: Twenty-first century game design.
II. Boon, Richard, 1973- III. Title.
  GV1230.B38 2005
  793.9—dc22

                              2005006412

Printed in the United States of America
05 7 6 5 4 3 2 First Edition

CHARLES RIVER MEDIA titles are available for site license or bulk purchase by institutions, user groups, corporations, etc. For additional information, please contact the Special Sales Department at 781-740-0400.

Contents

Acknowledgments

The authors would like to extend their grateful thanks to Ernest Adams; Erwin S. Andreasen; Owain Bennallack, editor of *Develop* magazine; John Burns at Halliwells; Neil Bundy; Ian Chard; Dylan Cuthbert and James McLaren at Q-Games; Lizzie Haines; Stephen Hey and everyone at Head First; Nicole Lazzaro at XEODesign; Richard Leinfellner at Electronic Arts; Dave Morris; Hirofumi Motoyama; Matt Mower; Jenifer Niles and Lance Morganelli at Charles River Media; Rhianna Pratchett; Brian Robertson and Alexia Bowers at Ternary Software; Kevin Saunders; Adrian St. John; and Adria Smiley.

We would also like to offer grateful thanks to Lawrence Schick's *Heroic Worlds* (Prometheus Books, 1991) for its insightful and exhaustive history of tabletop role-playing games; to Moby Games (www.mobygames.com) for their invaluable record of video game details; the Killer List of Videogames (www.klov.com) for their comprehensive list of arcade games; and to everyone who participated in the three surveys and scores of case studies during the research phase that lead to the DGD1 model being developed.

Preface

The veteran game designer and artist Paul Jaquays, who is currently working on the art for *Age of Empires III* at Ensemble Studios, and also worked on a number of early table-top, role-playing games and numerous video games with Coleco, was often asked how he got into such an unusual line of work. After spending some 10 years pondering this question, he said, "I'm still at a loss for an adequate explanation. I think it's just that I'm not qualified to do anything else."

A certain mystery still surrounds game design, and although much has been written on the subject, the formal study of game design practices in a definite sense is still in its infancy. Since professional game design is just a little over a century old, we can hardly be expected to have come to grips with every aspect of a field that dips its toes into both art and science, and much that has been written either takes a very global view, and is therefore somewhat vague on the specifics, or a very detailed view, and is therefore slightly parochial in its focus.

In many ways, this book is merely a polished record of the debates and discussions that have grown out of the working partnership of creative minds at International Hobo Ltd (ihobo for short). The company was formed to combine the talents of game design and narrative in one place, with an eye to letting the methods fuse organically. Certainly, ihobo is one of the few game design companies in existence with a philosophy of game design that is founded largely on subjectivity, rather than objectivity, which is curious and unusual. We have tried not to fall into the easy trap of dogma and recognized that most discussion is involved in providing or clarifying the language used in description. As Wittgenstein observed, words do not have absolute meanings, but rather the meaning of a word is how it is used.

We have always been inspired by Japanese game design, in part because of the natural elegance that the majority of Japanese video games display. The games of *Treasure* and *Takara*, for example, manage to be rewarding and entertaining despite being developed on a budget that many U.S. game developers would spend on their E3 convention presentations. However, it is likely we will never see a definitive book on game design from a Japanese author, because when Japanese game designers do publicly discuss their methods, they display a kind of holistic thinking that defies decomposition into methods, and what the Western audience seems to crave is precisely that—a mechanistic approach that can be acquired or emulated.

The philosophy of Zen Game Design, which is introduced at the start of this book and goes on to silently shape its structure throughout, is perhaps our attempt to express our impressions of what sound game design practice should be about and was doubtless inspired by our own bastardized impression of what underlies Japanese game design practice. It was particularly gratifying to have the original article on Zen Game Design translated into Japanese (by Q-Games President Dylan Cuthbert), because it allowed discussion with many Japanese observers of the games industry that otherwise would not have been possible.

The DGD1 (Demographic Game Design 1) model of play types grew directly from the application of Zen Game Design. Once we had determined that understanding the needs of the audience was an essential step to understanding the motivation for game design, we knew we had an obligation to conduct research into the needs of that audience because so little research had been previously done, or at least, published openly. There are suggestions that certain companies have detailed audience models that are used internally, but if this is the case, they are not discussed publicly.

We hope that a reader of this book finds it complementary to other game design books—that while other books talk about how to design a video game, this book teaches *why* to design a video game (or any other kind of game) and how to design for a specific audience. We also hope that it might provide a missing link between the process of design and the people whom that design ultimately benefits—the players of games, in their many guises, and the developers and publishers of games, whose livelihoods depend on satisfying the needs of those players.

If people working in the games industry sometimes seem defensive about their jobs, it is perhaps because games are often considered a lower form of media, not worthy of the same esteem that is reserved for fiction, film, and theatre, although this is doubtless a prejudice born of the apparent youth of the medium of video games, and of a fundamental failure to recognize the importance of play in all its many forms to culture and society—although the work of Roger Caillois tells a very different story.

If game designers, like Paul Jaquays, are at a loss to determine how and why they have ended up committing their lives to the craft of game design, they need only turn to the wisdom of Toru Iwatani, the creator of *Pac-Man*. At GDC 2004, he ended his talk by stating his simple philosophy on the importance of game design: "You were born to give people enjoyment. It is very important."

Introduction

By Ernest W. Adams

You are holding in your hands a groundbreaking and important new work in the theory of videogame design. It is, as far as I know, the first time a book on design has attempted to understand the player's desires and motivations in an orderly fashion; to move beyond rules of thumb, hidebound conventions, and what "everybody knows" about gamers. *21st Century Game Design* approaches some of interactive entertainment's most compelling problems in an entirely new way. In this book we take the extraordinary step of examining the personalities of the players themselves, and we then extrapolate from those personality types to arrive at a coherent theory of design. To understand why this is important, we need to look back into our history, and see how the videogame business got to where it is today... and what went wrong along the way.

THE SHADOW OF THE PAST

The earliest computer games were not "designed" in any formal sense; they were just written. They were built in the 1960s, back before the microprocessor was invented, and when people said "computer" in those days, they meant a mainframe: a hulking machine in a sealed room, tended by engineers in lab coats. But the first computer games were written by those same engineers for their own amusement. A programmer would hack out a few hundred, or at most a few thousand, lines of FORTRAN or BASIC code and share it with his friends. Computer games were entertaining, but no one thought there might be an industry in them. Writing them was often as much fun as playing them. Since all the players were other programmers, opening up the code and tweaking it after the first few play-throughs was a normal part of the gaming experience.

When personal computers appeared, they were initially purchased by hobbyists—early adopters, in marketing terminology. These were technically inclined, computer-literate people who were expected to program their own machines and enjoy doing it. They began by porting the original mainframe computer games onto their own systems. The culture of sharing, modifying, and hacking together new games for the fun of it spread from the workplace to the home, and from a few hundred specialists to hundreds of thousands of people.

That was the genesis of computer gaming. It was a wonderful, joyous time, a time of innovation and experiment. It defined the way we think about creating interactive entertainment. It established precedents that continue to influence the videogame industry even now, nearly forty years later. And like the aftermath of a really great party, we've been paying for the damage and mopping up the mess ever since.

FOR WHOM DO WE DESIGN GAMES?

The relaxed attitude of the early game developers, of creating games primarily for themselves, and partly just for the fun of creation, is still prevalent in the videogame industry today. Even though it's now a multi-billion-dollar business employing thousands of people, our creative drive is largely guided by passion and instinct rather than professionalism and planning.

There's an old, old dilemma that every writer faces: Do I write for myself, or do I write for my audience? Creating for yourself, expressing yourself however you feel inclined to do so, is the mark of an artist. Artists receive a certain respect in the Western world, but they often starve, too. Creating for an audience, trying to please the masses, is the mark of an entertainer. Yet, entertainers sometimes are thought of as hacks, cranking out work for the money, who don't deserve the same respect as an artist. But they're the ones who make a steady living.

Despite the indisputable fact that the game industry builds games for an audience—the customers who will buy them—most of us in the business still think of ourselves as artists rather than entertainers. On the programming side, the work doesn't pay as well as other high-tech industries; you can make a lot more money programming for defense contractors, or consumer software companies, or engineering firms. On the content side, creating artwork or music for a videogame clearly offers more freedom than doing it for advertising or for some company's PR department. When you take into account the inescapably lower pay, the greater aesthetic freedom, and the greater respect that artists get over entertainers, there is a natural inclination to see ourselves as artists, and this further reinforces that idea that we should really be making games for ourselves. We're not doing it for money, so we must be doing it for love.

This situation would not matter much if the demographics of the game industry matched that of the population at large; but they don't. Among game developers, young men predominate by a wide margin. There are comparatively few women, and almost no one over fifty. Most developers are white, middle-class, and based in western and northern countries (with the notable exception of Japan). South Americans, Africans, South and Southeast Asians, and the peoples of the Middle East and Mediterranean rim are so underrepresented among game developers as to be distinctly unusual when one does appear at a game conference or trade show.

The result has, predictably, been thirty years of games built by young white western men for other young white western men. These games reflect the culture, worldview, and indeed prejudices of their makers, and often don't appeal to people outside that particular demographic. The market has become supersaturated with these games, while other demographics go unserved.

And even the "young white western men" market is not really well understood. Not all young men are alike. They prefer different challenges. They have different amounts of money and time. In eight years of working for Electronic Arts, I never once saw a really thorough, properly-conducted market survey. Our understanding of our players was based on guesswork and hunches.

HOW SHOULD WE DESIGN GAMES?

Videogames are frequently compared with movies, and there are a few surface similarities. Games are light entertainment purchased by people with leisure time to spare and money to spend on it. They entertain people using pictures and sound. Some of the crafts required to make a movie are similar to those required to make a videogame, particularly as regards creating the look, sound, and mood of the work. Yet there are far more differences than there are similarities, not least of which is that games are interactive, and that they require software engineering to build. A movie is, in essence, a strip of film playable in any cinema projector. A game is a piece of software playable only on a certain type of computing hardware—and there are hundreds and hundreds of such devices. All movies are viewed the same way: by sitting still, facing a screen, and paying attention. All games are played in different ways: the player's interaction with the game varies considerably depending on its content and design.

Games exist in a variety far more vast than movies ever could, from tiny little keychain toys like the *Tamagotchi* up to massively-multiplayer persistent worlds played by tens of thousands of people at a time. Some are played by individuals alone; some by pairs; some in teams. Some are cooperative, others are competitive. Some require extraordinary physical dexterity to win, and test no higher brain functions at all. Others require extraordinary intelligence to win, and require no physical skill at all.

Hollywood has had nearly 100 years to work out how to produce movies, and because all movies are delivered by the same machinery, they have become very good at it. The videogame industry has had far less time to learn how to design a much more mutable product. Because games are so manifold, it has proven extraordinarily difficult to determine how a game should be designed. The design work required for a large, narrative-driven game on a personal computer is almost entirely different from the design work required for a wacky, coin-operated driving game in a video arcade. There is simply no standard way to go about it.

THE ESSENTIAL CHALLENGE

These, then, are two of the most critical questions the videogame industry finds itself facing today: for whom do we design games, and how do we do it? These are issues that *21st Century Game Design* seeks, for the first time, to address in a serious way. The answers are not simple; this book is not entitled "Design Your Own Videogame in Five Easy Steps." Rather, it's a thorough exploration of an important subject that the game industry *must* come to understand if it is to survive the major changes that lie ahead. Read it with close attention. You will be rewarded.

Part I

Audience

Before we can learn about game design, we must learn about the audience for games. All cultures play games—those games vary considerably, but all share certain common traits [Caillois58]. Many games are cultural artifacts passed down by word of mouth, and from parents to children through early play. The notion of a game (or at least of structured play) might date back thousands of years, but the notion of a game designer is a comparatively recent one.

Before the twentieth century, the idea that someone could make a living from creating tools for entertainment would have been strange, and in fact, George Parker (probably the world's first game designer) had to attempt to sell his first game to confused book publishers, before finally being encouraged by his older brother, Charles, to self-publish. Parker Brothers came into existence in 1888 and was a huge success. Throughout the early 1900s, dozens of games were released, some of which—such as the card game *Pit* (Parker Brothers, 1903)—are still available today. But it was not until the company acquired Charles Darrow's *Monopoly* (Parker Brothers, 1935) that games truly found a mass market audience. *Monopoly* went on to sell more than 100 million copies [History05], more than double the sales any video game has achieved to date [GameState03].

Although much has been written on the subject of game design as a technical process, very little of what has been written has touched upon the fact that games exist primarily to satisfy the needs of an audience. The first five chapters of this book serve to discuss the nature of game design in the context of an audience and go on to discuss specific audience models, and in particular the DGD1 demographic model, which is the first detailed audience model produced specifically to inform game design decisions.

1 Zen Game Design

WISE BLIND ELEPHANTS

"Five wise, blind elephants were discussing what humans were like. Failing to agree, they decided to determine what humans were like by direct experience.

"The first wise, blind elephant felt the human and declared, 'Humans are flat.'

"The other wise, blind elephants, after similarly feeling the human, agreed."

WHAT IS GAME DESIGN?

It would be tempting to think that it is readily apparent what the process of game design involves, but anyone who has looked into it has learned that if you ask one hundred people to define game design, you will get one hundred different answers.

Rather than attempt to force a consensus (an endless and fruitless task), for the purposes of Zen Game Design, we shall invent a definition:

Game Design is the process of coordinating the evolution of the design of a game.

Game design components can come from a number of different participants, including the producers, the programmers, and the artists, as well as the game designers themselves. The game designer's task is sometimes to create missing components, sometimes to integrate conflicting components, and sometimes to ensure that all the components combine to create the desired gameplay experience. This task exists for the entire length of the development process; very rarely does the designer's job end before the game goes to master.

WHAT IS ZEN GAME DESIGN?

Zen Buddhism is a branch of the Eastern religion in which the underlying message is implied rather than stated. Indeed, one of the key concepts in Zen Buddhism is that enlightenment cannot be expressed in words, because you must make a leap beyond the literal—it must be experienced, not learned.

It also includes the idea that there is no objectively correct and definitive perspective on anything—all experience is relative.

This idea forms the basis for Zen Game Design.

The Principles of Zen Game Design

Zen Game Design is built on two basic tenets, which can be summarized:

1. There is no single method to design.
2. Game design reflects needs.

These are the short forms of the principles. There is also an implied "zeroth" tenet:

0. There are methods to game design.

This caveat might seem trivial, but some people have no appreciation for the work of the game designer or believe that the distinction between a game designer and a programmer is irrelevant. It might be true than some programmers can carry out game design, but it is also true that some programmers can draw. That doesn't mean there is no distinction between programmers and artists.

THE FIRST TENET: THERE IS NO SINGLE METHOD TO DESIGN

Depending on your perspective, this principle seems either abundantly obvious or blatantly incorrect. Remember, even though someone might hit upon a good method for game design, that fact does not mean that the method is applicable to all cases, that it will always be relevant, or that it is equally useful with all types of games.

The long form of this principle is as follows:

The more methods you explore, the more options you have.

This is the nub of the concept. If you use one game design method, you have only one way of looking at a problem. If you have explored a dozen different game design methods, you have 4,096 (that is, 2^{12}) different ways of looking at a problem! (This statement is supposed to be evocative, not to be taken literally.)

The more different game design methods and philosophies you study, the closer to an infinite set of game design choices you get.

Seven Varieties of Design Methods

When we talk about "the design," what we are really referring to is the design documentation. This is roughly equivalent to an abstract specification in industrial software development and offers the same advantages. Even though the design documentation is almost certainly maintained by a single individual (usually the game designer), design isn't the sole prerogative of the game designer by any stretch of the imagination. It's the game designer's role to *coordinate* the design process.

We could summarize more ways to approach game design, but the following represent seven common methods. For each, a grossly simplified expression of the method is given.

First Principles

A game that is developed from first principles takes a long view of the design process. The steps could be described as follows:

Goals → Game World Abstraction → Design → Game

Using this method, you start by determining what you want to do, and then you determine the nature of your game world abstraction. Only when you know the nature of the intended game world abstraction do you proceed to design and then implementation.

Clone and Tweak

This is perhaps the most common design method in use. The steps could be described as follows:

Existing Design → Modified Design → Game

In essence, you pick an existing game (generally someone else's), adopt the pre-existing game world abstraction, and then modify it to suit the needs of the "new" game.

It's quicker and easier than creating a whole new design concept and for this reason is quite appropriate to many short time-budget games projects, and for sequels. Why start from scratch when you can learn from your previous abstractions and improve upon them? However, prestige products (also know as *AAA games)* are generally expected to achieve more than a simple reworking of previous game designs.

Meta-Rules

Some game designers attempt to produce a set of *meta-rules* to inform design, often with the goal of provoking debate. The implied method is generally as follows:

Meta-rules → Design → Game

Two very different examples of a meta-rule approach are Noah Falstein's "The 400 Project" [Falstein01] and Ernest Adams' "Dogma 2001" [Adams01].

"The 400 Project" is involved in identifying "rules of game design" and ascribing to them a hierarchy of precedence so that some rules trump other rules. The approach can produce some interesting discussions that can help inform design decisions, which is probably the greatest value of this method.

"Dogma 2001," by contrast, was not intended as an all-encompassing design method, but rather as a mental (and perhaps pragmatic) exercise for game designers to provoke original thought and return the game design focus to the design, and away from technical issues.

Any collection of meta-rules can be a useful method to employ, provided you recognize that these "rules" are not universal laws, but rather formalised observations. It is also doubtful that any design process can proceed using only this method.

Expressing Technology

In developers without an in-house designer, design can often be more about finding roles for new software technology. *Quake* (id Software, 1996) is an example of a game that demonstrates the use of this method. The method can be expressed simply as follows:

Technology → Game

Often, this method is combined with a Clone and Tweak approach. It's not a very interesting method from a design point of view, but it can be useful—although your technology has to be top-notch if you are going to produce something worthwhile.

The Frankenstein Approach

When you have to abandon your first design and start from scratch after you've already produced a sizeable chunk of software or art, the Frankenstein approach comes into its own. *Conkers Twelve Tales* becoming *Conkers Bad Fur Day* (Rare, 2001) is a good example by all accounts, and *Half-Life* (Valve, 1998) also seems to have made use of it. The method works principally as follows:

Materials → Design → Game

Like many methods, it generally works in concert with other methods. A game designer might be involved in producing an entirely new game world abstraction, or it might be a simple case of a well chosen Clone and Tweak.

Obviously, this method is primarily used to rescue a project in trouble, but it can also be used to produce a new game from existing materials by bringing in a new game designer to reorganize and abstract a new design from the existing materials.

Story-Driven Design

Games such as the classic text adventure *The Hobbit* (Melbourne House, 1982) and more recent adventures like *Broken Sword* (Revolution, 1996) and *Shenmue* (Sega, 2000) use a method in which the story to be told drives forward the design process. The method can be expressed as follows:

Narrative → Design → Game

Although this has been used mostly with adventures, any game with a plot can benefit from the use of this method.

Note that the narrative can be generated by the employment of a variety of different methods. One of particular note is *design-integrated narrative*, a first principles approach which can be expressed as follows:

Goals → Game World Abstraction → Design-Integrated Narrative → Game

Here the designer (possibly with the aid of a writer) identifies both game and narrative goals as an initial step, produces a game world abstraction to support those goals, and finally develops the narrative and game designs in parallel.

Iterative Design ("Design by Committee")

Under the right circumstances, iterative design can be a very powerful method, expressed briefly as follows:

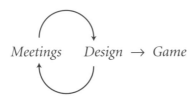

Meetings   Design → Game

Using this method, the development team creates a design version, holds meetings to revise the design, and then repeats until the game is complete or the budget is exhausted.

It can produce excellent games. It can also cause projects to overrun time and cost budgets and get cancelled. Historically, many more projects are in the latter category than in the former. In short, be very cautious about using iterative design as your core design method.

THE SECOND TENET: GAME DESIGN REFLECTS NEEDS

Why should it be that there is no single, ultimate solution to the game design dilemma? It is because every game is experienced by more than one person. Perhaps if you were creating a game that only you would play, you could develop a single, perfect design method—provided of course your tastes don't change...

The long form of this principle is as follows:

Game design must be egoless, balancing the desires and needs of all participants.

The idea that the game designer must be egoless might come as a shock to some, especially since many game designers hide a secret belief that they are the greatest game designer in the world. (However, unless your credit cards read "S. Miyamoto," this is unlikely to be the case.) But to really understand this principle, we need to look at who are the participants in a game project.

Participants and Advocates

The notion of a *participant* describes anyone with an interest in the project—it could be the development team, someone with a financial stake in the project (such as the publisher), or the audience. All these people participate in some portion of the game's life—both before and after release.

However, it is self-evident that it is impossible for every participant in a game to be involved in the design process. Because of this fact, certain participants function as *advocates* for groups of participants. For example, the external producer generally acts as the advocate for the publisher.

Saying that the game designer's role should be egoless is in effect saying that the game designer doesn't reflect their personal needs in the design process; they act as an advocate for *all* participants to the best of their ability. They do this at the design level, while the producer does this at the production level. In this way the role of producer and game designer are closely related, but they are not identical.

To be a good game designer is therefore to listen to and comprehend the needs of the many different participants in the development process.

Seven Varieties of Participants

Who participates in a game project?

The Audience

The audience's goal is to enjoy the game, and whatever else you do, you must satisfy this participant! Since you cannot truly know the audience's attitudes to a game before it is released, you need models to allow you to make informed decisions.

The most basic audience model in use is as follows:

"All game players think like me."

This is entirely useless unless you are the only person who is going to play the game. More sophisticated models recognize demographic groups and attempt to learn the tastes and needs of these groups, for example:

Casual, Hardcore

> Basic demographic split

Hardcore, Cool Gamer, Mass Market

> EA demographics

New Hardcore, Lifers, M&M's, Generation Next, Social Gamers, Golden Gamers
> Bennallack demographics [Bennallack02]

Focus groups can help provide feedback from the audience as well—but it must be mediated intelligently. The goal of a focus group is to assess audience response—not to yield control of the design to a dozen strangers!

Since you generally have no formal advocate for the audience in a typical game design process, the onus might fall upon the game designer alone to attempt to fulfil this role.

Publisher (Advocate: External Producer)

The publisher's goal is to get the best return on their investment—*and it is never too late for a publisher to pull the plug if they will not get a return on their investment.* The usual advocate for the publisher in the development process is the external producer; their role is to represent the needs of the publisher in terms of reducing the cost of development and maximizing the profit (since both these work towards a better return on the publisher's investment).

Some developers resent the publisher's involvement (or interference) in the development process, but this is generally because the external producer is trying to usurp control of the design process. When an external producer acts wisely, as an advocate for the publisher's needs, there is not a problem.

Just in case, developers are advised to follow the lead of U.K. development studio Steel Monkeys and have a clause in their contract allowing them to dismiss the external producer if they are unsatisfied. Getting the right advocate for the publisher's needs makes the whole process progress more smoothly.

Developer (Advocate: Producer)

The internal producer mirrors the role of the external producer, acting as an advocate for the developer as a whole. The developer's goals vary. They want to get money for salaries, certainly, and they might (but not necessarily) want to turn a profit as well. But for the most part, the developer's goal is to professionally produce a game, so meeting milestones and satisfying the publisher are inherent goals.

From the producer's point of view then, the developer's interest in the design is that it should be achievable, and as project status changes, changes in the design might be required. It is then the game designer's role to adapt to these changes.

Programmers

The goal of the programming team is to implement the game, and as such, they need the power to interact with the design and ensure that it is realistically implementable. In many cases, the programmers are also representatives of the audience, but, like focus groups, this does not mean that they should dominate the design process. Neither should their views be ignored.

It is desirable for there to be an advocate for the programming team as a whole (the lead programmer, usually). Issues that the programming team need to report can then be advocated on their behalf, which is more efficient than each programmer trying to influence the design process individually, although this is less of an issue with smaller teams.

Artists

The artists parallel the programmers and also benefit from an advocate (a lead artist) to bring forward their issues. The producer should be able to turn to the artists for advice on art and animation issues in the same way they can turn to the programming or design team for advice on their specialities.

Marketing/PR

The goal of the marketing department is to sell the game to as many people as realistically possible. This can mean being an advocate for the audience, but more often it means ensuring that the game is a product that can be marketed.

Like it or not, the marketing and PR teams are important participants in modern game development. With this idea in mind, it is desirable for them to have an advocate in the development process, rather than having them try to make changes to the game for marketing purposes when it is realistically too late to do so.

Since few marketers are design-literate, the game designer or producer sometimes has to act as an advocate on behalf of them. The important point is that you have dialogue between marketing/PR and the development team at some level.

License Holder

These days, more and more games have an extra participant: the license holder. The license holder's goals are to ensure that their brand gains something from the game, and also (like the publisher) to make money from it.

The situation is parallel to marketing—the license holder should be represented in some form, and the producer or game designer should be an advocate for them when necessary. Once again, keeping dialogue open throughout development is preferable to showing the finished game to the license holder and then being forced to make changes when they are most expensive. It is always cheaper to fix problems at the design level, and therefore always preferable to resolve issues earlier rather than later.

Example of Participants

An example can serve to clarify the concept of participants and advocates. Consider a hypothetical game and the design issue of save games. Assuming a basic demographic split model, you can see the following model with respect to save games:

Casual audience: They want to be able to save anywhere, any time, because they are fitting game playing into their life and want to be able to pick it up and put it down.

Hardcore audience: They are willing to play for long periods of time, and their interest in save games is that the save mechanism does not destroy the challenge of the game.

Programmers: Their chief concern is that the save mechanism be technically feasible. The relevant data to be saved depends on the game world abstraction, so it is worth considering the required functionality of save games at an appropriate early stage and then acquiring the programming team's approval of the intended solution.

Developer/Publisher: With respect to save games, which are usually not a major drain on development resources, the developer and publisher act as advocates for the perceived audience for the game. They can do this crudely by imitating what other companies have done or in a sophisticated manner by studying the market.

Artists/Marketing/License Holder: With respect to this issue, these participants have no special role, and do not need to be advocated.

The game designer, having looked at the needs of the participants, is thus better informed to make a decision on how the save game mechanism should be designed.

RETURN TO THE WISE, BLIND ELEPHANTS

At the start of this chapter, we told the parable of the five wise, blind elephants who, wondering what humans were like, tried to learn by direct experience. The moral of this story is that an individual's perspective dramatically affects their opinions on all things.

You cannot learn objectively about anything—including design. You can only be aware of your limitations and be willing to talk to (and more importantly *listen to*) the other participants in the design process.

By learning many different methods, the game designer has a varied toolkit; by learning the needs of many different participants, the game designer has a balanced outlook. Somewhere in between the two lies Zen Game Design, and the goal of making better games for everyone.

2 Designing for the Market

In This Chapter

- Demographic Game Design
- Market Clusters and Audience Models
- Market Vectors
- Design Tools for Market Penetration
- Phases of Market Penetration
- Conclusion
- Endnotes

Why is game design often overlooked as an important factor contributing to game sales? Perhaps because when most people in development companies talk about "good game design," they mean "game design that produced a game I really like." This sort of subjective validation of game design is of no use in business, which thrives on repeatable methods based around capturing a target audience—the market. Unable to see the profit resulting from "good design"—especially since many allegedly well-designed games fail commercially—most businessmen ignore design entirely.

Design is not suggested to be the only (or even the primary) factor in the sales of a game. Marketing, for example, is hugely important in making a product visible in a crowded market. Similarly, the sales of a game depend greatly upon the budget for development. A game developed on a budget of $100,000 should not be expected to achieve sales figures equivalent to a game developed on a budget of $5,000,000. However, mechanisms such as word of mouth transmit individual opinions of a product, opinions that will be swayed by the design content of the game.

Therefore, we face a great need to make game design relevant to the business side of the game development process. Once the ragtag market has stabilized, we will have plenty of time to pursue the artistic side of game development, but for the time being, that is a luxury we cannot afford. We would not see inventive film-makers like the Coen Brothers were it not for commercially motivated film makers like Spielberg and Bruckheimer, because the commercial success of a medium clears the way for artistic expression, not the other way around.

DEMOGRAPHIC GAME DESIGN

A first step is to consider a criteria for success—what is a successful design? Notions such as elegance, a criteria famously applied to the design process by Ernest Adams, are great aspirational concepts, but less useful for business purposes. Systemic production rules, such as Noah Falstein's "400 Project," provide neither a success criteria nor aspiration and are useful mainly as a means of provoking discussion.

The concept of *demographic game design* is that game design inherently targets an audience, and therefore the success criterion for a design is how effectively it satisfies the needs of that audience. This factor is not directly related to sales figures and is not intended as a means by which to consider the success of the game as a whole—only the success of the design. If the target audience is satisfied by the game (which can be determined by appropriate sampling techniques), the design can be considered a success.

However, before these criteria can be applied we must know the demographics that are available to be targeted, so the first step in demographic game design is to study the audience. If the game designer is to act as a player advocate in the development process—as if they are an elected politician reflecting the diverse needs of their constituency—they must first acquire a useful audience model.

A Warning on Statistics

It has often been said that you can make statistics prove anything you want, and this is true—provided the people you are talking to lack the critical faculty to see the flaws in the presented argument. Nonetheless, statistical principles are a vital part of modern business and science. Quantum mechanics, which all modern computing depends upon, is essentially statistical in nature, and even the concept of "species" is not a Platonic ideal, but a Gaussian distribution of diverse life forms arranged into clusters, which we choose to term "species" only by convention [1].

The most important thing to remember when dealing with statistics of any kind is that showing a correlation (a connection between two events, details, or tendencies) does not prove causality; it is merely a clue to something interesting. For example, in one famous incident a statistician found a statistically significant correlation between babies and storks in Switzerland. Storks were consistently nesting on houses with newborn children. This fact did not prove that babies were brought by storks, of course, and on investigation it was discovered that the houses with newborn babies were kept warmer than other houses. This extra warmth attracted the storks. The lesson is that statistical correlations tell you nothing of the underlying causal mechanisms.

The other important aspect of statistics is that statistical data about a group tells you nothing about individuals in that group. For example, it is well known that the majority of college students drink alcohol, but this statistic does not allow you to know whether any given college student drinks alcohol. Reasoning about the general tells you nothing about the specific.

The advantage of statistics is that whatever does not average itself out to insignificance in a given set of data is a tendency that can be counted on. For example, statistical analysis has demonstrated to the movie industry that roughly 50% of the audience of a profitable film return to see a sequel, allowing for strategies involving producing cut-price sequels for short-term gain.

MARKET CLUSTERS AND AUDIENCE MODELS

The notion of a *market cluster* (or *market segment*) originates in marketing. In recent years, with the advent of narrowcasting channels such as specialist TV stations and personal e-mail, cluster analysis has fallen out of favor in marketing, but the technique still has value in other disciplines. The basic principle is to analyze a data set containing information on a particular group of people and look for common traits that when taken together define a coherent group or cluster.

For example, the vacation travel market identified three distinct clusters: the demanders, whose priorities are exceptional service; the escapists, who want to get away and relax; and the educationalists, who want to see new things, experience new cultures, and so forth. These categories emerged from a cluster analysis on data taken from a pool of vacation makers; this data was then sorted by a clustering procedure. Note that the categories were named *after* the cluster analysis—the names were created to capture the feel of an abstract cluster of people who shared some common traits.

This cluster analysis approach is one of the more formal ways of producing an audience model, but a simpler method exists that anyone can apply: observation and hypothesis. In essence, you observe many different people from the audience (or look at statistical data in general) and draw a hypothesis from the observation. In science, this would be followed with an attempt to validate the hypothesis. Alas, in the games industry, many hypotheses are treated as a priori facts. However, provided you remember that such a hypothesis is only a working assumption *and needs to be tested to determine its value*, we find nothing wrong with building an audience model in this way.

Hardcore and Casual Split

This is the most basic audience model at use in the games industry today. It is in essence a consensual hypothesis—that is, a hypothesis which the majority accept as factual—and almost all people working in the games industry know what is meant by the *Hardcore* (or Core) market and the *Casual* market. Some data at use in the industry might confirm this split, but since no formal definition for each group exists, it remains in essence a hypothetical model.

The essence of Hardcore players can be summarized as follows:

- Buy and play a lot of games
- Game literate (that is, familiar with the conventions of current games)
- Play games as a lifestyle preference or priority
- Turned on by challenge
- Can be polarized—that is, a large proportion can be made to buy the same title

Capcom characterized the Hardcore approach at the start of *Resident Evil* on the GameCube (Capcom, 2002) as "Mountain climbing." This ego-neutral characterization was used at the start of the game to determine which players were Hardcore in their approach and therefore required greater challenge. Selecting this option ran the game at a higher difficulty level.

On the other hand, Casual players can be summarized as follows:

- Play few games—but might play them a lot
- Little knowledge about game conventions
- Play to relax, or to kill time (much as most people view TV or movies)
- Looking for fun or an experience
- Inherently disparate—cannot easily be polarized

Capcom characterized the Casual approach in the GameCube *Resident Evil* as "Hiking." Players who selected this option played the game at an easier setting, allowing them to have more fun and enjoy the experience without the greater emphasis on challenge (which often equates to greater emphasis on repeated failure).

The full wording of the sorting question at the start of this game is as follows:

Question: Which best describes your opinion about games?
I.   MOUNTAIN CLIMBING—Beyond the hardships lies accomplishment.
II.   HIKING—The destination can be reached rather comfortably.

The value of this somewhat unusual question over a straight choice between "Easy" and "Normal" (or "Easy" and "Difficult"; or "Normal" and "Difficult") is psychological. A Hardcore player faced with "Easy" versus "Normal" will pick "Normal," but a Casual player is equally likely to pick "Normal," thinking that choosing "Easy" makes them deficient in some way. The choice between "Normal" and "Difficult" is likely to cause some Hardcore players to select "Normal" (on the grounds that "Difficult" settings are for replay value) and then complain that the game is too easy. Finally, a choice between "Easy" and "Difficult" is likely to mislead both Casual and Hardcore types as they try to decide which of these two options is the normal setting.

In principle, the advantages of this approach are that tailoring the gameplay to the audience—and sorting the audience correctly—improves the reception of the game, equating to stronger sales. Unfortunately for *Resident Evil* on the Game-Cube, the slow-burning sales of the platform somewhat interfered with the actual unit sales. However, informal observation shows that Hardcore players were satisfied with the degree of challenge they received in "Mountain climbing" mode, while Casual players had no difficulty completing the game in "Hiking" mode.

This example clearly shows the value that even a simple audience model can have when used to approach the design process. The sorting question was a novel approach, and although it provoked some confusion in game-literate reviewers, the basic approach seems sound and could be refined to a more subtle approach.

Genre Models

Another hypothetical model in common use throughout the games industry is the genre model. In this, we assume that the audience primarily buys games of a particular type, and those types are referred to as "genres," much as films and books are divided into genres according to their tone and content.

For example, the popular (Hardcore) Web site GameFAQs divides games into the following genres:

- Action
- Adventure

■ Driving
■ Puzzle
■ Role-playing
■ Simulation
■ Sports
■ Strategy

These genres are often divided into sub-genres, which further define the content of the game.

On the surface, this approach seems valid—you can certainly quickly acquire data on the relative sales of games of the given genres and thus make market decisions based upon these categories (or another set of categories).

However, an essential problem exists. As mentioned before, the Hardcore is game literate, but the Casual market is not. In this sense, the Hardcore can connect a game with its genre type, but the Casual market does not buy on the basis of genre at all, looking instead for a game that appeals to them on other terms.

A parallel with the film industry exists. Films are also divided into genres, but the majority of the audience base their film-going decisions not on the basis of genre, but on the basis of which stars are in the film. The "pulling power" of an actor or actress mostly drowns out the effectiveness of genre. For example, romantic comedies are relatively popular (based on total box office receipts), but a romantic comedy without a recognizable star or enough advertising money being spent is generally doomed to obscurity.

Also, you have the issue that genre categories are extremely vague. "Action" would seem on the surface to include both first-person shooter (FPS) and platform games, for example, despite the fact that both types of games attract an entirely different audience. You could use more precise genre categories, but the more precise the genre category, the more subjective the definition becomes. This is because genre definitions are inherently subjective in nature—you cannot objectively measure the gameplay content without specifically defined tests, and any genre system built from specifically defined tests will inevitably disagree to some extent with the mental conception of these genre categories in almost all people who encounter them.

The biggest danger with using the genre model is to assume that if a game from one genre attracts an audience of a certain size, and a game from another genre attracts an audience of a certain size, then a game that combines these features will have a much larger audience. This is the set intersection error: if 70% of people like apple pie and 50% like cherry pie, the likelihood of someone wanting to eat cherry and apple pie is likely to be around 35% (the intersection value of the two separate sets), that is, much lower. So in an audience of 100 people, where 70 like apple pie and 50 like cherry pie, an apple and cherry pie is more likely to appeal to about 35 people (the intersection), not 120 people (the sum). Although expressed in these terms it might seem obvious, it is a surprisingly common mistake throughout the game industry.

This doesn't mean that a game can't mix elements between genres (apple and cherry might turn out to be very complementary flavors!); only that combining the core gameplay of two disparate games is a dangerous endeavor. *Mace Griffin: Bounty Hunter* (Warthog, 2003) tried to combine the first-person shooter genre with the space shooter genre; *Haven: Call of the King* (Traveller's Tales, 2002) combined multiple genre types (including platform, driving, space shooter, and even rhythm action). Both games performed poorly in commercial terms, despite relatively high production values.

We face, however, a danger inherent in ignoring the genre model completely. The game literate Hardcore (who buy more games than the more numerous Casual players) often buy a majority of titles in a genre they have become personally committed to. If a game defies genre boundaries, it might struggle to polarize the Hardcore, and therefore suffer in terms of sales. If, however, it defies genre boundaries and goes on to succeed, it will nucleate a new sub-genre in the minds of the Hardcore audience, which is market gold dust. The original *Resident Evil* (Capcom, 1996) and the *Tony Hawk's Pro Skater* series (Activision, 1999 onwards) both benefited from this effect, founding the pseudo-genre of *survival-horror* (a term which Capcom created themselves for that game) and the sub-genre of *extreme sports*, respectively, and going on to exert brand dominance in these new market segments.

Electronic Arts' Audience Model

The world's largest game publisher (at the time of writing), *Electronic Arts (EA),* has publicly discussed at least one of their audience models, based upon their own internal data and research [Leinfellner03]. This can be considered a theoretical model—that is, it has been devised to explain specific trends in data and is not a pure hypothesis. It can be seen in Figure 2.1 and has evidently evolved from the Hardcore-Casual split hypothesis.

Figure 2.1 alludes not only to the market segments, but also to the relative size of these clusters: the Hardcore gamer cluster is seen as the smallest, and the Mass Market Casual gamer cluster is the largest. Additionally, Figure 2.1 alludes to the way in which game sales are propagated through the market (the dominant market vector), that is, Hardcore gamers influence the Cool gamers to buy games, and the Cool gamers influence the Casual gamers to buy games.

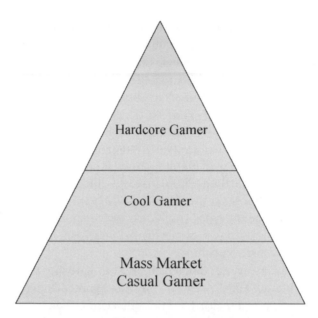

FIGURE 2.1   An audience model used by EA. This diagram is based upon material discussed by Richard Leinfellner at GPDC in Liverpool, October 2003.

The three clusters are characterized as follows:

Hardcore Gamers: This cluster reads the specialist press (magazines about games), plays demos, rents games before buying (especially in the U.S. market) and can play as many as twenty-five games (or more) each year.

Cool Gamers: A typical Cool gamer has a Hardcore friend who is their primary source of advice about buying games. They are part of big peer group, are swayed in their buying decisions by the opinions of this play group, and tend to play the current top ten hits in the gaming charts.

Mass Market Casual Gamers: The least game literate cluster in this model consists of a huge market of people who are in general swayed in their opinions of games by Cool gamer recommendation and TV advertising. They play predominantly the current top three hits in the gaming charts.

This model clarifies several key points. First, ignoring the needs of the Hardcore market to reach the larger mass market is a risky prospect, since the Hardcore gamers are the initial point from which awareness of a game in the market as a whole originates. Second, a large enough advertising budget to reach the Mass Market Casual gamers is justified only on a game that is capable of being enjoyed by this group. Spending a lot of money on marketing a game that can appeal only to the Hardcore is to commit a strategic business error.

The disadvantage of this model from the point of view of design is that it says very little about the design needs of these clusters. Knowing that the Cool gamer demographic is influenced by the Hardcore tells us very little about what design elements are needed to appeal to this group. However, it is a stepping point from which we can proceed to investigate the pertinent design aspects. This is understandable, since design issues were not the primary reason for the construction of the model, which is intended as a tool for understanding the market dynamics.

ihobo Audience Model (2000–2003)

Up until the end of 2003, the audience model used internally at International Hobo Ltd. (referred to as the "ihobo audience model") is the one presented in Figure 2.2. Like the EA model, this ziggurat-style depiction shows both the influence and size of the cluster. The model evolved out of market research and case studies and, like the EA model, is theoretical and not hypothetical in nature.

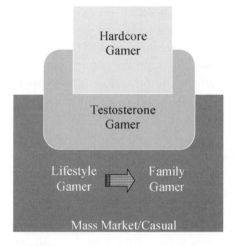

FIGURE 2.2 The audience model used by International Hobo from 2000–2003.

The two square groups—Hardcore gamer and Mass Market/Casual—are related in the same means of influence as two adjacent layers in the EA pyramid model. That is, the Hardcore gamer is the primary source of influence for the Lifestyle and Family gamer (which are divisions of the Mass Market/Casual audience). In addition to the vertical influence, a horizontal influence exists in the Mass Market/Casual layer—the Lifestyle gamers can influence the Family gamers. The Testosterone market segment is a special case that straddles the Hardcore/Casual divide, but is highly pronounced and therefore worthy of attention.

The clusters are characterized as follows:

Hardcore Gamer: As mentioned in the Hardcore-Casual split model, Hardcore gamers' primary concern is challenge, and they are in general looking for games to provide a satisfying level of difficulty. No control mechanism is too complex for a Hardcore gamer, provided they like the core game activity. They are the principle game evangelists and serve a vital role in the market because of this.

Testosterone Gamer: This group is predominantly male and consists of people with both Hardcore and Casual tendencies. The defining trait of this group is a content fixation: these players are most interested in games that focus around cars and guns, and also in games built around player versus player competition (such as the fighting genre). Complex control mechanisms can be tolerated, but not to the same degree as the Hardcore. They have the potential to influence the Lifestyle and Family gamer clusters in the rare cases that their tastes in games correspond to the tastes of the Casual clusters.

Lifestyle Gamer: These are broadly equivalent to EA's Cool gamer but are characterized here by their game design needs. Lifestyle gamers want fun, enjoyable activities in their game, and they don't in general want to be prevented from progressing through the games they play. Easy to grasp control mechanisms are essential. They are also interested in good stories, a trait not dominant in the previous two clusters. Like the Cool gamer cluster, Lifestyle gamers need a game that feels socially acceptable to play—they will (as a generalization) not play anything that could embarrass them in the eyes of their peer group.

Family Gamer: The large but disparate Family gamer represents parents buying games for their children, which they might play with them or might play the same games alone in their spare time. They are primarily looking for entertainment, and control mechanisms must be exceptionally simple. Like the Lifestyle gamer, they enjoy a good story, but this is unlikely to motivate their purchasing decision. They are not in general interested in anything shocking or outlandish and prefer the familiar to the esoteric. They almost never buy games for themselves, and most games they play have either been purchased by a relative (usually an older son or daughter) or were bought for their children.

Note that that we have included no child clusters in this model. This is because the market segments were defined by *purchasing* habits, and since children generally have their games purchased by parents, the Family gamer demographic incorporates the child clusters in an indirect fashion. However, the children might fit the Hardcore, Testosterone, or Lifestyle demographic type, and therefore, the Family type characterizes not the children themselves but the extreme fringe of gaming—in essence, people who are encountering games only because of their children.

The application of this audience model uncovered a number of different design issues extremely pertinent to market economics, all of which are discussed later in the section "Design Tools for Market Penetration."

MARKET VECTORS

A *market vector*, in the context we are discussing here, represents a particular route through which awareness of (and desire to purchase) a game spreads throughout the audience. Both the EA and ihobo audience model are built upon identifying the relative influence of the clusters, and these paths to audience are market vectors.

The concept was brought to the attention of the game community by EA's most prominent game designer, Will Wright, who observed that the route through the marketplace that *The Sims* (Maxis, 2000) took was not what might normally be expected of a game. Figure 2.3 demonstrates the process observed in *The Sims* propagation through the market.

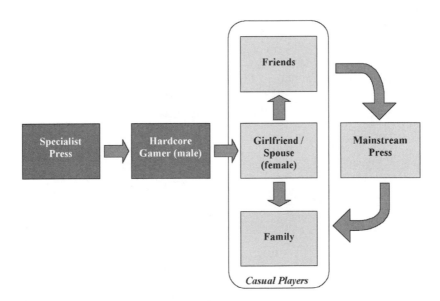

FIGURE 2.3 The market vectors for *The Sims*. Hardcore audience is marked in a dark shade, Casual audience in a lighter shade.

First, anticipation for the game was high among the Hardcore because it was something a little different, it had long-term authenticity due to the *Sim* label, and the specialist press had done much to draw attention to and hype the game prior to release. This led to the Hardcore audience buying the game in reasonable numbers. They did not, on the whole, like the game. Most played it for a very brief period of time, albeit in an obsessive fashion for the duration the game had their attention.

Although not especially taken with the game, many of the Hardcore had girlfriends, who either saw the game by watching their boyfriends play or were given the game by their boyfriends when they were finished ("here's something you might like"). The girlfriends in this context were indicative of what is termed the Lifestyle gamer in the ihobo audience model—people who play games, but are not especially game literate, and generally depend on other people's opinions to influence their purchasing decisions.

The girlfriends were not especially interested in the gameplay per se, but enjoyed the materials of the game for other reasons. They enjoyed decorating houses and, in particular, creating their own "soap opera" stories in their heads. They then showed the game to their friends and family, thus expanding the audience of the game out into the mass market—catalyzing primarily by word of mouth. EA backed this with advertising, but not until the game had already achieved most of its success. In fact, so successful was the game that it caught the attention of the mainstream press, which further increased the awareness of the game and drove the sales mechanism further.

The market vector in this case was as follows:

1. Specialist press
2. Hardcore gamer
3. Hardcore gamer's girlfriend or spouse (Casual gamer)
4. Friends/Family of the preceding (Casual gamers)

With a second round of propagation occurring once the phenomena had reached sufficient size:

1. Mainstream press
2. Casual gamers

The success of this game, which is in effect a virtual dollhouse, was not anticipated (in fact, EA was reluctant to back the project), and the fact that the game supports an audience 70% of which are female [2], which is decisively not the norm in the games market, should have been a sign to the publishing community that a large untapped market existed. Sadly, most publishers consider this game to be an anomaly and do not appear interested in pursuing the market vector it presented.

To be fair, purposefully targeting the female Lifestyle gamer in a game design is a definite problem in that it might be a recipe for alienating the Hardcore gamer required to initiate awareness of the game. On the other hand, it seems highly likely that intelligent design could produce a game that targets the (predominantly male) Hardcore gamer in a different manner than the female Lifestyle gamer within the same materials, perhaps by the use of a "sorting question" as used in the GameCube *Resident Evil* or by building a "challenge layer" on top of a predominantly sandbox world.

Indeed, this was the structure *Grand Theft Auto III* (DMA Design, 2001) used to hit Hardcore and Lifestyle audiences (with the Testosterone included in this case, thanks to the focus on cars and guns), although Lifestyle penetration was somewhat lower in this case because of the Testosterone slant. The sequels in the *Grand Theft Auto (GTA)* series have gradually adapted to better fulfill the goal of hitting both the Hardcore and Casual market segments.

Evangelist Clusters

We talk of an *evangelist cluster* as a market segment that can catalyze interest in a game with other clusters. The key evangelist clusters that can be used to build a market vector are as follows:

Specialist Press: Game magazines and Web sites. A powerful force, but they evangelize only to the Hardcore, so their usefulness is limited (although not to be underestimated).

Mainstream Press: Much more potent than the specialist press, but much harder to get interested in games. Usually, only when the popularity of a game has already reached high levels can the mainstream press be interested, but there are exceptions. Sony cleverly involved the mainstream press in promoting *EyeToy: Play* (Sony, 2003) by playing upon the novelty value of the new peripheral, for example, although clearly only a company of Sony's size could achieve this level of press influence.

Hardcore Demographic: Currently the single most influential evangelist cluster. They are the game designer's best friend and worst enemy, because if you give the Hardcore gamers everything they want, you create a game that only the Hardcore gamers are capable of playing. We would broadly estimate about a million Hardcore gamers in each major territory (for example, U.S., Europe, Japan). These can be polarized up to about 75%, but are usually not penetrated more than 50%—meaning that only up to about 500,000 unit sales can be attributed to the Hardcore for any given game in a given territory [3].

Target Clusters

The rest of the market (the mass market) can be considered to be *target clusters*—the larger audience one is trying to catch:

Testosterone Demographic: The easiest target cluster to reach, because their content needs are so basic, and marketing knows many techniques for hitting this cluster. We estimate about three million Testosterone gamers in each major territory; however, they can rarely be penetrated by more than 50%, and usually only penetrated at perhaps 33%, thus contributing no more than a million unit sales except in rare cases.

Lifestyle Demographic: Currently the most desirable target cluster in many ways, because perhaps some ten million Lifestyle gamers exist in each major territory. The bad news is that most developers and publishers have little or no clue how to design for them, and penetration of this cluster is generally low—under 10%—although when a game becomes a fad for example, *Pokemon, GTAIII*), this penetration can rise to 50% or more.

Family Demographic: This market is huge (perhaps some thirty million in each major territory). However, the degree of penetration is generally less than 5%, and the Family demographic almost never polarizes to any great degree. Still, even this small share is equal in size to the Hardcore or Testosterone, which accounts for the relatively high sales (up to 1,500,000 units) of cartoon license games and similar products, despite their lack of popularity with the Hardcore.

Clearly, it follows that any game to have sold significantly in excess of a million units must be appealing beyond the Hardcore and Testosterone clusters, although it should be noted that the numbers provided are not based on solid data and should be considered speculative at best. Also, the ambiguous nature of the Family demographic (being both the parents and the children) blurs the usefulness of this cluster in considering market vectors.

Thinking in terms of market vector allows a game designer to consider who is being targeted by a game and adjust the design accordingly. It also allows for cooperation between the design team and the marketing team, in principle at least. But it is not, and probably never will be, an exact science.

DESIGN TOOLS FOR MARKET PENETRATION

The application of audience models to the process of design, and the corresponding analysis of audience attitudes (by case studies, surveys, and so forth) has led to a number of concepts that allow the game designer to think about design in terms of market penetration. However, most developers and publishers still treat game design as an engineering process with no influence on sales or market appeal.

In this section we look at new ways of thinking about a game's design that directly connect to the market penetration that a game might achieve.

Gameplay versus Toyplay

The game industry, perhaps in part because of its assumed name, has been obsessed with the notion of *gameplay*, although this has for the most part been an ill-defined term. The veteran game designer Sid Meier, perhaps most famous for adapting Francis Tresham's board game *Civilisation* (Hartland Trefoil, 1980) into computer form and publicly attaching his name to it (perhaps to distinguish between the two games), gave one offhand definition that is oft quoted, namely that "a game is a series of interesting choices." However, this definition is highly limited. After all, *Snakes & Ladders* and *Beggar-My-Neighbor* (traditional board and card games, respectively) offer no interesting choices, yet are still games.

Games on the surface seem very similar to toys in that both are tools for entertainment. The decisive difference between a toy and a game seems to be some inherent degree of performance in a game. This might or might not mean a victory condition—it does in *Snakes & Ladders*, for example, but it does not for *Dungeons & Dragons*, which is a different kind of game altogether.

We therefore choose to define a *toy* as a "tool for entertainment" and a *game* as "a toy with some degree of performance." Every game that can be conceived includes some degree of performance, either in the form of victory conditions to be achieved, failure conditions to be avoided, or metrics to measure progress. This in turn leads to two useful definitions: *gameplay*, defined as "performance-oriented stimulation," and *toyplay*, defined as "unorganized stimulation."

Up until now, the games industry has been focused on different approaches to gameplay—in fact, insisting that this is the most important aspect. However, *The Sims* is clear demonstration that there is a demand for toyplay—for freeform, non-goal–oriented play activities. Furthermore, the playground world of *GTA* also speaks of toyplay, as do many online community games where progress is a largely optional element of involvement in the world.

The gameplay is what (in general) drives the Hardcore cluster to a purchasing decision, and therefore, it cannot be ignored as long as there is no reasonable market vector that does not intersect at some point with the Hardcore. It is also a draw for the Testosterone, in so much as competition is a motivating force for this cluster.

But the Lifestyle and Family clusters can equally be hit by toyplay—and in fact, it might be easier to target these clusters by including toyplay elements than by trying to design gameplay that they will enjoy. Certainly, looking at which games have been especially successful in the recent market suggests that toyplay is a game design goal worth pursuing.

Finding ways to combine gameplay and toyplay in the same game offers better options for reaching a mass market audience than trying either in isolation.

Control Issues

Not all players exhibit the same level of ability in terms of game control. The less time a person spends playing games, the fewer controls skills they are likely to have developed relative to more active gamers—and control mechanisms become more complex with each new generation of machine (for consoles at least). It is not lack of ability per se that causes these difficulties, but a disinclination in the Casual player to persevere with difficult controls, because they make the game less fun. As such, one key tool for market penetration is sensitivity for control mechanisms.

The difficulty of control in a game can be considered by calculating the dimensionality of control of a game. This concept is discussed at length in Chapter 7.

Play Session Length

The *play session length* for a game is a measure of the length of time that a typical instance of playing the game can last. Note that it is either a minimum time, or a mean time, not a maximum. As ever, this definition is largely subjective.

In games with discrete levels, the duration of an average level can be considered the play session length, except in cases where the levels are so long that multiple saves are required, in which case the average "time separation" of the save points should be used instead. In a game with no restrictions on saving, the play session length should be considered the average length of time that a typical game activity (a fight, a race, etc.) takes to complete.

Hardcore players play games for extremely long periods of time—days at a time in some cases. The length of the play session is not an issue for Hardcore players, except that they occasionally have to stop and do other things. With this in mind, minimum play sessions in excess of an hour are problematic, because too much progress is lost from quitting (or too much frustration engendered in an attempt to reach a save point).

Casual players, however, do not want long play sessions. They generally play for shorter sessions, and therefore a game that forces a long play session upon them can be badly received. A minimum play session of 10–15 minutes seems best to accommodate a mean play session length of about an hour. This is a typical outing in a game for a casual player, but they often need to put the game down at a moment's notice, hence the shorter minimum play length.

Keeping play sessions short is clearly vital for mass market appeal, a fact that Nintendo seem to be aware of. Almost all Nintendo games are designed to be quit at any time, and with core activities that are completed in minutes.

Play Window

The companion to play session is the *play window*. This is a theoretical value representing the amount of time a game's audience as a whole spends playing the game. This value is impossible to accurately calculate, but can be estimated by observing player tastes via sales charts, FAQ pages, magazine letters pages, forums, and so forth. Strong throughput of net traffic regarding a game is indicative of a long play window—players are still playing their game long after they have bought it.

The Hardcore demographic is key to this, as they prefer to play games to completion. Thus all replay value, any experimentation, time spent playing with cheats, or time spent finding hidden features can extend a game's play window.

A long play window is highly desirable, because the longer the game is in circulation, the more opportunities exist for potential new players to encounter the game through an "over-the-shoulder" viewing of another player with the game. However, it is particularly important that the Hardcore players are getting a long play window, because these are the primary evangelists for any game. (A Casual player might well play a game on and off for over a year—but they do so privately, and generally don't talk to other people about it.)

Because our primary concern with the play window is the Hardcore, tricks such as hidden bonuses (at almost any level of obscurity) are very powerful ways of expanding the play window. The reward for each need only be minimum for a Hardcore player *who has taken a liking for the game* to spend the time to seek it out. Of course, this time is wasted if the Hardcore player does not like the core gameplay.

Difficulty levels can be used to expand play window. Perhaps the most successful display of this has been *GoldenEye 007* (Rare, 1997), since the game's three difficulty levels each introduced entirely new objectives (within the same missions), and the game provided new rewards with each difficulty level. Each playthrough at each difficulty level was like a whole new game, despite the reuse of resources.

Replay value is another powerful way to expand the play window based on reuse of resources, but it requires some caution. The majority of players play the game only once, so the majority of the game should be accessible from a single playthrough. However, a variety of different characters (provided each has either a different narrative thread or different abilities) can dramatically explode the total play time. *Resident Evil 2* (Capcom, 1998) used this technique well, and *Dynasty Warriors 3* (Omega Force, 2001) pushes the technique to absurd limits, reusing different sets of seven levels from a set of twenty-three with thirty-two different characters for an exceptionally long potential play window.

Recently, online functionality has emerged as the newest way to expand play window. Playing against other opponents in online play can be a powerful draw to some Testosterone gamers (and some Hardcore), dramatically expanding the play window. However, many such games have limited appeal outside of these groups, which somewhat reduces the value of these features.

If a game doesn't have a long play window, it can struggle to propagate out to a wider audience than the Hardcore—"good but short," a common appellation by game reviewers, has been the tombstone of many games. No matter how much the Hardcore gamers like it, if they aren't playing it for long, they will soon be playing something else, which means they won't be evangelizing the game very effectively. Exceptions to this happen, but of the top twenty best-selling games of all time, the only one with a (relatively) short play window is a popular book/film license.

PHASES OF MARKET PENETRATION

Having looked at clusters, market vectors, and tools for taking advantage of these methods, it is worth looking at a breakdown of the typical phases a game must go through to achieve market penetration:

I **Hardcore Penetration:** During this phase the game must include challenge, progress, and depth. If the play window is too short, the market vector likely ends here.

II **Hardcore Evangelism:** To expand significantly past the Hardcore and into the Casual market, the game must in general have one of the following:
- Lifestyle appeal (for example, fad value)
- Easily accessed fun
- Strong marketing
- Strong license

III **Casual Penetration:** During this phase, the game must provide fun, toys, and a short minimum play session. It is during this phase that publishers know they have a hit, so this phase often triggers a second wave of marketing, which further drives uptake.

IV **Casual Evangelism:** If the game has exceptional power to penetrate the market, the Casual market ends up evangelizing the game, which almost guarantees mainstream press attention as well. The maximum audience for a game that can penetrate this deeply into the market is limited only by the maximum demographic appeal (about 1.5 million for Testosterone games, 8 million for Lifestyle games, and up to 30 million for a megahit that works with all clusters).

Of course, identifying these phases tells us nothing about how to design games that can travel "all the way," but thinking in terms of the different target clusters and, crucially, building ever more sophisticated audience models that can reflect game design issues offer that potential.

CONCLUSION

The demographic models presented here are simplistic, but serve to demonstrate the role that demographic game design can play within the games industry. The chapters that follow present a more fully rounded demographic model, designed specifically to judge player taste at the design stage of a project.

Demographic game design shows great potential. It might create new niches within the market by allowing games a greater chance of squarely hitting their audience. This might lead to shifts in game playing habits, which in turn will lead to new demographic models and new narrowcasting options for sales. Commercially viable diversity is a key need for a thriving games market. This in turn creates new development models.

It might be possible to target the Hardcore sector (who tend to express the belief that gameplay is more important to their gaming satisfaction than aesthetic elements) with cheaper games that show less graphical flash but provide gameplay keyed specifically to Hardcore tastes. Similarly, if the Casual market can be targeted directly, it might be possible to create more "toyplay" oriented products that appeal to this market. It might even be possible to create games that straddle the needs of these markets and provide different play needs to different audiences within one product. And it is likely that wholesale increase in gaming literacy will promote further integration of game styles into all markets.

Perhaps more importantly, demographic game design can be used to stabilize the market. Hitting demographic targets more accurately means less wasted investment, which means more and better games of all kinds. This also helps stabilize game developers, who, given a tool with which to more accurately target consumers, might be able to offset the growing cost of development by pinpointing their audience and making the games that the players want to play.

ENDNOTES

[1] There is no universally agreed upon definition of species, and several competing schools of thought exist. Certainly, no definition of species is entirely objective, or can be applied without some application of judgement [Wikipedia04].

[2] The fact that 70% of players of *The Sims* are female was informally reported by Richard Leinfellner, Vice President in Charge of Production at Electronic Arts Europe in 2003 [Leinfellner03].

[3] All numerical estimates for cluster size in this chapter are International Hobo Ltd. game audience estimates from 2003, based on informal analysis of sales figures.

3 Myers-Briggs Typology and Gamers

In This Chapter

- The Myers-Briggs Dichotomies
- The Sixteen Types
- The Mass Market Audience
- Conclusion
- Endnotes

All game designers bring their own assumptions to the process of game design. We each have our own perceptions of what makes a game "good" or what constitutes "good design," based for the most part on our own preferences and observations. Perhaps the most productive way to move beyond our own assumptions is to consider the process of game design from a psychological perspective—if we look at different aspects of psychology in people in general, that in turn will have lessons to teach us about game design.

This chapter looks at one such approach, by examining the mass market audience in terms of the Myers-Briggs typology, specifically the Myers-Briggs dichotomies, the simplest form of this psychological model, and therefore the most convenient starting point for this kind of research. Naturally, the Myers-Briggs model is not the only set of personality traits that could be used as a basis for such a study, but it has the advantage of being a widely supported form for which a wealth of data and research already exists. In particular, data as to the relative frequency of the different Myers-Briggs preferences is widely available, allowing meaningful statistical statements to be made [CAPT02].

In the next chapter, we will look at how applying the Myers-Briggs dichotomies to the game audience reveals certain trends in game players, but for the time being it is more important to get to grips with the basic nature of the Myers-Briggs model. The assumption in this chapter is that all types of people play games, but that the nature of games they enjoy, and the frequency with which they are likely to play games, varies according to their personality preferences.

THE MYERS-BRIGGS DICHOTOMIES

Before we can look at what Myers-Briggs suggests for games design, it is worth explaining briefly the nature of the system. Myers-Briggs typology is a scientific method of classifying individuals into sixteen different personality types, based upon their psychological preferences. These sixteen types are identified by denoting an individual's preferred trait from four pairs of traits, and it is these pairs of traits which form the Myers-Briggs dichotomies.

Developed in the 1940s by Isabel Myers and Kathryn Briggs, Myers-Briggs typology is based upon the work of Carl Jung. It was later transformed into a formal behavioral science, mostly thanks to the work of Dr. David Keirsey, a psychologist from Princeton University, whose book *Please Understand Me* rocketed the system into the public consciousness in the U.S. It is estimated some two million people take the Myers-Briggs Type Indicator (a registered trademark of Consulting Psychologists Press, Inc.) instrument each year [KYT03] for various reasons, including career guidance, candidate assessment, and psychiatry. Virtually all the Fortune 1000 companies in the U.S. use the system for team building and employee relations [HireGolden03].

The system is built upon four pairs of traits that are considered complementary and distinct. All eight of the Myers-Briggs traits—introversion, extroversion, sensing, intuition, thinking, feeling, judging, and perceiving—are present in *all* individuals to different degrees; Myers-Briggs tests (more commonly referred to as inventories or instruments) [1] assign one of sixteen unique types to an individual based upon their preferred functions within this set. That is to say, a person's Myers-Briggs type is an indication of their preferred approach to situations, although every individual can draw upon all eight resources in different situations.

In modern Myers-Briggs research, the tendency is not to look at personality through the reductionist approach used in the dichotomies but to take a holistic view of the sixteen types as distinct patterns. For personal growth and career counselling, this holistic approach can be seen as vastly superior, but for the purposes of demographic research, the reductionist approach is the only viable option.

We now look at each dichotomy and its corresponding two functions to establish the definition of the terms [2].

Extraversion versus Introversion (E versus I)

These mental preferences are concerned with what has been termed "energy consciousness" or "energy orientation." The part of a person that is concerned with the outer world of activities, people, and things corresponds to the Myers-Briggs trait of Extroversion, abbreviated to the letter E. The part of a person that is concerned with the inner world of thoughts, interests, ideas, and imagination corresponds to the trait of Introversion, abbreviated to the letter I.

The nature of the Extroversion function can be characterized as follows:

- Tendency to act now and think later
- Feeling deprived when interactions with the outside world are cut off
- Motivated by the people and things around oneself
- Enjoying experiencing a wide variety of different people and relationships

The converse trait, Introversion, can be characterized as follows:

- Tendency to think first, then act
- Needs to take regular private time to "recharge batteries"
- Motivated internally; external world might be ignored in favor of internal thought processes
- Enjoys one-to-one communication and relationships

In Western society, we see roughly 50-50 split between people who express a preference for Extroversion and those that express a preference for Introversion, and this split is approximately the same in both male and female subjects.

Sensing versus Intuition (S versus N)

These preferences are concerned with how an individual takes in information. Those who prefer Sensing (S) prefer clear instructions and information, rely on common sense, and are mostly connected to the present. They are firmly grounded in conventional consensus reality. Conversely, the Intuition (N) preference reflects a tendency to draw upon information of a more abstract or conceptual nature, and an interest in the imaginative possibilities of the future.

The nature of the Sensing function can be characterized as follows:

- Mentally living in the present
- Applying "common sense" is the automatic response
- Memory tends to recall rich details of past events
- Improvises solutions based on prior experience
- Prefers clear and concrete information and dislikes "fuzzy" information

The corresponding trait, Intuition, can be characterized as follows:

- Mentally living in the near future
- Creating imaginative new approaches is the automatic response
- Memory tends to be based around patterns, contexts, and connections between events and outcomes
- Improvises solutions based upon theoretical models
- Comfortable with "implied information" and guessing the meaning of "fuzzy data"

About 70% of the Western population expresses a preference for Sensing over Intuition. There is a slightly greater incidence of preference for Sensing in female subjects [3].

Thinking versus Feeling (T versus F)

These traits are concerned with how people make decisions. The Thinking (T) aspect is an objective, detached approach. It functions systematically, operating from factual principals to draw conclusions in a logical fashion. It is the essence of linear reason. The Feeling (F) aspect is a more subjective, attached way of making judgments. It draws from personal emotional responses, awareness of the impact actions have on other people, and personal values in order to draw conclusions.

The Thinking function can be characterized as follows:

- Instinctively uses facts and logic in a decision-making process
- Focuses on tasks to be completed
- Objective analysis comes naturally
- Considers conflict to be a natural part of relationships

The Feeling function can be characterized as follows:

- Instinctively applies personal emotions (and the impact on the emotions of others) in a decision-making process.
- Focuses on the consequences to other people
- Subjective values tend to override objective perspective
- Unsettled by conflict

Across the entire Western population, these two functions are roughly equal in preference. However, Feeling is preferred in about 70% of females, whereas Thinking is preferred in about 60% of males. It is not at all clear whether this reflects a fundamental biological difference or merely the cultural bias that asserts the emotional role upon females and the objective role upon males.

Judging versus Perceiving (J versus P)

These traits are considered to constitute an individual's life management orientation. Both traits are used by all people to process information, organize thoughts, make decisions, and otherwise manage one's life. However, as with the other functions, individuals tend to prefer one mode over the other. The Judging (J) approach is about approaching the outside world with a definite plan of action and reaching a state of closure, while the Perceiving (P) style is about taking the outside world as it comes, being adaptable and remaining flexible to new possibilities.

The Judging approach can be characterized as follows:

- Plans first, and then moves into action
- Focuses on tasks one at a time—completes meaningful task segments before moving on
- Avoids stress by staying well ahead of deadlines
- Uses targets and routines to manage life

The Perceiving approach can be characterized as:

- Plan as you go
- Enjoys multitasking; can have many different activities on the go simultaneously
- Works best close to the deadline
- Avoids commitments that might interfere with freedom, variety, and flexibility

The Judging approach is marginally preferred over the Perceiving approach (about 55%), with no apparent distinction between males and females.

THE SIXTEEN TYPES

Given that four different preferences can be chosen for any individual (one for each of the axes), these are often used to form a four-letter acronym that represents the Myers-Briggs type preferences of that individual. A vast array of analyses of the sixteen types is available, and it is beyond the scope of this chapter to go into depth. However, the significance of the types can be seen in the following job tendencies, based upon a table published by the U.S. Department of the Interior [USDI00]. For ease of use, the terms used by Bates and Keirsey to provide a conceptual summary of each type is included in brackets [Kiersey78]:

- **ISTJ (Trustee)**
  Management, accounting, engineering, electrician, dentist, pharmacist, school principal, file clerk, stockbroker, legal secretary, computer operator, computer programmer, technical writer, police officer

- **ISFJ (Conservator)**
  Counselling, ministry, library worker, nursing, secretarial, curators, bookkeepers, dental hygienists, paralegal, artist, interior decorator, retail owner, musician, elementary school teacher, physical therapist, social worker

- **INFJ (Author)**
  Playwright/novelist/poet, psychologist, librarian, special education teacher, editor/art director, graphical designer, marketer, mental health counsellor, dietician/nutritionist, research, architects, interpreter/translator

- **INTJ (Scientist)**
  Scientist, management consultant, economist, computer programmer, administrator, mathematician, psychologist, neurologist, civil engineer, intellectual properties attorney, inventor, financial planner, judge

- **ISTP (Artisan)**
  Commercial artist, carpenter, surveyor, firefighter, private investigator, pilot, police officer, chiropractor, computer repair person, race car driver, computer programmer, electrical engineer, coach/trainer, software developer

- **ISFP (Artist)**
  Jeweller, gardener, potter, painter, landscaper designer, bookkeeper, physical therapist, mechanic, surveyor, chef, forester, crisis hotline operator, elementary school teacher, beautician, typist, botanist, marine biologist, social worker

- **INFP (Questor)**
  College professor, researcher, legal mediator, social worker, holistic health practitioner, occupational therapist, human resources, minister/priest/rabbi, psychologist, writer/poet/novelist, journalist

- **INTP (Architect)**
  Architect, strategic planning, writer, lawyer, software designer, financial analyst, college professor, photographer, logician, systems analyst, neurologist, physicist, psychologist, computer programmer, database manager, chemist, biologist

- **ESTP (Promoter)**
  Promoter, entrepreneur, franchise owner, real estate broker, chef, land developer, physical therapist, stockbroker, news reporter, firefighter, pilot, insurance agent, electrical engineer, aircraft mechanic, flight attendant

■ **ESFP (Entertainer)**
Musician, flight attendant, floral designer, real estate agent, child care, social worker, fundraiser, athletic coach, veterinarian, secretary, receptionist, teacher, occupational therapist, travel sales, public relations specialist, waiter/waitress

■ **ENFP (Journalist)**
Journalist, newscaster, speech pathologist, ombudsman, clergy, career counsellor, character actor, marketing consultant, musician/composer, artist, human resource manager, advertising account manager, dietician/nutritionist, massage therapist

■ **ENTP (Inventor)**
Venture capitalist, actor, journalist, investment broker, real estate agent, real estate developer, politician, literary agent, restaurant/bar owner, art director, computer analyst, advertising creative director, radio/TV talk show host

■ **ESTJ (Administrator)**
Government employee, auditor, project manager, officer manager, factory supervisor, computer analyst, electrical engineer, stockbroker, construction worker, industrial engineer, funeral director, cook, security guard

■ **ESFJ (Seller)**
Retail owner, sales representative, telemarketer, caterer, flight attendant, bookkeeper, medical/dental assistant, elementary school teacher, minister/priest/rabbi, insurance agent, child care provider, professional volunteer

■ **ENFJ (Pedagogue)**
Career counselor, sales trainer, travel agent, program designer, corporate/team trainer, child welfare worker, social worker, recreation director, politician, entertainer, recruiter, artist, newscaster, writer/journalist, librarian, psychologist, housing director, interpreter/translator, occupational therapist, sales manager

■ **ENTJ (Field Marshal)**
Personnel manager, labor relations, management trainer, corporate team trainer, financial planner, program designer, attorney, administrator, office manager, sales manager, franchise owner, investment banker, mortgage broker, consultant

It should be noted that the jobs given are representative of typical jobs people of the relevant types pursue, and therefore many jobs cross over between different types, because personality type does not dictate job, and all that can be observed are prevailing patterns.

Having established briefly the nature of the Myers-Briggs typology in general, and the dichotomies in particular, we are ready to look at how these traits apply to the way different people approach games and, hence, how they might impact on game design decisions.

THE MASS MARKET AUDIENCE

Much talk is given throughout the games industry (and its associated academic areas) about the fact that games are now reaching a mass market audience. In one month in 2002, *Grand Theft Auto: Vice City* (Rockstar North, 2002) sold more than one million units in the U.S. territory alone—only 116 games had sold more than one million units *in total* since 1995 in the same territory [4]. These volumes of sales, although less than sales figures during the early days of consoles for various reasons [5], are considered to mark the entry of computer games into the mass market because of the rise in the scale of sales across the market as a whole.

The Myers-Briggs typology represents a continuum of individuals, and as such no evidence exists that any area on that continuum does not play or will not play computer games of some kind. Similarly, no region on this continuum does not to some extent read books, enjoy films, or watch TV. Entertainment media can work for anyone, although the reasons why a particular instance is enjoyed can vary according to the individual.

However, some evidence suggests that one part of the continuum buys more, plays more, and talks about computer games more than any other—the Hardcore, who have been the mainstay of the video games industry since its inception.

Hypotheses of Hardcore Cluster

Hardcore gamers are alleged to be the main driving force behind the entire computer gaming industry. They are usually considered male, between 14–28 years old and are characterised by placing games at the top (or near the top) of their priorities both for spending money and for spending time. They are considered to have very high technical knowledge of computers in general and games in particular, and they can be most clearly defined by the number of games they play in a year, which in some cases can be as high as eight different games a month [Megagames03].

Examination of Hardcore gamer attitudes to games (and life in general) reveals a few key points:

- They are willing to spend a considerable amount of time playing games on their own, which in Myers-Briggs terms strongly implies an Introvert orientation.
- They are predominantly logical and methodical in their approach, suggesting a Thinking bias.
- They are strongly goal-oriented, suggesting a Thinking bias.
- They are highly critical of games and attempt objective arguments on the subject, suggesting a Thinking bias.
- They enjoy conflict in a game situation, suggesting a Thinking bias.

- They are willing to spend considerable time on a single problem within a game and are willing to repeat a portion of gameplay repeatedly until they get it correct, suggesting a Judging bias.
- They tend to overachieve within the goal-space the game creates, suggesting a Judging bias [Pelley00].

These observations lead to the hypothesis that the Hardcore demographic cluster can be characterized in terms of Myers-Briggs dichotomies as Introvert, Thinking, and Judging—or I_TJ (the underscore denoting a "wild card" for the S-N dichotomy). If this hypothesis holds water, we can make an assessment to what proportion of the population as a whole falls in or near the Hardcore cluster by combining the proportions of INTJ and ISTJ populations. These figures combine to suggest the Hardcore cluster should be no larger than about one-sixth of the population as a whole, about 10% of females and about 20% of males [6]. Certainly, anecdotal evidence suggests a link between the ISTJ type and computer games [Craig03].

This is not the only potential model for the Hardcore cluster, however. Some statistical evidence suggests that the mode Myers-Briggs types for Massively Multiplayer Online games are ISTJ and ISTP [Watt03]. This might mean that the Hardcore could be characterized as Introvert-Thinking only, which would combine to suggest a maximum of one quarter of the population could be in this cluster, about 15% of females and almost exactly a third of males [7].

One other point worth mentioning in connection with these two hypotheses is that the Hardcore cluster is considered to correlate with strong computer knowledge and jobs within the computer industry. It is worth noting, therefore, that the four Myers-Briggs types associated with the job of computer programmer are ISTJ, INTJ, ISTP, and INTP [USDI00].

These hypotheses provided the motivation for a study into the gaming audience that is discussed in the following chapter. This study revealed some merit to both of the hypotheses, but crucially, other Hardcore players did not fit these patterns. It is from unexpected discoveries such at this one that a model grows and develops, and as such the key point to note at this stage is that the apparent nature of the Hardcore cluster appears to correlate with the main personality types associated with the people who make games—the programmers.

Regardless of the underlying structure of the demographic clusters, looking at game design from the point of view of the different functions in each of the Myers-Briggs dichotomies gives us useful ideas as to how to design for a mass market audience. Because the mass market is expected to be part of the continuum as a whole, and not a regionalised cluster like the Hardcore, we must expect to encounter all (or almost all) of the Myers-Briggs traits in the game audience. It follows, therefore, that designing for a mass market audience must balance these traits—rather than rely heavily on Thinking-style game design features, as is currently the norm.

In the next four sections, we look at each of the dichotomies, and the implications on game design.

How Games Are Played (E versus I)

The vast majority of games are being played by Introverts—people for whom the Introvert function is dominant are capable of spending vast durations on their own doing solo activities, such as playing single player games. This does not mean that people more influenced by the Extrovert trait do not play games; however, anecdotal evidence suggests that Extrovert-style gamers play games when they are bored, while Introvert-style gamers play games as a willing preference [8].

In recognition of the domination of the Introvert trait over games as a whole, the majority of games are designed with Introvert assumptions in mind. Games are designed with the intent of being played over a long period of time, and over long play sessions. Often, little thought is given to players who are trying to play the game for short, intermittent periods of time. Many games rely on the player to maintain their own model of the game world (and game goals) in their head. To cover for some Extrovert players, it might be wise to provide support within the game so that the player does not "forget what they are doing" if they return to the game after a long absence. The presence of a clock inside all consoles would even make this a functionality that could be detected and applied.

Extrovert-preference gamers do enjoy and participate with games in a social situation. Extroverted people tend to enjoy parlor games, for example, and games that can be integrated into a social situation are those that might be most enjoyable to extrovert players. Some anecdotal evidence suggests that couples play games together, sharing the gameplay ("pad passing")—often with one half of the couple being an Introvert-preference, and the other being an Extrovert-preference. No hard data exists to verify this phenomenon, however.

On a wider scale, however, some games appeal primarily to the Extrovert gamer. Most famous of these are the dance mat class of games, as characterized by *Dance Dance Revolution* (Konami, 2001). The essentially physical nature of these games appears to appeal to Extrovert-preference gamers—they are willing to get up and perform in public, while Introvert-preference people often feel uncomfortable when attention is drawn to them in public.

These dancing games were not anticipated to be a huge success. They took off in Japan (a culture that easily polarizes towards new ideas, making it an excellent breeding ground for innovation) and spread to the West primarily in the arcades, where specialised hardware is a necessity in today's modern market. Here in the arcades they attracted a cult following among Extrovert-preference gamers, who loved getting up and "performing" on the machines. (The fact that it was good exercise also helped, because Extrovert-preference people are generally more motivated to keep fit because of their bias towards the external world).

No company anticipated the success the dance mats would have in the marketplace. In 2001, dancing mats could be acquired in the U.K. only by ordering online. The following year, they were on sale in all the major games retailers. The reason for this delay might have been the overdependence upon Introvert-style thinking. The dance mats provided an Extrovert-preference game, and no one predicted that such a thing was possible.

Learning and Problem Solving (S versus N)

The information processing dichotomy of the Myers-Briggs model relates to game design most strongly in the area of problem solving and the player's patience with gameplay elements—an issue that is relevant to most game genres, because problem solving is one of the key recurring gameplay elements in a variety of game styles. Furthermore, the information processing dichotomy dictates to some extent how the player learns to play the game—this has relevance to every game, because as game complexity has increased, tutorials have also increased in abundance and complexity.

In a learning environment, Sensing-preference people are patient with routine material, which suggests in a game environment the same sensibilities dominate. Conversely, Intuition-preference people are patient with abstract or complex material [Pelley00]. In the context of game tutorials, a Sensing approach might be to have a series of linear exercises that teach game controls and game elements. Intuition-preference people on the other hand are used to perceiving patterns and connections and can to a great extent be left to intuit game controls and mechanics on their own. However, given the overwhelming dominance of the S-trait (70% of population irrespective of gender), it would seem vital to include structured, straightforward tutorial elements. Wherever possible, these should be structured to allow Intuition-based players to draw their own conclusions—although underlining any critical game rules would seem vital in all cases. (A *critical game rule* can be considered a condition that must be known for the player to progress at a certain point in the game structure.)

Many vocal Hardcore players show impatience with linear, structured tutorials, suggesting that these players are functioning in this regard with the Intuition-trait, but we have no way of knowing which proportion of the Hardcore is affected. (On the basis of the Hardcore cluster hypothesis, we would expect this to be only about

30% of these players, but given that the N-trait is associated with journalism, many game reviewers are likely to fall in this camp). The implication is that a good tutorial environment should be designed to be approached both from the routine exercise angle and the learn-by-experimentation method. Perhaps the most powerful method is to include a series of exercises that each teach an element of the game world, accompanied by player-solicited assistance to provide guidance for the Sensing-preference player. The majority of platform games do indeed employ such an approach and remain one of the most popular game genres [9].

When it comes to problems in the game world, we can assume that the Sensing approach to problem solving is likely to be a straightforward common sense or trial and error affair. This does not mean that Intuition-type puzzles (those that involve lateral thinking) cannot be included in a game, and of course, because every person has the Intuition trait to some degree, a few puzzles of this kind do not present a problem. However, when the game relies consistently on intuition to solve problems, rather than the application of taught methods or common sense solutions, it is biasing itself away from the majority of its possible players. Perhaps these puzzles should mostly be used for secondary rewards, and less for the main progress within the game structure. Since *Super Mario 64* (Nintendo, 1996), most platform games require players to complete only about three quarters of the puzzles and challenges, allowing players to pick their own battles.

The Sensing-person's reliance upon "common sense" and attraction to the familiar might be a factor in the enormous success of games based around cars or car-type vehicles. Few things in life are as familiar to people in the West as cars, as they form a part of every day life for the majority of people. The operation of vehicles in a game tends to be equivalent to the operation of a real vehicle (steering, accelerator, and brake), making this an easy skill for anyone to pick up (although it must be noted this observation applies even if Myers-Briggs typology is ignored).

The issue of complexity in game design also points to a greater need to reflect Sensing-preference issues. Intuitive people are patient with complex materials, but those for whom the Sensing trait dominates do not do so well when faced with an unfamiliar and complex game world. Simplicity, both in interface design and core game mechanics, must be considered a desirable trait; Intuitive players might persevere with a game with a steep learning curve, but the majority of players will not (and if the Hardcore cluster hypothesis holds, then complexity yields no advantage with even the Hardcore players).

Motivation (T versus F)

The decision-making dichotomy tells us about how different players experience motivation within a particular game space. In a learning environment, Thinking-preference people have been shown to learn best when given clear, objective goals and rationales, while Feeling-preference people respond best when receiving personal encouragement [Pelley00]. Here, we can see a clear distinction between the currently prevalent "Hardcore game design" philosophy, which has a tendency to focus on goals and objectives (often collected as a "Mission" with some side goals), and a more mass market approach, which seeks to balance objectives with encouragement. No matter how clearly defined an objective is, Feeling-preference players become discouraged when facing a problem they cannot solve, which might ultimately put them off a particular game.

The issue of encouraging the player is a key point that presents certain problems. Direct encouragement of the player ("You're doing great!") might work in a game designed for a predominantly Feeling-preference audience (we can imagine such dialogue in a licensed *Barbie* game, for example), but the Thinking-preference player might be patronized by such an approach. Up until now, games have been able to rely on Thinking-preference approaches because the majority audience has been male and the majority of male players are biased towards Thinking (60%)—and of course, from the point of view of either of the Hardcore cluster hypotheses, the majority of players (and game creators) appear to display Thinking preference.

Incorporating design elements that reflect the needs of Feeling-preference players seems to be a sound strategy for appealing to a wider audience. Perhaps the most powerful method of doing this at the moment is to award the player useful, aesthetically appealing or fun things within the game space. Such rewards are effectively presents, and these constitute encouragement for Feeling-preference players—and are liked by Thinking-preference players where they provide a competitive advantage. A wide variety of rewards—some giving advantages in the game world, some presenting additional entertaining elements, and some purely for aesthetic reasons (for example, different clothing for the central character)—seems like a win-win approach to encouragement.

Note that making the player collect generic power ups that are used to progress in the game with no additions to player abilities is not a very good approach. This sort of situation is common in lazily designed generic platform games—usually a multi-tiered currency situation where the player collects a number of items of type A, B, or C in order to earn items of type X, and when a certain number of items of type X have been collected, the player can progress. The collectibles are really acting only as keys, and few players are especially excited about collecting keys. Earning enough to progress in some measurable way can work as an encouragement if the player knows the targets from the start; otherwise, it is more likely to feel like a restraint on progress. In either case, collecting items of type A, B or C will never constitute much encouragement if collecting them cannot ever give the player something useful, aesthetically appealing, or fun.

On the other hand, this type of key-oriented gameplay provides a very clear goal to players, and so can be of use in attracting certain types of players. It might be that the popularity of the platform game is in part rooted in the simplicity of the goal structure—"find and collect items that look like this."

Variety of collection and simplicity of goal can be combined. Compare a situation where items A, B and C are collected as a contribution to a literal currency within the game world; if they can be used to purchase items in the game (both useful, fun and decorative), the player creates their own motivation by seeing what is on sale and then goes out to collect enough to purchase what appeals to them. The items acquired can then act as mechanisms to acquire the key-type items, if desired. Because they are functioning as a currency, and not a key system, you have the added benefit that the collectibles can regenerate (in a key system, regenerating pickups of these kinds allow the player to progress by doing the same thing over and over again, which is undesirable). With regenerating rewards scattered throughout the world, the player receives encouragement just for playing the game—no matter what they are doing. This can be considered an ideal case, but the game designer should beware of what happens after everything has been purchased and the currency has become irrelevant.

At a subtler level, a game can do much to hold the loyalty of a Feeling-preference player simply by providing a regular "pat on the head." These are simply clues that the player is on the right track. If dialogue is a part of the game design, game characters can provide encouragement through conversation—merely the recognition that the player's actions have had an impact on the fictitious characters in the game world constitutes a powerful pat on the head for Feeling-preference players (whether or not the effects on the people were positive or negative!). If they are navigating through unfamiliar terrain, a distinct change in the environment near the way out functions as a pat on the head and a common sense aid to completing the challenge. Similarly, subdividing large goals into smaller steps provides a pat on the head at each stage as the player is told they have progressed (perhaps by an audio cue, or text message). As we will see later, this is also of benefit when approaching Perceiving-preference players.

Another aspect of motivation worth considering is a Game Over screen. No game need necessarily include a Game Over screen, but they exist as an artifact of an earlier era of game design when such things were essential, especially from arcade games in the period from 1971 to about 1985. After 1985, arcade games were more likely to contain a Continue screen, inviting the player to put in more money. In the arcade, this made sense as a revenue generator (although it might have had negative consequences for arcade culture as a whole). On a home computer game the player has already purchased the software—the Continue screen should be the default exit condition for any home computer game that has a structure requiring an exit status (though it should be noted that many games' structures require no exit status unless the player wants to stop playing).

The relevance of a Game Over (or Continue) screen for Feeling-preference players is that the emotional effect of such a screen is ambiguous criticism. The player has clearly failed—although no reason for failing is usually provided (and if it were, this might be even more disliked by a Feeling-preference person). Thinking-preference people enjoy giving and receiving critical analysis (although not necessarily about themselves in a personal sense), while Feeling-preference people are much more likely to take critical analysis personally—even when the criticism connects to them only indirectly [Pelley00]. With this in mind, we can posit the idea that the frequency that the Game Over/Continue screen is displayed affects the motivation experienced by a Feeling player. If it comes up often, the Feeling-preference player will feel criticized (especially if they cannot see anything overtly wrong with their approach). The Thinking-preference player on the other hand is more likely to analyze their performance and spot possibilities for improvement, becoming discouraged only when they feel they have exhausted all possibilities (because at that point the goals have become obscure).

Part of the success of the *Legend of Zelda* series of games (Nintendo, 1986 onwards) might be attributable to the games' willingness to allow the player to fail without excessive criticism. For example, a fatal fall in many games would bring up a Game Over/Continue screen. In *Zelda*, a fatal fall is "charged" by a tiny cost in the player's life score. Although falling over and over again would bring up a Game Over screen, for the most part "instant death" is not a factor in a game of *Zelda*. This doubtless helped contribute to the games' appeal in a wider audience, and the games' mix of clear goals and regular and varied encouragements made it well balanced in regards of the Thinking and Feeling traits. It should also be noted that the *Zelda* games traditionally use an advanced key system for progression and also all use a currency system (primarily used to charge players to play mini-games).

Goal-Orientation (J versus P)

The life management orientation dichotomy connects to games specifically in the area of goal-orientation. Judging-preference people tend towards strong goal-orientation, while Perceiving-preference people tend towards process-orientation [Wellspring03]. This means that the Judging-preference player is playing primarily to complete objectives, while the Perceiving-preference player is playing to improve their abilities and completing goals is largely just a method of demonstrating their progress. The I_TJ Hardcore cluster hypothesis suggests that Judging is a Hardcore trait, and certainly a vast majority of games seem to be designed with a more goal-oriented than process-oriented structure. Indeed, Perceiving-preference players are extremely comfortable with open games (those with no clear end condition) and stop playing when it feels right for them to do so. Judging-preference players seem to prefer games they can definitively complete ("beat"), and where Judging traits are highly dominant over Perceiving traits, the player might not stop until they have completely beaten every aspect of the game.

This connects with research that demonstrates that Judging-preference people tend towards overachievement, while Perceiving-preference people are at greater risk for underachieving in an academic situation [Pelley00]. Note, however, that Perceiving underachievement in academic situations might result from academic structure being generally geared towards goal-orientation—especially where exams are used as the dominant method of assessment. It in no way implies that Judging people are "superior" to Perceiving people, just that in a goal-oriented situation, Judging-preference people are motivated to score highly and complete more goals than are strictly "necessary." It is simply the nature of their life management preference.

Whether or not the Perceiving-preference players are a key element of the Hardcore, many games are designed with an intense bias towards Judging. For example, *Rogue Leader: Rogue Squadron II* (LucasArts, 2001) has a structure that means that the player must complete everything within the game *at the highest possible level of achievement* in order to see everything—a situation palatable only to those strongly influenced by the Judging trait. Furthermore, effectively game-critical power ups are hidden within the levels in a needle-in-a-haystack fashion adding an element to the player's required progress that can only possibly be goal-oriented, never process-oriented. Had this game not been supported by the *Star Wars* license, it is questionable that it would have performed adequately in the mass market.

Game structure is inherently tied to the Judging-Perceiving dichotomy, and in this area games have made good progress. The linear approach to game structure (levels must be completed in strict linear fashion) is thankfully ceasing to be the prevalent concept in game organization. Such a structure inherently favors those who tend towards the Judging approach, because these people happily focus on a single task, no matter how tough, while those who tend towards the Perceiving trait are much more likely to postpone unpleasant tasks as often as possible [Pelley00]. Postponing unpleasant tasks for a game often means stopping playing, which means shorter play windows and worse word of mouth, equating to fewer sales.

This particular observation suggests that the original Hardcore demographic in the early days of computer games (1971 until around 1989) might well have strongly correlated with the I_TJ Hardcore cluster hypothesis, because all games (or almost all) were strictly linear in structure. It might be that since then the Hardcore has expanded to include Perceiving-preference people, but equally possible is that the shorter, smaller games inherent with this early era of gaming led to a "pick and

choose" approach for Perceiving-preference players at the level of the games them
selves, rather than internally to each game.

The most appropriate game structures for a mass market audience are those in
which the players can pick and choose what they are going to do, but must complete a proportion of the material to progress and complete the game—as with the
aforementioned typical platform game structure. Such a structure supports the
needs of both Perceiving- and Judging-preference players, and regardless of the
nature of the Hardcore cluster, accounting for both needs leads to a greater proportion of potential players and, hence, greater potential sales. It is perhaps only the
structure, and not the core gameplay, that have loaned platform games this market
success.

The success of the *Tony Hawk's Pro Skater* franchise (Neversoft, 1999 onwards),
not only in terms of its commercial success (these games have sold around two million copies in the U.S. territory alone), but also in terms of its capacity to influence
the design of other games, might be in part due to the incorporation of this type of
structure. Although the *Tony Hawk* branding was doubtless a major facet in catalyzing the success of the game, name brand alone cannot sell a game, as *David
Beckham Soccer* (Rage, 2001) indicated.

Also worth noting in connection to the Judging-Perceiving dichotomy is the
GTA series on PS2 (DMA Design/Rockstar North, 2001 onwards). These games
provide about half of the game materials (a large chunk of the city, a selection of
vehicles and weaponry) from their outset. Missions become very difficult quite
quickly, but the player can enjoy the game without playing the missions at all. This
strikes an interesting balance between Judging and Perceiving trait issues—the
goal-oriented, Judging-preference players can persevere with the missions, while
the process-oriented, Perceiving-preference players can play around in the game
world, pursuing their own personal entertainments. Although this balance is by no
means the only factor contributing to the games' success, it is certainly a highly beneficial element of the game design.

In the light of analysis of this dichotomy, it might be the case that a linear game
structure has no place outside of the Hardcore audience anymore. Inevitably, in a
linear structure the player gets held up at a certain point—not a problem for those
who are predominantly Judging in their approach, but a potential disaster for Perceiving-preference players.

Challenge versus Fun (TJ versus FP)

A final point worth raising is that of game difficulty—a scale that ranges from chal-
lenge at the difficult end to unstructured fun at the other. From a TJ perspective
(Thinking-Judging traits dominant), the challenge is likely to be a key issue: the
Thinking trait is associated with a focus on tasks to be completed and an acceptance

of conflict as a natural state of affairs, and the judging trait is associated with goal-orientation, suggesting that people with both these traits dominant are more comfortable at the challenging end of the difficulty scale.

Conversely, from an FP perspective (Feeling-Perceiving traits dominant), fun is likely to be the key issue. The Feeling trait is associated with involvement in emotional states and subjective experiences, and the Perceiving trait is associated with process-orientation and an avoidance of difficult tasks. An FP-preference player is therefore more likely to be interested in the fun offered by a game.

The vast majority of games up to this point have apparently been designed in a TJ-style (which further suggests that the I_TJ model for the Hardcore is stronger); there have been very few FP style games. The one possible exception might be *The Sims* (Maxis, 2000)—a game with no formal goal-orientation that is mostly focused on relationships between its virtual characters. This virtual dollhouse game is, at the time of writing, the best-selling PC game of all time, selling ten million copies for that format [GameState03]. As it is the only significant FP-style game on the market [10], we cannot help but wonder if its success can be chalked up to having no real competition in a largely unexplored market space.

With so few FP-style people involved in games development, it is perhaps unsurprising that games in this style are so rare, but this does not excuse the overlooking of this vital, underdeveloped market. Perhaps a certain Hardcore blindness when looking at games blocks exploration of what might be the most profitable unexploited market. The problem is that without sufficient marketing spending (which *The Sims* could draw upon thanks to being published by Electronic Arts, the world's largest publisher [Donovan03]) games have difficulty reaching a market without evangelization by the Hardcore, who are almost certainly Thinking-biased, even if they are not Judging-biased.

This suggests that one of the major battlefields of modern design will be balancing the needs of TJ-style and FP-style players and creating games that can be approached in a variety of different manners, thus appealing to a wider audience. Whether the Hardcore can be made to polarize for a game in this style (and hence act as an evangelist cluster for such a game) remains the biggest unanswered question. Perhaps we will discover new evangelist clusters capable of proselytizing games to the other facets of the market, but at the moment this remains a matter of pure speculation.

CONCLUSION

Though the game designer's innate sense of good design will always be of vital importance to the creation of good games, in a market so potentially vast, it seems foolish to assume that a single designer can please every facet of their intended audience without putting specific thought into the nature of that audience's preferences.

Games have traditionally evolved along the lines of genres, meaning that new types of games tend to appeal to the same people who liked the previous versions. Certainly, an identifiable sector of the games-buying public can be classified as Hardcore gamers. So, by considering different requirements of different players, game design can expand its repertoire, presumably expanding its potential user base at the same time.

Use of the Myers-Briggs dichotomies can provide a useful way in which game designers can understand players different from themselves. By turning their skills to creating ways of entertaining a wide variety of players, designers can explore new avenues for games. Creating FP style "play" games is one possibility in the future of games, as is creating more F style character-driven games. By examining different types of players, many new game styles might emerge.

Alternatively, use of the personality typing systems might allow large budget AAA products to please wider audiences. By using simple design elements to balance features for different players, the greatest number of players can be attracted to the product, and further financial success can be achieved.

Thus, understanding the game-playing audience allows artistic furtherance of games and also shows new ways to compete commercially in an expanding market.

ENDNOTES

[1] *Test* implies that answers can be right or wrong. Because all responses are valid in a set of questions intended to identify Myers-Briggs type, *instrument* or *inventory* has emerged as preferred terminology.

[2] Information in the following four sections is adapted from the Personality Pathways site [Pathways03a], [Pathways03b].

[3] Incidence of Sensing preference is 70–75% in females, 65–72% in males [CAPT02].

[4] Data from confidential sales data. The month in question was December, so Christmas sales effects should be taken into account.

[5] Sales figures from the early NES era (1985–1988 in the U.S.) were larger for the top titles because it was a captive audience (no competing platforms), and because of the best games being bundled with the hardware, thus receiving artificially inflated audience penetrations. For example, the best-selling console game of all time is *Super Mario Bros.* on the NES, which sold 40 million copies—but this game was bundled with the console and therefore represents sales figures unlikely to be repeated [GameState03].

[6] ISTJ represents 11–14% overall, 7–10% female, 14–19% male; INTJ 2–4% overall, 1–3% female, 2–6% male. This suggests 15% of population, 10% female, 20% male, based upon figures from the Center for Applications of Psychological Type [CAPT02].

[7] ISTP represents 4–6% overall, 2–3% female, 6–9% male, INTP represents 3–5% overall, 1–3% female, 4–7% male (based upon figures from the Center for Applications of Psychological Type [CAPT02]). Combining with data from [6], this gives 24% of the population in total, 15% females and 33% males.

[8] From surveys and interviews with gamers conducted by International Hobo Ltd. during their research for the DGD1 model.

[9] Six of the twenty best selling games in the U.S. (1995–2002) and seven of the top ten best-selling games of all time (across all territories) are platform games.

[10] You can find, of course, other toyplay games such as the *Sim City* series (Maxis, 1989 onwards), but these tend not to typify what is being crudely expressed by FP tendencies here. Rather, these can be considered to typify TP toyplay tendencies. This point will become clearer in the context of the next chapter.

4 The DGD1 Demographic Model

In This Chapter

- The Research
- Analysis
- Play Style
- Distribution of Play Styles
- Conclusion
- Endnotes

The philosophy of Zen Game Design has at its heart the notion of reflecting the needs of participants in the process of game design. Arguably the most important group of participants is the game audience, and because you cannot ask them personally to participate, an audience model is needed in order to make intelligent assumptions about their needs.

This leads to the inevitable goal of building new and better models of the audience. Because each model reveals something new about the psychology and needs of the audience, every study is worthwhile. However, most studies are relatively vague, or focused on marketing (that is, promoting the desire to purchase, rather than meeting gameplay needs) and in most cases are never made publicly available.

Having conducted studies to further its understanding of the game-playing audience, International Hobo Ltd developed its own demographic model—the

DGD1 (Demographic Game Design 1) model. The goal was to provide a tool to aid in *market-oriented game design*, that is, maximizing the appeal of a game to targeted demographic groups by incorporating elements specifically designed to meet their needs.

THE RESEARCH

After the groundwork of the application of Myers-Briggs typology to games was investigated and a hypothesis to guide the research was formed, a study was initiated. The basic hypotheses (that Hardcore tendencies would relate to an Introverted, Thinking, and Judging bias or to an Introverted and Thinking bias) were used to direct the study.

The survey was comprised of two components: a 32-question Myers-Briggs personality test, used to estimate Myers-Briggs type, and a short questionnaire, used to determine elements such as game purchasing and playing habits.

Part of the questionnaire asked for the individual's assessment as to whether they considered themselves "Hardcore gamers," "Casual gamers", or had no idea. In the final results, it was assumed that any Hardcore gamer could identify themselves as such, and everyone else who played/purchased at least one game a year was considered "Casual."

Some individuals reported that they only purchased games for their family or did not play games at all. These were considered inapplicable to the purpose of a survey aimed at classifying the gameplay needs of the audience and excluded from the results.

Participants were recruited by gathering the survey data as part of a competition to win games. This was advertised at Web sites that were known to have a number of Hardcore players frequently visiting, and also at "comper" sites (places that catalog competitions on offer). These latter sites had been used previously to gather information about the ihobo "Lifestyle" and "Family" demographics in a previous survey and were considered an excellent source of data on Casual players. This provided a good mix of Hardcore and Casual respondents. Additionally, a number of students from four different university game courses participated in the survey, which provided additional diversity to the data.

A little over four hundred participants took part in the study, and about one-fifth of these were also contacted for follow-up interviews to gather case study data (naturally, all names used in connection with the case studies are not the real names of the participants) [1].

In addition, during the study, a source of additional data was found in the form of a database of players of Massively Multiplayer Online role-playing games.

This database was actually focused on gathering Bartle data (a typology applied to players of MMO games), but included Myers-Briggs type data—allowing an additional three thousand cases to be gathered with respect to the online gaming audience. However, this data lacked the additional information gleaned in the main study [2].

It should be noted that the data from the main study was not necessarily a representative sample of the population at large; although correlations between Myers-Briggs type and play habits could be gathered, data about the relative frequency of the types in the population at large would always be subject to sampling errors. As a provisional study, this was considered an acceptable cost.

ANALYSIS

Cluster analysis provided very sketchy and incomplete results, but it indicated certain trends that were then followed by more direct methods. It became apparent that the patterns between Hardcore and Casual gamers were almost identical in respect to the Thinking-Feeling axis and the Judging-Perceiving axis, while the other two components (Introvert-Extrovert, Sensing-Intuition) showed a general trend that applied across the whole model.

With this in mind, four clusters of play style were identified:

- **Type 1 Conqueror (TJ)** relating to all ISTJ, INTJ, ESTJ, and ENTJ players (typical jobs for these players include management, engineering, computer programmer, scientist, consultant)
- **Type 2 Manager (TP)** relating to all ISTP, INTP, ENTP, and ESTP players (typical jobs for these players include broker, planner, lawyer, computer programmer, firefighter, architect)
- **Type 3 Wanderer (FP)** relating to all INFP, ENFP, ISFP, and ESFP players (typical jobs for these players include social worker, artist, therapist, services, teacher, musician)
- **Type 4 Participant (FJ)** relating to all ESFJ, ISFJ, ENFJ, and INFJ players (typical jobs for these players include retail, marketing, teacher, counselor, journalist, librarian)

(The four Myers-Briggs categories included in each type are listed in order of frequency of occurrence in the survey.)

These four types relate directly to four distinct play types, but in practice this should be seen as a continuum of play as shown in Figure 4.1 and not strict pigeon holes. By relating the Myers-Briggs data to data regarding preferred play, the specifics of each play type emerged. (The four play types are not mutually exclusive; one or more can be enjoyed by each individual player.)

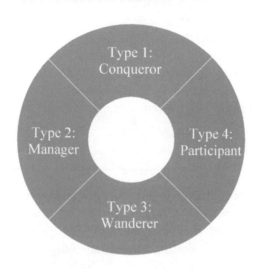

FIGURE 4.1   The four play styles of the DGD1 model.

The original hypothesis that motivated the study was largely disproved. Although the Introversion bias that was predicted was verified in the study, the Thinking bias was not. Rather, Thinking bias was associated with two types of play (Type 1 Conqueror and Type 2 Manager). The research found a Hardcore cluster associated with *each* of the four types of play—the common identity of the Hardcore clusters seemed to be related to a bias towards Introversion (which was predicted) and a bias towards Intuition (which was not).

Before the four types are explained in full, the Casual/Hardcore split (as it related to the DGD1 model) requires explanation.

Hardcore versus Casual

Previously, it was assumed that different styles of game appeal to Hardcore and Casual players. However, the survey data shows that while a distinct split between Hardcore and Casual players exists, each of these groups contains a class of player that fits one of the four types discussed (Types 1, 2, 3, and 4).

The demographic types can be separated into two sets—Hardcore (subtypes H1, H2, H3, and H4) and Casual (subtypes C1, C2, C3, and C4), as shown in Figure 4.2.

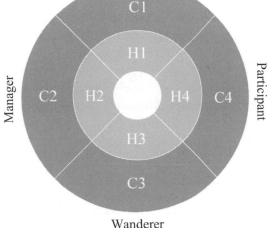

FIGURE 4.2 The two sets of subtypes within the DGD1 model, dividing the model into eight clusters.

In terms of the DGD1 model, the split into Hardcore and Casual sets requires some brief mention.

Hardcore players, according to DGD1:

- Buy and play many games
- Enjoy longer play sessions—regularly play for long periods of time
- Enjoy challenge, progression, and game mastery
- Tolerate a high dimensionality of control (that is, complex controls) because they have played many games and absorbed the skills involved
- See game playing as a lifestyle preference, and talking about games is a social component of their lives

Casual players, according to DGD1:

- Buy fewer games, buy popular games, or play games recommended to them (usually by Hardcore friends)
- Enjoy shorter play sessions—play in short bursts

- Prefer having fun, or immersing themselves in an atmospheric experience
- Generally require a low dimensionality of control (for example, driving games, puzzle games), although C1s are often an exception
- See game playing as another time-passing entertainment like TV or films; Casual players might use or refer to games in social situations with Hardcore friends

Both type and subtype are vital to a player's enjoyment of a game. Type determines the kind of gameplay they prefer, while subtype describes how they play. The game designer must take both into account.

A Type 3 Wanderer Casual player (C3), for example, is likely to enjoy a game design that is appealing to a Type 3 Wanderer Hardcore player (H3), but they might also require an easier difficulty level, an allowance for shorter play sessions, and other Casual-friendly features.

PLAY STYLE

Four different play styles are identified by the DGD1 model.

Type 1: Conqueror

TJ: Myers-Briggs Thinking & Judging Preferences

Conqueror (or Type 1) play involves winning and "beating the game." In single-player games, completing the game generally counts as winning, while in multiplayer the goal is to beat the other players—either way, winning is the most important factor in Type 1 play. Players who enjoy Type 1 play love the feeling of domination, or of knowledge, and enjoy being the person who their friends (or even strangers) turn to for advice about games. Games like *Half-Life: Counter-Strike* (Valve, 2001) were often listed as favorites, as well as computer role-playing games (RPGs) such as the *Final Fantasy* series (Square, 1987 onwards), by players who preferred Type 1 play.

The psychology of players preferring the Type 1 Conqueror play style appears to be directly related to what Nicole Lazzaro of XEODesign has characterised as "Hard Fun," that is, gameplay related to meaningful challenges, strategies, and puzzles [Lazzaro04]. Lazzaro identifies the emotions of anger, frustration, and boredom as key emotions associated with this style of play—but significantly also identifies *fiero* (or personal triumph over adversity) as a key emotion [Ekman03]. Fiero is that feeling of euphoria you experience when a difficult challenge has been overcome—the feeling that makes you raise your arms in the air and shake them triumphantly (something most sports fans experience when their team scores from behind). Players preferring Type 1 play do not necessarily need to experience anger prior to fiero, but they must have had to apply themselves.

For this style of play, the greater the challenge the greater the reward. It perhaps directly correlates with Capcom's "Mountain climbing" approach, which had previously been assumed to encompass the whole of the Hardcore. However, as we will see, other Hardcore players are not tied into this feeling of fiero, and in fact, some actively desire easier gameplay experiences.

Type 1 Conqueror style play attracts goal-oriented players—a stated goal is a challenge to be overcome—and they take whatever steps are required to fulfill that goal once it has been brought to their attention.

Hardcore (H1)

Predominantly INTJ, ISTJ

The H1 cluster represents a player who is often interested in completely understanding and completing the game. The idea of not completing a game that they have committed to is somewhat alien to them. Action games are popular, as are computer RPGs, among the more Intuitive H1 players. In the case studies, Sally characterized the general approach of the H1 player: "I won't finish the game until I've seen everything." They have a genuine desire to see and do everything—not just to win, but to utterly conquer the game in every sense. Because completing "everything" can be a common self-imposed goal for the H1 player, these are among the few types of players willing to spend time trying random combinations of game components in the hope of finding hidden elements (provided the game has made it known that hidden elements are there to find).

Games that do not provide enough materials for seeing everything to feel satisfying and a game that never demonstrates any significant challenge can be equally unimpressive. To some extent, the H1 player wants the game to kill their avatar—because only by reaching their limits in some way can they then come back and overcome that challenge. If the game does not demonstrate its difficulty to the H1 player, they are often completely oblivious of the degree of performance they are achieving (relative to another player).

For the most part, the H1 player seems mostly interested in overcoming their own challenges. Players of arcade games before the introduction of "pump and play" often competed with themselves to beat their own scores. "I used to go to the arcade every week," states Colin, "and play the same games each time. I was trying to do better than I did the last time." This approach of attempting to "beat oneself" seems to be largely an H1 style approach.

The Myers-Briggs types that dominate this cluster (INTJ, ISTJ) are two of four types that research has shown to be common to programmers, and indeed, Type 1 gameplay dominates current game design assumptions in most developers and publishers. In some cases, it seems that this has been identified as the only style of "legitimate" gameplay—which is a dangerous state of affairs in an industry where development costs are growing exponentially and audience sizes are growing linearly.

The H1 cluster showed much higher Sensing tendencies than the other Hardcore clusters, suggesting that the tendencies of the C1 cluster (discussed next) are bleeding into the H1 cluster (perhaps, in fact, two subtly different tendencies are at work here).

Casual (C1)

Predominantly ISTJ

Players fitting the C1 cluster seem mostly interested in competition and winning (or having fun by competing to win). C1 players are proportionally more Sensing than their Hardcore counterparts, and therefore likely to be involved in direct competition. First-person shooters and competitive racing games appeal to the C1 audience.

The interest in computer RPGs does not greatly extend to the C1 group, although they might still play them. A more visceral style of play is called for. In single player games, fiero is still the payoff the player is attempting to experience—although they might be oblivious to this. It is not uncommon for a C1 player (or a Type 1 Conqueror player in general) to be found cursing and hating a game that they later purport to have been a "great game." If the game does not challenge, it is somehow lesser in their eyes.

Unlike the H1 subtype, players fitting the C1 subtype seem more interested in interpersonal competition. They show more of a liking for what Lazzaro characterizes as "The People Factor" [Lazarro04]—especially the emotion of *schadenfreude* (gloating over the misfortune of a friend)—but are still primarily interested in overcoming a difficult challenge. However, whereas the H1 cluster represents players likely to seek fiero in single player games and in personal challenges, the C1 player seems more actively interested in seeking it in multiplayer situations. "I want a way to crush my opponents," Pete said in his interview, "A skill level with no roof." This is a typical C1 approach—winning is not enough; opponents must be utterly defeated, humiliated, and crushed underfoot.

Laughing at other people's misfortunes is a commonly enjoyed experience. Games that allow the player to snipe at random people are enjoyed for an almost comedic value, provided the game is not portrayed in super-realistic terms. This indeed contributed heavily to the success of the *GTA* series (DMA Design/Rockstar North, 1997 onwards), which was heavily enjoyed by Type 1-oriented players, especially C1s. The opportunity to create carnage appears to be an appealing aspect of the C1's play style.

Unique among the Casual clusters, the C1 players tolerate complex control systems (as indicated by the willingness to play twin-stick controlled first-person shooters on consoles). This is perhaps due to the fact that this cluster has been catered to in games to a high degree for some time—hence the audience (even the Casual audience of this Type) has built up a high degree of familiarity to common game components. Alternatively, C1-oriented players might persevere with unfamiliar control systems for reasons similar to those for which they play games in the first place—they refuse to be beaten.

This familiarity has a negative aspect, however—the C1 player is likely to be highly annoyed with a game that does not meet their expectations. Deviations from the norm had better contribute to amusement or fiero, or they are likely to be used as criticisms. Although C1 players might say they are looking for originality, their purchasing habits and favorite games reveal a different pattern, and a few new ideas in an established framework might be more effective than an entirely new approach (which will inevitably be interpreted in terms of the established forms).

The Type 1 Style of Play

The following sections summarize the Type 1 Conqueror play style.

Progress: Rapid Advancement

Players preferring Type 1 play want to improve their abilities in the game world—to get stronger and better. The addictiveness of computer RPGs for H1 players might be tied to the numerous ways these games support constant improvement of the core characters, creating a feeling of rapid advancement from what is in fact a laborious process of selecting the best equipment from a large pool of options. Because the payoff is to feel stronger and more able to conquer, the relative tedium of the process is overlooked—a means to an end. Similarly, the C1 player wants to receive better weapons and power ups in the games they play (first-person shooters are a staple of this group).

Story: Plot or Irrelevant

Type 1-oriented players are focused on plot events, or in the case of C1 players might believe that story is not important in a game. Although H1 players might talk about "good characters," their favorite games show a focus on typical wish-fulfillment stereotypes—the stories they identify as good are mainly those which feature plot twists and intrigue, not strong character-based stories.

Social: Online

Type 1-oriented players can be characterized as the "vocal hardcore" who enjoy arguing with other players about games at online Web sites and the like—even in social situations they feel a certain need to "win" (in this case, win the argument). Online play is no barrier to Type-1 play; the player need not see or know their opponent to achieve satisfaction after a victory, though it is likely that all players prefer to play with friends.

Type 2: Manager

TP: Myers-Briggs Thinking & Perceiving Preferences

Manager (or Type 2) play revolves around a strategic or tactical challenge. Players who prefer this style of play are interested in the mastery of the game—that is, the process-oriented challenge of learning how to play well. Whereas the Type 1-oriented player wants to beat the game, the Type 2-oriented player wants to master the methods of the game. Winning is to some extent meaningless to the archetypal Manager if they have not earned it. A key distinction between Type 2 and Type 1 play is that even when the game has been mastered, the Type 2-oriented player is likely to continue playing for enjoyment—because they enjoy the experience of being the master of a particular game. The Type 1 Conqueror player is likely to stop when they feel they have beaten the game (when there is no more challenge to be overcome); a Type 2 Manager player is more likely to try and beat the game again, putting their higher degree of mastery into practice, and enjoying the process of play.

Type 2 Manager play works well in open games (games with no specific endpoint), especially strategy and construction/management games. A game environment in a game providing good Type 2 play often consists of many different elements that can be employed in different ways. As such, pure Type 2 play is more common in PC games than in console games, in that these games often feature interfaces supporting many different options for interaction, from which many different strategies can be employed.

Although multiplayer games seem less appealing to Type 2-oriented players, multiplayer games that attract both Type 1 Conqueror and Type 2 Manager players (that is, those with a strategic level as well as a competitive level) produce interesting dynamics. Initially, the Type 1 players might dominate (by finding the easiest advantages), after which the Type 2 players devise strategies to overcome these advantages, if this is possible. This then presents a new challenge to the Type 1 players to overcome, and so forth.

Hardcore (H2)

Predominantly INTP, ISTP

Players in the H2 cluster are especially motivated by a desire for strategic gameplay. Games such as the *Civilization* series (Firaxis, 1991 onwards) and the *Homeworld* series (Relic, 1999 onwards) occurred on the "favorite game" lists of many players in this cluster. They are looking to be presented with a set of tools and a series of challenges that they can master by acquiring or honing their skills. Adventure games were also listed as favorites for many H2 players; many reported a certain sadness that the classic adventure game genre is no longer well supported, and classic adventure games were also reported as favorites.

"Hard fun" is again an issue, but the H2's motivation is less likely to be the pursuit of big "payoffs" of fiero and more likely to be tied to strategic mastery and overcoming puzzles. Len characterizes the H2 style: "I'm looking for games that allow you to play for hours without getting bored, to be challenging, but not impossible, and to have a lot going on without being overwhelming." Unlike the H1 player, the H2 player is likely to stop playing if the game presents too difficult a challenge. They are not willing to endure the same degrees of anger and frustration as a Type 1 Conqueror player. Although they might experience the same satisfaction from fiero, if this emotional reward is hard to reach, they are more likely to stop playing that particular game and instead choose another. Nonetheless, H2 players display degrees of patience that other players rarely exhibit.

The desire to complete everything is less important to the H2 than the H1; because the Type 2 Manager player is more process-oriented, the activities that keep their attention are almost always those with the capacity to refine a technique. Searching an environment for hidden features is therefore not greatly appealing to an H2 player—unless this searching somehow makes use of techniques that the player has learned to master. Then the search becomes a chance to enjoy the degree of mastery they have attained and an opportunity to devise new strategies using the tools the game has provided.

Any problem a Type 2 game throws at the H2 player is interpreted as a challenge to overcome by devising a stratagem. Obstacles that cannot be overcome methodically, or recurring negative events for which no strategy can overcome (or minimize the effect of) in general reduce their interest in playing—but a considerable payoff is achieved each time they devise a strategy that is effective.

The appeal of adventure games to this cluster probably lies with the logical challenge presented. Although these games often do not appear process-oriented, in general the player is given an inventory of items that can be used to interact with the world. Intuiting the meaning and purpose of a found item presents a form of strategic challenge that generally is not found in other games, and most players preferring other play types do not enjoy this kind of gameplay where the goal and methods often have to be deduced, rather than being clearly stated.

This cluster includes the other two Myers-Briggs types that are common to programmers (INTP, ISTP), and therefore it is unsurprising that strategy and construction/management games are well catered for in the products currently on offer in the marketplace. Indeed, whole studios appear to exist whose programmers are primarily Type 2 in orientation—companies that specialize in strategy games of all kinds.

Casual (C2)

Predominantly ISTP

Similar in their needs to their H2 brethren, players who fit the C2 cluster are less Intuitive and hence more comfortable with familiar settings. Realism is desired, and construction and management games are enormously popular. These are the players that helped drive Maxis' *SimCity* series (from 1989 onwards) to success. However, it would be wrong to conclude that the C2 player is interested only in strategy and simulation games, as the gaming tastes of this cluster overlaps significantly with that of the C1 cluster.

Lacking the same degree of game literacy as their H2 counterparts, simpler control methods might be preferred, but highly complex interfaces are acceptable because these interfaces are usually accompanied by highly complex sets of game components that support the Type 2 Manager strategic style of play.

C2 players have considerably less patience with being stuck at a game than H2 players. Getting stuck usually heralds a loss of interest in the game. "I want a feeling of steady progress, no matter how crap I am at playing it," Leo explains. "I want the game to adjust to my level, giving me a sense of being challenged but not walked over." He adds: "I prefer strategy to arcade." This neatly characterizes the C2 approach to games, although many players in the C2 cluster enjoy arcade as well as strategy games.

All Type 2-oriented players enjoy the feeling of building something, but the C2 is more likely to want to actually construct something, while the H2 player is content to "build" a more ephemeral construct—a viable strategy or a flexible combination of strategic units. If the game tries to interfere with what the player is building (by the addition of disasters or other random events), this might be interpreted by an H2 player as a challenge for which a defensive strategy must be devised; a C2 player is more likely to experience the feeling that the game is "stomping on their sandcastle" and lose interest.

In terms of games that appeal to both C1 and C2 players (especially driving games, which share an appealing sense of wish fulfillment to most male players), the difference between these two clusters can be found in their attitude to challenge. The C1 player tends to demonstrate the Type 1 tendency to tolerate fail-repeat gameplay in their quest for fiero; the C2 player is more likely to put aside a tough challenge, do something else for a while, and return to it later. Games with relatively smooth difficulty curves can appeal to both the C1's desire for fiero and the C2's desire for mastery.

The Type 2 Style of Play

The following sections summarize the Type 2 Manager play style.

Progress: Steady

The archetypal Manager player wants to feel they are making steady progress; they do want a degree of challenge, but they often give up if it gets too hard for them (or in the case of H2s, if it seems that no strategy can be applied reliably against a particular recurring problem). Progress can be measured by the acquisition of new units or abilities, or simply by an improvement in their capacity to overcome by strategic thinking. However, they do not generally desire to reach a state whereby they can always beat the game—the game must rise to their level of challenge.

Story: Plot

Much like the Type 1-oriented player, Type 2-oriented players enjoy the story of a game on an intellectual level and are therefore more motivated by issues of plot than of character. Unlike most other types, the Type 2 player is likely to enjoy political intrigue and other socio-political elements to plot and setting.

Social: None?

If a social side to Type 2 Manager game activities exists, it was not found in this survey. Some Type 2-oriented players appear to participate in multiplayer games, but it was by no means the norm.

Type 3: Wanderer

FP: Myers-Briggs Feeling & Perceiving Preferences

The player who enjoys Type 3 Wanderer play is a player in search of a fun experience. Whereas players oriented towards Type 1 and 2 play are looking for a challenge, the Type 3 player is looking for enjoyment, or a unique experience. They won't play a game they aren't enjoying and, in fact, stop playing the moment it ceases to be fun. Genre did not seem to be an issue for these clusters—although the *Super Monkey Ball* series (Sega/Amusement Vision, 2001 onwards) and games in the *Zelda* series were often mentioned. The former is likely enjoyed because of the variety of mini-games offered; variety is definitely desirable.

Type 3-oriented players seem to connect with what Lazzaro characterizes as "Easy Fun" (associated with the emotions of wonder, awe, and mystery) and also with "Altered States" (emotions generated from perception and behavior) [Lazzaro04]. Although an easy challenge entertains, the Type 3 Wanderer needs to be able to give up and do something else. Any requirement for "jumping through hoops" in a game—any linear sequence of problems to be overcome—is likely to damage that game's ability to deliver Type 3 play. Like the Type 2 players, if the game ceases to meet their needs, they stop playing. The Type 3-oriented player can take a dislike to a game within minutes of playing, or even from just seeing someone else playing it.

Fiero does not appear to be a factor for players preferring Type 3 play; indeed, because hard problems are likely to cause them to give up, they rarely experience the emotional reward of fiero, and they avoid games that are obviously challenging in this way. It is the altered state of perception that attracts them—the imagination of being in another world or the strange experience of becoming one with an abstract play experience (something most Tetris players have experienced after a long play session). They enjoy the feeling of everything falling into place around them— ideally because of their contribution to the process. Toyplay is vastly more important than conventional challenge-oriented gameplay.

Unlike players who prefer Type 1 Conqueror and Type 2 Manager play, the Type 3-oriented player seems relatively likely to play single player games with other people. They enjoy contributing to the process of progressing through a game and can even enjoy being a spectator for an atmospheric, story-oriented game. In many cases, if the Type 3-oriented player gets stuck in a game, they might turn to a Type 1 or 2 friend to help them out (especially in cases of Type 3 Wanderers whose romantic partner is also a game player). Several case studies found Type 3-oriented players who played games with friends or significant others—this might be a result of the general level of difficulty most games are pitched at (which in turn probably relates to the dominance of Type 1- and Type 2-biased individuals involved in making games). It must be noted, however, that methods of gameplay were not the focus of the case studies, and it might be that players preferring all types of play sometimes play in a 'pad passing' style with friends.

In the population as a whole, Myers-Briggs Feeling-Perceiving preferences are more associated with females than males, and indeed, the Type 3 approach to games might seem to some as "feminine." Nonetheless, the survey demonstrated that Type 3 Wanderer play is evidenced in both men and women, and that gender is not strictly an issue. However, there may be a large untapped market of female Type 3-oriented players for whom the current focus on Type 1 gameplay and male-fantasy settings is highly off-putting.

Hardcore (H3)

Predominantly INFP

The most Intuitive of all the groups looked at, players in the H3 cluster appear to be dreamers who want the game to dream with them. They consider themselves Hardcore because they play a lot of games, but unlike H1 and H2 players, they often consider games to be too hard. They show an interest in finesse—completing a section of the game is not as important as having "done it right," that is, in an aesthetically or stylistically pleasing manner. The more the game assists them, the better to some extent—whereas a Type 1-oriented player enjoys mastering a complex control mechanism (such as a fighting game), a Type 3-oriented player generally wants to press a single button and have something pleasing happen.

Story and setting can be of vital importance, as the whole atmosphere of the game is a factor in enjoyment. Once H3 players become emotionally invested in the characters of a story, they are hooked on the desire to see the story progress. This is a goal in itself. Barry said of this: "After I grow tired of a game or get stuck, if there is a story, I always cheat through the rest of the game to find out what happens!"

This is not to say that the H3-oriented player requires a story, however, as the puzzle game genre includes many examples popular with this cluster. Provided a game is providing an experience they enjoy, H3-oriented players happily play that game for lengths of time disproportional to the usual assumptions. The game does not need to provide new challenges—more of the same is acceptable. *Bust a Move/Puzzle Bobble* (Taito, 1995) is a perfect example of an H3 game drawing from the "Altered States" type of enjoyment. It exhibits brightly colored, fun environments, and an intuitive core play mechanism by which the player produces satisfying changes in the environment.

H3 players seem able to become exceptionally skilled at a game that they enjoy playing, but this is not the same as desiring a high degree of challenge. Games for the H3 audience need to progress at a gradual pace, or the players feel left behind, lose interest, and play something else. H3 players typically play many games at once and often think nothing of playing a game for only a few hours in total before trying something new.

Casual (C3)

Predominantly ENFP

C3 players appear to have similar tastes to the H3s, but are usually less game-literate and therefore find it harder to enjoy many games. They need their games to be supremely easy; they want to feel they are accomplishing something in the game world, but do not specifically need to be challenged. Games for the C3 player are supposed to be a way to relax.

Alice gives a classic example of the attitude of a C3 player: "Games should be relaxing in every way while still giving you the feeling of accomplishing something." They want to feel that things are progressing (otherwise they become bored), but they don't want to have to struggle to achieve that progress.

Because the games currently in the market rarely meet the needs of C3 players, when they find a game they like, they are likely to play it for a considerable amount of time—often far in excess of what the H3 can attain. The H3 player is likely to find new games to grab their attention, but the C3 player encounters few games targeting them.

The C3s are undoubtedly the most recent battlefield in terms of brand dominance and new audiences—although most publishers are struggling to understand how to reach this audience because their only business strategy is to watch what succeeds and then clone it. Targeting this audience is a particular problem, however, in that most games reach a Casual audience only by way of Hardcore evangelist clusters (primarily consisting of vocal Type 1-play preferring players)—and the easiness of play that C3s desire is anathema to the fiero-dominated challenge experience that the evangelizing players seek. New market vectors are required to hit this audience more effectively.

The Type 3 Style of Play

The following sections summarise the Type 3 Wanderer play style.

Progress: New Toys

The Wanderer-oriented game should supply new and fun things to do. Its players don't want to complete everything; they generally want to try new things. They are much more interested in toyplay than gameplay, and they love games that present a playground for them to experiment within. The continuing success of the platform game genre might be in part due to the fact that the standard structure consists of a playground in which not everything need be completed—a situation well suited to Type 3 play. The fact that most are loosely story oriented and present colorful and imaginative environments is likely another factor.

Story: Character/Emotion

The Type 3-oriented player is generally not interested in the plot so much as the character and emotional elements. They want to identify with the characters and share in their emotional journey—although few games deliver this experience. In many games, they invest their own emotional meaning to the game world (especially in toyplay games).

Social: Talk about What They Like

H3 players talk to other gamers about what they like and enjoy; C3 players might show other players what they are enjoying. In both cases, arguments are hated and avoided at all costs. Although some magazine reviewers in the specialist press are H3 players, for the most part the demographic associated with Type 3 Wanderer play is an invisible part of the gaming audience.

Type 4: Participant

FJ: Myers-Briggs Feeling & Judging Preferences

Despite being the largest group in the population at large, people who prefer Type 4 Participant play represented the smallest cluster in both the survey and the online data. In truth, we know very little about these players, except that the more Intuitive among them seem very story-oriented, and the more Sensing-biased appear to play games only as a social experience, for example, something like *Dance Dance Revolution* (Konami, 1999). They want to participate either in the story the game is offering or with other players in some emotional context.

It is possible that the H4 and C4 groupings are in fact two completely different styles of play—because the H4s seem largely concerned with story-oriented games such as computer RPGs, while the C4s are more concerned with fun multiplayer or social experiences. However, so little data was gathered from this cluster (or clusters), it is difficult to draw conclusions.

Hardcore (H4)

Predominantly ESFJ?

Very little data arose from players in the H4 cluster, making it difficult to say anything about them in confidence. Myers-Briggs FJ-types are very much focused on "doing the right thing" in the real world, and games might feel frivolous to them. The more Intuitive H4 players seemed very focused on computer RPGs—perhaps because these were the closest they can find to a game that gives them a feeling of participating in the development of the story.

Competitiveness is not greatly desired. "I like games where collaboration is primary and competition only secondary," Perry noted. Like the Type 3-oriented players, fiero is not necessarily desired, but they appear to show much greater willingness to persevere with a game. In this respect, they sometimes resemble the Type 1 Conqueror player in their tenacity.

Casual (C4)

Predominantly ESFJ?

These players seem mostly to enjoy playing games as part of a group. They might enjoy playing co-operative games, but they also seem to enjoy competitive multiplayer games—provided the other players are in the same room. The social experience is vital, what Lazzaro calls "The People Factor." Amusement is the key—laughter is much more common in groups of players than in players on their own [Lazzaro04], and the C4 player appears to desire that form of social entertainment. Games that simulate a social environment are also a good fit to this cluster. *The Sims* (Maxis, 2000) almost certainly succeeded thanks to the support of C4-oriented players.

Despite the emphasis on social play, online multiplayer does not appear to appeal to players in the C4 cluster. Rupert said: "I want either a strong multiplayer element (on consoles, not online), or an interesting, immersive storyline in single player." Indeed, the Massively Multiplayer Online Role-Playing Game (MMORPG) survey data showed that Type 4 Participant players were the smallest minority. If the people are not physically present, it doesn't feel like a social experience to this group of players.

The Type 4 Style of Play

The Type 4 Participant play style can be summarized as follows.

Progress: Narrative

Players exhibiting Type 4 preferences appear to be interested in changing emotional states—either of a group of players or of a group of characters within the game world. It might be that these are two separate tendencies that have been erroneously conflated into a single typing.

Story: Character/Emotion

Much like the Type 3 Wanderer, players who prefer the Participant style are interested in the characters in the game—but they appear much more likely to want to feel in control of how the story advances. They do not appear to be content with being told a story; they want to interact with the story in some manner.

Social: Multiplayer

Players who prefer the Participant style appear to thrive on a good multiplayer game. As previously noted, they do not tend to enjoy online play—they must relate with other players face to face.

DISTRIBUTION OF PLAY STYLES

Figure 4.3 shows proportions of each cluster of players preferring a specific play type in the survey. It is difficult to know from a single survey how much of the bias towards the Type 3 play orientation found in this survey is a result of an underlying bias in the population and how much is a bias in the sampling, but it is clear that the pattern is the same in both Hardcore and Casual players.

It is quite likely that the survey did not attract sufficient numbers of Type 1 Conqueror players, because these players are early adopters and less likely to want to enter competitions to win games. However, it is also possible that the Type 3

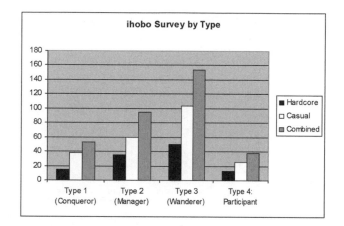

FIGURE 4.3 Proportions of people surveyed fitting each of the four play styles.

Wanderer player exists in large numbers and is currently poorly serviced by the games industry.

The scarcity of Type 4 Participant players is curious and hard to interpret. It might be that they do not enjoy games or that their play needs are not being met by the current market. More data is needed before a conclusion can be drawn, and a new audience model might make these issues redundant.

Comparisons to Control Data

Figure 4.4 shows how the proportions found in the survey compare to the expected distributions in the general population, based upon other Myers-Briggs typology studies. The data gathered regarding players of MMORPGs is also shown for comparison.

Survey data represents this study, while Bartle data is from the (independent) study of players of MMORPGs that included Myers-Briggs data [2]. In analyzing the data relative to the control, understand that the control data represents distributions of Myers-Briggs tendencies in the population at large; therefore, an assumption has been made that the correlations between Myers-Briggs type and Demographic Game Design type hold as a general case.

The biggest surprise here is that the Type 4-oriented personality is the most common in the population at large, but rare in both sets of survey data. This seems to indicate quite strongly an issue to be explored—either fewer Type 4 Participant players are drawn to games, or the games that Type 4 players are looking for are not currently being made or being well distributed.

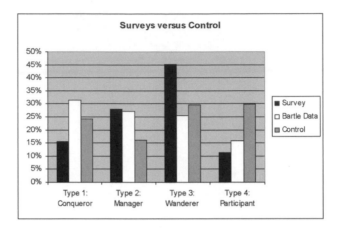

FIGURE 4.4 Proportions of play style preference as implied by the survey, by Bartle survey data, and by control data.

The low proportion of Type 1 Conqueror players in the survey probably represents a sampling error (the Bartle data is probably more accurate in this case), but the Type 2 Manager and Type 3 Wanderer players do appear to exist in large numbers. A follow-up study would be invaluable to interpreting this data accurately.

Gender

Figures 4.5 and 4.6 show the percentages of male and female players found in the survey data.

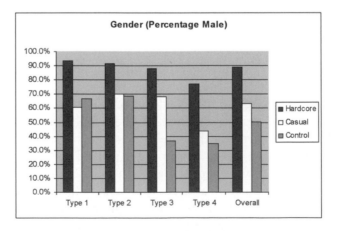

FIGURE 4.5 Percentages of male players in the Hardcore and Casual sets of data and in the control data.

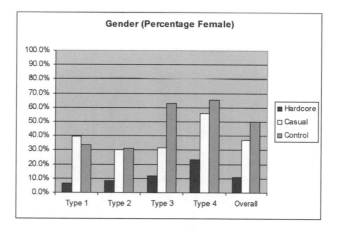
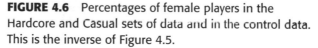

FIGURE 4.6 Percentages of female players in the Hardcore and Casual sets of data and in the control data. This is the inverse of Figure 4.5.

Unsurprisingly, players preferring all Types were predominantly male, but the Casual sets included many more female players—37% female overall rather than 11% in the Hardcore. Clearly, gaming is opening up to a wider, more gender-varied audience—the fact that *The Sims* attracts an audience that is purportedly 70% female is a clear indication of the maturing nature of the game market [Leinfellner03].

C4 was the only group in which women outnumbered men (56% female, 44% male), but this might reflect the bias in the population at large (65% of people in the general population who match the Myers-Briggs type associated with Type 4 Participant play are female). Again, the dearth of information on the Type 4-oriented players makes any conclusions very difficult without resorting to further studies.

Introversion versus Extroversion

Figure 4.7 compares each play type in terms of the number of people in the survey showing a preference for Introversion.

If you look at the degree of Introversion, the pattern is striking. The online players were the most Introverted, then the Hardcore, then the Casual. A continuum exists between these groups towards the population norm, and this fits the prediction that game players are predominantly Introverted—the only prediction from the original hypothesis to hold true in this data.

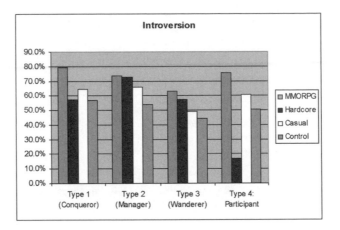

FIGURE 4.7   Percentage of people surveyed showing Introverted preference in the MMORPG survey data, the Hardcore and Casual sets, and the control data.

The anomaly with the H4 cluster probably results from the small number found in the survey, but might actually reflect the completely different gameplay needs of these players—namely a bias towards social interaction through games ("The People Factor") over challenge or experience. Anecdotal evidence suggests that traditional "parlor games," such as Rob Angel's *Pictionary* (originally released by Parker Brothers, 1986), appeal to the Type 4 Participant player—a style of gameplay rarely provided by computer games. The possible exception of this might be the *You Don't Know Jack* series (Sierra, 1995 onwards), which has obvious parallels with *Trivial Pursuit* (Horn Abbot, 1982 onwards), one of the best-selling games of all time, having sold more copies than any computer game ever manufactured [3].

It is hardly surprising that a form of entertainment that for the most part consists of an individual staring at a screen should demonstrate a bias towards Introversion; however, this assumption has not previously been demonstrated by empirical evidence.

The results show that the Casual players, too, were slightly more Introvert than the population as a whole, suggesting quite strongly that Introversion is a trait that predisposes people to game playing of all kinds.

Conversely, Extroverts do play games by themselves, but usually only when there is no one else around. "I usually play games at night, when everyone has gone to bed," Ardan reported. This might sound like a Hardcore response, but in fact, Ardan worked a night shift at a local hotel and therefore frequently found himself with no one around to interact with. He passed these times by playing computer RPGs.

This behavior can be seen as roughly equivalent to the way Extrovert-biased people use TV and films as a means of passing time enjoyably. They are exceptionally unlikely to undertake long play sessions of games in the way that Introvert players do.

Earlier computer games were largely targeted at Introverts, but as the mass market has been tapped, a greater balance has been achieved. We have recognized, for example, that many players want to play games only for short period of times in each session (an Extrovert-style approach). Some publishers have even begun to tap directly into Extrovert style games, such as Konami's *Dance Dance Revolution* series (from 1999); something the market has largely ignored up until this point.

Intuition versus Sensing

Figure 4.8 compares each play type in terms of the number of people in the survey showing a preference for Intuition.

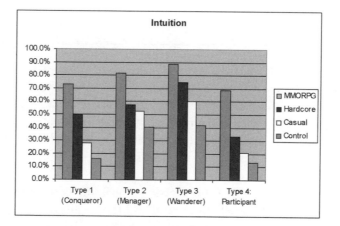

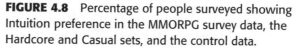

FIGURE 4.8   Percentage of people surveyed showing Intuition preference in the MMORPG survey data, the Hardcore and Casual sets, and the control data.

In the population as a whole, Intuitive-preference is outnumbered 3 to 1 by Sensing-preference [CAPT02]. Not so among gamers. A continuum exists between the online players (most Intuitive) through the Hardcore players to the Casual players—who show a similar distribution to the population as a whole. Clearly, Intuition constitutes an important factor in Hardcore and Online players.

People who are Intuitition-dominant are pattern-seekers, and in games, they enjoy working things out for themselves—Type 1 Conqueror and Type 2 Manager players with an Intuitive preference enjoy puzzle solving and lateral thinking, while Type 3 Wanderer players embrace more abstract gameplay. Intuitive players persevere with longer learning curves and more complex game mechanics. They are imaginative and drawn to creative, original settings.

Conversely, people who are Sensing-dominant want to know what they are supposed to be doing at all times. Clear instructions and (often) a lower level of complexity are vital, as is familiarity of setting (real world or a familiar license setting). Sensors are also more motivated by issues of branding and popularity. When a game seems like "the next big thing," a Sensing-preference player is more likely to buy it—they often enjoy participating in fads and crazes.

Older computer games were very much focused on Intuitive-style gameplay—especially Type 1 Conqueror Type 2 Manager style puzzles. However, publishers such as EA have recognized the value of targeting the Sensing audience (without identifying them as such) by, for example, taking the abstract content of a game such as *Quake* (id Software, 1996) and repackaging it in a familiar setting for *Medal of Honor* (DreamWorks Interactive, 1999).

CONCLUSION

Making games to please a specific audience has always been a commercial goal of the games industry, but audience requirements have formerly been judged by the assessment of sales and of the apparent popularity of previously released games of a similar genre. Thus, large numbers of games are created to satisfy Type 1- and 2-oriented players (specifically H1 and H2 players), as these players are served by the video games specialist press and are also the types that correspond to the vast majority of game programmers.

In recent years, due to the growing availability of gaming systems (driven by the success of Sony's PlayStation brand and the increasing ubiquity of both PCs and consoles in the home), many more people have become exposed to video games. For example, one widely documented trend involves girlfriends of game-playing males taking up the controller out of curiosity. As gaming continues to lose its "geek" tag, such trends will continue.

To expand the market for video games, we require wider audiences, but it will not be possible to target these directly. A new approach is required, designing games that still appeal to the core demographic, but also appeal to a wider market whose needs can be very different. Market-oriented design can help any project succeed commercially by assessing the audience for a product before design is initiated. In such a situation the chance of catalyzing sales to a wider audience will be greatly increased, relative to a game which is focused on one small part of the audience.

It would be invaluable for another party to follow up this data with a new survey to verify the results (perhaps in the United States where Myers-Briggs data is widely known already), although the underlying observations are independent to the distributions of players preferring each type. Although this initial study shows intriguing results, it needs independent verification and more research to advance the underlying model.

One possible next step would be to devise a test that explores the elements of Myers-Briggs in direct reference to game playing. The case studies showed that there were people whose lifestyle orientation and gameplay orientation did not seem to match, for example. Often their gameplay orientation matched the Myers-Briggs type they belonged to during their teenage years. Alternatively, several deeper analyses of the Myers-Briggs typology could be used to provide a more detailed analysis of the audience in relation to psychology (aspects of which will be touched upon in the next chapter).

What is clear is that designers who design games solely to please their own sensibilities are unlikely to create genuinely mass market games. For lower budget games, this poses no problems, because a large, acknowledged audience for "traditional" video games (that is, those demonstrating Type 1 Conqueror and Type 2 Manager play) exists. But when designers consider the mass market, more consideration must be used when designing games for their intended audiences. The DGD1 model is intended as a tool to expand the perspective of game designers when tackling the diverse needs of players.

ENDNOTES

[1] The survey included 286 male subjects and 122 female subjects. 194 subjects were age 18–25, 81 subjects were age 26–33, 55 subjects were age 34–41, 36 subjects were age 42–49, 27 subjects were age 50+, and 15 subjects were less than 18 years of age. Case studies were a representative cross-section. Data was collected between 2002 and 2004, with the bulk of the survey data in 2003.

[2] Bartle type information in connection with Myers-Briggs typology collected, collated, and reported by Erwin S. Andreasen, reported with permission and with grateful thanks. No direct correlations between Myers-Briggs type and Bartle type were found—a preference for Exploration seemed to be endemic to the system.

[3] *Trivial Pursuit* has sold 70 million copies [Trivial05]; the highest selling video game of all time is *Super Mario Bros.* (Nintendo, 1985), which sold 40 million copies [GameState03].

5 Player Abilities

In This Chapter

- The Experience of Flow
- Types of Games
- Temperament Theory
- DGD1 Model and Temperament Skill Sets
- Conclusion
- Endnotes

Once we have decided to view the audience as a varied group of individuals who, at a statistical level at least, share some commonalities, we are at the beginning of how to use an audience model to inform game design decisions. The DGD1 model presents one such approach by drawing upon Myers-Briggs typology as its foundation to produce a set of categories to which the game audience can be said to belong. Of course, such a model works only when considering an entire audience, not an individual, because the variety at the level of individuals bleaches out the details that can be observed in larger populations where statistics can be applied.

Before looking at how to conduct design with an audience model for reference, we need to consider in more detail what different players are capable of doing.

What are their strengths and weaknesses? What are their goals and ideals? What gives them enjoyment? The previous chapter provided a general overview of the nature of the four player types described by DGD1, but we still have to understand how they relate to each other.

This chapter initially discusses the concept of *flow* as a means to understand what players want from their individual play experiences. Next, we look at different types of games and see how this relates to both flow and the needs of the different types of players. Finally, we use Temperament theory to explore the hypothetical skill sets of different player types. By comparing these skills sets with game and play types, we can begin to form an impression of what individual players want from their games and therefore hopefully deliver those requirements more efficiently.

THE EXPERIENCE OF FLOW

It is often said that the goal of a game is to "deliver great gameplay," an adage that is both seductive and misleading. If players have different needs from a game, what is "gameplay"? If it is a synonym for an enjoyable play experience, then we should expect there to be many different types of gameplay (and, as previously observed, of toyplay as well).

The psychologist Mihaly Csikszentmihalyi, a professor and former chairman of the Department of Psychology at the University of Chicago, conducted research into what he called *optimal experience* or *flow*. The essential hypothesis of his work is that in certain mental states we feel a complete and energized focus in an activity, accompanied by a high level of enjoyment and fullfillment in what we are doing. The term *flow* comes from the way many of the participants in Csikszentmihalyi's studies described the state: "going with the flow" or similar phrases [Csikzentmihalyi90].

Csikszentmihalyi identifies seven characteristics of the flow experience, not all of which need be present together for flow to be experienced:

- The subject is undertaking an activity that they believe they can complete
- The subject is able to focus their concentration completely on the activity
- The activity has clear goals
- The activity has direct feedback
- The subject experiences a sense of effortless involvement, such that worries and concerns vanish
- The subject feels that they are in control of the activity
- Subjective experience of time is altered

Not all of these components need to be present together for flow to be experienced, but collectively they represent the common traits of the flow experience [Csikzentmihalyi90].

Anyone with a passion for playing games, or who has interviewed or studied those that have such a passion, will recognize many of these components as common to the playing of video games, and that the state of flow can be correlated with a highly enjoyable (and immersive) play experience.

Csikszentmihalyi suggests that certain activities are conducive to flow because they were, in effect, designed to make optimal experience easier to achieve—by having rules that require the learning of skills, setting up goals, providing feedback, and making control possible. These elements are common to almost all video games.

This hypothesis suggests, therefore, that to provide an enjoyable experience, a game should endeavor to place the player in an optimal experience, or at the very least, provide a framework that makes an optimal experience more likely to occur.

Difficulty

The psychology of optimal experience comments on what happens when the subject falls outside of the flow experience: when the subject faces challenges for which they have insufficient skills, they experience anxiety, and when the subject faces challenges for which their skills are excessive to the needs of the challenge, they experience boredom. Figure 5.1 illustrates the nature of this relationship.

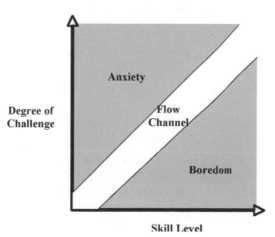

FIGURE 5.1   The flow channel is the balance point between skill level and the degree of challenge, according to flow theory. When challenge exceeds ability, anxiety results, and when ability exceeds challenge, boredom results.

Figure 5.1 immediately suggests that the inclusion of a choice of difficulty level (where technically viable) is always of some benefit. Because the skill level of the players varies wildly, offering different skill levels increases the chance that the game can provide an experience of flow (or approaching flow). However, this immediately presents issues. How will the player know what skill level they have before playing the game? Will a Casual player (with low game literacy) think of changing the difficulty level if the game bores them?

Furthermore, we anticipate that a player's skill level with a game increases as the game is played, which seems to imply that the difficulty of the game should increase as the game progresses. But we cannot know how fast the player will learn, and we can be certain that different players will learn at different rates. Therein lies the danger of a linear structure: if the player's skill level does not rise at the same rate as the game difficulty, the game begins to become a source of anxiety, and the player stops playing if no other motivating factor to continue exists.

In the case of players preferring a Type 1 Conqueror style of play, their desire to conquer, to beat the game, might overcome any anxiety at being out of their depth. Indeed, players preferring Type 1 Conqueror play seem to thrive on difficulty, and in some cases purposefully take on more demanding tasks to rise to the challenge of overcoming them.

Conversely, players preferring Type 3 Wanderer and Type 4 Participant styles of play show no such desire for "victory at all costs." If the game stresses them out, and they find nothing else that they can do in the game world, they are more likely to stop playing—and indeed, might lose interest in video games altogether if their conception of games is that this particular experience is typical of what they offer.

But as we have already noted, Type 3 Wanderer and Type 4 Participant play is often more related to toyplay than to gameplay. To understand what flow means in the context of toyplay, it is necessary to look in more depth at the nature of play itself, which we will do later in this chapter.

Goals and Feedback

Two particular elements of the flow experience are worth special mention. Presenting clear goals and providing feedback are properties of the activity being undertaken and not qualities of the participant (or the participant's experience). Therefore, it's easy to assume that providing goals (and feedback in regard to goal completion) is a universal component of game design. Indeed, Noah Falstein's 400 Project lists as its first meta-rule: "Provide Clear Short-term Goals" [1].

Case studies do demonstrate that a desire to know what one is expected to do is a common trait among all players, but it is not always the case that the player's chief concern is the goal. Type 1 Conqueror style play (and to some extent Type 4 Participant style play) tends towards an inherently goal-oriented style of play, and games intending to meet these needs should provide clear goals and the feedback required to inform players that they are on track. However, the Type 2 Manager and Type 3 Wanderer styles of play, with their emphasis on process-orientation, seem to operate in a different fashion. It has been noted that players preferring a Type 2 Manager play style often have an affinity with puzzle solving and adventure games [2]. In these cases, the short-term goals are often obscured; instead, the long term goals are made apparent. The most rewarding puzzles for these players are often those in which the overall goal is made explicit, but the mechanism by which this problem is solved is left for the player to deduce, using the tools they have at their disposal (often a set of objects, a collection of tools, or in some cases, a set of topics of conversation). Here, what is desired is clear feedback rather than clear short-term goals. The use of detailed error messages in adventure games, to provide clues that the player is on track, demonstrates this tendency.

Type 3 Wanderer play, which can tend towards a desire for toyplay, or at the very least has little patience for repeating the same activities over and over again, does benefit from clear goals—but often with the purpose of liberating the player from guessing what to do next. A common comment among players preferring Type 3 play is that "the game should always make clear what you should do next," and the conventional platform game, with its emphasis on finding and collecting similar looking tokens, delivers on this front. However, when players preferring Type 3 play in such games are observed, they do not immediately set out to collect all the tokens, but rather explore and experiment with what has been placed around them, using the tokens merely as a means of telling whether or not they are finished in a particular area. The goal and the feedback in this case are closely related because the goal is physically embodied as a token.

A player preferring Type 3 Wanderer play generally has no patience with being stuck in a game (if they are game literate, they turn to a FAQ, or purchase a strategy guide when they buy the game; if not, they likely stop playing). Conversely, the Type 2 Manager player might elicit great enjoyment in being stuck on a puzzle—provided, of course, they eventually deduce the solution to the problem, and that the solution is logical. This reflects the difference between the Thinking tendency and the Feeling tendency in Myers-Briggs typology, the former correlating with logic and the latter with value systems.

The common trait is not so much that goals must be clear (although this is generally an advantage) but rather that the player should not become stuck—facing a single problem that they cannot solve and for which no feedback exists to guide the player to a solution (with the possible exception of Type 1 Conqueror players, who might feel a greater payoff of fiero from facing an apparently insurmountable problem).

Therefore, a dynamic between goals and feedback exists. Choosing to favor clear short-term goals (as Falstein suggests) reduces the need for detailed feedback, but you can also choose clear long-term goals accompanied by more complete feedback (which might be more suitable for Type 2 Manager players) or a recurrence of the same goal with changes in the manner in which it is achieved (as seen in the classic platform game structure, which appeals to players preferring Type 3 Wanderer play).

Of course, in toyplay, no goals exist except those that the players create for themselves. This behavior can be seen very clearly in players of *Halo: Combat Evolved* (Bungee, 2001) who in some cases have evidently spent some considerable amount of time devising methods of rocketing their vehicle ever higher into the air despite the fact there is no game reward for doing so [3]. To understand how flow relates to toyplay, it is necessary to look in more detail at different kinds of play.

TYPES OF GAMES

The noted sociologist Roger Caillois studied games in many different cultures and identified four distinct categories of play (or categories of games, because Caillois extended this term to describe any activity that produced entertainment or enjoyment and was fundamentally outside the normal activities of daily living) [Caillois58].

Agon, or competition, is a collection of games (and sports) whose primary motivation is to test the player's abilities against others (or against a particular challenge) so that victory can be achieved. Caillois suggests that the desire for agon asserts itself in children as soon as the personality manifests—children in all cultures can be seen competing to see who can hold their breath for longest, for example.

Alea, or chance, is named after the Latin name for the game of dice and is seen as the counterpart to agon. Whereas the outcome of a competition of agon is that the best competitor wins, in pure alea, each competitor has an equal chance of winning. In a game of pure alea, "the favor of destiny" determines the outcome, and the player is (Caillois asserts) entirely passive.

Mimicry, or simulation, is based upon forgetting, disguising, or temporarily shedding your personality to assume another. Beginning in cultural practices such as the wearing of masks and culminating in aspirations to the role of the actor, the essence of mimicry is in pretending to be someone or something else. This is another tendency that can be seen in children at a young age.

Finally, *ilinx*, or vertigo, consists of momentary attempts to destroy the stability of perception and inflict temporary panic upon yourself. The root of this can be vertigo, or sharp acceleration, or speed, or even sudden surrender to a destructive urge—practically anything that temporarily abolishes conscious thought. It can be seen in children who spin around solely for the pleasure of being dizzy when they stop.

Caillois was not writing at a time when video games existed in any meaningful way, and his motivation was to produce a sociological model based upon the links between the games people play and their means of social control; he compares, for example, the use of mimicry and vertigo in primitive societies to the use of agon and alea in more complex societies. Although fascinating, this part of Caillois' work is considerably beyond the scope of a book on game design.

However, his categories of games have much to say about the nature of games of all kinds, and video games in particular. As well as the four types of play described previously, Caillois identifies a degree of turbulence or order in the nature of play. At one extreme, he identifies a quality he calls *ludus*, in which the characteristics of the play experience are mediated by rules. Its polar opposite he terms *paidia*, the primary power of improvisation and play. Immediately, we can see that ludus can be related to gameplay and paidia to toyplay. Clearly, the distinction between these two approaches to play extends beyond video games and reflects human tendencies on a wider scale.

Figure 5.2 shows the general manner in which the four types of games can be subdivided according to the degree to which ludus or paidia dominate. The examples listed are summarized from Caillois' observations of play activities that are common to a variety of different cultures.

	AGON (Competition)	**ALEA** (Chance)	**MIMICRY** (Simulation)	**ILINX** (Vertigo)
PAIDIA (Spontaneous play)	Spontaneous races	Counting out rhymes, Heads or tails	Masks, Disguises	Children 'whirling', Swinging
LUDUS (Structured play)	Sports	Betting, Lotteries	Theatre	Skiing, Mountain climbing

FIGURE 5.2   Examples of activities fitting Caillois' four categories of play in relation to the degree of formal structure implied by ludus and paidia.

Agon and Mimicry

Immediately, we can see that the notion of agon and its inherently competitive spirit correlates directly with the tendencies we see implicit in the Type 1 Conqueror style of play. As noted before, players preferring a Type 2 Manager style of play are generally also open to Type 1 play experiences, and agon extends to Type 2 play, although here the desire to win is a product of the desire to demonstrate mastery, rather than the simple desire to conquer associated with Type 1 play.

Conversely, the Type 3 Wanderer and Type 4 Participant styles of play are not enormously involved in agonistic struggles for superiority or victory. As mentioned, when Type 4-oriented players do participate in competition (such as in a racing game), it is often for the feeling of participation, and winning or losing is a secondary concern.

Instead, we see the tendencies of mimicry manifesting in Type 3 and Type 4 play. Games such as *The Sims* (Maxis, 2000) rely almost entirely on mimicry to support play, and the desire for a unique experience associated with Type 3 play also relates to mimicry; the experience results from imagining you are something other than yourself.

There appears, therefore, to be a clear split between agonistic play with the Type 1 and 2 play styles and mimicry with the Type 3 and 4 play styles.

Alea in Video Games

Curiously, Caillois does not associate alea with children—perhaps because his focus tends to be on alea in the form of gambling, which is less applicable to children who have less of a notion as to the meaning and consequence of money. However, in analyzing games, alea does seem to be prominent in appealing to children. Classic children's games such as *Snakes and Ladders* or card games such as *Beggar-My-Neighbor* have no skill in their play at all—the winner is determined entirely by chance, either through a series of die rolls or as the mechanistic consequence of the sequence of cards dealt. The appeal of such games is in part due to their simplicity, but also through the freedom of any participant to win. A young child playing his or her parents at chess is likely to lose; at a game of chance, they have equal likelihood of victory.

In video games, we also see games targeting younger players allowing more influence of chance. *Kirby Air Ride* (HAL Laboratory, 2003) features a high degree of chance in the outcome, particularly in its City Mode, in which players rush around a landscape picking up whichever vehicle they please to compete in a randomly selected game. The winner is largely a matter of whether (by chance) the player has managed to choose the correct vehicle for the challenge that is selected. Adult players might find this arbitrary outcome unsatisfying, but younger players are more willing to abide by an outcome determined by chance.

Similarly, *Ribbet King* (Bandai, 2004) presents a heavily modified game of golf in which the greens are littered with hazards and features that behave in somewhat unpredictable ways, so that each shot can result in an unexpected outcome—often a much better outcome than might be first imagined. The game is clearly targeting a younger audience, although the anarchic appeal of the game does extend to older players.

Players expressing a preference for Type 1 Conqueror style play seem the least willing to tolerate alea in their games. A desire for total control over their avatar or elements under their control is dominant, and any random elements are likely to be disdained. This corresponds to the split that Caillois identifies between agon and alea—the former awards victory to the most qualified participant, while the latter gives each participant an equal chance of victory.

Conversely, players preferring Type 2 Manager play seem more willing to allow a certain degree of alea into their games. Games such as the *Sim City* series (Maxis, 1989 onwards) often include disasters that affect the nature of play. Such aleatory components might be frustrating to Type 1 players, but in Type 2 play where process is more important than outcome, the chance to test skills against an unexpected problem is more welcome.

Similarly, players preferring Type 3 Wanderer play seem more willing to accept some random elements. Because the desire for an experience outweighs the desire to win, freak occurrences can be enjoyed provided they tend towards happy accidents and not random obstacles. The aforementioned *Ribbit King* has a certain appeal to players preferring Type 3 play because of the unexpected outcomes it presents, and puzzle games such as *Tetris* (Atari, 1988) and the *Bust a Move* series (Taito, 1995 onwards) are generally enjoyed by Type 3 players. These games do not present puzzles in the sense that Type 2 Manager players enjoy (logic problems) but rather present a sequence of randomly chosen pieces that the player must then decide what to do with. The emphasis once again is on process, rather than goal, and the presence of chance is inherent to the nature of play.

Appealing to Ilinx

Strictly speaking, most video games cannot induce ilinx, which is, in effect, a physical sensation. However, in the arcades several games have drawn upon the sense of vertigo to add to their appeal. Perhaps the most famous of these is *Space Harrier* (Sega, 1985), which used hydraulics to provide physical sensation to the player's movements in the game world. In a broader sense, however, any game that appeals to a sense of speed is appealing to ilinx in broadening its appeal, and games such as *Burnout 3: Takedown* (Criterion Games, 2004) succeed in part because of the sheer sensation of high-speed motion that the games induce.

This type of appeal seems to be universal, and not linked to any particular play style. However, it is by necessity tied to mimicry because without appealing to physical apparatus to invoke vertigo, the game must trick the mind into believing it is being rocketed around at speed. This is a trick achieved primarily by a willing suspension of belief, which these days we are wont to call immersion. In some respects, immersion is a correlate of mimicry—that to some extent the immersed player believes they are performing the game activities, rather than noticing their actual activity (sitting in a chair pressing buttons on a controller).

Flow and Mimicry

Figure 5.3 shows the broad correlations between Caillois' types of game and the DGD1 model. Having related Type 1 and 2 play styles with agon (and gameplay) and Type 3 and 4 with mimicry (and toyplay), we are faced with the question of how mimicry relates to flow.

Type 1 Conqueror Agon	**Type 2 Manager** Agon (with Alea tolerated)
Type 4 Participant Mimicry	**Type 3 Wanderer** Mimicry (with Alea tolerated)

FIGURE 5.3   The relation between the four play styles of DGD1 and Caillois' categories of games.

In the case of Type 3 Wanderer play, we have the notion of finesse, which seems to relate to mimicry: whereas other players might be content to use their game skills to complete goals, a desire in Type 3 play seems to be to carry out actions in a pleasing fashion. It is only marginally satisfying for a Type 3 player to complete a goal, but highly satisfying to complete a goal in a fashion that looks and feels appropriate to them.

Conversely, in the case of Type 4 Participant play it is hard to see where flow can come from. *The Sims* presents no goals, per se, and what is achieved is whatever players choose to set as their goals. In the absence of clear challenge, how can the model of flow be applied?

Any player has superior abilities in certain areas, and flow is more likely to result when players use these skills during play of a game; they feel in control of the play experience and are more confident of their abilities as they play. Where these skills relate to mimicry, the overall motivation seems to be the feeling of authenticity engendered by the simulation, rather than the achievement of specific external goals.

As we have seen, two of the seven key aspects of the flow state are as follows:

- The subject is undertaking an activity that they believe they can complete
- The subject feels that they are in control of the activity

These two aspects clearly relate to the concept of skill but need not relate to externally defined goals.

During gameplay, the player attempts to overcome the challenges presented by the game. In toyplay, however, the player chooses their own challenges. By defining their own goals, the player has taken more direct control of the activity than if the goal were specified for them. What motivates these self-imposed goals is the spontaneous creativity of paidia, and for players preferring Type 3 and 4 play, this is geared towards mimicry. In effect, flow can be achieved through mimicry by making authentic simulation the goal, and all player-created goals are subsequent to this desire in this context. So, while the goal of agonistic gameplay is to win, the goal of toyplay is satisfying mimicry.

Therefore, if flow occurs at the balance point between challenge and ability, and we have established the nature of both agonistic challenges and the demands of mimicry, we must now look at what abilties players employ to meet their goals. What is needed is some notion of the skills that are used by players in different situations, and to investigate this we can look at temperament theory.

TEMPERAMENT THEORY

In some respects, temperament theory dates back to the ancient Greeks, but in its modern form begins with David Keirsey's work (which we have already encountered in connection with Myers-Briggs typology) [Keirsey78]. For our reference to temperament theory, we refer to the work of one of Keirsey's students, Linda Berens, who has done much to make this complement to Myers-Briggs typology accessible to a wider audience.

Temperament theory is based around a model of four recognizable patterns or configurations of behavior. In its modern form, it is not a case of placing individuals in a box, per se, but rather observing that we utilize these four patterns in different situations, and with varying degrees of comfort. It is common for practitioners of temperament theory to claim that one temperament is a person's "true self" (which, it is claimed, is a predisposition from birth) and the other temperaments can be acquired as part of the developed self. Ultimately, from moment to moment, we have a contextual self that utilizes the patterns of behavior we have available according to the needs of the situation [Berens00].

Although we can observe a relationship between Myers-Briggs typology and temperament theory (which we will discuss shortly), temperament should not be confused with personality type. When we talk about temperament, we are always referring to patterns of behavior (or patterns of emotional responses) and not patterns of perception or judgement. Also, although some evidence does exist for temperament being set at birth [Keirsey78], some debate on this point still exists, and we should focus on the patterns that have been observed, rather than the underlying biology behind it, which remains ill defined [4].

The Four Temperaments

The four temperaments are known by various names, but the four we shall be using are *Rational*, *Idealist*, *Artisan*, and *Guardian*.

The Rational temperament is based around core needs of knowledge and competence, along with the notions of mastery and self-control. It correlates in Myers-Briggs typology terms to the dominance of the Intuition and Thinking traits (NT) and is associated with a set of *strategic* skills.

The Idealist temperament has core needs of unique identity and a search for meaning and significance. It correlates with Intuition and Feeling (NF) in Myers-Briggs terms and is associated with a set of *diplomatic* skills.

The Artisan temperament is based around core needs of freedom to act and the ability to make an impact and is correlated with Sensing and Perceiving (SP) in Myers-Briggs typology. The skills associated with this temperament are referred to as *tactical*.

Finally, the Guardian temperament is based around core needs of membership (or belonging) and a sense of responsibility or duty. It correlates with Sensing and Judging (SJ) in Myers-Briggs typology and is associated with a *logistical* skill set.

Figure 5.4 summarizes this information and includes the (somewhat unwieldy) terms that Keirsey coined for the four temperaments.

Note the approximate percentage of the population associated with each of the temperaments [CAPT02]. The Guardian temperament represents as large a proportion of the population as all the other temperaments combined.

The Four Temperament Skill Sets

What we are particularly interested in is the skills that are associated with the different tendencies, as these have the most to say about the skills we can expect a particular gaming audience segment to possess.

Temperament (Berens)	Temperament (Keirsey)	Myers-Briggs Traits	Skill Set	Approximate Percentage of Population
Rational	Promethean	NT	Strategic	10%
Idealist	Appolonian	NF	Diplomatic	15%
Artisan	Dionysian	SP	Tactical	25%
Guardian	Epimethean	SJ	Logistical	50%

FIGURE 5.4 Summary of the four temperaments, giving their names as expressed by Berens and by Kiersey, as well as the associated skill sets.

Strategic skills (Rational temperament) include the capacity to think ahead to possible contingencies and factors and then design processes for achieving objectives, to identify the ways and means to achieve a well defined goal, and to mobilize and coordinate the actions of others to implement a strategy. These skills are generally associated with the capacity to imagine how to reach a future state. It is easy to see how these skills relate to the playing of video games, which frequently require the player to perform these exact actions. It is also notable that the majority of programmers' Myers-Briggs type preferences equate to the Rational temperament and hence to this skill set.

Diplomatic skills (Idealist temperament) include the capacity to strive towards unity by resolving conflicting issues while honoring individual uniqueness, having empathy, and viewing a situation at a level of abstraction to find how different views are similar. Because these skills are primarily interpersonal, they do not immediately relate to most gameplay situations, except perhaps in social games such as Massively Multiplayer Online games. However, the capacity for empathy suggests an ability to identify with character-driven stories, and therefore to play a game for the unfolding of interpersonal relationships and character development.

Tactical skills (Artisan temperament) chiefly revolve around the capacity to read the current context and then skillfully manage the situation. If the Strategic skill set is concerned with planning ahead, the Tactical skill set is concerned with taking action. It is about taking action according to the needs of the moment, planning the next move (not several moves ahead), and executing actions in response to the varying demands of the situation, going around obstacles when necessary. Like the Tactical skill set, these clearly correlate well with video game situations, especially those in which the player is assigned charge of only themselves, and not multiple units.

Logistical skills (Guardian temperament) are based around getting the right things and the right information in the right place at the right time, in the right quantity, and to the right people. Logistical skills are also concerned with optimizing and standardizing—finding ways to carry out the same activities in a more efficient fashion—and are connected with sheltering and protecting in order to provide safety and well-being. This is another case that connects well with many video game situations. We can see this sort of behavior in the Real-Time Strategy (RTS) games such as *Command & Conquer* (Westwood Studios, 1995) that are primarily won by optimizing your production to overwhelm the enemy and also in the lifestyle management play of *The Sims*.

Figure 5.5 summarizes the skills associated with each temperament.

Skill Set	Temperament (Berens)	Skills
Strategic	Rational	Think ahead, plan ahead Identify the means to achieve a goal Coordinate actions strategically
Diplomatic	Idealist	Resolve conflicts while recognising individuality Empathy Find similarities through abstraction
Tactical	Artisan	Read the current context and manage the situation Work out the next step and take action Improvise to overcome problems
Logistical	Guardian	Organising and meeting needs Optimising and standardising Protect and ensure safety

FIGURE 5.5 The skill sets associated with each of the four temperaments.

DGD1 MODEL AND TEMPERAMENT SKILL SETS

Looking at the DGD1 model through the model of temperament produces certain patterns that offer us a way of considering the skills associated with different play styles. It should be noted, however, that the DGD1 model is specifically intended as a model of audience and not a model of individuals, and therefore you should not substantiate yourself or others into the DGD1 model. It can be applied only when considering a group of individuals large enough to be considered statistically.

To compare temperament with the DGD1 model, it is necessary to make an assumption as to the composition of the segments. To make straight comparisons, we consider the Hardcore audience segment as reflecting Intuition (N) and the Casual audience segment as reflecting Sensing (S). This choice results from extrapolating the statistical tendencies found in these groups, but is a fairly crude approximation at best, and you should bear in mind that having a majority of the members of a particular set display a preference for one of these traits is not the same as assigning all members of that set a preference for that trait. For the purposes of exploring what temperament theory says about the DGD1 model, however, it will suffice.

Using this assumption, we can associate each of the play types of the DGD1 model with a combination of skill sets, as shown in Figure 5.6.

	Hardcore	Casual	Combined
Type 1 Conqueror	H1 Strategic	C1 Logistical	**Type 1 Conqueror** Strategic-Logistical
Type 2 Manager	H2 Strategic	C2 Tactical	**Type 2 Manager** Strategic-Tactical
Type 3 Wanderer	H3 Diplomatic	C3 Tactical	**Type 3 Wanderer** Diplomatic-Tactical
Type 4 Participant	H4 Diplomatic	C4 Logistical	**Type 4 Participant** Diplomatic-Logistical
	Hardcore Strategic-Diplomatic	**Casual** Logistical-Tactical	

FIGURE 5.6 The relationship between the play styles of the DGD1 model and the skill sets of temperament theory.

Flow and the DGD1 Model

Flow provides a useful model regarding player enjoyment and its generation through play, and temperament theory allows skills to be matched to the DGD1 play types, allowing further investigation of why different players enjoy different game styles. We are now in a position to look at how to encourage flow in the different types and subtypes of the DGD1 model; for each type we have a pair of skill sets that can be assumed to apply.

Type 1 Conqueror (Strategic-Logistical)

For Type 1 play, we are inherently expecting players to be seeking agonistic play—they want to overcome challenges or defeat enemies. Flow is therefore to be found in utilizing Strategic and Logistical skills to bring about victory.

Combining these skill sets creates a situation in which gameplay is guided by the capacity to see in advance how to address the problems (Strategic), but for which solutions can be found by repeated action, gradually optimizing towards a solution (Logistical). When these skill sets are working together (as we assume they are in Type 1 play), flow need not occur in a single attempt at a particular challenge but rather over the repeated attempts to overcome a challenge.

RTS games are an excellent example of this combination of skill sets and indeed can in principle be played either way—strategically or logistically. The games that have achieved the most commercial success within the RTS genre tend to always include the capacity to win by mastering the means of production, as in the *Warcraft* series (Blizzard Entertainment, 1994 onwards), but also contain the capacity to be played in a strategic fashion. Similarly, games such as the *Gran Turismo* series (Polyphony Digital, 1997 onwards) combine a strategic element (determining which car, or car parts, to buy at any given time) and a logistical element (mastering the courses by repeatedly playing them).

The actual needs of the player vary according to whether they lie closer to the Hardcore or the Casual end of the spectrum. We would expect a player typifying the H1 subtype to find flow primarily through the application of Strategic thinking. Such a player can be left with a deficit of information provided the goal is clearly defined, as part of the strength of the Strategic skill set is devising a solution to a clearly stated goal. However, we assume that such a player also has access to some Logistical skills and with this comes the willingness to undertake the same challenge repeatedly, provided each iteration provides some progress towards the goal. Because the payoff of fiero—triumph over adversity—is paramount, as long as victory can be achieved (and sufficient feedback to ascertain that progress is being made is given) there might be no limit as to how many iterations of play are attempted before victory. In fact, more failed attempts implies a greater payoff of fiero when victory finally comes—provided, as noted in the definition of flow, sufficient feedback suggests steady progress towards victory through the process of optimization.

However, Strategic skills can also be used to recognize that a given approach is completely flawed and entirely new solutions can be devised. Once again, the key is feedback. For this, replay features (especially at a strategic level) are invaluable. A good example can be found in the *Dynasty Warriors* series (Omega Force, 2000 onwards), which ends each battle (whether it succeeds of fails) with an overview map showing the movements of all the key military units. When the battle has been lost, for example, because the player's top general has been defeated, watching this replay allows the player (with the application of some strategic thinking) to determine a new strategy. This map provides the feedback necessary for the H1 player to formulate a new strategy.

Game bosses exemplify this aspect of Type 1 Conqueror play—especially pattern bosses (which require the player to develop a strategy by observation and trial-and-error). H1 players happily try multiple strategies against such challenges and play as many iterations as necessary to achieve the fiero payoff, providing their strategies receive some feedback (for example, parts of the boss flashing when damage has successfully been caused).

The Casual counterpart—the C1 subtype—has the preferences reversed; therefore, Logistical skills take precedence over Strategic thinking. Immediately, this suggests that goals must be more clearly delineated, as the strengths now lie in optimization, not in devising solutions. Such a player is presumably better suited to being faced with a situation in which they know what to do, but that they must do well to pass. The *Dynasty Warriors* games are no longer appropriate—because progress is not made by optimization, but through devising new strategies. Instead, they require games that can be optimized—if failure occurs, the player can immediately deduce a superior approach without having to think in terms of larger patterns.

In the case of RTS games with production of units, the optimization is provided by mastering the production process. On the first visit to a level, the player is learning where everything is. They might fail, but next time they know where to go. Next, failure might result from the decision to build the wrong units. But because the number of units types is limited (and RTS games rarely *require* clever combinations of units for victory, even though sometimes they might be useful), the player can try again and build different units. Gradually, through a guided process of trial and error, victory is achieved. Critically, the optimal approach discovered in one level can then by applied to a different set of challenges. It might fail for slightly different reasons, but in gradually optimizing a solution to one problem, the player is learning a method that gives them a head start in optimizing a solution to the next problem.

In FPS games, optimization is possible if levels are short or small enough to encourage the player to try again after death, or if the game offers quick saves (that is, the option to save wherever and whenever the player wants with just a key press or similarly simple action—as most if not all modern PC-based FPS games do). In either case, the player learns from successive encounters with opponents who behave in predictable ways. For example, the core set of enemies in *Doom* (id Software, 1992) represents a recognizable, recurring opposition. Different combinations of enemies in different physical circumstances provide challenge; should the C1 player die, they attempt to optimize by playing again, taking into account the circumstances that led to their last death.

If a quick save option is available, optimization is also possible through choice of where to save (a choice usually based upon how much work has been done and how much ammo and health remains). If not, the player must optimize over the entire level. Watching C1 players play a game like *GoldenEye 007* (Rare, 1997), it is usual to see them slowly build a pattern or routine through which to run to beat a level. The number of attempts this pattern requires to be optimized to the point at which the level can be beaten depends upon the difficulty of the game relative to the player's skills.

What the Type 1 Conqueror style of play has in common in respect of flow is a willingness to fail and repeat the same action to some degree. With the emotional payoff of fiero increasing with the degree of challenge (provided the goal can be reached and the player does not find themselves out of their depth—that is, anxious and hence giving up in angry frustration), such players are perhaps alone in their tolerance for repetition of the same challenge. Many Type 1 players report having been in a state equivalent to flow when the game gives them a challenge they fail, but believe they can work out how to defeat.

Type 2 Manager (Strategic-Tactical)

With the Manager types we are coupling the ability to plan ahead (Strategic) with the ability to act in the spur of the moment according to changing situations (Tactical). This differs from the Type 1 Strategic-Logistical skills in that repetition is less important because standardization and optimization (the Logistical skill set) are not directly represented. The result is that players of the Type 2 Manager tendency tend to show natural aptitude to games, coupled with a willingness to give up and try a different game if the one they are playing ceases to amuse.

There are few games for which the alliance of Strategic and Tactical skills is not an advantage, and both of the examples we gave for Type 1 Conqueror play apply. Both FPS and RTS games present a constant stream of new situations, for which the Type 2 Manager player can in general find a solution on the fly, or at least with a minimum amount of replay. This further underlines the connection between the Type 1 Conqueror and Type 2 Manager style of play, in that Type 2 play tends to comfortably incorporate much of what suits Type 1 play. The distinction (when viewed through the model of temperament) is that with Type 1 the approach is repetition until completed, while with Type 2 we assume a greater capacity to deal with the situations as they evolve, using the Tactical skill set's natural adaptability. If the Type 1 play style suggests mastering RTS games by mastering production, the Type 2 play style suggests mastering RTS games by outmaneuvering the enemy and spontaneous battlefield strategy.

In terms of achieving flow, a marked separation exists between the H2 and the C2 subtypes. The Hardcore side of Type 2 Manager play seems very much focused on delivering the payoffs of pure Strategy and displays a marked preference for games in which the player has as much time as they need to solve a particular problem. This seems to be the flow of Type 2 play, familiar to many dedicated players of state-space games such as chess, or of turn-based strategy games. Lost in thought, the H2 player's state of flow seems to lie primarily in the search for a solution, a procedural approach that is as much concerned with mastering the process as in achieving victory.

The constant reoccurrence of the *Civilization* series (Firaxis and others, 1991 onwards) in the favorite game lists of players fitting the H2 profile, and the reports of players losing themselves in the unfolding of the empire-building process therein, seems to suggest that this kind of experience produces flow in these players. Similarly, the lamenting of the lost golden age of adventure games (another common theme in interviews) suggests that solving puzzles is a definite flow experience.

To encourage flow in H2 type players, a sufficiently strategic battlefield seems to be required. This battlefield should be one in which the player has the time to come to their own decisions without feeling rushed, and one in which the complexity of interactions is such that it can be viewed as a complex process and not merely as a case of finding the optimal strategy. Alternatively, a set of puzzles can be presented (again, ideally without time limitations). The trouble is, very few of the other clusters connect well with direct puzzle solving, which does not tend to lend itself to a solution by optimization.

Conversely, the C2 subtype's emphasis on Tactical skills over Strategic skills (which are likely to be present but downplayed) seems to achieve flow in the midst of action. The Tactical skill set provides the capacity to be placed in a situation and to think spontaneously about the action to be taken. Some planning ahead might occur, but as often as not such a player is relying on their general competence to see them through. Time to make a decision is neither here nor there; action proceeds at its own pace.

Sim games of various kinds can be enjoyed because these seldom require excessive strategic planning and can be approached as a set of situations to be resolved. But with the desire for agon present (albeit not as pronounced as in the Type 1 Conqueror players), any kind of competitive arena can be enjoyed.

Flow occurs when faced with a sequence of situations for which the solution falls naturally out of the action. Driving games of all kinds seem to provide this, as does any game in which competence is sufficient to provide victory (which is a majority of games in the modern market). The key in this instance appears to be clear short-term goals; flow can occur when the player loses the distinction between themselves and their avatar and merely lets themselves be carried along by the tasks which are placed in front of them.

Type 3 Wanderer (Diplomatic-Tactical)

As already noted, the Diplomatic skill set does not seem to directly reflect most video game situations, but the root temperament of Idealist also has the core need for unique identity, which connects with the Type 3 Wanderer cluster's desire for a unique experience. What this Type suggests, therefore, is a group of players with the tactical competence to deal with situations as they come but without the Strategic or Logistical skills to support perceiving the solution to a goal, or optimizing a solution through repetition. This connects well with platform games, for which the activities required to progress are usually explicit, and the player simply must resolve the situations presented to them.

Distinctions between the Hardcore and Casual subtypes do not seem to be particularly pertinent here, and, in fact, the conditions for flow are very similar to the C2 subtype discussed previously (which shares the Tactical skill set). However, as we noted before, the Wanderer's primary concern is unlikely to be agon, and more likely to be mimicry.

Therefore, the flow of the Wanderer lies in willing suspension of disbelief (or immersion)—the capacity to lose oneself in the artificial world that is presented. The general preference for toyplay over gameplay does not represent a lack of desire for progress (on the contrary, the Wanderer is likely to become annoyed or bored if they cannot progress) but rather a general desire to lose oneself in the game world, rather than to lose oneself in the game mechanics.

In designing games to elicit flow for Wanderers, clear short-term goals (or an overarching goal with repeated subgoals, as in platform games) appear to be desirable because they remove the need to constantly puzzle out what to do next. The player can quite literally wander around the game world and see what they find.

Game mechanics should be subtle, or hidden in the background, and the environments presented should be designed to operate as playgrounds—places that the player can explore at their leisure, achieving their goals almost as a side effect, rather than the purpose, of their play.

An exceptional example of this can be found in one of the earliest levels of *Mischief Makers* (Treasure, 1997) known as "Clanball Land." The level is, in fact, a tutorial of the many different ways the player's avatar can interact with items in the game world; however, it is presented as a playground, and the player encouraged to experiment. The level is almost entirely absent of agon (and no hazards are present to cause failure), but contains ample toyplay if you lose yourself in the carnival.

The appeal of platform games to this cluster almost certainly reflects the ease with which Wanderers can achieve flow in these games, which present simple acts of competence often in a varied playground world that the player is free to explore at their own pace and, to some extent, to set their own level of challenge.

Type 4 Participant (Diplomatic-Logistical)

The Type 4 Participant's desire for social play connects strongly with one of the core needs of the Guardian temperament (from which we derive the Logistical skill set for this play Type), which is rooted in a need to belong. Because little is known of the H4 subtype (if indeed it can be said to exist), any discussion of the Participant must focus on the Type as a whole.

Though numerous toyplay games exist, the only direct examples of games supporting Type 4 play are *The Sims* and *Animal Crossing* (Nintendo, 2001). This type of player is not often targeted by games companies. The flow of *The Sims* lies in losing yourself in caring for the virtual people that you have emotionally connected with. This is an experience of mimicry and not of agon, because no inherent competition is present. It is also almost entirely toyplay.

Animal Crossing delivers play in similar fashion to *The Sims*, but also includes many more activities that the player has direct control over, such as fishing and catching insects, many of which also support a kind of Type 1 Conqueror play. The common element between Type 1 and Type 4 styles is play that lends itself to optimization, and indeed the core play activity in *Animal Crossing* can be seen to be optimizing the production of personal wealth in order to buy furniture to decorate your house and ultimately to pay off your mortgage and thus acquire a bigger living space.

Flow can also be found in the Participant's love of emotional involvement. Invested in a story, a Participant can lose themselves in a game, but lacking the Strategic or Tactical skill sets, solutions must yield to simple optimization (or fall naturally out of continuing to play) and cannot present obscure puzzles or difficult challenges. These are likely to move outside of the Participant's skill set and therefore cause frustration (anxiety) that ultimately causes them to stop playing.

Similarly, the Participant can lose themselves in a social situation. Games using Sony's EyeToy peripheral certainly seem to appeal to the Participant audience, but it is hard to imagine them playing it alone. The flow of the EyeToy is the similar to the flow of the performing artist—the special relationship between the performer and the audience.

Hardcore and Casual Clusters

We can also extend our comparisons to include the Hardcore and Casual clusters as a whole. C1 and C4 represent the Logistical skill set, while C2 and C3 represent the Tactical skill set; hence, the Casual audience can be seen as the Logistical-Tactical combination. What is notable in this situation is the absence of Strategic skills (and hence the ability to figure out the solution to goals or problems) and the absence of the Idealist's desire for unique identity. What this suggests is that the Casual audience is best approached with familiar settings and content, and with gameplay that revolves around optimization or thinking on your feet.

Conversely, the H1 and H2 subtypes represent the Strategic skill set, and the H3 and H4 subtypes represent the Diplomatic skill set. What this suggests about Hardcore players collectively is that they desire original and unique games, or games that reflect their own sense of identity (the Idealist temperament of the H3 and H4 players) and also show a capacity for solving problems on their own and finding the steps required to reach a goal (Strategic skill set). Turn-based RPG games that combine story with purely strategic play, such as *Final Fantasy Tactics* (Square, 1997) and the *Front Mission* series (Square, 1995 onwards), fit this audience well, and adventure games with their combination of problem solving (Strategic thinking) and story (for Idealist appeal) also seem a better fit with this audience than with the more mass market Casual audience.

CONCLUSION

The model of flow allows us to hypothesize about how to satisfy a player's needs—by keeping the play experience within the boundaries of their skills, thus avoiding the boredom or anxiety of being unchallenged or out of one's depth, respectively. Caillois' types of games lead us to the idea that players of video games are chiefly engaging in either agonistic (competitive) activities or in the process of mimicry (simulation) and suggest that different skills apply in each case. Also, we have seen how alea (chance) can be added to help a juvenile player win or to increase variety and how ilinx (vertigo) can add to the appeal of a game experience by simulating the sensations of speed and acceleration.

To give a video game player an optimal experience—to keep them in the experience of flow—we must be careful therefore to deliver an experience that uses their skills and abilities to produce the kind of gameplay or toyplay that they desire (either the challenge of agon or the escapism of mimicry). Temperament theory allows us to relate the different play styles of the DGD1 model with specific skills (and desires) pertinent to the sphere of video games, and thus allows us to reason about how to provide a satisfying play experience.

Because the play styles identified by DGD1 cross the boundaries between the highly game-literate Hardcore players and the mass market Casual players, each type shows an alliance of skill abilities that manifests in certain games more than others for each style of play. Successful games, in general, need to meet the Strategic and Idealistic needs of the Hardcore audience, while still providing gameplay that yields to Logistical or Tactical solutions or toyplay that satisfies through identification with characters or situations.

Games that are intended to target a purely Hardcore audience (thus, games targeting a smaller market, but one whose members are more likely to purchase and therefore a more stable market) should hit their optimal balance of appeal when they combine the capacity for strategic thinking or problem solving with an experience with a unique identity—something new and original. But such games in general might not be suited for the mass market.

Games that are intended to target the mass market must court both the Hardcore and the Casual audience (unless marketing or licensing allows the Hardcore audience to be ignored) and as such must deliver some element that appeals to the Hardcore (either unique identity, capacity for strategic benefit, or both) and also has the capacity to keep the Casual player in a state of flow (either via repetitive Logistical play or flexible Tactical play, or both). This can be readily achieved in games of agon appealing to the Type 1 Conqueror and Type 2 Manager play styles and should also be achievable to the Type 3 Wanderer and Type 4 Participant play styles through an appeal to mimicry, or identification with characters within the game world.

No game can perfectly satisfy all the different play styles equally, but by understanding how to keep players in a state of flow, and hence a state of satisfaction with their play experience, we move closer to understanding the purpose of game design—to meet the needs of the audience by delivering experiences that they feel competent to complete and for which the resolution is ultimately satisfying.

ENDNOTES

[1] It should be noted, however, that the meta-rules of the 400 Project are not intended to be read in any particular order [Falstein01].

[2] Adventure games, with their emphasis on puzzle solving, were prominent in the replies for players preferring Type 2 Manager style play in surveys of favorite games.

[3] Cover disks on the *Official Xbox Magazine* frequently feature videos of players attempting such behavior. We can assume that for every player who went to the trouble to submit a video recording this behavior, hundreds more attempted it in private.

[4] It is common in modern psychology to equate apparently inborn traits with genetic predisposition. However, although the evidence that genetics encodes for proteins that affect development is overwhelming, nothing is really known about the relationship between proteins, biological development, and behavior. Until this knowledge gap is bridged, it is premature to refer to behavior as being genetic in origin.

Part
II Design

Game design reflects the needs of the participants in a particular project, which include the audience as well as those involved in making the game. Having seen the diversity of the audience for games and looked at specific ways of modeling that audience's needs and abilities, we are now ready to look at the specifics of the game design process.

Game design does not lend itself to a strictly mechanical examination, because games, which are tools for entertainment, are not subject to universal laws. As the needs of the audience change, so must the needs of game design. It is already the case that a guide to designing arcade games in the 1970s and 1980s would be of little application to a person wanting to work on the design of a modern video game—the factors that applied have changed completely, in terms of the influence of technical considerations, commercial issues (such as the decline of the coin-operated machine as the primary medium for video games), and diversification of the audience.

Nonetheless, any process can be examined, and the chapters in this section serve to consider the nature of game design and the specific issues that apply in video game design, such as the creation and application of game world abstractions, issues relating to interface design, and the question of how a game is structured. All these issues relate to the audience in some fashion, but they are more specifically involved in understanding the process of game design.

6 Foundations of Game Design

Game designers meet a lot of people who say they want to be game designers. Usually, they are players of video games who are drawn to the idea of getting to decide what goes into a game and believe that a game designer is the person who makes these decisions. The truth, however, is that game designers rarely decide what a game will be about, what genre it will be, who the central characters will be, or any of the other factors which frame the creation of a game. This situation has been the case since the end of the era of "bedroom programmers" (individuals who would design, code, and create graphics and sound for their games on early home computers) and is unlikely to change.

A game designer creates paperwork that specifies the design details of a game, but they do not usually get to decide what goes into the game. Those decisions are made either at a higher level of the "chain of command" or made by the entire team as a group. The game designer might be charged with the task of producing a coherent design that ties together all of the elements required to make the game work and might create inventive mechanics to integrate the game elements, but they do not control the development of the game.

So if the game designer does not decide what the game is about, what does the game designer do? What are the basic game design skills that the designer uses to craft a design document, and why is game design as essential to the development process as programming or art? This chapter looks at the foundations of game design, the video game development process, some basic game design skills, and the core of the role of the game designer.

THE PHASES OF DEVELOPMENT

The complete process of video game design tends to consist of four discrete phases. The first of these, *concept*, involves the creation of the game idea and framework in the broadest strokes. The second phase, which can be called *initial design*, involves expanding the concept into a more complete design document. The third phase is the period of *expansion*, when the game design grows to accommodate all the desired features, and the final phase is *contraction*, when the more ambitious features are lost in a desperate attempt to meet the milestone schedule.

Phase One: Concept

Most games begin either with a developer pitching a concept to a publisher (usually supported by a tech demo), or with a publisher looking to produce a game for a license they have acquired (for example, a popular film license). As a result, the game designer's first task on any game is usually to create a concept document that encapsulates the desired high-level details and expresses an initial concept of gameplay.

Because of the developer-publisher relationship, the publisher is usually at the top of the development chain of command. Publishers want to create a product that will make as much money as possible and attempt to influence the development process towards this goal. In point of fact, the publisher very rarely has any way of knowing what will sell well and has to rely essentially on guesswork. Therefore, most publishers assess projects in terms of the risk of the project not being completed (or not being completed on time), and their chief role in the development process is to ensure that game milestones (development targets) are made on time.

As a result of this situation, the people who generally determine the high-level details about a game are at the management level of the developers, but they do so with the goal of interesting a publisher. Each developer has their own way of approaching this. Some have management staff who perform this and other duties; others allow the development teams themselves to determine the broad strokes of a game in a democratic manner. Even if the team is in charge of determining the shape of the game, they usually have to win approval for the project from someone in the developer's management staff.

All these factors—the developer's need to determine the overall shape of a game, and the need for publishers and developers to have some tangible basis for discussion—create the need for a concept document. These documents vary in size from one page to a dozen and serve to present a broad-strokes overview of a game. Concept documents contain the high-level details of a game and the basic gameplay mechanics—enough to give an idea of how the game might work. Depending on its size, it might cover the user interface, the core mechanics, the game structure, and the narrative component of the game, where appropriate.

Phase Two: Initial Design

Once a publisher has agreed to fund a project (and in some cases even before this point), the concept document becomes insufficient, and a design document is required. This transition can result from an expansion of the concept document— filling in the blanks that were only implied in the concept, for example—or the design document can be an entirely new item of documentation generated using the concept document as a general overview.

When developers make games without a dedicated game designer, the game design document generally gets put together by someone during the early stages of development. In these situations, the document is often being created only in order to get the game design approved by the publisher (or in some cases the platform licensor, if it is destined for a console); after this point, the document falls by the wayside as an artifact of development. This state of affairs suits only the least ambitious game projects, or those projects that are driven solely by technology.

Initial design without a game designer is usually a series of meetings between various development staff (or, in the worst case, all the staff). Everyone has ideas they want to incorporate, and a large number of these ideas pull in radically different directions, leading to the usual problems associated with committee-driven design. The final results can be worthwhile if the team is talented, has good communication skills, has sufficient patience, and if sufficient time is budgeted to warrant such an approach.

Conversely, a lone game designer (or, even better, a small design team) can complete the initial design in a relatively short period of time, without leaving out the views of the rest of the team. By initially discussing the game with the individuals involved in the project, the game designer or design team can learn the desired traits and then work to incorporate them into a coherent initial design document.

Phase Three: Expansion

Once an approved initial design is in place, programming and art creation can proceed, and the period of expansion begins. In practice, the initial design phase can sometimes be omitted (especially if the game is technology driven) or the expansion phase can occur as part of the initial design, with the programmers and artists starting work only when the paperwork is principally complete. More commonly, some programming and art work begin at the concept phase, because of the need for tech demos to convince publishers of the value of the project; in other words, by the expansion phase, a prototype already exists.

The game designer has more work to do during the expansion phase than at any other time. Every aspect of the concept must be expanded, and every point of expansion must be built on sound design principles, be realistic for the programming team to implement, and be reasonable for the artists to render (where applicable). When the process is working smoothly, each iteration of the design documents receives feedback from the programming, art, and production team until the design is complete.

For larger projects, the documentation expands to the point whereby it is no longer helpful to keep it in a single document. It can splinter into main design documents, level design overviews, narrative documents, agent reference lists, and art specifications—a vast variety of documentation.

Phase Four: Contraction

At a certain point during development, it is no longer tenable for the game to continue to expand, and the contraction process begins. Either management puts a freeze on the game, refusing to allow any new features to ensure that the game is delivered on time, or the project has already started to slip from its milestone schedule and the game design must shrink to make allowances for the delays. From hereon in, the game begins to contract.

This is when the most difficult part of the game design process generally begins (although shrewd design work in the earlier stages can relieve some of the difficulty). When it becomes apparent that not all the high-level features that the team (or management) wanted to get into the game are feasible, the game designer must determine what is essential to the design and what can be removed. They are often unhappy with what must be lost in the contraction, but with good design skills, the game can be significantly improved by this process.

Contraction allows the game design to become more focused. The features that get thrown out first are often those that seemed like a good idea but do not support the core of the design, resulting in a tighter design. At its best, contraction improves the final game; at its worst, the process strips the game design of anything interesting. It is therefore a critical part of the design process and must always be taken into consideration.

EXAMINING THE DESIGN PROCESS

Game design is characterized by an early, abstract phase (concept); a period during which the game acquires its outline and core features (initial design); an extension phase that increases the level of detail and completeness (expansion); and a simplification phase that focuses and tightens the design (contraction). Programming and art creation can begin at any stage, but preferably tend towards starting in the expansion phase, not counting any materials put together for a tech demo.

The amount of freedom a game design has to move in the expansion and contraction phases can be referred to as the *elasticity* of the design. A design in which all of the features support the core concept of the game can be described as *tight*, whereas a design that contains an exhaustive collection of features can be described as *extensive*.

Each of these concepts—tightness, elasticity, and extensiveness—are worth closer examination, as each has a role in the process of game design.

TIGHT DESIGN

Although we tend to think of the role of game designer as referring solely to video games, the process of game design has been around for at least a hundred years. Many video game designers started as game designers in another medium. Substantial level design in *Doom* (id Software, 1993) and *Quake* (id Software, 1996) was carried out by Sandy Peterson, who also created the popular *Call of Cthulhu* (Chaosium, 1981) tabletop role-playing game; Julian Gollop's *Chaos* (1984) was based upon a board game he had created; and game design luminary Warren Specter produced tabletop role-playing games and board games for Steve Jackson Games prior to working on video games.

Board game designer Klaus Teuber has stated that when he redesigns his board games, his goal is to simplify the game without losing any of its essence [Gamewire04].

This is the purpose of tight design—to use the minimum quantity of elements required to support the desired gameplay. Teuber's most famous creation, *Die Siedler von Catan/Settlers of Catan* (Franckh-Kosmos Verlags, 1995), demonstrates the benefits of tight design with its simple set of mechanics that supports diverse gameplay, and the board game has sold more than three million copies around the world. Game designers often cite it as an exemplary case of elegant design.

The epitome of tight game design comes with card games, and creating a card game for an arbitrary audience is an exemplary exercise in tight design. What makes card games so useful in this area is that the creative freedom is limited by the available materials. You have only fifty-four cards to use—four suits, thirteen values, plus jokers (potentially), plus a few peripheral options such as score or use of a table. Because the "hardware" we have available is so simplistic, successful game design is almost guaranteed to be tight.

Designing Card Games

What are the design components of a card game? The players, the hand, the deck, the discards, the cards in play, the turn sequence, the rules, and the meta-rules. Decisions in each of these areas define the nature of the card game.

A card game can have one, two, four, or many players. Although in principle a card game can be designed for three players, in practice most new card games are designed for either solo play or two or more players. Designing a game for exactly three players would dramatically restrict the chances to play it, so this would be an unusual choice for any game. Some examples of different player choices include *Solitaire* (1 player), *Beggar-Your-Neighbor* (2 player), *Poker* (2 or more players), and *Bridge* (4 players).

The hand denotes cards the players keep to themselves. Not every card game has a concept of a hand. For example, *Memory* begins by all the cards being dealt onto the table, and players take turns trying to find cards of matching value out of the cards in play. In general, however, each game has rules about the hand. *Beggar-Your-Neighbor* begins with a hand equal to half the cards in the deck, and *Bridge* begins with one quarter of the cards in the deck. Each of the *Poker* variants, on the other hand, has a certain hand size—generally from two to seven.

The deck and the discards define the flow of cards in the game (though as with hands, not every game has a deck and discards). In most games, new cards come from the deck and go to the discards. In general, discards are out-of-play. However, games such as the many *Rummy* variants allow new cards to also come from the discards (and indeed, the prime difference between most variants of *Rummy* is in the degree of access to the discards that the player is allowed, for example, top card only, all discards, etc.).

"Cards in play" can mean cards in front of a particular player that apply only to that player, or cards on the table that affect every player. As with other elements, not every card game requires cards in play, whereas other games (such as *Solitaire*) get almost all of their gameplay from the cards in play.

The turn sequence dictates both the order of play and the allowable actions. The most common system is that each player takes a turn in a clockwise sequence, but many other options are available. Some *Poker* variants, for example, vary the order of play according to the nature of the betting, and *Bridge* and many *Whist* variants have a turn sequence dictated by victory in the previous turn (known generally as a "hand"). The allowable actions state how the hand and cards in play can change during the course of a player's turn.

Finally, the rules and the meta-rules dictate the nature of all remaining interactions. Rules dictate the meaning of individual cards, sets of cards, and the state of play, as well as how the game is won or lost. The rules of *Poker*, for example, dictate that a straight flush is the strongest hand, followed by four of a kind, flush, straight, three of a kind, etc., and (in most variants) they dictate that the strongest hand wins. If a card game has a scoring mechanism, the rules dictate this.

Meta-rules are modifiers to the general rules. When *Poker* players decide that, for example, deuces are wild, they have added a meta-rule to the rules. The distinction between a rule and a meta-rule is largely one of interpretation, but in general a meta-rule is something that can change according to the desires of the players, while a rule defines the nature of the game. What people call "house rules" are functionally equivalent to meta-rules.

Between these eight factors, a card game results. The simplest games, like *Beggar-Your Neighbor* (also known as *Beggar-My-Neighbor* or *Strip Jack Naked*) are deterministic and suitable for entertaining only children, because the rules mean that the player has no choice in the outcome; there is as much skill in such a game as there is in rolling dice and determining who has the highest score (although such aleatory play becomes more meaningful to adults when money is at stake). The most accessible games strike a balance between skill and luck (most *Rummy* variants fall into this group), and the most enduring games are simple to learn but support a wide variety of play styles (as is true of most *Poker* variants) [Hoyle46], [Penguin79].

Tight Card Games

To produce a tightly designed card game, you need to make a decision in at least three of the eight aspects of card game design. (You must have either a hand or cards in play, there must be a turn sequence of some manner, and there must be rules to dictate the end of play.) You can be certain that the game is tight by keeping each of the given aspects as terse as possible, but what most game designers find when they experiment with creating card games is that a very basic set of design components produces ambiguities or problems that require clarification or refinement.

When the volume of additions to the design components exceeds the initial set of components, the game design has gotten out of control. At this stage, the game might possibly be fun to play, but it is difficult to learn and almost impossible to spread to a wider audience. It might be a card game, but it is no longer a tight card game, and as such its "shelf life" is limited. We can say that the mechanics have become slack.

Tight game design is not only elegant, but it is easier for arbitrary players to learn to play. This accessibility is the main commercial advantage of tight design in video games, but tight design also means that little development time is wasted developing secondary components that the game does not actually need. Many video games suffer from slack design, often as a result of a committee-driven design process—the aspiration to accommodate all the desires of a development team can be disastrous if no one is looking for the subset of ideas that lead to a tight design.

Anyone involved in (or wanting to be involved in) video game design can learn much about tight game design by experimenting with card games. With such a small set of options to play with, these games can be created quickly, and the distinctions between a tight card game design and a confused and cluttered card game design are easy to identify. Working in such a constrained state space discourages slack design, and every game should work towards tight mechanics if it is ever to reach a wide audience.

Goals of Tight Design

Tightness is a concept we have defined as the property of having all (or the majority of) features in a game's design support the core concept. It is a desirable property for all game designs, because a tight set of mechanics is easy to learn, but it is especially desirable in video games where the cost of implementing game mechanics is high and therefore you do not want to commit to developing more than is necessary.

We have seen that it is easier to produce a tight design for a card game than for other types of games, because the number of design components is limited, which forces a certain economy. You can produce card game designs that are not tight but still fun, just as you can produce a video game that is fun to play, but has a giant learning curve. The fact that a game is fun to play does not necessarily justify the game in a commercial perspective, though. A fun, complex card game costs nothing to design or implement—a complex video game is very expensive to develop and must reach a large audience to justify that expense.

By keeping to the goal of tight game mechanics, the video game designer reduces the cost of development, improves the accessibility of the game to a wider audience, and ensures that the game play feels elegant and interconnected. Because tightness cannot be measured, it is a subjective concept, and you must acquire an aesthetic to judge its presence and absence. We find few better ways to acquire this perspective than by experimenting with card games.

ELASTIC DESIGN

The form that best expresses the concept of elastic design is that of the card-based board game, characterized by games such as *Fluxx* (ICE, 1998), *Illuminati* (Steve Jackson Games, 1982), and trading card games like *Magic: The Gathering* (Wizards of the Coast, 1993). These games are primarily comprised of a set of cards sometimes (but not always) used in conjunction with a set of counters. The basic game design principles are almost identical to card games, the chief difference being that each card has its own unique identity carrying with it the capacity to alter, expand, or change the rules of the game.

Fluxx is the epitome of the form, consisting as it does of four clearly identifiable types of cards. Keepers are privately owned cards in play, New Rules are publicly owned cards in play that alter the state of the rules, Goals are publicly owned cards in play that specify the winning conditions, and Actions are cards that have an immediate effect when played. The game offers an entertainingly variable play experience as the changing state of the rules makes each game unique—for example, changing the number of cards drawn or played, forcing players to play a card randomly, causing people to exchange their hands, and so forth.

Designing Card-Based Board Games

When creating a game in this form, the card mix is the main design problem (because the core game mechanics usually write themselves). For the game to be fun to play, players must be able to draw interesting cards throughout the game, they must frequently have meaningful choices to make, and (most importantly) no card should upset the balance of the game play. In many games of this style, certain key card types must occur with a certain frequency or else the game mechanics break down (for example, in *Magic: The Gathering* the land type must appear approximately one third of the time if a deck is to be playable).

During the design process, the game designers are usually working towards a set card limit, often dictated by the production method (which generally involves printing onto cardboard sheets that are then die-cut into individual cards, with a fixed number of cards per sheet) and the cost of manufacture. This target number of cards is usually fixed, but might change throughout the development process. The problem this target number represents is that designers always have many more possible cards than the target; they must throw out a certain proportion of the cards in development.

This is the principle of elasticity in action: having more resources than you need with the express purpose of whittling the set of components down to the best minimal set that the production constraints allow. In practice, some of the initial set of cards will prove unbalanced or unworkable and will have to be thrown out, and sometimes play testing suggests new cards that would greatly improve the play mix. In an elastic design situation, this freedom to make changes must be anticipated.

Types of Elasticity

When elasticity is expressed by a freedom to throw out components, we can call it *contractile elasticity*; when elasticity is expressed by a freedom to add new components, we can call it *expansile elasticity*. When both these properties exist in unison, the game designers have total freedom to redesign the game during the development process, a situation that is extremely common in board game design, but that is both rare and expensive in video games.

Limiting elasticity generally implies that the game will not be as good as it could be, whether the game is a board game or a video game. The elasticity of design can be preserved in a card-based board game because the cost of each iteration of the design is trivial compared to the cost of manufacture. Each iterative print of the prototype cards costs very little, and the largest cost in this situation is the time and resources required for adequate play testing.

In video games, this is rarely the case. This kind of flexibility in video games is significantly more expensive, although some designs can benefit from cheaper elasticity through the use of paper prototypes. If a subset of the game mechanics can be expressed in a board game of some kind, this allows for cheap testing of the mechanics involved, although this option is generally limited to highly abstracted games. Eric Wujcik, creator of many tabletop role-playing games including *The Palladium Role-Playing Game* (Palladium Books, 1982) and *Teenage Mutant Ninja Turtles and Other Strangeness* (Palladium Books, 1985), observed that reality is too complex to simulate completely, although computers narrow the gap with every passing year [Schick91].

Expansile elasticity in video games is generally the purview of the most expensive products, those that are destined to be considered AAA. Only AAA class games can justify the budget requirements attached to the freedom to add new details and features during the development process. Every video game project would benefit from this freedom, but in reality only the big budget games can afford it.

Contractile elasticity, on the other hand, is essential in all video game design. Game designs must have the freedom to contract because the actual time it takes the art team and, in particular, the programming team to implement a particular design cannot be calculated, only estimated. Unexpected difficulties, delays, bugs, and other problems all contribute to slippage (a delay in the release of the game) unless the design has contractile elasticity built into it.

In the worst case, the contraction of a game design means the loss of design features, which can invalidate the core gameplay. This is a situation all game designers want to avoid, and with this in mind, all video game designs must include a degree of contractile elasticity. They must be designed to allow for certain elements to fall out as the contraction period of development takes its toll on the project.

Goals of Elastic Design

We have defined elasticity as the freedom to make changes during the design process and have identified distinctions between expansile elasticity—the freedom to expand the game design—and contractile elasticity—the ability for the game design to shrink without developing problems as a result of the loss of design components. Contractile elasticity is desirable in all video game projects to allow for inevitable changes in the development cycle.

The development of card-based board games is inherently elastic, as game balance is a product of maintaining an effective card mix, and it is both simple and inexpensive to change this card mix for that particular style of game. Video game design should always aim to include elements of contractile elasticity, and this inclusion is a non-trivial design process. Remove too many elements of a design, and the remaining features no longer form a coherent whole. Conversely, expansile elasticity is easy to carry out, but generally applies only to the big budget, AAA games.

Because we have already demonstrated the value of tight design, it follows that the vast majority of video game designs need to be tight-elastic. Most games are not AAA, and most games have a strictly limited budget for development. If they can't be delivered inside that budget, they might not be completed at all. Tightness is desirable because it ensures that the game design is constructed around a complementary core of supporting game mechanics, but at the same time making the core mechanics tight removes a certain freedom for contraction, effectively limiting elasticity. Finding a way to balance tightness with elasticity is a useful skill for game designers to develop.

EXTENSIVE DESIGN

Extensiveness is a property that is sometimes mistaken for good design. Any game with many different features, many activities supported, and a wide selection of choices in the player's core actions can be described as having an extensive design. In the sense that extensiveness gives the players options, greater freedom, and a reduced feeling of being constrained, it is a desirable property. Realistically, however, these benefits can be costly to develop, and if the game does not also feature the properties of tightness and elasticity, extensiveness can be the downfall of the entire project.

Extensiveness is not an antonym for tightness; any extensive game can be simultaneously tight, provided a coherent logic to the confluence of the game mechanics exists. However, games that lack extensiveness tend towards tightness; we can describe such designs as compact or concise, and concise design is inherently tight. Tightness is a property that you start with in abundance and that diminishes as new game mechanics are added that don't support a consistent core set; extensiveness is a property that starts in total absence but always increases as new mechanics are added—irrespective of the nature, tightness, or quality of the mechanics that are added.

The concept of extensive design is epitomized by the tabletop role-playing game. Although creating a complete role-playing game is a tremendous effort as merely an exercise, every video game designer would do well to look at several role-playing games to get a feeling for the concept of extensive design. It is not that the quality of game mechanics in role-playing games is particular good (it is generally quite patchy); rather, it is the quality of extensiveness that can be found in relative abundance.

Tabletop Role-Playing Games

The basis of all role-playing games is captured in *Contract* (Discordia Incorporated/ Infamy Games, 1998), which was created as an attempt to boil the nature of this game form to its minimal form. The minimal form of the tabletop role-playing game (hereafter, abbreviated to RPG) is a social contract between the referee (often known as a games master) and the players; the players implicitly agree to let the referee decide how their actions will develop the story, and in return the referee implicitly agrees to provide either entertainment, or impartiality, in their role as mediator and chief storyteller.

Contract embodies the observation attributed to E. Gary Gygax that if RPG players ever realized that they could do everything by themselves, the game designers would be out of a job. The fact of the matter is, however, that most games masters require some mechanics to help them run the game world, and most players feel more comfortable trusting the games master's role as referee when some random-driven mechanics provide a framework. The aleatory appeal of dice rolling is also part of the appeal and ritual of tabletop RPGs. Most RPGs are therefore concerned with providing a set of mechanics to simulate the game world and most (but by no means all) provide a set of mechanics for use with dice to simulate events.

The archetypal RPG provides its mechanics in a set way, and this method has been inherited almost wholesale by the computer RPG (cRPG). This form is constructed by creating a character role for each player, which is expressed in terms of attributes and/or skills—usually in terms of numbers attributed to qualities of personality, physical prowess, or talent. The mechanics provide a number of rules and/or tables for relating these attributes and skills to various game tasks, most specifically combat, which is usually the most detailed part of any RPG rulebook.

Eric Wujcik suggested that the trickiest balance in RPG design was combat realism versus playability, and this holds true in video games. In one of his essays he states: "Real-life combat is a model that can't be applied directly, simply because it's too deadly or (if accurately simulated) too time consuming" [Schick91].

RPG Templates

The most famous model of extensiveness in RPGs is E. Gary Gygax's *Advanced Dungeons & Dragons* (TSR, 1978). In this, so many tables, mechanics, and gameplay details were provided that the rules spread out across three different volumes comprising more than 460 pages (and later gaining more volumes adding ever-more detail). Ironically, the combat mechanics at the core of *AD&D* are largely biased towards playability over realism. The bulk of the mechanics are concerned with providing tools for the games master to create adventures, and trying to compensate for the inadequacies of the core mechanics at expressing much beyond combat.

AD&D, like *Dungeons & Dragons* (TSR, 1974) before it, is considered a "class and level" system. These systems are the basis of the majority of cRPGs because "class and level" systems are easily accessible (and also because the exponential experience system behind most level systems can be fiendishly addictive to some players, especially those with a preference for Type 1 play). The other most prevalent style of RPG is the skill-based system, which is usually excellent at simulating non-combat situations, because such systems have a general skill mechanic for resolving tasks by comparing character skills with a die roll by some method.

Chaosium pioneered arguably the most famous of the early skill-based systems, which they called Basic Role-Playing—the backbone of their successful *RuneQuest* (Chaosium, 1978), *Call of Cthulhu* (Chaosium, 1981), and several other RPG systems. In these, the mechanics are simple—skills are represented as percentages, and success or failure is determined by a die roll. The simplicity is enviable, but the problem with this mechanic is that most die rolls end in failure, which makes storytelling somewhat fatalistic unless the games master is generous with what the players can achieve without having to roll dice.

Percentage-based skill systems are often extensive by virtue of the need to interpret the meaning of the percentage levels of the various skills. Many games systems that use this approach provide supplemental mechanics for each and every skill, providing the games master with potential assistance with problem situations at the cost of greater reliance on mechanics. These systems are of very little use in video games where percentage systems seem somewhat capricious. If the player reaches a locked door, for example, the game cannot make a single random determination as to whether the player can break into the door unless other guaranteed means of entry exist—and if reliable methods for getting past the door do exist, the random chance of breaking in becomes both incongruous and superfluous.

Converting Mechanics

The inapplicability of most RPG mechanics to video games stems from the key distinction between the two forms. An RPG uses simple mechanics because it (in general) uses dice as its random source, and because it works best when the random mechanics are used only when dramatically appropriate. A video game uses comparatively complex mechanics because (a) they can and (b) video games must model all interactions in the game world, not just those that are dramatically interesting.

Despite this, RPGs are tremendous examples of extensive design, frequently attempting to cover almost every situation that might present itself with some form of mechanics. Like an extensive video game design, they end up focusing on those situations likely to occur, or those that support the core expected game activities. In a game where combat is a key activity (true of most RPGs, perhaps unfortunately), even the variety of combat situations are covered extensively.

An excellent exercise for any would-be video game designer is to take an arbitrary RPG and convert it to a concept document. This forces the subject to consider many useful questions: What are the core game activities? How much expressiveness can we support in the game actions available to the player? Which mechanics will convert well to a video game setting? Because one is dealing with source materials that already have mechanics specified, the resulting process presents more game design challenges than simply coming up with a concept document from scratch.

The Cost of Extensiveness

The reason RPGs display such a high degree of extensiveness is that it is a property that is cheap in that form of game. They are generally printed as books, and the cost of adding another page of rules material is trivial compared to the total cost of each print run. The same page of additional game mechanics added to a video game design could add another man-month of programming, art, and QA, adding at least an additional $20 thousand to the cost of the project.

In fact, a video game must have substantial development resources (both in terms of budget and of team size) if it is to express any degree of extensiveness, and this can make it a highly undesirable property for many projects. This is not to say that the audience does not desire extensiveness—to a certain extent it is expected that all AAA games deliver a high level of extensiveness—but the acquisition of extensiveness might cost tightness. Therefore, it is a property to be approached with some caution.

No video game can ever be as extensive as a tabletop RPG, at least until AI can accurately simulate human intelligence (which is unlikely to happen during the lifetime of any reader of this chapter). Despite this gap, studying RPGs can show how to achieve a high degree of expressiveness using only a simple core of central mechanics, and this is the goal of extensive design: to support a considerable number of player activities using the same core resources.

Dangers of Extensive Design

We have defined extensiveness as tending towards a wide variety of features and activities expressed in the design. Although extensive designs can easily lose tightness, you can produce tight-extensive designs provided the game designer always keeps in mind the principles of tight design when adding in new features. Extensiveness is a luxury that in general can be afforded only by AAA designs, because only these big budget games can expect to implement more than a core set of mechanics. The presence of extensiveness usually implies contractile elasticity, which is always desirable in development.

Tabletop RPG's are replete with extensiveness, because of the cheap cost of including many options in a game form that is printed as text. By comparison, extensive video game design is always expensive to develop, and as such, game designers must be careful when they have the freedom to produce extensive designs. Analyzing RPG design can be a useful step towards identifying both the benefits and pitfalls of extensive design.

When tackling extensive design, the game designer must keep in mind the principle of tightness to ensure coherence in the resulting project, but often need not worry about elasticity, which is usually inherent to extensiveness. The expansion phase of video game development tends towards extensiveness, and the extent to which this growth is allowed to proceed must be in proportion with the budget for the game. The game designer might desire to focus on extensiveness over tightness, but to do so is to be negligent in the designer's duty to the game.

THE PRESENTATION DILEMMA

One quandary facing many video game designers working on typical products is that their design work generally includes some features that are outside the core mechanics but that potentially make for interesting new gameplay. The problem with these unnecessary new ideas is that the full implication of the mechanics might not be clear until much later in the development process, making their inclusion in the game somewhat risky. Because they do not want to lose these desirable features, they expend some effort in making these points essential to the game design—with a corresponding loss of elasticity.

Many of these features are doomed to be cut, and the honest way to present them would be to mark them as optional or discretionary design components. However, designers are reluctant to do this because they know from experience that cuts have to be made at some point and optional components are the first to go. They might just as well cut them at the initial design phase, because in the extremely unlikely event that additional time is left at the end of development, the time can always be used for spit and polish, and tweaking time can be more valuable to a project than new design features.

The presentation dilemma is precisely this: should you include new, interesting, and innovative design features if you know they are going to be cut later in the project? Perhaps the best answer to this question is the following: "If you know they can be cut, the features cannot be part of the core design." In an extensive design, you might have the luxury to include such features and see what happens, but in a typical tight-elastic design, you don't. Cut everything you can live without.

Instead of gambling on getting additional design features into place, the most prudent approach is to allow for contractile elasticity in the peripheral design elements (for example, the level structure). In a game organized on a level basis, figure in some levels that can drop out of the design without the need for excessive restructuring. These components can afford to be optional because publishers expect a certain minimum play time for every product and therefore cuts that affect game length (play time) are less likely to be implemented than cuts that effect core design features.

CONCLUSION

The game design process begins with a tight concept, for which expansile elasticity is present in abundance because the concept is largely incomplete. The initial design phase begins the growth of extensiveness, which must be curtailed in most game projects but is allowable in AAA games. Focusing on tight mechanics in the initial design phase makes it easier to remain tight throughout the development process by identifying the core elements of the design conception. During expansion, extensiveness must be controlled in proportion to the development budget, and the designer must ensure that contractile elasticity is present or else the inevitable contraction phase will be unable to adjust to delays and problems resulting in development.

As espoused in the philosophy of Zen Game Design, the game designer has a duty to design responsibly; they must balance the needs of the game with the desires of the development team, while simultaneously attempting to anticipate the needs of the game's audience. Striving for tight game designs, innovation should be focused at the micro-level with a goal of producing consistent, integrated core mechanics that provide a high degree of expressiveness. Elasticity is essential, tightness is desirable, and extensiveness is a dangerous property that is needed in the most expensive game projects, but must be secondary to maintaining tight mechanics.

Every game designer wants the opportunity to be inventive, but such unbounded creativity can be the most expensive part of any video game project. AAA products might have the luxury of inventiveness, but most games are not AAA and must emphasize reliability of design over ingenuity. Restraint is one of the greatest talents any game designer can possess; when it is coupled with instincts for tightness and elasticity, it is the height of the game design art.

Resourcefulness is still of value in game design, and every design, no matter how modest, has room for creativity. If designers sharpen their skills in tight-elastic game design, they can be certain that when they earn the freedom to carry out extensive designs, they will be able to design in a manner that demonstrates all three traits: tightness, extensiveness, and elasticity.

Returning to Eric Wujcik for one last piece of game design wisdom: "Add only those new elements that are necessary for the game. Aim for the minimum of innovation" [Schick91]. The foundation of game design is in providing the right design work for the project, not in trying to dazzle with unfettered creativity. All game designers have a duty to the project that must always take precedence over their desires as players of games, and that duty is the core of the game designer's role.

7 Principles of Interface Design

In This Chapter

- Five Golden Rules
- Five Cautions
- Learning Curve
- Subjective Metrics of the Action Space
- Concept Models
- Immersive Menus
- Tutorials
- Conclusion

The creation of the game interface is a crucial step in the design process. A game interface defines all the ways in which the player can interact with the game and is arguably the single most important element of a design. A weak, disorganized or overly complex interface is a barrier to enjoyment for all players (especially the Casual gamers), and therefore every interface should strive to be as simple as is feasible to express the required game actions.

There are three basic components of the interface design for any game:

Front End: This is the term applied to all menus and screens that occur outside of gameplay. In essence, the front end takes the player from the title screen of the game to the point that gameplay begins, but many games have front end screens that are, in effect, part of the game itself (especially those in which the game levels are not hermetic, and elements cross over from one section of gameplay to the next).

In-Game Menus: These are a set of menus and screens accessed in-game, often from a pause menu, but sometimes as part of the game space. The same principles that apply to front end design can, in general, be applied to the in-game menus, and for some PC games the distinction between front end and in-game menus can be minimal. However, the in-game menus form part of the game mechanisms (and therefore can present issues of suspension of disbelief), whereas the front end is usually distinctly separate from the game world.

Control Mechanism(s):   The way in which the player controls their avatar or other game entities is dictated by a control mechanism. Many games have just one control mechanism, but it is not uncommon (especially in sports games) for a game to have multiple control mechanisms at use.

In this chapter, we look at the general principles of interface design, of menu design (front end and in-game), and of control mechanism design. Having laid the groundwork, we discuss how a designer can take into account the needs of different demographics in interface design. Because the game interface effectively connects the player to the game, interface design is of great importance in the designer's goal of creating games that provide enjoyment to specific audiences.

You should consider many issues when working on an interface design, although three in particular are worth considering in detail:

Simplicity: The principle of *simplicity* is that an interface should be as simple as is possible to support the required degree of actions. The more tightly designed a game is, the easier this goal is to achieve, and the more extensive the design, the harder this goal becomes.

Expressibility: The principle of *expressibility* is concerned with the degree of options and choices of action that the player has in the game world. The more extensive a game design is, the greater expressibility is required in the interface. Therefore, an essential tension between simplicity and expressibility exists in all interfaces.

Learning Curve: The *learning curve* is a conceptual measure of how hard it is to learn to control or use a game. The classic formulation is to see learning curve as a chart with time along the x axis, and players' level of mastery along the y axis.

Throughout this chapter, the terms *button* and *key* can be considered synonymous: a button refers to an interface switch on a console controller or joystick, while a key refers to a keyboard switch, but functionally these are simply binary switches that are used in the interface.

FIVE GOLDEN RULES

The following are a set of basic suggestions for constructing interfaces. Although we have characterized them as "Golden Rules," remember that these are just suggestions—they should not be taken as a dogmatic attempt to define eternal rules.

Rule 1: Be Consistent

Although it sounds self-evident, all too many games do not ensure that their controls maintain their functionality across all contexts. If functionality remains consistent, the player need learn the controls only once. If the functionality is different in many different contexts, the result is either an excessive learning curve or player irritation.

Most importantly, ensure that all menus are operated using essentially the same controls. Choose how the players accept a menu option and how they go back up a menu level, and stick to this convention rigidly. The player must be confident that a certain button will do what they expect it to do.

One powerful method for consistency is a concept model for the interface device—we will discuss this later.

Rule 2: Use the Simplest Interface Feasible for the Gameplay

Always strive for the maximum number of different actions in the smallest set of controls. Indeed, although it is tempting to make use of every button on a controller (or every key on a keyboard!), the core controls of a game should strive to use as *few* buttons as possible.

Imagine you are teaching someone to play the game verbally: you should be able to tell them the basics to get started in two or three sentences ("move with this, use this button to do this, and the other button to do that"). Other controls should be picked up while playing (or be purely cosmetic).

In striving for the balance point between simplicity and expressibility, simplicity should be given the edge—it's almost always better for an interface to be easy to learn rather than full of bells and whistles. Even a game developed for a Hardcore cluster (say, a game exhibiting complex Type 2 Manager play, targeting primarily H2 players) is competing against similar games of the same type; the player always wants to engage with the play elements of the game rather than interface, no matter how game literate they are.

Along the same lines, don't add actions that you don't need—and *never* add an action just because other games of the same type do. Many FPS games use a jump button, despite jumping being peripheral or even distracting to the core activity of many of these games. If your game doesn't need it, you should generally leave it out. However, it might be worth considering whether a common feature meets a particularly player need before cutting it—in the case of jumping in FPS games, players might feel artificially constrained if their avatar cannot reach a platform that could realistically be jumped onto.

Metrics for measuring the degree of simplicity of an interface are discussed later in this chapter.

Rule 3: Draw from the Familiar

Don't reinvent the wheel. If an interface style already in use that the audience knows about fits the situation, use that as a starting point. For example, the standard Windows-style WIMP (Windows-Icons-Mice-Pull-down menus) environment is fine for PC sim games. If you replace it with something else, it had better be easy to learn and offer significant advantages. The same rule applies to icon design. You can use many internationally recognizable symbols to improve the player's immediate comprehension of your interface.

Of course, if you are targeting the mass market, you have to be careful because what the Hardcore consider to be a widely known interface style might be entirely unfamiliar to any given Casual player.

One last caveat: as with so many issues of competence, the development team cannot assume that their audience is as skilled with a particular control scheme as they are. Issues of dimensionality of control, discussed later, cannot be ignored, no matter how familiar a control mechanism seems to the development team.

Rule 4: One Button, One Function

Each button or key should have a single defined function; the player should know when they hit a particular button roughly what it should do. The range of expressible actions can be expanded by having context-sensitive functions. A context-sensitive 'Action' button, whose functionality changes according to what the player's avatar is next to, means that only one action results in any given situation. (Ideally, an icon indicating the nature of that action should be displayed on screen so that the player does not need to guess its meaning.)

When this rule is not followed, controls are considered to be *overloaded*. In *Jet Set Radio* (Smilebit, 2000), the interface is beautifully designed except for the overloading of the left trigger, which is used for both camera control and spraying graffiti. This means that you cannot move the camera when you are close to a graffiti tag, which can frustrate many players.

These issues will be examined in more depth in relation to concept models later in the chapter.

Rule 5: Structure the Learning Curve

Casual players can get swamped if you attempt to teach them all the controls from the start, and therefore it is advisable to stagger the learning curve. Introduce the player gradually to both in-game functionality and interface controls, ideally within the main gameplay, but if that's not possible, make sure the player is encouraged to play the tutorial before they start play.

We discuss both learning curve and tutorials later in this chapter

FIVE CAUTIONS

To complement the five "Golden Rules," here are five cautions that represent game design "red flags" to be checked for.

Caution 1: Shortcuts Are for Advanced Users Only

In PC games, avoid requiring the keyboard for the main interface (with the possible exception of the cursor keys and the space bar). You should generally provide some way (no matter how contrived) to achieve an action from the mouse alone. That doesn't mean you shouldn't include keyboard shortcuts, because the advanced user will certainly want them, but few mass market players want to memorize a list of keys before they can play.

On consoles, consider providing advanced elements of the control mechanism that allow the player to achieve certain actions more quickly, such as *GoldenEye 007*'s (Rare, 1997) ability to trigger mines by hitting the A and B buttons simultaneously. Hardcore players find themselves wanting to do certain things more easily after they have played a lot and can be frustrated by the *absence* of shortcuts. (In addition, the discovery of such shortcuts deep into the play window of a game gives its audience a tremendous sense of involvement and expertise.)

Also bear in mind the fact that players have to remember shortcut controls (generally a problem that applies only to PC games). Keyboard shortcuts suffer often because the only sensible key for an action is the letter it begins with—and certain keys go quickly. A, S, D, and W are commonly used for movement keys, for example, although Casual players generally expect the cursor keys to perform this function.

Don't settle for a contrived solution, such as using the second letters, because this won't help the player at all (especially when the game is being translated into other languages). Try arranging them in sensible spatial clusters on the keyboard, or renaming the game action so that it can begin with another letter (although again, this might present issues when the game is localized).

Ideally, allow the player to define or redefine their own shortcuts for all the main game actions, although in console games this can be tricky for various reasons, not least of which is the more rigorous QA protocols that are applied. For console games, a set of predefined control options is usually the best solution.

Caution 2: Icons for Speed, Text for Clarity

Icons are great for immediate recognition, provided the player knows what they mean. Casual players don't generally have the patience of the Hardcore, so it is wise to ensure that you provide a text description for all your icons (either as a tool tip in a PC game, or in a help line somewhere on screen, or if all else fails, as a page in the manual).

The front end for *SSX* (EA, 2000) is a good example of using both text and icons to produce a pleasing interface that is simple to use. Each menu consists of a horizontal row of icons, which, where possible, clearly relate to what they represent. Beneath this row is a pictorial representation or other display pertaining to the option currently selected—for example, when the row of icons is used for character selection, the attributes of the currently selected character appear in the center of the screen. Similarly, when selecting courses, a picture of the course is shown. Finally, at the bottom right of the central display area, the meaning of the currently selected icon is shown in text, so that the player never has to guess what the current icon means.

When icons are used in the game world, the player can generally be left to divine their meaning on their own, provided the risk of letting the player experiment is minimal (that is, no cost accrues to the player for experimenting). However, when the icons require controls to activate, some guidance is required. In *Grand Theft Auto* series games (DMA Designs/Rockstar North, 1997 onwards), for example, this occurs when the player is carrying a weapon, but standing over an icon of the same weapon type (for example, they are carrying a chainsaw and standing over a pool cue, which are both types of melee weapons in the game). In this situation, a non-interactive alert box in the top left of the screen tells the player which control allows them to switch weapons.

Similarly, if an icon is activated only when a control is pressed, the control can be displayed over the icon when the player is close enough, or the game can cycle between showing the icon and the control as happens in *Crimson Skies: High Road to Revenge* (FASA Studio, 2003).

Caution 3: Allow Skipping of Non-Interactive Sequences

You might want the player to see your expensively rendered cut scene, but they might not care—or they might have seen it a hundred times before, especially if its between a save point and a tough boss. Provide a method to skip cut scenes, but don't use a control the player might hit by accident.

Game designers encounter some issues with this, however, because some cut scenes contain essential story or game information that the player must see. Acceptable compromises include a menu option "movie viewer" that allows you to see any cut scene already seen, and only allowing the player to skip cut scenes they have already seen (requiring the game to save data on which scenes have been seen, the overheads for which are largely trivial). An example of both can be found in *Eternal Darkness: Sanity's Requiem* (Silicon Knights, 2002), which has three different versions of its framing story so that on repeat play the player sees a mix of new and old cut scene material. The game permits a cut scene to be skipped only if the player has never seen it before and also includes a movie viewer option to show all of the cut scenes already seen.

It is also important that skipping a cut scene doesn't happen by accident. If one of your core game controls skips a cut scene, players might cancel the cut scene just as it occurs! On consoles, using Start/Pause to skip a cut scene is becoming an accepted convention; on PC, ESC is the obvious candidate for skipping, situated as it is at a fair distance from the rest of the keys.

Caution 4: Provide Options and Save Options

Options allow the player to tailor the interface to their own needs. Despite the name, they are not optional to the game design and are a vital part of the interface, especially when designing for a Hardcore audience. Try to allow the player to customize everything that doesn't affect the core game play—you can never be certain what might annoy a player in your interface design.

If the controls are customizable, remember to transfer secondary actions. *Black & White* (Lionhead, 2001), for example, allows you to redefine the control for the move operation (normally on left mouse button), but if this is done, the player loses the double left-click function that allows you to jump to a particular location directly.

Also, make sure you save all the options. The player doesn't want to reconfigure every time they start playing the game. Ideally, maintain a player profile for anyone who might be playing the game, and save their options separately.

Caution 5: Document It!

Even though most players don't read the manual, they will turn to it if they have a problem or want to find out if such-and-such a thing is possible. Good documentation saves your players much frustration. A Hardcore player might be willing to go online to get the answer to an interface question from a FAQ, but everyone else is more likely to turn to the manual.

LEARNING CURVE

How hard a game is to learn determines to a considerable degree who ends up playing it. Complex games appeal only to Hardcore players, except in rare cases (flight simulators, for example, have a niche audience who tolerate complexity for the sake of realism). To appeal to the mass market, simplicity is king. The learning curve is a way of thinking about the impact of interface complexity on the player.

To a certain degree, the learning curve is a product of both simplicity (simpler interfaces have shallower learning curves) and expressibility (the more expressive the game, the steeper the learning curve), but one other key factor exists: how familiar the techniques used are. Using techniques that players already have some familiarity with always eases the learning curve—but beware. While you can count on a Hardcore gamer to know all the current interface styles (including complex forms such as twin stick/mouse-keyboard first-person shooter interface), you cannot count upon the mass market to have the same skills.

Examples, such as those depicted in Figure 7.1, can depict some basic points.

The three learning curves shown in Figure 7.1 represent three different types of situations with regards to learning an interface. The solid line represents the "optimum" learning curve—players achieve a steady level of mastery over the controls as the game progresses, with the interface elements being introduced gradually. The dashed line represents a more typical situation: the player has a lot to learn at the beginning, resulting in a very steep learning curve—the player is effectively thrown in at the deep end. Despite this being a common state of affairs, it is not a good sign for a commercial game. Games with steep learning curves like these rarely penetrate beyond the Hardcore.

The dotted line represents the effect of prior player knowledge on learning a game, specifically when the interface is in a form the player is already familiar with. Initially, the player already knows much of the control scheme of the game, so learning doesn't really take place fully until later, and less overall learning must take place. Most of the learning is the player adapting to the specifics of the game itself.

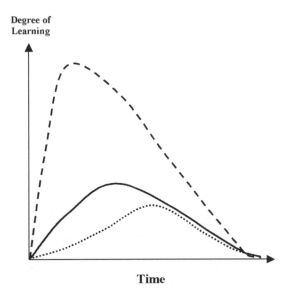

FIGURE 7.1 Three different learning curves for hypothetical interfaces. The solid line is the archetypal "optimal" learning curve, the dashed line shows the learning curve for a complex interface, and the dotted line represents the effect of prior knowledge in attenuating the learning process.

Note that knowledge of different interfaces is not evenly distributed, and therefore profiles like the dotted line *cannot* be planned for except in rare cases. One such exception is a game for PC under a Windows operating system. Because the player already knows the basis of operating a WIMP interface, you can use this in your game with some confidence of prior player knowledge.

Figure 7.1 showed learning curve with respect to achieving mastery, but you need to understand another aspect of learning curve: the point in the game that mastery is achieved. Figure 7.2 demonstrates this point most clearly.

The solid line in Figure 7.2 shows a good learning curve for a game—the player steadily learns controls in the early part of the game, but before the halfway point the emphasis changes from learning to enjoyment of the game. The dashed line shows a somewhat frustrating style of learning curve: the player is taught a set of tough controls, but just as they get to grips with those, they are expected to learn something knew. Learning progresses throughout the game, so that the player has managed to master everything only by the very end. Although this might potentially work with a Hardcore audience, it is an awkward approach. Learning what to do is not what most players want to be doing: they want to be actually doing it.

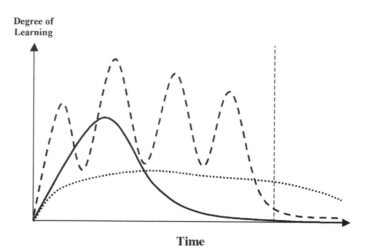

FIGURE 7.2 Learning curves with respect to mastering an interface. The solid line shows a well-paced learning curve, the dashed line a game that is constantly providing the player more and more things to master, and the dotted line a game that is easy to learn but with hidden complexity.

The dotted curve represents a "quick to learn, lifetime to master" interface. The player gets to grips with the controls quickly and easily, but still has much to learn. The player continues to uncover features of the interface organically as the game progresses. This was the approach taken with *Ghost Master* (Sick Puppies, 2003)—letting the player learn and master all the controls they needed relatively quickly, but imbedding complexity in the nature of the actions that the ghosts could carry out. Most players had not learned even a fraction of the capabilities of the ghosts' powers by the end of the game. In principle, this would have stood the game in good stead for future add-on packs, leaving much left to play with.

For *Ghost Master*, this was a mixed blessing. That the controls were relatively easy to master was a success, but the hidden extent of the ghosts powers proved problematic, because it invited criticism of the game based on ignorance (because even at the game's completion, the players still had much they had not come to understand). Typically, the idea that powers affected the world as a system, rather than as individual actions, was difficult for some players to appreciate (especially where game assumptions preceded experimentation). Perhaps more effort could have been expended to allow the player direct access to some of the knowledge locked up in the "organic world" that the game used, although it is equally likely that Hardcore players who thrive on micro-management would have struggled to adapt to the more holistic system used in *Ghost Master* without specific assistance.

The bottom line is that numerous learning curves can be made to work, but in general, learning should be seen as something to keep manageable. Sharp peaks on a learning curve diagram show periods where many players are struggling to achieve anything; this sort of frustration is to be avoided wherever possible.

SUBJECTIVE METRICS OF THE ACTION SPACE

The *action space* of a game is a projection of all the possible activities that can be carried out within the game world. The more different actions possible (and the more different operational modes the game uses), the larger the action space. One way of representing an action space for control mechanisms is to imagine all the controls the player has as the leftmost column of a table, and all the different contexts within which the controls might be used as the topmost row of the table.

For menus, rather than controls, the action space can be considered as a flowchart (or similar representation) that shows all the possible states that the menu system can be in. This applies equally to the front end and any other menu screens at use in the game.

The total action space is therefore the sum of all control mechanism action spaces and all the menu action spaces.

As a general rule, we want to keep the action space as small as possible, to keep the learning curve of the game as low as possible, but we want a sufficient degree of expressibility within this space that the player can do anything that is relevant to the game.

To assess interface design, it is useful to apply metrics that "measure" certain properties of the action space defined for the game. For control mechanisms, a good metric is dimensionality of control, while for menus, action depth is a useful metric.

Dimensionality of Control

The concept of *dimensionality of control* is a measure of the degree of complexity inherent in a control mechanism. It is a numerical figure representing the number of dimensions inherent to the interface mechanic presented to the player. Although it is derived in an essentially subjective fashion, any formulation can be used as the measure, because games are measured relative to one another.

The main component of the dimensionality of control is the number of degrees of freedom of movement inherent to the control mechanism. For example:

Tetris (**Atari, 1988**):   This has essentially one degree of freedom of movement—the blocks move only left and right.

The Legend of Zelda: A Link to the Past (**Nintendo, 1987**):   This game is presented in top-down 2D projection and has essentially two degrees of freedom of movement—the player can move left, right, up, and down.

GoldenEye 007 (**Rare, 1997**):   In its default configuration, this game has two degrees of freedom of movement—the stick changes the direction faced and moves in that direction. (Strafing and tilting the view up and down are also provided as an additional component, but in this control mode are entirely optional.) In its other configurations it has four degrees of freedom of movement—the player can adjust their view in two dimensions, move in and out of that plane, and strafe left and right.

Half-Life (**Valve, 1998**):   This game and other PC first-person shooters are based around four degrees of freedom—two degrees of view and two degrees of movement. (Although it might seem strange to have more than three degrees, remember that these control mechanisms simulate both the facing of the avatar and independent planar movement.)

In addition to the degrees of freedom to move, dimensionality of control must take into account any other dimensions to control:

- Different ways of moving along a line of some kind (such as strafing, throttle-based velocity, or time control) constitute an additional full dimension of control.
- Any *enfolded* control aspects, such as discrete rotation, accelerator-velocity, or jumping, can be considered an additional half a dimension of control.
- Atomic actions that are non-spatial can be considered to add dimensions equal to one quarter of the number of actions.

Deciding what constitutes an "enfolded" aspect is in general a judgment call; however, a simple test is as follows: if you plot a chart of this property, does it fit on one axis and consist of a limited set of values? So, for example, discrete rotation is an angle that is another dimension, but is enfolded because it is non-spatial and limited to set values. An argument can be made that velocity control should constitute a full dimension of control; however, the intuitive familiarity of an accelerator system (cars, etc.) and the fact that the range of velocities is fixed and limited in most games make this reasonable as a half dimension. However, a throttle system—where the speed and the setting of the control are different—should be considered a full dimension because of the added complexity.

Jumping, similarly, can be shown on a single axis (varying height), but the profile is fixed and therefore can be considered a half dimension. Note, however, that jumping generates a half dimension from one control, while most other enfolded elements use two controls, making this a special case.

Continuing with our previous examples:

Tetris: The player can rotate blocks left and right, so we consider this an addition half a dimension (discrete rotation).

The Legend of Zelda: A Link to the Past: In this game the player has a number of different actions in the game world, but all from two buttons. These two atomic actions add another half dimension to the controls.

GoldenEye 007:   The controls gain an additional half dimension from selecting weapons, and another half from atomic actions. (In the basic configuration, you also have an additional dimension from strafing and from vertical adjustment of view, although players using this configuration tend not to use these components of the interface.)

Half-Life: This game adds to its basic controls various added functions including swimming with unique separate controls (+1), jumping (+0.5), ducking (+0.5), weapon changing (+0.5), four additional essential atomic actions (+1), and a large number of optional additional controls that can be ignored.

This makes these four games, by this measure of dimensionality of control:

Tetris: 1.5 dimensional.

The Legend of Zelda: A Link to the Past: 2.5 dimensional.

GoldenEye 007:   3 dimensional in the basic configuration (two degrees of movement, plus weapon select, shoot, and action), and 5 dimensional in the advanced configuration.

Half-Life: 7.5 dimensional (in the PC configuration).

The recent explosion of controls included in games has meant that the trend in dimensionality in control has increased with each new controller—as game designers insist on using all the controls available to them. The NES controller could support only 2.5 dimensional play; the PlayStation controller offers up to 4 dimensions from its two analog sticks, 1–2 dimensions from the D-pad, 1–2 dimensions from the face buttons, another 1–2 dimensions from the shoulder buttons, and a final 0.5 to 1 dimension from the stick buttons for a staggering maximum of 11 dimensions of control (although typically a game using all buttons will be only 7.5 dimensional, because very few actions like jumping can be considered to add 0.5 dimensions from a single control).

A summary of this particular system of evaluating dimensionality of control can be found in Table 7.1.

TABLE 7.1 Dimensionality of Control

Element	Type	Dimensionality
Control	1 dimensional (left-right)	+1
	2 dimensional (left-right, up-down)	+2
	3 dimensional (left-right, up-down, in-out)	+3
	3 dimensional (2D view that extends off the screen, for example, space shooter controls)	+3
	4 dimensional (2D view, 2D move, for example, first-person shooter twin sticks/mouse keyboard)	+4
Additional Movement	Strafing mechanism (2 buttons)	+1
	Throttle-type acceleration (2 buttons)	+1
	Height control (2 buttons)	+1
	Leaning (2 buttons)	+1
Enfolded Dimensions	Jumping	+0.5
	Accelerator-type acceleration (2 buttons)	+0.5
	Discrete rotation (1 or 2 buttons)	+0.5
Atomic Actions	Any other action (1 button)	+0.5 per 2

Of course, not all actions in the game world are essential. To count control of the radio stations or beeping the horn as part of the dimensionality of control in *GTA* is unfair, because they are aesthetic elements, not gameplay elements. This suggests it might be worth thinking in terms of core dimensionality of control and full dimensionality of control for some games. *GTA*'s core controls (for the driving element) are 1.5 dimensional (steer left and right, plus half a dimension for velocity), with another 5 dimensions in optional components (2 dimensions of optional camera control, 0.5 dimensions from look left or right, and 1.5 dimensions from atomic actions).

Different demographics can handle different degrees of dimensionality of control; as a rough guide:

Casual players: In general these players can cope with between 3 and 5 dimensions of control.

C1 players: Players fitting this cluster can be expected to deal with 7 dimensions of control, or more if they are built upon an already learned mechanism (for example, FPS control has become so ubiquitous, they can handle 9 or 10 dimensions if built on this interface configuration). Many, but by no means all, C2 players also fit this profile.

Hardcore players: These players can (in general) handle 9 dimensions of control without any difficulty and can master more if sufficiently motivated, with potentially no upper limit. H3 and H4 players prefer fewer dimensions, however, and 5–7 is recommended for these clusters.

Games targeting the mass market have significant benefit from introducing controls gradually, because the player masters a low dimensionality of control interface mechanism before having it expanded. Although this might annoy H1 (and possibly H2) players (who apparently like to be put in at the deep end), it is worth bearing in mind for other target clusters.

Thinking in terms of dimensionality of control, it becomes clear that the player shouldn't be the only force in charge of the camera if you want to hit a mass market audience. If the game controls the camera, but the player can adjust it, you are just adding an additional 2 dimensions of optional control, but if the player must control the camera, you are adding an additional 2 dimensions of required control. This probably means the game can no longer appeal to C3 or C4 players.

The reason so many companies produce third-person games using a twin stick control mechanism with no automatic camera control can be attributed to the fact that the majority of game developers routinely play PC first-person shooters (which usually have at least 5.5 dimensions of control, and generally much more) and therefore have an exaggerated sense of what the normal player can handle. This trend might ultimately be doomed for the mass market (but might survive for niche markets, such as pure Hardcore games) because any such game is going to have a minimum of 5 dimensions—and that assumes that only four face buttons are used for controls.

Credit must be given to Nintendo for keeping dimensionality of control low in their games, which are always targeting the maximum possible market (especially in terms of age range). Although it is doubtful they couch these design decisions in terms of dimensionality of control, it is clear they have recognized the limited degree of control the mass market can master, relative to the Hardcore. It is notable that Nintendo's only FPS series, *Metroid Prime* (Nintendo, 2002 onwards), does not use a twin stick control mechanism, although the full control mechanism for this game does offer the same high degree of dimensionality control of other FPS once mastered. A parallel can be drawn with *GoldenEye* (which was also on a Nintendo platform) with its low-dimension default control mechanism that expanded into full FPS style controls.

Action Depth

What dimensionality of control is for a control scheme, *action depth* is for a menu system. Simply put, the depth of a particular action can be defined as the number of subactions required to execute that action. For example, opening a pause menu by pressing Start would be at depth 1, quitting a game from the pause menu is at depth of 2 (open the pause menu, then select quit).

In general, every action should be at the lowest depth achievable, and all common actions should be within a depth of 3 or less. Minimizing action depth makes the interface easy to learn and fast to navigate and minimizes player frustration.

The principles of action depth should be applied to the front end and to the in-game menus. For example, you do not want the action depth to continue playing a game to be more than 1, except in rare cases. Similarly, it is desirable to allow the player to start playing a game from the title screen with very little menu navigation, and most games default to having the new game option as the default. However, it should be noted that if an extant save game exists, it is often better for "continue" to be presented as the default option on the title screen; the player needs to start a new game only once in most cases, but continues an existing game frequently. New game can be offered as the default option only when no extant save game exists.

Making the player go through all of the previous menus before returning to play should be avoided, and wherever possible the most common options should be immediately available at the end of a section of gameplay. *Wave Race 64* (Nintendo, 1996) allows the player to change the course or their chosen watercraft from a menu at the end of each race, minimizing the action depth of the most common options by offering them on a menu displayed after each race.

Mandatory replays should also be considered carefully, because you are committing the player to an extra action just to continue playing. Perhaps the optimal approach for replays in terms of action depth is demonstrated by *SSX*, which plays the replay automatically behind the results screen and offers the player a menu on this screen from which they can choose to restart the level, view the replay (without the results overlay), see the records, or quit.

Action depth can also be applied to control mechanisms. Consider *Turok 2*'s (Iguana, 1998) radial weapon select, which is always around depth 1, versus its contemporary rival *GoldenEye*'s linear sequence of weapons, where depth increases as you acquire more weapons. The latter style has become the norm in console FPS games because of a perceived need to select a weapon and move at the same time—a product of the extreme Hardcore attitude of many FPS players. The *Turok* wheel is a superior choice for a more mass market audience: holding a button brings up a radial menu; the player then selects their option, and releases the menu button. Although only eight different options are allowable in this system, it offers much shallower action depth, and it is notable that the system was revived for *Ratchet & Clank* (Insomniac, 2002), which presumably was hoping for a mass market audience.

Any number of systems can be defined for measuring action depth, and your choices of how to do this can affect how you think about the interface design. If you consider selecting to be half an action and pressing a button or key to be another half action, it is apparent that using a single key to close a window as a shortcut generally halves the depth of exiting the menus when you have finished. Try to use a system that reflects the factors most important to the interface in question. If you add depth for loading times, for example, you are more likely to spot the need to include a restart option on the game over screen, so the player doesn't have to reload to play the level again.

The point of thinking in terms of action depth is to spot where the player might end up spending too much time wrestling with the interface and then simplify.

CONCEPT MODELS

A *concept model* is a framework that can be taught to the player that assigns a single role to each control. For example, a very simple concept model for a simple game might be as follows:

- Stick → Move
- A Button → Action
- B Button → Attack

Now it might be that the A button carries out different actions in different contexts, but if the player thinks of it as the "Action" button, they learn simply that pressing this button will carry out most actions. Similarly, "Attack" might mean different things in different situations, but by learning it as "Attack" the player always knows that the Attack button performs an offensive move.

In general, a concept model emerges from looking at all the actions that need to occur in the game world and then grouping them according to functionality.

Designing Concept Models for Multiple Platforms

Increasingly, games are appearing cross-platform (or multi-format)—that is, they appear on multiple different consoles and possibly on PC as well. In this situation, it is vital that the concept model can be applied to all the different platforms the game will appear on.

As an example of what happens when this point is overlooked, consider *Turok: Evolution* (Acclaim, 2002). The concept model for this game was worked out for the PS2, and the functionality then converted for the other formats (GameCube and Xbox).

The clearest sign that multiple formats were not considered occurs with the GameCube version. Next Weapon and Previous Weapon are control concepts that belong on related buttons. On the PS2, the four face buttons are part of a set of four, and any two adjacent buttons can be paired for these functions. But on the Game-Cube, the A and B keys are paired, and the X and Y buttons (which are grey and kidney shaped) are conceptually a different element of the controller. However, *Turok: Evolution* on the GameCube assigns Previous Weapon to B and Next Weapon to Y. This is counterintuitive; it would have been better to assign these two functions to X and Y because they are part of the controller that imply related (and lower priority) actions.

The same problem occurs in the flight controls in *Turok: Evolution*. Bank Left is assigned to B, and Bank Right is assigned to X, with weapons on the shoulder buttons. Speed Up and Slow Down are assigned to A and Y. It makes considerably more sense that Bank Left and Bank Right be assigned to shoulder buttons so that the Left shoulder executes Bank Left and the Right shoulder button executes Bank Right. Speed Up and Slow Down can then be grouped on the grey X and Y buttons, with A and B firing weapons. Curiously, the game options include an alternate configuration that does take into account these issues; why it is not the game's default is a mystery.

One could argue that the motivation for the contrived flight control configuration was to keep the concept model for A (fire) the same. But as the only control that maps between configurations, this seems misguided. It is likely that the game design favored the PS2 version because this was the platform that greatest sales would be expected for (on account of a larger installed base), but given the role of the Hardcore as evangelists and the tendency for Hardcore players to buy games on the most technically advanced platform they own, this was probably a mistake.

Whenever a concept model needs to map across multiple formats, consider the nature of the control devices on all formats and identify the common elements and features that can be used. The control schema must be compatible with the control devices with the fewest number of controls if all the target platforms are going to have adequate control methods.

IMMERSIVE MENUS

Whereas a front end menu is almost always a simple list of options, menus appearing inside the game world need not resemble the classic list of text. Indeed, a growing trend is towards imbedding menu functionality within the game world in a form that seamlessly integrates with that world. We can consider such an approach an *immersive menu.*

An early example can be found in *The Legend of Zelda: The Ocarina of Time* (Nintendo, 1998) in which the shops displayed all the items for sale on shelves that can be seen by the player as they move around the world. When talking to a shop keeper, the menu functionality manifests by allowing the player to move around the shelves to select what to buy, as if their avatar were scanning the shelves with their eyes. This is a more immersive approach than the classic overlaid text menu that had predominated before 3D games began to become the norm. Clearly this kind of approach is rooted in mimicry, and as such, it can be assumed that attempting this kind of interface is a decision to incorporate elements that appeal to players who enjoy Type 3 Wanderer and Type 4 Participant play.

Another example of moving away from menu selection and towards immersive menus (or functionally equivalent situations) can be found with the *Tokyo Xtreme Racer* (*TXR*) series (Genki, 1999 onwards). Racing games prior to this generally allowed the player to select a race from a conventional menu front end. *TXR* turns this assumption on its head by letting the player drive around a world (based on the Tokyo highway system) within which many other cars are on the roads. Specifically marked cars represent a race—to trigger it, the player has merely to drive up behind them and flash their headlights on and off. This triggers a brief sequence as the two cars acknowledge each other and pull alongside, and then the race begins. The mechanic elegantly discards the need for a front end menu to select races and increases the degree of immersion experienced by the player.

Similarly, the *GTA* series have used their game worlds as a surrogate menu system. Missions are not selected from a menu, but are represented by spotlights in the world at large that the player drives to and stops within to trigger the mission. Another example within this series of games can be seen with the shop and wardrobe functionality in *Grand Theft Auto: San Andreas* (Rockstar North, 2004). Here, the menu system for dressing up exists both in text and in graphical display: the avatar walks into the wardrobe and then emerges wearing the selected item. Sadly, this system was marred slightly by the long load times associated with trying on clothes, which reduced the elegance of what was otherwise a sound approach to making a menu system more immersive.

We have already noted how these kinds of approaches favor mimicry over agon, and it is interesting to note that *Need for Speed Underground 2* (Black Box,

2004) provides a choice of game modes. One offers the immersive world approach of *GTA* whereby tasks are selected by driving around the world to certain points. The other strips away this layer of mimicry and replaces it with a conventional menu system. Reviewers have been divided on the two approaches, and this likely reflects a split between the agon-motivated Type 1 and 2 styles of play, and the mimicry-motivated Type 3 and 4 styles.

TUTORIALS

Once an interface design has been constructed, some thought must be given as to how the player learns the game. To date, no unified tutorial design philosophy has emerged, and the many different approaches have advantages and disadvantages to each. Much of the decision as to which way to go should depend upon the nature of the game and the nature of the target audience. In general, Casual players are patient when being told rules, while Hardcore players (specifically H1 and H2) greatly prefer to experiment for themselves.

Control Flashcard

The simplest form of tutorial is a *control flashcard*, where the game controls are shown on one screen. Game demos often use a control flashcard at the start of the demo to brief the player of the controls. The flashcard can also be shown on the loading screen, as in *Crimson Skies: High Road to Revenge*.

Incredibly cheap and simple, it is not recommended as a replacement for a tutorial, not least of which because it is often a somewhat indigestible way of delivering information—too much is shown to the player at once and players don't know what is of primary importance and what is an advanced control. Multiple flashcards each showing one element of the controls, as seen in *Beyond Good and Evil* (Ubisoft, 2003), improve this situation somewhat, but might leave players wondering what the other buttons do.

However, it is well worth including a control flashcard as a reminder for the player somewhere in a game, as happens with *Tak and the Power of Juju* (Avalanche Software, 2003) and other games that have a control flashcard available from the pause menu. It allows the player to check the controls without having to look in a paper manual.

Training Movie

This is another simple form of tutorial where the player is shown a short film that briefs them of what to do. In general terms, it is suited only to situations where the game is very simple to pick up and hence a short briefing suffices, because in other situations the player should be afforded the chance to experiment with the controls they are being taught.

A good example of the training movie can be found in *Kirby Air Ride* (HAL Laboratory, 2003). Each of the game's three modes has a short training movie that is between 60 and 90 seconds long. The most important information is given right at the beginning and the least important at the end, so that the player generally has the gist of the game without having to watch the entire movie. The tutorial is played the first time a mode is selected and the first time a mode is selected after not having been accessed for a considerable length of time and can also be selected by the player manually using the "How to Play" option on the front end menu for that mode. One of the reasons this approach works well with this game is that the control scheme is very simple—just the stick and a single button—and the implementation of the training movie format in this game is practically optimal.

Less effective is the training movie in *Tak and the Power of Juju*, which briefs the player about the controls in the two snowboarding levels. The movie is several minutes long and occurs in the middle of play, thus breaking the player out of the game in a somewhat unwelcome fashion. The movie is necessary only because the snowboarding sections are essentially a completely different game.

Training movies are of most use on games where the availability of storage space is very high, especially console games that often have more data storage on their media than is needed. On portable devices and mobile phones, their applicability is more limited. They are also a great cost-saving move, because a training movie is almost invariably cheaper to construct (in terms of man hours) than a playable tutorial. This is presumably the reason that *Tak* uses a movie to introduce the secondary gameplay of the snowboarding levels, but a detailed playable tutorial for the main gameplay.

Linear Exercises

In this style of tutorial, information is given to the player as a series of exercises, each of which teaches one element of the interface. This has the huge advantage of being comprehensive and straightforward, but might lead to Hardcore players' (or any player who picks it up quickly) becoming frustrated with the slow pace. Players who display a preference for Sensing (which can be assumed to be the entire Casual audience) prefer this style of tutorial.

To allow for some freedom for Hardcore players to proceed at their pace, it is often worth including the capacity for players to skip exercises. This can be doubly beneficial, because it generally implies that earlier exercises can be returned to as well—thus allowing the player some degree of control over their tutelage.

Goal-Oriented Tutorials

This is a variant on linear exercises in which the exercises run in series, each with a goal. Completing each goal is required for progress, so the player must (in principle) have learned what they need if the goals are all completed. The downside of this approach is that the player might fluke the goal in a way the designers never intended and not learn the required mechanic. Plus, the issue of how the use of the control in question is to be conveyed to the player still exists. Nevertheless, this technique does not alienate any particular cluster of players.

Common techniques for teaching the player within a goal-oriented tutorial are context-sensitive commentary and help signs (both of which are discussed later in the chapter). Alert boxes that pop up near the start of each segment are a functionally equivalent, if somewhat clumsy, alternative.

It is also possible for goal-oriented tutorials to be structured in a parallel fashion, for example, if the player is given a list of goals to be achieved. This can work for any audience group provided the number of elements being taught at any given time is kept low, although it is likely to be preferred by Hardcore players (whose game literacy often gives them a head start in learning how to play a game) and especially H1 players who have a desire to advance rapidly and might become impatient if constrained. When multiple goals are provided simultaneously like this, the player should always be provided access to a list of their goals (often from a pause menu).

Help Signs

A common technique in Nintendo games is to have all the help written on signposts in the game world that the player can read or ignore at their leisure. This has the huge advantage that experienced players can ignore the boards, but has several disadvantages. First, if the player doesn't find a particular board, they do not learn a particular element of the interface. Second, the player might pick up most of the interface easily, but still need advanced tuition—this leads to players' having to read every board, even though most of them are telling them things they already know.

The method works relatively well for Casual players, and Hardcore players (especially H1) are likely to simply ignore it and make their own way. However, placement of the signs is absolutely critical. Ideally, if the player *must* learn a particular mechanic, a barrier should be placed in front of the player at a mandatory point with the help signs nearby to provide instruction, much as in a goal-oriented tutorial approach (and, as already mentioned, the two methods readily combine).

Imbedded Manual

An *imbedded manual* is simply a situation where the text of the game manual (or a secondary manual created specifically for imbedding in the game) is provided that allows the player to read about game functions in the game world. This can be considered in many ways a more detailed version of Help signs and a less immersive solution.

Games targeting Type 2 Manager players (especially the more complicated PC sim or strategy games) benefit greatly from the inclusion of an imbedded manual, and H2 players in particular have the patience to explore a manual at their leisure. H1 players, by contrast, might feel obligated to read all the manual material presented to them, even if this frustrates them, and Casual players generally look at manuals only when they are stuck.

In games targeting a more mass market audience, the imbedded manual can be softened by breaking up the text into smaller segments. The *Resident Evil* series (Capcom, 1996 onwards) uses a system whereby the player is provided short notes that introduce gameplay elements gradually as the game progresses. In this approach, it is similar to the Help sign approach, except that the player generally has access to all the notes they have collected from their pause menu, thus they gradually build up a complete imbedded manual.

Context-Sensitive Commentary

In this approach, the player is told about interface elements only when they first use them. The usual source of the commentary is generally a character in the game world, if only to avoid undermining the game's narrative abstractions. The need to have a character as the voice of such commentary is inevitable if all speech is to be recorded, although avoidable if the game presents it as text (usually only seen in games with large amounts of script, such as RPGs, or games made on much smaller budgets).

This approach can work well—except when the nature of controls to be taught means that many things can be encountered simultaneously. In this situation, it becomes difficult to know what to tell the player, and worse, the player might encounter huge "info dumps" of tutorial instructions all at once. Early versions of the *Ghost Master* tutorial suffered from this problem to a near-terminal degree, but fortunately adequate blind testing smoothed out many of the problems before the final release.

As already noted, this approach works best when combined with the goal-oriented approach; the context-sensitive instructions can be delivered when the player approaches the part of the game world in which that knowledge is needed to overcome the goal.

Checklist with Prompts

This is based around the idea of ticking off an item in a list when the player has learned a particular action. The list in question need not be seen by the player if the criterion for ticking off an item is sufficiently inclusive. In a sense, it is a version of the parallel goal-oriented approach, in which the "checklist" is expressed in the game world as goals. The advantage of this approach is that the player can be prompted with context-sensitive dialogue whenever they need a particular action. When the player has definitively demonstrated that they can do a particular action, it is "ticked off," and the player is no longer prompted.

The challenge with this approach is ensuring that the checklist condition is a sufficient test that the action was learned. For example, this approach was used in the aforementioned *Ghost Master* tutorial and worked fine with many players. However, in several cases the player had apparently learned how to change the view (thus ticking off the instructions relating to camera control), but had in reality merely pressed the wrong control.

Staggered Complexity

This is a technique used in the *GTA* games, as well as many games developed by Nintendo. In this approach, not all the functionality of the interface is "switched on" at the start of the game, and controls are added as they are needed. This has simplicity on its side, but care must be taken in just how the player is told about the controls: in *GTA*, text is displayed in an alert box in the top-left corner of the screen. If the player is involved in something that requires their full concentration, these instructions can be missed, leaving the player permanently in the dark. (The pause screen menus allow some of this text to be reviewed, but Casual players are unlikely to think to look.)

Care must also be taken that players who replay the game are not annoyed by the actions blocked to them at the start. Controls should be introduced relatively quickly wherever possible (unless the game elements they refer to are not encountered until later and then they can be deferred).

CONCLUSION

The importance of good interface design cannot be overstressed. Any game design can be ruined by a thoughtless, overcomplicated, or inconsistent control scheme, and a badly structured front end can hinder a game's chances at market by alienating curious players before they reach the meat of the product. From a point of view of first impressions, these elements are vital in convincing the player that they are playing a carefully created product that is worth their time.

It is vital that a game interface is designed with that product's target audience in mind. Different players have markedly different needs from a control scheme. For example, Hardcore players (especially H1) actively require character actions to deliver a sense of competence and might be frustrated when the game offers them insufficient options for controlling their character. Conversely, Casual players require simplicity (delivered via a low dimensionality of control), and those who favor Type 3 and 4 play generally want an interface that favors mimicry.

The degree of complexity in the control interface might determine the extent of a game's possible audience, *regardless of other game elements*. As such, interface design requires significant thought at the earliest possible stage of development.

8 Game World Abstraction

In This Chapter

- Motivations for Abstraction
- Abstractions of World
- Conclusion
- Endnotes

The practice of *game world abstraction* is the core of the game designer's work during the early parts of the design process, and the maintenance of that world abstraction is an important factor in any changes to the design during development. Game world abstractions state the rules of the world the game is set in: the nature of the game world, the players' potential interactions with that world, and the manner in which that world is represented. Because the entirety of reality is too complex to be simulated in a game, it must be abstracted, and it is because of this abstraction that game mechanics are required.

No game has ever been produced without a game world abstraction. For example, consider this summary of the game world abstraction for *Pac-Man* (Namco, 1980):

> *The world consists of a linear series of 2D mazes; a small yellow circle (Pac-Man) moves around these mazes scoring points for eating dots, with a new maze beginning when all the dots have been eaten in the current maze. Pac-Man is opposed by a set of colored ghosts that attempt to home in on Pac-man's position; if they touch him, he loses a life. If Pac-Man eats a power pill, the ghosts turn blue, during which time the ghosts can be eaten and attempt to run away from Pac-Man. Any ghosts that are eaten become eyes that float to the center of the current maze and turn back into ghosts; Pac-Man scores points exponentially for eating multiple ghosts in succession. At the end of a power pill's duration, ghosts flash white before returning to their original colors and state of invulnerability. Periodically, fruit appears and bounces around, and Pac-Man can eat these for extra points. Both Pac-Man and the ghosts can go off the edges of a maze and appear on the opposite side of the screen.*

This is practically the complete game world abstraction for *Pac-Man*—and indeed for many other games in that sequence. To convert the preceding summary of abstraction so that it describes *Ms. Pac-Man* (Midway, 1981), for example, you need add only the following:

> *Every few levels, a short cut-scene tells the love story between Pac-Man and Ms. Pac-Man: first, how they met, then their courtship, and finally the arrival of Baby Pac-Man.*

Summaries in this form read exactly as descriptions of gameplay because game world abstractions specify what can and cannot be done in the game, but the art of creating game world abstractions is much more subtle than simply describing the gameplay. What sounds good on paper might be unfeasible, unplayable, or unimplementable in practice, so responsible abstraction is essential. Game designers need mental tools to think about the abstraction process to avoid the pitfalls and bring out the strengths of a game and to accurately bias individual game world abstractions to their target audiences.

MOTIVATIONS FOR ABSTRACTION

The abstractions that are used in game design are sometimes motivated at supporting play, sometimes intended to improve immersion, and sometimes originate in technical issues. In general, the abstractions in use are in constant change—in part because of technical advances, in part because an expanding (or changing) game audience requires different approaches, and in part thanks to general selective pressures (as the more appropriate or preferred abstractions win out over clumsier approaches).

Technical Limitations

The first thing that must be understood is that you cannot do whatever you want for the simple reason that you face hardware and software limitations. You cannot yet design a game in which you engage in free and open conversation with the non-player characters (NPCs) because artificial intelligence and dialogue synthesis is not that advanced yet (and will likely not become so any time soon).

The history of video games is littered with abstractions that have resulted from technical limitations, such as the use of 2D sprites in 3D games such as *Wolfenstein 3D* (id Software, 1992), which was published at a time when significant polygonal 3D was not viable on most PCs, or the arcade game *M.A.C.H. 3* (Mylstar, 1983), which used a laser disc to provide landscapes, but overlaid 2D sprites for the player's plane and the enemy targets. Similarly, early arcade games are presented in a 2D third-person view simply because it was not viable to render in 3D until the first vector hardware was produced—and when these games, such as *Tail Gunner* (Cinematronics, 1979), did arrive, the 3D models were restricted to wireframes.

Even in modern development, when polygon budgets can reach ten million or more, abstractions for technical restrictions still exist. Games tend to forget which items have been smashed in the game world, as happens in the *Grand Theft Auto* series (DMA Designs/Rockstar North, 1997 onwards) because it is a tremendous cost in terms of memory to record data regarding everything that has been broken.

Budget Limitations

The limitations that apply to most projects are not due to the limits of technology (because most game projects are inspired or at least affected in part by what is currently capable) but to limitations of budget. Not every game is a AAA project that is allowed a multimillion budget; most games must be developed within a particular price range, and as such, serious limitations are implied. Even at the top end of the market, where development costs can run to $5 million or more—*Shenmue* (Sega AM2, 2000) reputedly cost $20 million to make [1]—severe limits still apply to any project.

Although producers want their game designers to know how much everything is going to cost, in reality, it is not the game designer's job to provide costing, develop project schedules, and so forth (except in the cases where the director or producer of the project is also the game designer). As such, game designers should just get a general feel for the scale and the scope of the project and adjust their expectations accordingly. If project budgets were more widely publicized, it would perhaps be possible for a more detailed analysis to be carried out, but as it stands, we must content ourselves with crudely dividing the market into different tiers.

At the top end of the market are those projects that are referred to as AAA ("triple A") games, which can cost anywhere from $3 million to $8 million dollars or more. Such projects are intended to be the cream of the crop, although in point of fact, many are commercial failures (that is, they do not make back their development budget). Less than 10% of games produced are responsible for about 50% of all revenue generated by games, and of these the top 2.5% are responsible for 25% of the revenue generated [Parker03]. When designing for AAA games, the game designer can generally set out with high expectations and expect to rein in those expectations only in response to the needs of the programming and art teams.

Below the AAA games is what can be considered the high-tier market. Here, games are developed for something in the region of $1 to $3 million. Many such games are license adaptations, that is, games that use a pre-existing intellectual property (IP), such as a film or TV show, and develop a game around it. Usually developed on schedules of 18 months or less, these games are often quite profitable, in part because the attached IP helps limit risk and in part because their lower development cost implies lower break points (that is, the number of copies that must be sold to make back costs). When designing for this market, designs must be lean and efficient, as most games are aiming to pass themselves off as being AAA games, even though they are developed for a fraction of the cost.

The mid market consists of games developed for somewhere between half a million dollars and $1 million. Very few console games are at this budget scale, as these are generally more expensive to make (in part because of the cost of development equipment for console games) and also because the share of profits that the hardware licensor requires cuts into profits. Most games are for PCs, and most games are targeting either a Hardcore audience or a clearly defined Casual audience (probably through the use of licensed IP once again). The game designer is usually given limits based upon what software engine can be licensed, or has already been put together by the developer, and the game design is about how to use these tools to best effect.

The low tier market consists of projects developed for under a half a million dollars, but usually more than $100 thousand. These games are much like the mid market in microcosm, and the technical limits of the software tools available very much determine what can be achieved. Games for handheld platforms can often be found in this market, because the technically simpler platforms allow for cheaper development, although, as ever, development cost continues to escalate as the hardware becomes more powerful.

Games developed for under $100 thousand are generally for mobile phones. In this market, the technological limits usually severely restrict what is possible, and the games often resemble the games of 20 years ago or more because of the step down in technological capabilities.

The budget that a game has for development is the severest limitation. Except for certain U.S. developers who are allegedly allowed to develop games without reference to budget, every game must operate within the restrictions of budget, and as a result, when choosing the game world abstraction, the game designer must take into account whether their decision is going to add to the cost of the game, and whether or not the abstraction is viable given the hardware or engine limitations they must work within.

Goals

As well as abstracting in order to stay within limits, we also use game world abstractions in response to achieving certain goals. Often, a game begins with a vision statement that states the overall goals of the game project. Although profit is the primary motivation for most game development, the vision statement helps develop the project's identity, and deciding upon this at an early stage helps constrain the options for development to a manageable subset, as well as provides focus.

The goal of an elegant game world abstraction, therefore, could be said to be to meet the needs of the vision statement, but this is a definition that provides little help, because every game has a different guiding vision. Instead, we can consider the goal of an elegant game world abstraction to be to meet the needs of its audience, within the scope of the vision statement.

In an agonistic game that is to be played by a single player, the abstractions must provide the player with a fair chance of success and a degree of challenge suited to the needs of the players in its target audience (which might vary considerably).

In an agonistic game that is to be played by many players, the abstractions must work towards the goal of giving all players an equal a priori chance of victory—which is to say, any imbalance between the players initial chances of winning must in general be minimized (else the game tends towards alea, and not agon).

In a game of mimicry, the abstractions must in general work towards suspension of disbelief, as immersion is more important than balance of play. If the game's vision statement values mimicry over agon, then the choice of abstractions should reflect this bias.

In a toyplay game, the abstractions should support freedom to experiment over constrained challenges, or in a game where toyplay is to be supported (but complementary to gameplay) the abstractions should not limit the player's freedom to experiment without interfering with the essence of its challenges.

ABSTRACTIONS OF WORLD

Although there are no limits to the number of different types of abstraction that can be put to work in a game, certain areas stand out as being particularly relevant to games (at least in their current forms). This chapter examines high-level abstractions—those that specify the overall shape of the game world and the nature of the player's interaction with that world. The next chapter looks specifically at abstractions that relate to the player's avatar and the avatar's direct interactions with the world.

Logic and Reality

The choice of logical abstraction can be one of the most important decisions with respect to determining the appeal of the game. The logic that underpins the game determines the reality of the game world and as such is the most basic element of the game world abstraction. You can make at least three sensible choices, each with its own implications. You also face the ever-present danger of the game displaying *capricious logic*, where the game logic is inconsistent—a state of affairs that often occurs in games by virtue of either poor design or as a result of the pressures of development.

Realism

Although "realistic" is an adjective players often use to describe a game, it is in fact quite rare for a game to attempt realism. Flight sims such as *Microsoft Flight Simulator* (subLOGIC/Microsoft, 1982 onwards) are built around realism as their raison d'etre, and indeed enjoy a thriving niche market. However, such realistic simulators are always targeting a loyal but relatively small audience of enthusiasts. They sell consistently and make back their costs, but never set the charts afire with fast sales or millions of units shipped.

You might ask how it can be considered an abstraction if the game is using a factual basis, but because not all elements of reality can be modeled, the choice of factual components constitutes a game world abstraction. For example, a flight simulator might accurately model the physics of flying a plane, but weather effects are almost certainly abstracted in a fashion to make them *seem* realistic, rather than based on real atmospheric physics. This is perfectly sensible—the amount of work involved in accurately simulating atmospheric physics would certainly not be justified. Players of flight sims are interested in the realism of controlling a plane, and the weather need only feel realistic.

Accurate physics are the basis of almost all attempts at realism, because the components of physics are founded on mathematics and are thus relatively easy to simulate, while other sciences either lack a firm mathematical basis or provide little gameplay options at this time. However, even the physics that are used are not wholly realistic. Games use Newtonian physics as the basis for their object interactions, even though this is only an approximation, because practically no game needs to deal with the complexities of special and general relativity.

The goal of realism, therefore, is to produce an experience that the player cannot easily distinguish from conventional reality. Realism seeks to deceive the player into believing that its world operates on real terms, rather than accurately simulating in the manner of a scientific model. Abstractions are still at work, but they abstract away those elements of reality that are troublesome, or that would cost too much (in terms of processor power or development time) to simulate accurately— or for which an approximation seems as real as an accurate simulation.

A game such as *Gran Turismo* (Polyphony, 1998) is an example of realism at work, with cars simulated using a level of physics realism that had not been seen before. The tagline for the game—*The Real Driving Simulator*—underlines this appeal to a sense of reality. However, even in this game the player is being hoodwinked. The physics model at work has been simplified to make driving easier, which can be easily seen by going to the options and turning the driving aids off.

Similarly, it is hard not to notice that cars in the *Gran Turismo* series always remain on the ground; no matter what you do, you cannot roll a car in one of these games, nor can you cause damage to the cars in any way. This is a result of the game's decision to use the makes and models of real production cars. Most car manufacturers are sensitive to how their vehicles are portrayed in games and do not want to have their cars seen to be smashed up, crashed, or in anything other than showroom condition. The terms of the legal licenses required for some of the makes of car to appear in the game prohibit the player from seeing them damaged or in a serious crash. In effect, the game design trades physical reality for the sense of reality engendered by using the real names and makes of cars.

By comparison, the *Burnout* series (Criterion, 2001 onwards) does not use the real names of cars, but uses general descriptions such as "super-mini," "sports coupe," or "roadster." This reduces the feeling of realism engendered by the use of real cars, but frees the developer to roll, smash, flip, and otherwise completely devastate their cars in some of the most visceral car crashes found in any game. So satisfying is this aspect of the game, that *Burnout 2: Point of Impact* (Criterion, 2002) introduced an entire mode (Crash Mode) dedicated to challenging the player to cause the largest and most expensive pileup imaginable.

It is also worth noting at this point that unless you are working on a AAA game, the game project probably cannot afford to acquire the licensing rights for many different makes of car, although you can create a game based upon a single model of vehicle, as happened with *F355 Challenge* (Sega AM2, 2000).

Another area where realism is achieved by using abstractions that seem realistic, rather than ones that are strictly real, is sports games. These generally attempt to fool the player into believing in the reality they present, but often have had to alter the nature of the world of the game for pragmatic reasons. Real physics are not used to simulate the reaction of the ball to the player's foot in a soccer game, for example, because it is assumed that the players are able to dribble with perfect accuracy, barring interference by the other players.

Realism, therefore, is still an abstraction, and the decision for a game to appear real sets up certain obligations for the game design in terms of creating an experience for which willing suspension of disbelief is particularly easy to achieve.

Neither should realism be the goal of every game. Realistic platform and FPS games, for example, are all highly unsatisfying gameplay experiences. In platform games, players have come to expect to be able to move their character in the air (and often to jump again even though they have nothing to push against), and to insist on realism would be frustrating to most players. Similarly, a realistic simulation of a World War II battle from the perspective of a single combatant would be bloody and brief.

A general expectancy is that greater realism appeals to the Casual audience, whereas the Hardcore audience is generally comfortable with more esoteric abstractions. We find some merit to this argument, but as we will see in the next section, designing to meet player expectations is often more effective than strict realism. Except for niche market products like flight simulators, games simulating real sports, or AAA products attempting a realistic spin in an already popular game style (*Gran Turismo*), realism should generally be avoided.

Using Player Expectations

Instead of an appeal to objective reality, we can build the logic and reality of a game to provide what players *expect* to encounter, not what they would encounter in reality. Ironically, suspension of disbelief can be higher in a game with this approach, because a person's reality is entirely in their own mind (and even those experiences of objective reality that they might have are mediated by their belief system).

A simple example is the sound of gunfire. People do not tend to immediately recognize the sound of real guns being fired because they are used to encountering it in a Hollywood context, and films prefer to make gunfire sound deep and resonant, rather than the hollow popping which is closer to reality.

Similarly, people expect sharks to attack everything that moves in the water. A shark is inherently interpreted as a threat in a game, whereas in reality shark attacks on people are extremely rare—the risk of death from lightning is thirty times higher than the risk of death from a shark [Burgess91]. But the expectation that sharks behave in a certain way is stronger in most people's personal reality than the facts of the matter.

The problem in an appeal to the player's personal sense of reality is that everyone's personal reality is inherently different, so we need a mechanism to generalize expectations. Fortunately, the logic of TV and film forms a canon of expectations that can be drawn upon with some confidence, as these media have replaced the fireside legend as our key sources of narrative mythology.

For example, the mythology of James Bond is fairly ubiquitous in Western culture. Villains attempt grandiose plans to achieve power or wealth (often just because they can), spies are sex symbols engaged in grand adventures, and henchmen can be cut down in swathes by the hero who emerges unscathed and with perfect hair from even the largest horde of attackers. It's a far cry from the reality of espionage, but it presents a mythology that can be drawn upon with confidence because the expectations associated with that mythology are well known.

The most commercially successful game to exploit this mythology in informing its reality is *GoldenEye 007* (Rare, 1997), which sold some eight million copies. On the lowest difficulty setting, the game provides numerous supports to give the player the feeling of being Bond, including an auto-aim so that the player need only point in roughly the correct direction and pull the trigger to shoot a foe. The game is not realistic (if you run into a room full of people firing guns in real life, you will die), but it presents the "reality of James Bond" in a fairly convincing fashion.

The media is littered with other equivalent mythologies. Animated films and TV shows provide a variety of different "realities"; from the slapstick violence of Chuck Jones cartoons to the family friendly Disney movie, we are all familiar with different approaches, and some of the most successful games have drawn from these established mythologies for their game reality.

The *Tomb Raider* series (Core, 1996 onwards) draws heavily from the treasure hunter mythology of the Indiana Jones movies (which in turn owes a debt to the 1950 MGM film *King Solomon's Mines* and other early treasure hunter movies), the *Grand Theft Auto* series has been inspired by the gangster and getaway movie paradigms, and *Halo: Combat Evolved* (Bungie, 2003) owes more than a little to the movie *Aliens*.

Because films and TV shows become part of the cultural canon, they can be drawn upon as the inspiration for the sense of reality and logic for a computer game with some confidence, provided the source is not too obscure.

Choosing a source mythology in this way gives the game a point of reference in making decisions as to how things work. For example, if one were to make a game whose mythology was inspired by space opera in the style of the old *Flash Gordon* movie shorts, it would be acceptable for foes to die in dramatic fashions yet return to face the player again with very little logical explanation, because this kind of situation is endemic to the chosen setting.

In appealing to a Casual audience (and hence shooting for a wide audience), the more common film and TV references are always a better choice, because appealing to player expectations applies only if the player is familiar with the "fake reality" one is attempting to embody. Sci-fi and fantasy should generally be avoided except when a major license is available (such as *Star Wars* or *The Lord of the Rings*) as these tend to be more esoteric. Conversely, the Hardcore is much more familiar with sci-fi and fantasy mythology, and in appealing to a predominantly Hardcore audience, you usually do better with this style than a real-world mythology.

Internally Consistent Logic

If a game is not going to draw from a well-known mythology, it should at least strive towards a consistent internal logical representation. *Pac-Man*, for example, does not resemble any sort of conventional reality, but its internal game logic is consistent and can be derived from observation. This indeed is the most important thing to remember if stepping away from the familiar metaphors and creating an entirely original game reality: the player must be able to derive the logical rules of the game world from observation, and these rules should remain consistent.

It is worth immediately noting that for a Western audience, choosing to abandon familiar mythology is immediately to turn your back on the Casual audience and to favor instead the Hardcore audience (with their desire for games to possess a unique identity). This seems to be less of an issue to some degree in Japan and other markets, where relentless innovation seems culturally more acceptable (perhaps because of a lesser cultural bias towards scientific materialism over philosophical subjectivism).

Indeed Japanese games often abandon familiar mythology in favor of an internally consistent logic peculiar to individual games. Hardcore game fans have called this kind of abstraction "Nintendo logic" [2], in reference to the design methodology behind many early Nintendo games, which frequently used a consistent internal logic with no bearing on reality. The failure of a film such as *Super Mario Bros.* is in part because the internal logic of a Mario game makes sense only in the context of a game: mushrooms make you grow in size, a hat makes an overweight plumber fly, and if it moves, you can kill it by jumping on its head. This is not the recipe for a Hollywood blockbuster.

It is important to realize that internally consistent logic is *always* desirable, whether the logic of the game draws from an attempt at realism, ancient or modern mythology, or an entirely original context. When a game shows no reliable logic, no real-world logic, and no mythological logic, or contains a blend of the three so that the player cannot learn consistently how they are expected to behave in the game world, it is behaving in a capricious manner that is sure to lead to player frustration.

Such capricious logic can occur when the player is not subject to the same advantages as the other game agents, or when the game agents are not subject to same disadvantages as the player's avatar. This highlights an interesting point about the player's needs: most players don't mind when their avatar is exempt to problems that other agents face, provided they do not lose out on advantages other agents get. The game is unfair only when the player does not get what they want. The player's expectations from the game are essentially selfish: they are the player, and they expect to be treated with a certain respect and latitude. After all, they expect an enjoyable play experience. The problem with capricious logic is that the player never fully learns the game's logical context, so their expectations are frequently disappointed, leading to player frustration.

Some small transgressions in this regard might be forgiven by the player if they are enjoying other aspects of the game world abstraction, but irritation results when players encounter frequent capricious logic (or are prevented from progressing because capricious logic conceals the means to advance in the game). This can often result because of trying to create gameplay by compromising the logic of the game world.

For example, *Black & White* (Lionhead, 2001) contains a puzzle in which some people are drowning in a part of the sea. Elsewhere in the game, the player had been able to pick up and drop people themselves, but at this point the player is forced to use their creature (a highly complex tamagotchi-like agent) to rescue the people. Because no game world reason exists for this limitation, it breaks the logic of the game world—and even if a justification were provided, it could still cause irritation in many players because bolting on justifications for a break in logical consistency is generally unsatisfying.

A similar problem occurs when a game allows an action in one case that inevitably leads the player to the question, "Why can't I do that elsewhere?" For example, *Fear Effect 2* (Kronos, 2001) has a door knob at one point in the game that can be shot off, despite the fact that every other door in the game is utterly indestructible. Not all game behavior can be completely generalized, but the player is assuming consistent world logic; if they encounter exceptions it undermines immersion, compromises enjoyment, and can potentially present an undesirable barrier to progress.

Capricious logic is never intentional: it always results from either a failure to provide a consistent logic system for the game world or from a failure to follow the prescribed logic system. In should be noted, however, that few logical abstractions are so definitive that no subjective element is involved in interpreting their application. It is in this area that game designers should perhaps be most open to constructive criticism during the development process, even if it makes their job that much harder to ensure some level of logical integrity.

This subjectivity is most apparent in dealing with ambiguous issues such as player knowledge, a problem that applies in many narrative-driven games. The player might know information about the game world that the character does not (perhaps because they have played it before). Should the player be able to take advantage of this information or not? The answer depends on the interpretation of the chosen logical abstraction and the overall goals for the game.

Teaching the Game Logic

Whenever the logic of the game world is not absolutely congruent with the most basic expectations (that objects fall when dropped, that sharp objects hurt, and that the player's avatar can swim), the game has an obligation to educate the player. The more the game draws upon puzzles for its appeal, the more vital it is to teach the player the logic of the game world.

As a general rule, Hardcore players (with their greater ability to think abstractly) are capable of dealing with more diverse logical systems than the Casual market, which should instead be delivered logic within its expectations, and the H1 and H2 subtypes of player are likely to be more willing to derive the logic of the game world on their own, while the H3 Wanderer would perhaps prefer to be told more or less outright what the scope of the world's logic contains.

In this regard, it is helpful to include challenges within the game world that teach the player the nature of the game's internal logic in gradual steps. Once the player has performed a task for which the logic of the situation is a requirement for completion, the player has learned something about the game logic which they can then apply in other situations. This can then be built upon with more elements of the game logic to build up a tool kit that the player can use to determine how they are expected to interact with the game.

For example, in *Tak and the Power of Juju* (Avalanche Software, 2003) the player is placed at an early stage upon a platform from which they have no way to progress unaided. On this platform sits an orangutan by a palm tree, which it plays with idly, pulling it down and releasing it so it snaps back up. Because the player cannot progress by any other means, they can quickly discover that standing on the palm leaf while it is pulled down by the orangutan allows them to be rocketed to a new area. This teaches part of the game logic: orangutans and palm trees can be used to send you to new areas.

The player is also taught that they can pick up and drop fruit by virtue of a simple challenge involving goats who butt the player away if they come too close. The only way to progress (in principle at least) is to lure the goat away by dropping fruit and then slipping past. This element of the game logic is then combined with the previous instance to provide a slightly more complex puzzle when the player later encounters a situation in which the orangutan and the tree do not send the player where they need to be, but another tree (sans ape) looks like it would do the trick. The player can use their knowledge that fruit can be used as a lure to entice the orangutan away from the first tree and onto the second, thus allowing the player to progress.

This kind of "bootstrapping" of game logic is essential in many games, but how it should be approached depends on the desired audience. The H1 and H2 subtypes with abstract reasoning and logic skills and a desire for agonistic challenge are willing to be placed in a situation and left to solve the problem on their own (provided, critically, the game provides sufficient cues to make it absolutely clear that they are in the right place).

For all players, and the Casual market in particular, repetition is the key. A particularly complex game situation might be remembered by the player because it stood out, but a trivial situation can easily be forgotten if it does not reoccur often enough to remain in the player's memory. In the aforementioned example of the goat in *Tak*, you can get past the goat without the use of the fruit. However, the game makes excellent use of the fruit as a game tool, and thus the player is taught what can and can't be done with fruit in a number of different situations.

It is often necessary to teach the player the internal game logic even when it might seem to the game designer to be entirely intuitive. It might seem obvious that falling a great height causes death, but many games do allow the player considerable latitude in falling. The reverse is doubly true—if the player is *expected* to fall a great distance, it is important to teach them when it is okay (and how to tell if it is okay).

Yoshi's Story (Nintendo, 1997), for example, uses the sound of rushing air to indicate when a fall will be fatal. Unfortunately, this logical abstraction is used only in a particular level, and in many places earlier in the game the player has no means of telling whether or not it is safe to drop down other than taking a leap of faith. If a game expects the player to take a leap of faith, it had better give the player abundant clues as to when this is necessary, else some players will inevitably throw themselves into oblivion as soon as they get stuck on any problem.

Some game designers believe that it is wrong to treat players like idiots, but unless the audience are H1 and H2 players with a high tolerance for repeated failure or for being left to puzzle things out alone, it is generally not a bad idea to imagine that the player needs some help figuring things out. The reason for this is that the assumptions the game designer applies in any situation are different from the assumptions each player makes, and the only pre-emptive defence against this is to consistently provide slightly more help than it is felt is needed.

The ideal solution is blind testing: getting nearly complete versions of the game to be played by a diverse sampling of players from the target audience is almost indisputably the best way to iron out problems of understanding, and developers should always plan to perform such trials at some point in development. It is also vital that the people conducting blind testing do not contaminate the data by talking to the test subjects. It is all too easy for someone emotionally invested in the game to make an offhand comment, but they will not be present when the game is exposed to a wider market, and it is precisely these knowledge gaps that blind testing is well-suited to discover.

Perspective

The perspective that a game is rendered in greatly affects the elements of the game design. This decision can influence all other aspects of the game world abstraction, and as such is usually one of the first choices to be made in a game design. Closely related are issues as to the nature of the player's avatar or the agents under the player's control, which we will discuss in the next section.

First Person

One of the most common perspectives used in games is first person. In this abstraction, the player does not see their avatar, but sees the world from their avatar's perspective. FPS games are the most famous examples of this form, and it is often included as a perspective in racing games, simply because it is easy in that particular case to add the view because the control mechanism does not need to change.

First-person games generally have only one avatar, although no technical reason exists that a game cannot be designed with multiple characters that can be switched between, something that is most commonly seen in the tactical squad-base FPS genre, for example, *Tom Clancy's Rainbow Six* series (Red Storm, 1998 onwards).

Originally, the first-person perspective offered a significant cost saving, because it meant that the player's avatar could not be seen on screen, thus saving the cost of developing animations for that character. More recently, AAA games have tended towards embodiment—the development cost of the projects is so large that the cost of animating the player character's physical extensions in the first-person view has become a lesser concern. *The Chronicles of Riddick: Escape from Butcher Bay* (Starbreeze Studios, 2004) embodies its central character to provide player identification with its star, Vin Diesel.

Today, the first-person view is usually chosen for purposes of immersion—the player's point of view is approximately the same as the avatar's, so audio can provide environment cues, and visual effects relating to equipment (for example, night vision) can be convincingly portrayed.

Unfortunately, it has several disadvantages. For example, field of vision is highly limited (falling from about 120 degrees in real life to about 60 degrees). The player does not see what they would realistically perceive because they lose both peripheral vision and the ability to turn their head easily.

Any game requiring the player to judge the spatial relationships of features within the environment (for example, a platform game) should generally avoid this perspective, as many players (especially Casual players) have difficulty judging spatial arrangements in first-person perspective. First-person platform games *tranquility* (Bill Romanowski, 1992) and *Jumping Flash* (Exact/Ultra, 1995) are notable exceptions, as in both cases jumps are exceptionally high, and either gravity is gentle enough for the player to control their descent (in the case of the former) or the view defaults to looking down at the apex of the jump (in the case of the latter).

Another minor issue is that because the viewpoint is first person, the projection must be 3D, so technically simpler platforms are generally not viable, although it is already the case that the cutting edge of mobile phones can manage simple 3D graphics, so this is perhaps a lesser problem.

The major problem with first-person perspective is dimensionality of control, which as we noted in the previous chapter is very high. Although it is possible for vision and movement to be connected, as happened in early FPS games including the default control mechanism for *GoldenEye*, the majority of FPS players have mastered the highly complex control mechanism required for independent movement and view and feel restricted if this is not provided.

This projection is no real problem for Type 1 Conqueror or Type 2 Manager players, but largely inappropriate for Type 3 Wanderers and entirely inappropriate for Type 4 Participants who require simple-to-master control mechanisms. It is ironic that an approach that lends itself to immersion is largely inappropriate for the audience for whom mimicry is most important.

Because the player has no external context to navigate by, first-person perspective also requires either an elegant map system or environments which are designed to help lead the player. The tendency for FPS games to be built on a linear path is in part recognition of the difficulties of navigating in first person. Additional abstractions can be used to help minimize this problem. For example, *Halo* had effectively linear levels in which the corridors had glowing chevrons imbedded in them that pointed in the direction the player was expected to travel, thus helping to keep the player on track.

In general, first-person perspective is a dangerous choice because it almost guarantees that the game will become an FPS or will be judged in comparison to FPS games. Although the most popular FPS games do sell millions of copies, and both *GoldenEye* and *Half-Life* (Valve, 1998) are among the highest selling games of all time, the general characteristic of the AAA games market to be prone to market failure applies especially here. To make an FPS is to compete with some of the biggest brands in the games market, and unless an FPS game has some exceptional qualities or a strong license attached, it is likely to fail to make back its costs.

Third Person

Third person is the oldest of any of the perspectives used in computer games. Using this abstraction, the player sees their avatar and controls them from a fixed or variable viewpoint. The aforementioned *Pac-Man* games all use this abstraction, as do more modern games such as *Tomb Raider* (Core, 1996). Platform games are perhaps the most well-known examples of this abstraction.

More versatile than first person, both 2D and 3D worlds can be supported, and the player is granted significantly more ability to judge their position and circumstances under this abstraction because they are viewing the action remotely. An added benefit with this abstraction is that narrative integration can be improved because exposition of the plot can be done easily within the game engine. (This is possible in first-person character, but it is generally less satisfying, and third-person cut scenes are generally used instead.)

Disadvantages are largely as a result of the extra work involved in animating and rendering the player's representative in the game world. This guarantees more art and programming work than a first-person game and either adds to the cost of the project or reduces the additional features that can be included. However, this is usually compensated for by much simpler control mechanisms, which imply the capacity to reach a much larger audience.

Initially, third-person was a technical abstraction because early games could not render in full 3D perspective until the advent of vector hardware, and a 2D game must by necessity be in third person. As hardware has improved and rendering in 3D has become ubiquitous, this has become irrelevant.

Players of the C1 and C2 types sometimes accuse third person of being "less immersive" than first person. However, it is generally the case that a wider audience can be reached with third person games because of the simpler control mechanism, and for the most part people seem to have no difficulty achieving a suspension of disbelief in third person, perhaps because TV and films are generally produced in this form and we still manage to emotionally identify with the characters, even though we rarely see literally through their eyes.

Both coordination within the environment and navigation around the world are greatly improved in third person, but you have issues in the way that the camera operates that need to be considered. In a first-person game, the camera viewpoint and the avatar viewpoint are identical, so the player has no need to control the camera. In third person, the avatar and camera are separate entities, with serious consequences.

If the game is to be set in large open spaces, the situation is usually manageable. The camera can follow the avatar, and if the avatar moves into the plane of the camera, the camera can gradually rotate to fall in behind, a technique that has become practically ubiquitous. However, if the avatar is close to a vertical plane, the view can be obscured, or the camera can occasionally see behind the landscape. These problems are soluble, but it inevitably implies that some of the project is spent fixing problems with either the camera functionality or the landscape.

If the game is to be set indoors, the situation is even more troublesome. Because the setting is surrounded by vertical planes, the problems with cameras are amplified. A common solution is to provide a fixed camera perspective indoors, such as is seen in survival horror games such as the *Resident Evil* series (Capcom, 1996 onwards). Here, a new problem manifests—when the player transitions from one fixed camera perspective to another, a jarring switch of perspective can confuse the player's sensibilities. As some players have noted of these games, "The camera is your enemy." This makes the fixed camera solution risky if the game is intended to reach the mass market, which is generally less patient with such problems.

It is also the reason that many of these games use a relative control mechanism (one in which the direction you must push depends upon the alignment of the avatar, not the position of the avatar in the world), which again tends to limit the effectiveness of such games to reach a mass market, for whom absolute control is generally preferable. Certainly if one expects to reach the Casual audience, it is better to default to absolute control and to provide relative control as an option.

The solution used in *Fatal Frame* (Techmo, 2001) is to keep the relative direction of the avatar constant when the camera shifts and adjust the relative meaning of the control only when the player releases the stick. The result is that control is absolute—but changes when the player releases the stick after a camera shift. Once the player learns to trust the game, this presents no problem, but many players naturally change what they do with the control stick when the camera shifts, thus amplifying the problem and making the game frustrating to play.

Perhaps the best solution for the problem of using third-person perspective indoors is seen in *Eternal Darkness: Sanity's Requiem* (Silicon Knights, 2002), which solved the problem by specially designing every environment so that a fixed camera angle would never cause a sudden transition. The view might bend gently around a corner or change when the avatar climbs up or down or passes through doors, but it never shifts suddenly. This makes for a very Casual friendly control mechanism, which is reliably absolute, but you can only guess at the level design skills that went into eliminating any camera problems. (An additional minor cost also exists in that some of the area under the camera is generally invisible to the player unless a first-person view is also included.)

The bottom line is that any game designer wanting to use a single avatar in a third-person perspective has to address some issues with the use of camera, and in part the solution depends upon the types of environment the game is to present. Choosing either an entirely exterior environment (or one that is mostly exterior and is cavernous when the avatar is in an interior space) with a dynamic camera or a largely interior environment with some kind of fixed camera solution seems to be an inevitable split.

One final point in respect of cameras in third person relates to their direct control by the player. The game literate Hardcore all but demands that they can control the camera to some degree—at the very least being able to rotate their view and probably to tilt the view as well. Some game designers have seen this as equating to first-person controls and have therefore neglected to provide any default camera control, as in *Freedom Fighters* (IO Interactive, 2003). Having no default camera control immediately alienates a large proportion of the Casual audience for whom dimensionality of control is a factor, and this should always be avoided except in a low budget game targeting only the Hardcore.

As a related point, console games in third person should always provide a control that centers the camera in the direction that the character faces; this is not only expected by the Hardcore, but also aids the Casual player in not getting confused when the camera behaves unexpectedly, by giving them a panic button to center their view. The usual warning about not overloading controls does not apply to combining a control to center the view with a control to enter a first-person "view" mode as the camera can be made to center first and then zoom to first person, as in *Ratchet & Clank* (Insomniac Games, 2002) and other games.

Other Third-Person Views

A variety of third-person views also apply to games, including the distant observer view common in RTS and sim games, top down and side on views, and isometric projections.

The *distant observer* or *god view*, in which the player sees the action from far above the play field and can hence see a great deal of what is taking place, is ideally suited to games in which the player controls multiple agents. Camera controls are generally simplified, if only because this view tends to be used with exterior landscapes, and the capacity to rotate (either in discrete 90 degree turns, or freely) and zoom are usually provided simply so the player can have more control over what they see. These views are always better suited to PC rather than consoles, because the mouse is practically essential for easy control in this view.

The distant observer view can be used in an interior location, however, as in *Ghost Master* (Sick Puppies, 2003), which is mostly set in haunted houses and other buildings. The player controls which floor they are looking at by using the Page Up an Page Down keys to "add" or "remove" floors of the house. In other words, the play area is effectively a series of stacked flat areas that the player can cycle between.

Fixed perspective views such as isometric are largely equivalent to the distant observer view, but can be used without resorting to a full 3D engine and are therefore still very much alive near the bottom of the games market where development costs are a major issue and anything that can be done to keep costs down is useful.

Top down and side on views are found pretty much only at the bottom of the market (on handheld platforms and phones, for example), or in quirky games such as *Vib Ribbon* (NaNaOn-Sha, 1999), which was graphically simple because the game software had to be able to run in the PlayStation's memory without any disk access, so the user could put whatever music CD they wanted into the PlayStation as the source for the game's audio and environments. This is perhaps unfortunate, because dimensionality of control in strict 2D controls is very low, and hence they can be controlled by a wide audience. However, as games consistently deliver beautifully rendered 3D locations, players seem less satisfied with the graphical restrictions of a 2D world.

Second Person

The term *second person* is rarely used in games circles, but some games use the equivalent of this perspective. Those sim games that represent the game world primarily in text can be considered to be using second person, for example, the *Championship Manager* series (Sports Interactive et al, 1992 onwards). The player is literally given the role of being a soccer team manager—the fact that the team in question is virtual does not change the fact that the player themselves fulfills the protagonist role without the presence of an avatar or a "god-like" viewpoint (as in the distant observer view). Fantasy stock market games are another example of the form, because the only difference between such a game and playing on the stock market is the fact that the money used is virtual.

Second person can also apply in a narrative form, as is the case with text adventure games , which literally cast the player into the story. With the decline of the text adventure as a commercial form, second-person narrative games have largely vanished, although *Majestic* (Electronic Arts, 2001) could be considered an ambitious (if commercially unsuccessful) attempt to explore this form, and interactive fiction keeps the text adventure alive as an art form, if not as a commercial market.

Commercially, the value of second-person games is quite limited (with the possible exception of sports manager games), but near the bottom of the market second-person games can eke out a profit because they are very cheap to develop, requiring very little art resources, and a modest amount of programming. *Uplink: Hacker Elite* (Introversion, 2001) is an example of the few games that manage to make second person work for them.

Avatars and Agents

In discussing the perspective used in a game, we have largely considered only those games in which the player controls a single character, but in a variety of games the player has multiple agents under their control, instead of a single avatar.

Computer role-playing games such as the *Final Fantasy* series (Square, 1987 onwards) give the player control of a team of characters (commonly referred to as a party, in reference to the terminology of tabletop role-playing games). Sometimes the player is given an avatar and additional agents are added to the party; sometimes the team of agents collectively form the player's avatar; the distinctions between these two forms are largely minimal. However they are organized, movement is still usually delegated to a single agent who acts as an avatar for the player when exploring.

Conversely, strategy and RTS games rarely give the player a direct avatar, but tend instead to give the player a pool of agents to command. These games tend to work best on PC, simply because a mouse is excellently suited to selecting groups of agents and therefore coordinating the actions of a large number of agents in parallel. The same is true of sim games, in which the player has no avatar but rather access to either a set of agents or a set of options with which to influence the development of the world, as in the *Sim City* series (Maxis, 1989 onwards).

Pikmin (Nintendo, 2001) is an unusual example that resembles an RTS in many ways, but gives the player a protagonist to lead the many hundreds of eponymous agents at the player's disposal. This approach allowed the game to function using a console controller instead of a mouse, although it was only a marginal commercial success.

Another unusual case is the aforementioned *Ghost Master*, which featured agents that while ostensibly under the player's control were capable of autonomous action. The game received some criticism from Type 1 Conqueror players because they were not given the capacity to completely control ("micromanage") the activities of the game agents, whereas it was well received by Type 3 Wanderer players who treated the ghosts in the game as toys that could be thrown into the world and experimented with.

All these games are based upon a third person, distant observer–type view, but you can use multiple avatars or agents in a first-person view, as in *Hired Guns* (DMA, 1993), which used four simultaneous first-person views, allowing the player to control four different characters at the same time. This approach is, however, very rarely used primarily because of the growing popularity of real-time play that complicates the form considerably except when multiple players are added.

The decision to use agents or a lone avatar (or some hybrid thereof) determines a fundamental split in the nature of the game, and as such is likely to be inherent in the very concept of the game. It is also likely to imply a choice of platform, because as already mentioned, games with large numbers of agents are generally tenable only on PC where a mouse is available.

It is worth noting that none of the highest selling games of all time give the player control of multiple agents. *The Sims* (Maxis, 2000) seems to be an exception, but even this gives the player control of only one agent at a time. The inescapable implication is that when targeting the Casual market, a single avatar is always preferable—and indeed because multi-agent games tend to have higher dimensionality of control, there are good reasons to expect this.

Nonetheless, games with multiple agents are still a profitable enterprise at all levels of the market, although it is hard to take market share away from the big brands in the AAA market such as the *Warcraft* series (Blizzard, 1994 onwards). Where they appear to thrive is in the mid to low market, targeting a primarily Hardcore audience (which might at times stretch to include the C1 Conquerors, although only if word of mouth among the Hardcore players and magazine reviewers elevates a game above its usual market reach).

Dividing the World

The world that is presented to the player is inevitably divided in some fashion. In part, this is due to technical considerations and budgetary limitations, but also you have good reasons for dividing the game area in terms of meeting player needs. C3 and C4 players, for example, do not seem to possess strong navigational skills and can become easily lost in a world that does not divide itself, and even though C1 players seem to enjoy finding their way, they seem to do better when faced with a slightly convoluted linear path, as is presented in most FPS games.

Levels

For many years, games were organized into discrete *levels*, and this approach still sees considerable use simply because it is technically simple to divide the game world in this way. The player is presented with a small area, and when they are finished there, they can be taken to another area. Certainly near the bottom of the market, few games are able to afford to do anything else.

Sometimes separate levels are disguised as being part of a larger world by joining them together to make a continuous level. This is functionally equivalent to a discrete level scheme, except that the player's attention is not drawn to the change of levels; they seem instead to be a moving around in a *continuous environment* (albeit a highly constrained continuous environment). Indeed, in a continuous level game the player can often go back to recent earlier levels, which is rarely the case in discrete level games. FPS games have used this structure often, offering more immersion than discrete levels, for example, in *Half-Life*.

Although the decision to use a discrete level abstraction is generally motivated by technical issues, it can be made into an asset. This is clearly demonstrated by *GoldenEye*, which is biased towards discrete level structure by virtue of limitations presented by the game license and the cartridge-based console format. However, this allowed the design of the game to make use of the discrete levels to provide gameplay elements tailored to this approach. For example, knowing that each level is hermetic allowed for each level to be designed with multiple objectives corresponding to different difficulty levels, enhancing and expanding the gameplay (as well as imbedding the long-term learning curve).

The success of *GoldenEye* demonstrates an important point: that the most complex abstraction is not inherently superior to the simplest forms. A continuous world (which we will discuss shortly) is not intrinsically superior to discrete levels, despite its higher level of complexity and immersive qualities, because discrete levels can be tweaked more easily than a larger game space and can be more easily navigated, which can be a considerable benefit. The key is in selecting a set of abstractions that support each other to create a coherent game world suitable to the needs of the target audience.

Domains and Worlds

When the game world is divided into a series of hermetic mini-worlds, we can consider a *domain* abstraction to be in use. 3D platform games make considerable use of this abstraction, as typified by the archetypal *Mario 64* (Nintendo, 1996), which sold a staggering 11 million units and is hence unsurprisingly widely copied both in form and structure.

In some respects, the distinction between levels and domains is somewhat arbitrary, but one of the key distinctions is that the domains are usually connected into a larger structure. They are almost always connected via a central hub (such as the castle in *Mario 64*) from which each domain can be reached.

The chief benefit is in the way the game feels to the player. The domain abstraction allows for a number of thematic mini-worlds (for example, ice world, desert world, underwater world) that can be made to seem to be real places in subtle ways. When this approach is used, it is always the case that each domain supports multiple challenges. In the case of *Mario 64* this was achieved by letting the player pick a challenge upon entry, although any of the challenges present was allowed in principle. Other games tend to scatter the challenges around internally, often using characters to trigger them as in *Jak & Daxter: The Precursor Legacy* (Naughty Dog, 2001).

By allowing the player to perform multiple challenges in the same place, the player is allowed to build more of an emotional attachment to the place. In a level-based game, the player is usually required to solve some challenge and then moves on, never to return. But in a domain game, the area of the domain feels more like a real location because many different things are going on within it.

This obviously offers little in terms of agon, but is highly beneficial for mimicry, and it is unsurprising that 3D platform games are a popular genre among Type 3 Wanderer players.

When domains are allowed to seamlessly overlap, as in *Jak & Daxter* or *The Legend of Zelda* series (Nintendo, 1986 onwards), the result is a *contiguous world*.

The relationship between domain and world in these cases is equivalent to the relationship between discrete and continuous level, with the same underlying factor: greater immersion.

Of particular note is the use of contiguous worlds in *Grand Theft Auto III* (Rockstar North, 2002) and its sequels, which have been some of the highest selling games of all time. *GTA: Vice City* sold some twelve million units, and it is predicted that *GTA: San Andreas* could sell as many as fifteen million units—sales figures that have not been seen since Nintendo possessed a near monopoly on games consoles back in the days of the NES.

These games are noteworthy examples of balancing the play needs of different audience demographics. Difficult-to-complete missions, largely constructed in a linear chain, provide agonistic play and considerable fiero for the Type 1 Conqueror players, while the cleverly abstracted game world provides a practically unparalleled setting for mimicry and toyplay. Indeed, many players who purchased the game have said in surveys and interviews that they do not bother completing the missions at all, and simply take advantage of the world provided to play within.

This is almost certainly indicative of a trend at the top end of the market, and we are likely to see many more AAA games that deliver this combination of agonistic challenges wed to mimicry and toyplay in an immersive world.

It is worth also considering the comparison between the *Grand Theft Auto* games and the less successful *The Getaway* (SCEE Studio Soho, 2002). Both feature a large city and the low dimensionality of control inherent to driving, yet *The Getaway*, despite ample marketing support from Sony, has failed to make such an impact in the market. *The Getaway* even uses a more realistic game world abstraction—directions are given by flashing indicators on the cars, and healing is effected (somewhat bizarrely) by leaning against walls.

The trouble with *The Getaway* is that it is organized in a fashion that can support only agonistic play. The player must undertake its challenges. They have a large world to drive around, but have nothing to do here—no toyplay, no real opportunities for rewarding mimicry. By comparison, the cities of the *Grand Theft Auto* games are packed full of toys and easy entertainments to keep the player amused.

Also, the choice for realism in *The Getaway* loses out to *Grand Theft Auto* because the apparent benefits of greater immersion are lost if the player becomes frustrated. It might be unrealistic to represent a gun in the world as a rotating circular icon (as it is in *GTA*), but it is readily understandable, easy to spot, and perfectly adequate for the needs of the game world.

If one is to develop a AAA game with a contiguous world, the real benefit does not come from the contiguity of the world, but the capacity for that world to support easily accessed toyplay and mimicry, thus appealing to a wider audience.

Maps

It is quite common at all tiers of the market to join a set of domains or levels by a central map or map area. Often, this is a budget-conserving measure (because it is wildly expensive to develop continuous worlds), but the map also has benefits to the players, in particular the ease of navigating around the world. The map in question might be fully interactive as in the *Final Fantasy* series, a highly abstracted environment as in *Super Mario World* (Nintendo, 1991), or might be a static screen as in many point-and-click adventures.

A map abstraction can provide additional gameplay at the map level. For example, *Discworld Noir* (Perfect Entertainment, 1999) featured a map that was fully interactive with the clues and inventory items, allowing players to gain hints and complete some game goals either from the map or in the main game areas.

However, as a general case, the map is simply a means of focusing development time on the core elements of the game.

Time

The approach to the passage of time, and the persistency of environmental status, is dominated by issues of budget and technical limitations. PC games (or games for the Xbox) have access to a hard drive, and therefore can record more data about the state of the game world, while consoles have inherent limitations that inevitably lead to worlds with a kind of environmental amnesia.

Resetting versus Dynamic Environments

The most familiar temporal abstraction in games is probably the *resetting* abstraction. Under this system, when the player exits and re-enters a location, it returns to a "ground state." The player can cause any number of legitimate environment changes while in the location, but upon exit, these changes are lost. This abstraction has particular value in simplifying puzzle design, because it ensures the player cannot get the game into a state from which they cannot complete their goals, but it is anti-immersive because in reality a cup of tea does not change back to water, tea leaves, and milk when we leave the room. Nintendo has always tended to prefer this approach, most notably in the dungeons in *The Legend of Zelda* series of games.

We also see resetting at work in games such as *Grand Theft Auto*, where the player has the capacity to damage the environment. Lamp posts can be knocked down, fire hydrants toppled, and all manner of vandalism can be enacted upon the world, but when the player's attention is moved elsewhere in the world, the damage is undone, and the world returns to its default state. In general, this is not an issue—who cares whether or not a lamp post is restored? It might be slightly more immersive to be able to see the results of one's rampages persist, but it is not a huge benefit to any player.

At the other end of the scale, a game like *Otogi: Myth of Demons* (FromSoftware, 2003) that records all the damage in the environment might lend itself to one inevitable outcome: levelling everything that can be destroyed so that what was initially a rich environment becomes a barren wasteland. Such an approach is okay in a game that is primarily concerned with agonistic fighting, but would not suit a game like *Grand Theft Auto,* which balances agon with mimicry.

Although dynamic environments in which changes are recorded permanently might seem appealing, unless the game benefits in some tangible manner, it is questionable whether it is worth doing, and all manner of play is disrupted by the capacity to destroy the environment. For example, all the usual means by which a player's movements can be corralled is lost in a game where the player can knock down any wall. This does not make such a situation worthless, but it requires some sound thinking to be implemented in a fashion that benefits the game.

It is also worth considering games where some of the environmental features can be destroyed or altered but not others. Here the lessons learned in considering game logic apply: the player must be taught what they can and cannot do, and the game must be consistent in its use of logic. For example, *The Legend of Zelda: The Ocarina of Time* (Nintendo, 1998) allows the player to use bombs to destroy some walls, but these walls are always clearly flagged with cracks or faults.

Persistent Worlds

The term *persistent world* has been applied to a number of MMORGPs. In essence, the persistent abstraction allows that the state of the world is permanent: temporal causality is not interrupted by abstractions of convenience (such as resetting). Objects remaining where they are left is sometimes the sole extent of the abstraction, but it has the potential to mean considerably more.

The first persistent worlds were the multi-user domains or MUDs of the late 1980s and 1990s. Text-based, these game worlds have inherent persistence because they are built on a database model; the underlying world is stored in the form of a database. Modern MMORPGs use a similar system for storing data, but the graphical environments necessitate a less expressive environment. They are generally focused on PC because of the technical limitations of consoles, but this is gradually changing.

The value for immersion in these games is apparent, but in general the appeal of the games rests in the social dynamic produced by collecting so many players in the same game space and has nothing to do with the persistence of the game world. However, the capacity for players to build their own embellishments in a persistent world is an effective way of heightening the player's emotional investment in the game, such as the houses players could build in *Ultima Online* (Origin Systems, 1997) and other massively multiplayer games.

The same benefits of persistence can be seen in single player games such as *Animal Crossing* (Nintendo, 2001), which allows the player to affect the comparatively small game world in a number of different ways, including planting flowers and trees, making signs, burying treasure, and most significantly through selecting and arranging furniture in their house. This is clearly a game of mimicry more than anything else, although the game also features a number of different money-making activities that are open to optimization, and hence the appeal of the game includes Type 1 Conqueror players, as well as Type 3 Wanderer and Type 4 Participant players.

Rewinding Time

Some games allow the player to "rewind time," either as a gimmick for solving game puzzles, as in *Blinx: The Time Sweeper* (Artoon, 2002), or to help the player, as in *Prince of Persia: The Sands of Time* (Ubisoft Montreal Studios, 2003). Although widely enjoyed by Hardcore players, the value of this latter feature to the wider market is questionable. In order for a short rewind of time to be of value, the cost of failure must be significant, which means such a feature can appear only in agonistic games with a considerable degree (or potential for) fail-repeat gameplay. This might work with a Type 1 (and possibly Type 2) audience, but it is unlikely to work on a wider scale. Still, *Prince of Persia: The Sands of Time* did not make a loss and was very popular with the Hardcore community, and hence the feature at least served to enhance the unique identity of the game.

Where rewinding time is most useful in terms of audience games is at the complete other end of the spectrum. In computer versions of solitaire card games, the capacity to undo moves makes the game a much easier proposition and hence lessens player frustration.

Abstractions for Passage of Time

Most games do not need to reflect the passage of time, but the more immersive a game is intended to be, the more valuable it is to represent changes as a result of time. Naturally, mimicry is supported by the inclusion of such features, but they must be considered carefully because they can accrue considerable developmental costs.

Changing between day and night is comparatively simple to implement and features in many games with continuous worlds, most notably *The Legend of Zelda: The Ocarina of Time* and the *Grand Theft Auto* series (which also uses weather to further enhance the sense of immersion). In such games, the most common abstraction is probably that 1 second of real time equates to 1 minute of game time, which produces a day which passes in 24 minutes. This approach suits any game that wants to support mimicry, but should in general not be coupled to gameplay.

It is almost always dangerous to require the player to be at specific places at specific times in the game world. *Shenmue* (which used a rate of just slower than 1 second per minute) just about succeeded in making this work, but it was recognized that the player needed to be given the capacity to control the flow of time, and this was added in the sequel.

Perhaps the most interesting case of an abstraction for passage of time is with *The Legend of Zelda: Majora's Mask* (Nintendo, 2000) in which the game is set over the same 3 days, which repeat indefinitely. This allows for some convoluted and fascinating set pieces as the player gradually acquires the means to change the key events that are unfolding, not unlike the movie *Groundhog Day*. The player is given several tools to control the passage of time, including the capacity to return to the start of the 3 days, to advance 12 or 24 hours, and also to advance time by shorter amounts by talking to certain characters. As rich as this game world is, it can be suited only to the Hardcore audience, because the abstract complexity is wholly inappropriate for a mass market audience.

On the wider scale, some games reflect the passage of time between days, such as with *Pokemon Silver/Gold* (Nintendo, 1999), which has different events on different days of the week. This is perhaps suitable for hiding features deep in the game space for H1 players (with their desire for knowledge) to uncover, but it would probably be wholly inappropriate for a game to restrict access to something critical for progress in this way without providing tools to advance time.

At an even wider scale, you have the changing of the seasons in *Harvest Moon* (Natsume, 1997) or *Animal Crossing*. In the latter, the passage of time is the same as in the real world, and the changes are solely for mimicry and to promote a sense of progress within the game space as different activities are available at key calendar dates. This sort of passage of time abstraction implies some considerable developmental costs because the graphics have to be changed to reflect the player's expectations, for example, that there will be snow in winter, but in both cases the changes are essential to the nature of the game. It can also be done solely for mimicry as with *Fable* (Lionhead, 2004) but this is likely to occur only for AAA products that have the budget to invest in such extraneous features.

As a general rule, abstractions for passage of time are used for mimicry and immersion only, but this does not mean they are not valuable. Because both Type 3 Wanderer and Type 4 Participant players appear more interested in this aspect of the game than in the direct challenges of the agonistic elements of game design, we can only assume that including features that on the surface seem decorative help enhance the appeal of the game. Of course, if the game is primarily targeting Type 1 Conqueror or Type 2 Manager players, the development resources implied might be better spent elsewhere.

CONCLUSION

This chapter has looked at some key abstractions that can be used to define the game world; in the next chapter we will look at abstractions that relate more directly to the player's avatar (or agents) and how they interact with the world.

The aspects of game world abstraction discussed in this chapter demonstrate the basic principles of game world abstraction and show how decisions in one area have significant impact elsewhere. Designers aim towards choosing sets of figurative representations that come together coherently to produce a well-rounded and self-consistent game world abstraction. This consistency is important, as every game requires a coherent set of abstractions. Otherwise, it falls into capricious logic and alienates its players.

ENDNOTES

[1] *Shenmue* is recorded as the most expensive game ever made [Guinness05].

[2] This term seems to have grown up out of the Internet community, and as such it is hard to attribute the term "Nintendo logic" to any one source. Nonetheless, a search for "Nintendo logic" in any search engine provides a substantial number of hits, suggesting the term has caught on.

9 Avatar Abstractions

In This Chapter

- Relationships between World, Avatar, and Player
- Abstractions of Avatar
- Conclusion
- Endnotes

The distinction between abstractions that relate to the avatar and those relating to the game world is one of convenience. Every aspect of the game world, avatar included, forms a part of the game world abstraction, and if a distinction exists, it is only that the player is allowed to form a much deeper emotional connection with the avatar (or player-controlled agents) than with any other aspect of the game world. The avatar is generally the player's only means of participating in the virtual world that is presented, and, as such, players routinely incarnate themselves mentally into their avatar's role.

This chapter continues the theme of game world abstraction by focusing on the role of the avatar in the game world, and thus how the player becomes connected to the game world. However, before discussing specific avatar abstractions, it is worth considering the relationship between the world and the avatar, as well as the relationship between the avatar and the player.

RELATIONSHIPS BETWEEN WORLD, AVATAR, AND PLAYER

It is important to understand the extent to which the avatar exists in a state of duality with the world. In a single player game, each part of the world is like Schrödinger's cat—it exists and does not exist until the player actually goes there and it is presented to the player. The avatar is therefore like a marker that says, "The player is paying attention here; everything else is hidden from them." In a very real sense, if a virtual tree falls in a virtual forest and no avatar is around to listen, the tree definitely *does not* make a sound.

Even in massively multiplayer games, the game exists as nothing but data except when something is there to act as an observer. The avatar makes the world by their very presence, and in the absence of an avatar to act as an observer, nothing but raw data exists. As far as the players are aware, however, the world is always there and continues to act and take action behind their backs. Anything that undermines this sense of existence is likely to undermine suspension of disbelief and therefore undercut player immersion.

Abstracting Behind the Scenes Action

Processing power is always a precious commodity in game development. Even though hardware continues to become more and more powerful, graphics, physics simulation, and artificial intelligence continue to rise in complexity in step with the increases in power. The result is that game designers must always be on the lookout for ways to conserve hardware resources by avoiding resolving a situation in the most complete fashion, which is by running a complete simulation. It is necessary to completely simulate a situation only when the player is present (as they need to witness what goes on around their avatar). Elsewhere in the world, the designer has a free hand.

This aspect can be seen very clearly in the *Dynasty Warriors* series (Omega Force, 2000 onwards), each installment of which simulates huge battles from Chinese history, with the player in control of one of the key officers in each battle. Where the player is present, the battles unfold according to the player's direct action—enemy soldiers are killed and are removed from battle, and the player receives damage from the soldiers as they manage to injure the player's avatar. However, the battle continues where the player is not present, and critically it does not proceed according to the same mechanics.

Although not readily apparent to most players, the mechanics used to simulate the battle "off camera" are completely different from the mechanics used to simulate the battle where the player is present. At the player's position, soldiers attack each other, defend and damage each other using exactly the same mechanics as the player's avatar, but the frequency with which they attack is determined by the

Morale statistic for the unit to which they belong. (This Morale stat is affected by the number of losses their unit has won, any victories that unit has won, and the overall state of the battle.) Wherever the player's avatar is present, units retreat from the battlefield only when their commanding officer is killed.

Behind the scenes, Morale is the chief determining factor used to simulate the outcome of a battle. In general, if two units with identical Morale meet each other in battle at a certain point in the world, this battle proceeds indefinitely until one of the two units suffers a loss of morale, thus tipping the balance in the contrary direction. Similarly, a unit with a high Morale score coming up against a unit with a low Morale score is always victorious—and the time it takes for that unit to achieve victory is proportional to other factors, such as the number of units present. Another critical difference is that the unit's leader cannot be killed independent of the unit itself while it is off camera; both the officer in charge and the unit are removed from the play field at the same time in the abstracted layer of the battle simulation.

At first glance, this seems like an oversimplification, but in the context of the game it works perfectly. Each battle has been balanced according to the nature of that battle—so mighty struggles are usually balanced almost perfectly so that the player's actions are the deciding factor in which side is victorious, whereas in historical "David and Goliath" battles such as the Battle of Red Cliff [1] when the player fights on the weaker side, they must work hard to overcome the numerical and morale advantage of the superior force. Crucially, the abstracted battle system adds to the player's experience: when an allied general calls for assistance, it often requires the player to review the strategic situation and consider if they are needed elsewhere in the battlefield.

Of course, this strategic layer to the game also limits the audience to which the game can appeal, because arcade competence in battle must be partnered with strategic thinking, and it is likely that the audience for the *Dynasty Warriors* games is primarily H1 and H2. Although in Japan where the Three Kingdoms historical setting is as famous as the stories of King Arthur in the West, the game has "implied IP," which allows its appeal to stretch much further, and the games are top sellers in the Japanese market.

In addition to abstractions at the scale of the whole battle, the *Dynasty Warriors* games also feature abstractions at the interface between the wide-scale battle abstraction and the game world abstractions that mediate the avatar's conflict with foes in face-to-face battle. In *Dynasty Warriors 2*, if the player dismounts a horse and then travels such a distance that the horse is no longer on the local map, the horse vanishes because this game (unlike its sequels) does not record the positions of horses except when they are in the player's immediate area. Similarly, when the number of soldiers present on screen outstrips the hardware's capacity to render all foes, the further away foes are not drawn on screen (and pop up when they come close). If these off-screen foes are archers, the game has an abstraction that allows them to still damage the player even though they are not physically being drawn. This can be a cause of great consternation in players who find they are being shot at by foes that they cannot actually see.

Similarly, the player's bodyguards attempt to follow the player around, but if the player jumps off a wall or otherwise distances themselves from their bodyguards, the guards are replaced at the edge of the player's local map a short time later to allow them to rejoin the player without the game having to calculate an actual path for them to follow in order to join up. A similar issue applies in *Tomb Raider* (Core, 1996) in which the creatures that the player is expected to fight are able to pass through walls when they are outside of the area being shown to the player because the game only simulates their position; terrain exists only in the game world where the player is present, because no wider scale abstraction deals with terrain that is behind the scenes.

These kinds of behind the scenes abstractions are of vital importance to sports games, which frequently must simulate the result of a sporting contest in a short period of time. In games that allow a season of a sport to be simulated, such as *All-Star Baseball* (Acclaim Studios Austin, 1999–2003), the game must provide a score result for games that it simply cannot emulate in full. The situation is even more acute in manager games: the *Championship Manager* series (Sports Interactive et al, 1992 onwards) requires much more data, and therefore the games require the player to wait briefly while the detailed simulation of play is completed for each game occurring behind the scenes.

In general, the more a game tends towards strategic play (and therefore an H1 and H2 audience), the greater a volume of mechanics are likely to be needed to abstract significant proportions of the game world off camera. This said, any game for any audience is likely to feature situations in which the game designer needs to produce a result behind the player's back, which is intended to seem seamlessly integrated with the player's experience of direct play (that is, avatar-world interaction) within the world. In this, the designer's skills in creating simple, robust mechanics are tested; the audience's needs are of lesser importance in these situations, so the designer should concentrate on developing mechanics that simulate the necessary factors in the simplest or most efficient manner possible.

Playing in Character versus Character Expression

The relationship between the avatar and the player is more subtle than it might first appear. In the Japanese market, it is most common for the avatar to be created as a persona in their own right—with a personality, history and identity over which the player has no influence. This creates the situation of *playing in character*, that is, the player has the choice to take upon the identity of this character as a role and to play the game as if they were this particular character, rather than playing as if their personality had somehow been implanted in their avatar's mind. This can be seen with absolute clarity in *Shenmue* (Sega AM2, 2000), which is the story of Ryo, and little or nothing the player does in the game world changes the unfolding of this story. Until the player settles into their role of guiding Ryo (rather than dictating his actions or personality), the game can seem very inflexible. Once the player gives themselves up to being Ryo, the game becomes a refreshing experience—play in the sense of theatre as much as play in the sense of a game.

Conversely, in the Western market it is more common to give the player the capacity to adapt the avatar to their needs. Nowhere is this dichotomy clearer than when looking at computer RPGs. Japanese RPGs such as the *Final Fantasy* series (Square, 1987 onwards) assign a character to the player, whom they are then expected to play, whereas Western RPGs such as *Fallout* (Interplay, 1997) allow the player to create the character themselves, providing a name and a unique identity. This is the essence of *character expression*—letting the player express their own needs and personality through the capacity to define or alter the appearance or nature of the central character.

Even when the player is presented an existing character in a Western game, such as in the *Grand Theft Auto* series (DMA Designs/Rockstar North, 1997 onwards), character expression still takes precedence over playing in character, which is to say that the player is never prevented from doing something because it would not make sense for that character to do so. Changes in clothes and choices in cars and accommodation are all provided to allow the player a degree of expression.

Both playing in character and character expression are largely connected with mimicry. The former is mimicry of a given character, and the latter is player-mediated mimicry, but the outcome is the same. As such, these choices are related to Type 3 Wanderer and Type 4 Participant play, but of course, even those players who prefer Type 1 Conqueror and Type 2 Manager styles of play still get some enjoyment from mimicry, just as a Type 3 or 4 player can still enjoy fiero when they overcome a particular hard challenge.

It does seem that the choice between these two styles of player relationship with avatar might be principally a cultural issue. It is possible that in the West, where the culture of unique personal identity is dominant, having the freedom to do what we want to do is taken as a universal. Conversely, Japanese culture places more emphasis on adapting to the needs of society, as failing to meet social expectations is a cause of great shame [Yoshimura97]. We can hypothesize, therefore, that cultural issues are behind this apparent split in approach to the relationship between avatar and player.

However, even in the West, the notion of playing in character can be significant. Table-top role-playing games might primarily be used by players to act out fantasies of power and control, but in a small proportion of groups of players these games become a narrative art form, in which taking on the roles of the character (playing in character) vastly outstrips the importance of doing what feels fun to the player (character expression) [Schick91]. The appeal of these games appears to correlate with the Intuition preference, and therefore with the Hardcore segment of the market (according to DGD1), so we can assume that games that primarily target the Hardcore have more of a luxury to choose playing in character as the nature of the avatar relationship to the player.

In general, however, when targeting a Western audience, character expression is to be preferred. It must be recognized that the implications of character expression are often quite expensive or even technically insurmountable. In games for which all dialogue is recorded, for example, it is not generally possible for the player to pick the name of their avatar, because speech synthesis is not yet advanced enough to allow in-game dialogue to be produced dynamically. Therefore, a certain degree of playing in character is inevitable if only as a cost-saving mechanism.

ABSTRACTIONS OF AVATAR

The game world abstractions that relate to the avatar, and the avatar's interactions with the world, define the nuts-and-bolts interactions between the player and the world. However, this separation of abstractions into abstractions of world and of avatar in this book is merely a convenience and should not be construed as anything other than a largely arbitrary split.

Mortality

The robustness of the player's avatar, or the player's agents in the game world, has a critical effect on the nature of the game. Because violent action is so prevalent, mortality issues figure quite prominently in a considerable number of games, and most of the related issues are concerned with agonistic and therefore with Type 1 Conqueror or Type 2 Manager play. However, the converse is inevitably true: if you want to support Type 3 Wanderer and Type 4 Participant play, it is necessary that avatar mortality does not become a barrier to mimicry.

Early arcade games generally required some sense of mortality in the form of a failure condition that marks the end of a game, because at some point the player was expected to put in a fresh coin and start a new game. This changed with the arrival of games such as *Gauntlet* (Midway, 1985), which created a whole new business model for the arcade. Instead of players spending a coin to play the game until they failed (or reached the end, if there was one), arcade games from this point switched to a *pump and play* system whereby the player could add more coins to continue playing. Although revenues initially rose, the Hardcore players were able to complete games more easily and therefore played for less time—resulting in a crisis for the arcades as their user base increasingly defected to home consoles for their gaming needs (though this defection wasn't helped by console technology slowly but tangibly catching up with arcade hardware).

Lives

The oldest mortality abstraction is in terms of discrete lives: when the player dies, they lose a life. This abstraction made sense in early arcade games (before "pump and play," at least) because the designer had to limit play time by some mechanism. As video games have matured, the lives abstraction has increasingly seemed like a legacy from an earlier era and is used with decreasing frequency with each passing year.

Even when modern games use a discrete lives system, this is usually in conjunction with a health abstraction (which we discuss in the next section), and it is easy to forget that early arcade games simply had discrete conditions that caused the player to die: if your ship comes into contact with an enemy or a shot in *Space Invaders* (Bally Midway, 1978), you die and lose a life. The same is true for *Asteroids* (Atari, 1979), *Defender* (Williams, 1980), and *Pac-Man* (Taito, 1980).

What characterized these early games was an exceptionally high risk of failure on the part of the player. Although expert players could "clock" *Defender*, for example, or play *Pac-Man* more or less indefinitely, the vast majority of players lasted for only a few minutes with each game. If they happened to enjoy this brief play experience, they would return and play again later.

It is no exaggeration to say that the vast majority of early arcade games reflected Type 1 Conqueror gameplay almost exclusively; the player failed often and had to learn (usually through a gradual process of optimization) how to progress further into the game or how to play it for longer. It is easy to see how the high risk play of these games supports the emotional payoff of fiero; when it is hard to complete even a single wave or level of a game, then fiero is achieved regularly, with each success (at least until the player expects to last a certain length of time—at this point, the player must strive to beat their own prior achievements to reach a point for which fiero has been earned). High-score hunting is also obviously fiero-related and has the added advantage of including a social aspect.

The process of softening the harsh rules of games that used the discrete lives abstraction was actually very slow in coming. One of the first signs of a change came when the player's avatar was granted a brief period of invulnerability after the loss of a life, signified by having the avatar flash briefly. While the avatar is flashing, it cannot be harmed. An early example can be seen with *Joust* (Williams, 1982) in which the player's avatar (a knight mounted on either an ostrich or a crane) flashes continuously at the point that it appears on-screen until the player presses a control. Thus, the player could decide when to come into the game—essential in the case of *Joust*, since entering into the play field at random would be highly likely to cause instant death.

However, by the mid 1980s discrete lives were already starting to decline in favor of a health abstraction. After *Gauntlet*, it was mostly just scrolling shooters that continued to use discrete lives as in *Nemesis* (Konami, 1985) and its sequel *Salamander* (Konami, 1986). These games presumably continued to attract an audience of players who enjoyed Type 1 play, as this was in essence the only style of play compatible with the high stakes implied by one mistake leading to instant death.

Health

The notion of health as a set of *hit points* or *HP* dates back to table-top gaming and predates tabletop RPGs, which inherited them from a common lineage. Nowadays, the use of hit points or a health bar is so common a game abstraction that players no longer question it. In reality, you cannot assess the state of being for an entity on a linear scale, but the abstraction is easy to understand and easy to implement, which makes it justifiably popular. The fact that the avatar does not die instantly allows more diverse styles of play to be supported as opposed to the pure Type 1 play of discrete lives.

You have enormous variety in how you choose both to scale and to represent the health mechanic. In a computer RPG, for example, hit point values are allowed to become very high, because the game wants to present the possibility of death, but the play is actually inconvenienced whenever the player is unfortunate enough to have their avatar die. Conversely, in fighting games a relatively small scale keeps the gameplay swift and challenging.

At the smallest end of the scale, the health is divided into so few units that each is represented iconically (a "wound" abstraction), which is useful when violence is to be avoided more often than embraced, or in cases where the loss of a wound can be physically represented to aid immersion, as in *Ghosts & Goblins* (Capcom, 1985) where the avatar loses their armor when first hit (and is seen running around in his underpants) and dies when they are hit a second time.

As a general rule, numerical representations of health (hit points in numbers, for example) are more appropriate for the Hardcore audience, and graphical representations of health (bars or lines of icons) are preferred for a Casual audience. The reason for this is that a Hardcore player might have reason to want to know how many hit points will be lost in a certain situation, whereas the Casual player is far more likely to care only that certain activities cost a lot of health or just a small loss. This perhaps relates to the Rational temperament's desire for knowledge, and therefore numerical representations of health should perhaps be constrained to games primarily targeting the H1 and H2 audience clusters.

In addition to atomic health representations (hit points or a bar), some games use a system whereby separate components have their own damage. This can sometimes be an aid to mimicry—it can feel more realistic if one is driving a vehicle, for example, if damage to the engine and tires is dealt with differently—but you face a danger if damage to individual components causes the avatar to function less effectively.

This is an issue of negative feedback that applies in any game that reduces the avatar's abilities as its health (or the health of its components) falls. At first sight, this appears to aid immersion and hence mimicry, but in fact, it generally adds to the agonistic elements of gameplay by raising the stakes: players cannot afford to take damage because the game becomes harder the more damaged they become. For the most part, situations where damage to the avatar decreases abilities favor Type 1 play over all other kinds for the same reason that the discrete lives abstraction does, namely it increases the risk of failure and therefore adds to the payoff in fiero.

When used responsibly, deterioration can be used to enhance mimicry, however. The *Resident Evil* series (Capcom, 1996 onwards) features a deterioration abstraction that does not affect avatar performance until the avatar is very close to death. Initially, the avatar begins to limp but movement rate is not significantly affected; then when the health bar is nearly exhausted, movement rate is seriously impeded. This serves the goals of mimicry quite readily, as rather than a continual process of negative feedback, deleterious effects of damage occur only near the point of death—and its manifestation in the game world serves as a cue for the player to heal their avatar.

It is worth noting also that the *Resident Evil* games (in common with most survival horror games) do not display health on screen during gameplay, so the changes to the movement animations for the avatar serve as the primary means of determining the avatar's current state of health. (The player can always check the actual status by pausing the game, where a display provides the state of health as a colored ECG-style display.) This is a good example of how health abstractions can be used to enhance mimicry (and hence appeal to Type 3 and 4 players).

Bipartite Health Abstractions

One special case in regard to health abstractions occurs when the health consists of two components that undergo sequential attrition. A very simple example of this happens with *GoldenEye 007* (Rare, 1997).

The game uses a standard health bar representation, but the health can only go *down*; it cannot go up. This serves to heighten dramatic tension, in that the player knows that damage they suffer is permanent and cannot be healed; other games with first aid kits and similar health-restoring elements encourage the player to be somewhat reckless, because sooner or later they will have an opportunity to heal.

If this were the only aspect of the health system, it would naturally favor Type 1 play by increasing the risk (and therefore the fiero), but it is coupled with a second health element represented by body armor. Picking up a body armor item adds as much additional health as the player has originally at the start of a level, via a second bar. Whenever a body armor power up is gained, the armor bar is completely refilled.

This is a simple example of a *bipartite health* system, and in this case the result is a system with a unique personality. For example, the player is encouraged to be extremely cautious at the start of each level, thus engendering stealth play, and once body armor has been found the player is free to risk a little recklessness. Type 1 Conqueror players benefit from the heightened tensions and risks of the underlying health mechanic, while other players have the benefits of a conventional health system in the form of the body armor mechanic. A sense of Bond-esque realism is also preserved; you find little logic in instant-heal health packs, but throwing on extra armor makes perfect sense as a way to protect an avatar.

In terms of appeal to a wider audience, the bipartite health system is improved upon in *Halo: Combat Evolved* (Bungie, 2001). Here, the same two components can be found—health and armor, although this time it is explained in game setting in terms of a futuristic energy shield. However, the shield portion of the player's health rapidly recharges if the player is out of combat for a sufficient period of time. The result is a health system that is much more forgiving than those usually found in FPS games; the player can restore up to half of their effective health by retreating from combat and waiting for their shield to recharge. By making the game more forgiving the appeal of the game stretches out to Casual and Type 3 Wanderer play styles more effectively, and tension is preserved for Type 1 Conqueror players because, once the shield is depleted, failure becomes obviously imminent (especially on the higher difficulty levels, where a concentrated barrage of enemy fire can reduce a pristine shield to nothing in seconds).

Another style of bipartite health occurs when the game features a non-ablative armor system, such as is used in the multi-award winning table-top battle system *Car Wars* (Steve Jackson Games, 1981 onwards). Here, hit points are represented in part by the armor on the vehicle. However, the player has the choice to replace some or all of the regular plastic armor with metal armor, which weighs considerably more but is non-ablative. Metal armor in this game does not decrease with damage, but rather subtracts from the damage suffered (although certain weapons and situations do subtract from the metal armor, but the rate of ablation is considerably less than with regular armor). The game balance in *Car Wars* is nearly perfect, and the choice between metal or plastic armor (or a composite of the two) is one of the more interesting decisions that the player faces when designing a car to battle with [2].

Computer RPGs sometimes make use of a similar system, whereby the armor the avatar wears subtracts from damage suffered (although they rarely have the partially ablative system used in *Car Wars*). *Kult: Heretic Kingdoms* (3D People,

2004) grants the player avatar certain abilities that allow individuals to permanently lower the armor of a foe when a critical result is achieved. This allowed canny players to deal with heavily armored foes by stripping them of their armor and thus making them easy prey. However, because this aspect of the mechanics was effectively hidden (because the player had no way of actually knowing the current armor level of their foe), this mechanic was largely lost on the game audience. In principle, at least, this should have helped support Type 2 play in a primarily Type 1 game, by offering more diversity of tactics.

Invulnerability and Immortality

It was some time before game developers hit upon the idea that it wasn't necessary for the player to die at all. The text adventure game *Jinxter* (Magnetic Scrolls, 1987) might have been the first game in which the player definitively could not die. The game was structured so that in any situation that the player might die, they were rescued but lost a certain proportion of luck. To properly complete the game, it was necessary to not make any of the mistakes that resulted in a loss of luck, but the basic idea was still that player mortality was not an essential element of game play. By the 1990s, LucasArts adventures had almost standardized the idea that the avatar in an adventure need not die, and perhaps only the *Broken Sword* series of adventures (Revolution, 1996 onwards) stuck to the idea that the avatar could be killed by bad player choices.

In other games, having a limited number of lives was not seriously challenged until *Super Mario 64* (Nintendo, 1996). In this game, the player had a number of lives, and when they lost a life they went back to the point in the hub from which they had last selected a domain to visit. When the player ran out of lives completely, they were still shown a game over screen, but they could start the game again, and all of their prior achievements remained completed. Something similar to this model had actually been used before with *Tir Na Nog* (Gargoyle, 1984), in which one could die in battle, but any achievements remained completed.

Gradually, game designers came to the realization that having a limited number of lives was not only unnecessary for certain games (in particular platform games), it was detrimental to mass market audience appeal. By *Jak & Daxter: The Precursor Legacy* (Naughty Dog, 2001), the notion of lives as an in-game currency had vanished completely. The player was effectively immortal—they could die over and over again, and nothing at all would be lost (except, perhaps, the player's patience). Various experiments had appeared previously in 2D platform style games—*Oddworld: Abe's Oddysee* (Oddworld Inhabitants, 1997) and *Heart of Darkness* (Amazing Studio, 1998) both allow the player to die, but fail to keep track of how many "lives" have been lost. The trend emerged even earlier in quest games—*The Legend of Zelda: A Link to the Past* (Nintendo, 1991) used a system in which the player can die any number of times, but their save file recorded the number of lives lost as a kind of score.

When targeting a mass market audience, this ratcheting of game progress so that player achievements cannot be lost under any circumstances is almost always desirable, and immortality (infinite lives) should almost always be preferred when targeting a Type 3 Wanderer or Type 4 Participant audience, where mimicry and immersive experiences outweigh agon and fiero as factors in player enjoyment. Only in Type 1 Conqueror play (and to a lesser extent Type 2 Manager play), where agon and fiero are more important, should the game allow for there to be something to lose when the player fails. However, it need not be in progress; just making the player have to travel to redo a task is often sufficient to heighten the sense of something being at stake in the case of failure.

Many games targeting a wider, mass market audience should consider whether or not it might be beneficial for the avatar to be invulnerable. In particular, in *GTA*-style games whereby the player's avatar takes charge of a variety of vehicles, the vehicles can have health, but the avatar itself can be made invulnerable. This allows for imbedding challenges within a playground world where the player need not feel the stress of having to lose their achievements when they die. An example can be found in *Simpsons: Hit & Run* (Radical Entertainment, 2003), which copies *GTA* but crucially removes the agonistic combat and replaces it with platform gameplay. The player's avatar in this game is invulnerable, and nothing the player does results in their death, as befits the mass market audience for such a game.

Time

The use of time as a limiting factor for game length is almost as old as the lives abstraction. *Road Champion* (Taito, 1978) is one of several early driving games to restrict the length of a play session by having a timer count down. This is functionally a mortality abstraction, and after the arrival of "pump and play," it was often the case that the distinction between health and time was limited. *Gauntlet* might have used a health system, but it was also set up so that the player's avatar's health ticked down slowly with time, thus forcing the player to keep topping up their health with coins (except for those players who could greedily steal all the food for themselves without having their co-players turn against them).

In modern games, it is rare for the overall sense of mortality to be related to time, but it is not uncommon for an individual challenge to be against the clock. This heightens the sense of risk and the tension of play, and therefore contributes to a more agonistic play experience. When the amount of time provided to complete a challenge is just enough, the result is play that appeals to the Type 1 Conqueror player with their desire for fiero. For a wider audience, a timer can be used to heighten tension, but in general the time provided should be vastly in excess of what is required when targeting a mass market audience, especially an audience to include Type 3 Wanderer and Type 4 Participant players.

In some cases a sense of limited time can be engendered in the player by sleight of hand. The remake of *Resident Evil* (Capcom, 2002) features a sequence in which the player is in an underwater area that will collapse if the player does not take action. Rather than a literal timer, the player is shown a gauge that signifies how long they have to act. The first minute or so of time constitutes about three quarters of the gauge's length, thus giving the player an intense spur to action, but the remaining portion of the gauge takes a considerable length of time to advance. Player tension is further heightened by visual and audio events, such as a shark banging into the barrier and a continuous siren. This is an example of using limited time for the purposes of mimicry, and these kinds of illusionary threats are well suited to a Type 3 or 4 audience.

Interacting with the World

Even from the earliest days of video games, some interaction occurred between the avatar and the environment. *Space Invaders* (Taito, 1978) has its famous barriers that are destroyed by both the shots of the invaders and the player's shots. This dynamic element of the environment does much to enhance the play experience; the extent to which the barriers are destroyed heightens the tension (and hence the fiero of victory), and also the fact that the player can choose to blast a hole in the barrier and shoot through from behind cover provides a game advantage to players who want to exploit it.

It is almost always the case that the means of the avatar's interaction with the world is limited in some way, because it is technically unfeasible for every aspect of the game world to be changed. Near the lower ends of the development budget scale, games must by necessity have more static environments, whereas AAA games are capable of allowing the player a greater capacity to have an influence on the environment, even if that influence occurs only in predetermined manners.

Hotspots

The term *hotspot* refers to a point in the game world where the avatar can interact with the world in a meaningful way. It might simply be the area around an NPC from which a player can trigger a conversation, or it might be a place in the world where a particular item or ability can be used to cause an effect that allows the player to earn a benefit or otherwise progress.

In early games, players had to determine the location of hotspots (another case of early video games having more appeal with H1 and H2 players, for whom overcoming a knowledge deficit can be an enjoyable challenge). By the heyday of point-and-click adventures, it was generally considered wise to at least allow hotspots to light up or show text when the mouse pointer was positioned over them. For example, the *Discworld* adventure games (Perfect Entertainment, 1995–1999) showed a text tag when the player pointed the mouse cursor at anything of interest, and clicking would cause a description of the entity in question to be read aloud by the central character.

In the former example, each hotspot was a unique case, but in other games a more systematic approach applied. *The Legend of Zelda* series (Nintendo, 1986 onwards) pioneered a system of codified iconography for hotspots, so that the player could identify the hotspots from certain observable features. In *The Legend of Zelda: A Link to the Past*, for example, the hook shot could be fired at certain metal ring features to allow the avatar to cross intervening divides. This iconography became slightly confused in the transition to 3D with *The Legend of Zelda: The Ocarina of Time* (Nintendo, 1998), where the hook shot functionality was expanded to include wooden objects and vines. However, not all wooden items and not all vines were legitimate targets for the hook shot in this game, and hence the iconography was inconsistently implemented. The situation was repaired in *The Legend of Zelda: The Wind Waker* (Nintendo, 2002), which contains one of the most consistently applied iconography for hotspots.

Having a consistent iconography for hotspots, however, applies only when the means of player interaction are limited (as is the case in the *Zelda* games, which feature a toolkit of items, and all interactions are with this fixed toolkit and the appropriate features). In the more general case, you always face a balance issue between player immersion and easy comprehension, because not everything that looks interactive to the player will be so and marking hotspots in too obvious a manner can undermine willing suspension of belief.

This particularly applies for survival horror games, where immersion is as important (or more important) than game challenge and a number of different solutions can be seen. *Resident Evil* prefers to make smaller or hidden hotspots (such as equipment in the world) glint or flash subtly. Conversely, the *Silent Hill* series (Konami, 1999 onwards) has evolved a solution whereby the avatar's head turns to face anything of interest. This is more immersive, but works only if the player is taught that this is the case—otherwise, the player is left to flail about in the environment, constantly clicking to determine where the hotspots lie.

In general, with the possible exception of the H1 and H2 audience who are willing to tackle puzzles with a higher degree of obscurity, it is the obligation of the game designer to ensure that hotspots are clearly conveyed to the player by some mechanism—either by highlighting the hot spots or by using a consistent iconography to identify them.

Cosmetic Interactions

When the player has the capacity to change the appearance of the game world in some manner, it almost always serves the play needs of mimicry. If the player can choose their avatar's clothing, that's a positive step towards mimicry, but if the player can change the color or nature of an element in the world at large, that gives the player more of a meaningful emotional connection with the world.

An example can be seen in *Jet Set Radio* (Smilebit, 2000) in which the player can choose or define their own graffiti. Then, when the player sprays tags in the game world, they see their own graffiti designs appear on the walls. This emotional connection is further enhanced by the cut scenes between levels, in which the action being viewed is set against a backdrop within which the player can see their own designs displayed.

Obviously, it takes time (and hence development budget) to include features relating to changing the appearance of the game world cosmetically, but when considering the Type 3 and 4 play styles where mimicry and emotional issues dominate, it is always a benefit. Indeed, one could say of *The Sims* (Maxis, 2000) that the appeal of the game rests in part upon the high degree of environmental customizability afforded to the player.

Avatar Abilities

The abilities available to the player's avatar or agents are one of the key determinants of the types of play a game is going to support. At the very least it is assumed that the avatar will be able to move and have either abilities to improve its negotiation of the environment (such as jumping), the capacity to cause damage to opposition (in a game where combat is a factor), or the ability to collect equipment or information and apply it in the world—or all of these abilities. The choice of which types of ability the avatar possesses is intimately tied up with the nature of the game, but the nature of how those abilities are allowed to *change* is more closely tied to the types of play the game will support.

Resources

The use of resources in games is practically universal, because having an internal economy to a game is often an essential element to promoting play. Sim games and many RTS games make considerable use of resource abstractions, and a vast number of games use a money-resource of some kind. Generally, the resources are used to purchase enhancements to the avatar, to build new game agents, or to add assets to the game world that affect avatar or agent abilities or production, such as buildings in RTS games. In this manner, they support Type 2-style decision making better than other play styles, although Type 1 play is often also supported because the process of resource generation can usually be optimized.

Resource abstractions never exist in isolation; for them to be meaningful, the resources must be applied to some other aspect of the game world. For example, in computer RPGs a financial resource can be spent to purchase better equipment, whereas in RTS games the resource-asset combination is practically ubiquitous.

Although they are mainly involved in supporting general gameplay, they can be used for mimicry or toyplay instead. *Azure Dreams* (Konami, 1998) allowed the player to use their money to build new assets for their home town, granting little gameplay advantage but offering a greater emotional connection to the game world—ideal for Type 3 Wanderer and especially Type 4 Participant players, because the building of these cosmetic assets heightens the player's emotional connection with the game world and its inhabitants, and in many cases the construction of these cosmetic assets is specifically requested by the other characters with whom the player has a relationship. It should be noted, however, that the core aspects of this game were totally unsuited to Type 4 play.

Of course, health and lives can also be used as a resource inside the game world, although the use of lives as a resource is becoming less and less common. The management of health, as previously discussed, is often one of the key elements in a game that features combat, and the placement of items to restore health and so forth is quite critical in balancing game difficulty. In general, however, the player never faces any active decisions about how to spend these resources, and so they generally form part of the substructure of the game world abstraction.

Power Ups

The classic computer game *power up*, which lasts for a limited time after collection, is the most common form of temporary enhancement of avatar ability. The duration might be timed, or the end point defined by some other activity (for example, an armor power up that lasts until the player is hit or suffers a certain amount of damage). The temporary nature of power ups supports Type 1 Conqueror play more than other styles as a general rule—the player has an obligation to act fast and use the power up as best as they can before it expires, and in the long term, the player learns to optimize the use of power ups through repeat play.

When games feature multiple power ups that are not timed in their duration, but last until the player dies (or some other condition), a more progressive system is in use. Under these circumstances, the player can reach a number of different levels of power within the game, but none of these states are permanent. 2D shooters in the mid to late 1980s made considerable use of this abstraction, typified by *Nemesis* and its sequels. However, since these power ups expire when the player dies, the result is an increase of the risk inherent in the game, and therefore this is another play style which appeals primarily to players preferring Type 1 play. In the case of *Nemesis*, the challenge the player faced rose in proportion to the volume of power ups the player had applied. This provided some balance of play, but it was still the case (especially in the later levels) that to die was often to accept that your game was effectively over, and for most players the game had to be completed on one life or not at all.

Both these approaches to power ups are rooted in the arcade. These methods have become accepted game elements thanks to the frequency of their usage, and they are by their nature anti-immersive because of the artificial nature of the abstraction. In reaching a more mainstream audience in the West, it might be desirable to tone down the unnatural qualities of these power ups, or at least define their operation within an expected logical framework. The use of a medical kit to heal within a game, for example, is generally acceptable to Western audiences despite the artificiality.

You can use power ups in a manner suitable for a wider variety of play styles. For example, *Super Mario 64* has a power up that enables the player to fly. Once the power up is picked up, the player is able to remain airborne as long as they want—but the power up ends when they touch the ground. Similarly, in *R-Type* (Irem, 1987) the player has three different choices of basic power up—a red, yellow, or blue power up, each one corresponding to a different type of attack. Once collected, this ability lasts until death, and the player can switch between the different modes by collecting a power up of a different color. (Although losing the ability at death seems harsh, the game contrives to provide a new power up immediately after each life begins.) This system supports Type 2 Manager play through giving the player the choice to select a different weapon type for a different situation, and Type 3 Wanderer play by giving the player different "toys" to experiment with.

Permanent Increases in Ability

Many games feature skill abstractions in which the avatar has a set of quantified abilities, as is common in computer RPGs such as *Fallout* (Interplay, 1997) or *Deux Ex* (Ion Storm, 2000). Almost infallibly, if the game includes skills, part of the gameplay relates to permanently increasing these abilities over the course of the game. Almost all such schemes originate with table-top RPGs, in which long-term progression in the game is almost always related to enhancement of the player character's abilities.

Perhaps the most common way of dealing with permanent increases of ability is a level-based abstraction, in which the player periodically advances a level and gains slight enhancement in ability when they do so. Another similar kind of permanent enhancement abstraction uses an embedded resource system (which usually has absolutely no meaning in the game world) to allow the player to improve their abilities by spending points acquired by some game activity.

Both these approaches are highly abstract (real people do not level up), and in principle their appeal is mainly with the H1 and H2 subtypes. However, so widespread has the class and level system become, partly because of the success of the *Dungeons & Dragons* table-top RPG (TSR, 1974) in its time and partly through simplified computer RPGs such as *Diablo* (Blizzard Entertainment, 1996), that the appeal has spread to a wider audience. Nonetheless, any game wanting to apply this kind of system is probably targeting the Hardcore and C1 play types only.

Furthermore, most of the character progression systems featured in computer RPGs are based upon an exponential system that is fiendishly addictive to Type 1 Conqueror players (and any player preferring Type 2 Manager play style), but can feel like a tedious treadmill to players preferring Type 3 Wanderer and Type 4 Participant styles of play if the game requires the player to commit to actions solely for the purpose of leveling up. If the spine of the game provides sufficient rewards for leveling to proceed apace, players seldom have an issue, but if the game periodically expects the player to spend time in the field solely for the purpose of gathering experience (as happens in many MMORPG games), players preferring Type 3 or 4 play can quickly lose interest.

An interestingly simplified version of permanent skill increases can be found in *Grand Theft Auto: San Andreas* (Rockstar North, 2004). Abilities power up automatically through the player action without the player having to make any decisions or deal with an abstracted level system. For example, the longer the player spends swimming underwater, the greater their ability to hold their breath. The player is informed of any significant changes in their abilities (in many cases, they are just reminded that their abilities are improving) by pop-up text boxes that contain information such as "Health—Upgraded. You can take more damage before dying," or "Bike Skill—Upgraded. You have less chance of falling from your motorbike." In terms of appeal to the mass market Casual audience, this kind of system is cutting edge and avoids the problems associated with leveling up in terms of appealing primarily to Type 1 (and Type 2) play styles while retaining the fun of continual improvement.

Inventories

Instead of abilities being inherent to the avatar, as in a skill system, an inventory abstraction grants avatars additional abilities according to the tools and weapons they have acquired. For example, a grappling hook can allow a special climbing action as in *Tenchu: Stealth Assassins* (Acquire, 1998). Abstractions of inventory are familiar to most players of games; as a tool-using species, homo sapiens perhaps think of problems in terms of "What tool can I use?", which makes inventory abstractions highly accessible. Because they are so common, and because they are only slightly abstracted from the familiar assumptions of the real world, inventory abstractions do not interfere with suspension of disbelief as much as some other representations.

Inventory systems present interface issues relating to how the contents of the inventory are accessed. One common approach (used in the aforementioned *Tenchu*, as well as in *GoldenEye* to select weapons or equipment) is to have a linear sequence of tools that can be selected through the use of keys to cycle through the list (sometimes with another key to select), and iconic representations on screen used to show the inventory options. This is more than adequate for the Hardcore audience and the C1 subtype, but for a more mass market audience a simpler option is recommended. If the number of items in an inventory are eight or fewer (or sixteen if two different keys are used), a *Turok*-style selection wheel can be used, as in *Ratchet & Clank* (Insomniac Games, 2002)—a relatively Casual-friendly option.

Another approach to inventory occurs in games for which equipment can be enabled and disabled, for example, armor can be put on and taken off or the settings of a weapon changed. Many computer RPGs use this approach to affect just about every ability present in the games. Although this approach can aid immersion by virtue of the apparent reality of equipment providing advantages, we have already mentioned a key problem associated with equipment and immersion, namely that having to deal with an inventory breaks the player out of role. In many games where equipment-based enhancement is encountered, the mechanism is very numbers-heavy, which further undermines player immersion. When the player can gain gameplay advantages by changing their selections frequently, the situation is dramatically worsened, and immersion suffers considerably, so in general this should be used only when the core audience is primarily H1 and H2.

Perhaps the best option for a Casual game audience is to abstract away from the need to select equipment at all. With a context-sensitive inventory, the player acquires equipment during the game but never has to select a desired object. Instead, the interaction of equipment with the environment is codified in such a way as to ensure unique cases result. This allows the player to just choose to act, with the appropriate object being used automatically. Having to deal with an inventory abstraction at all breaks the player temporarily "out of role," which is anti-immersive, and the context inventory abstraction avoids this problem, while simultaneously simplifying gameplay and making it more accessible.

Context-sensitive inventory abstractions are a desirable representation in terms of accessibility and playability, but they carry a terrific cost in terms of the requirements of the design. Every ability granted by an item of equipment must have a sphere of applicability completely separate to all other abilities—you cannot have, for example, two different ways to respond to a vertical surface or else overloading results. This requires considerable skill (and design budget) to make this approach tenable. The process can be simplified if overloaded situations inherently trump one another—for example, if the vertical surface can be climbed by using pitons or by using a grappling hook, and the latter is superior to the former in every way (faster, quieter, etc.). Nonetheless, there will always be some limitations. Hardcore players will find a context-sensitive approach frustrating if they ever feel that they cannot select the equipment they want, so it should be used with a certain caution.

In practice, it is usually not possible to make an inventory completely context-sensitive, but you can get close. *Fatal Frame* (Techmo, 2001) has an inventory, but the player need only use it to use healing items. All other items, such as keys and quest-specific items (and the stone mirror that resurrects the player if they die) are used automatically in the context for which they apply. (However, the lenses used to power up the player's camera are selected in an inventory-like fashion.)

The desire to keep the inventory system as simple as possible can lead to interesting design decisions. For example, in *Halo*, unlike in other FPS games, the player is restricted to carrying only two different weapons at any given time. Therefore, the inventory mechanic becomes a single button to switch between the two weapons the player is carrying (and a context-sensitive action to swap the currently selected weapon for a weapon the player is standing over). This reduction of choices would have caused considerable player complaints because of the reduced variety, but the developers have cleverly built in two other forms of attack as always accessible from a single button without having to use an inventory—the player has the capacity to use a grenade or to use their current weapon in melee (that is, to hit the foe with the butt of their gun) from separate keys. This approach is relatively Casual player friendly and gives the player sufficient options without having to break immersion by reliance on an inventory mechanic. It is also possible that the planning element introduced by the weapon restrictions appeals to Type 1 players as strategy via optimization.

Opposition

Although a game need not use opposition, in practice the presence of opponents in the game world is virtually ubiquitous. The opposition that a player encounters has more to do with the avatar than the world as a whole, in general terms, because without the player to pit against an opponent, they have no purpose.

Clearly, the chief purpose of opposition is to support agonistic gameplay, although it is worth remembering that opposition can be used for the purposes of mimicry—for example, if the foes are easy to defeat, but included solely for the purpose of heightening dramatic tension. The opposition directly relates to the avatar, because the avatar often gets to test its abilities only in the context of some opposition to face off against.

Fighting versus Avoiding Opponents

It is inevitably the case that some of the most complex game play elements that must be dealt with occur when the player is fighting opposition. Indeed, fighting games are based entirely around this interaction. It is clearly the case that fighting opponents is an agonistic activity, and as such its appeal is chiefly the domain of Type 1 Conqueror and Type 2 Manager players.

Conversely, the Type 3 Wanderer or Type 4 Participant player seems just as happy to avoid opponents, rather than feeling the need to fight everything they encounter. This is not to say that they will not fight opponents, or cannot enjoy doing so, but rather that merely testing your mettle against a foe is largely an agonistic pursuit and as such not of particular interest to players for whom mimicry is more important. However, when narrative reasons require battle to be joined (to defeat an opponent who is troubling one of the NPCs, for example), these players can enjoy the emotional payoffs associated with defeating a foe as much as anyone else.

A clear distinction exists between voluntary avoidance of foes and stealth gameplay, where the avoidance of foes has become formalized. This is a tricky area, because avoidance contains a thrill that extends beyond agon and into mimicry—the appeal of hide and seek appears to be universal among children. When dealing with issues of stealth, the primary factor is the cost of failure.

When failure to remain stealthy increases the game difficulty significantly, stealth has become a Type 1 play activity—because failure makes life difficult, however you defeat the situation presented, you achieve fiero in victory. The more the game requires the player to repeat a section of stealth gameplay until they get it right, the more biased towards Type 1 play the experience becomes. If any mistake results in failure, only players preferring Type 1 play are likely to enjoy it.

Conversely, succeeding in stealth is an agonistic reward in itself—getting through a section without being spotted delivers fiero much as any other victory would do so. Therefore one argument suggests that when targeting a heterogeneous audience with no clearly dominant play style, the penalty for failed stealth need not be insurmountable odds, but merely opposition that is of equivalent difficulty to the stealth activity itself, as is seen in the stealth sections within *Grand Theft Auto: San Andreas*. Most games for which stealth is a primary activity are likely to be targeting a Type 1 (or Type 1 and 2) preferring audience, however, and so the game difficulty need not be so smoothly balanced.

Bosses

The notion of a boss is peculiar to video games. It requires very little analysis to appreciate that by presenting a section of higher difficulty that must be completed for the player to progress, a game has chosen to favor agonistic play in general, and Type 1 tendencies in general. We find definite variety in player responses to bosses, with most Type 1 Conqueror and many Type 2 Manager players enjoying the challenge they present, and many players, especially of Type 3 Wanderer style, finding bosses in general, and difficult bosses in particular, anathematic to their enjoyment.

The pattern boss exemplifies the issue. Pattern bosses are designed to carry out a particular sequence of actions and generally are vulnerable to attack only at a certain point in this sequence. The pattern boss holds great appeal to the H1 and H2 subtypes, because it represents a (generally) simple puzzle to solve; the player observes the bosses actions, determines when best to strike, and then uses this knowledge to bring about defeat.

When designing for Type 3 players (for example, when designing platform games that generally take in Types 1, 2, and 3 in their audiences), pattern bosses can still be included, but it should always be readily apparent how the foe is defeated. (There is no harm in telling the player outright if, after a short period of time, they have not been able to damage the boss.) The goal here is for the pattern boss not to present an enormous challenge, but rather to be a mini-game for which victory is largely inevitable, but which the player is not fully cognizant of when they first begin.

It must be noted, however, that Type 1 players are likely to be disappointed by a game in which the bosses are too easily defeated. The emotional payoff of fiero is undercut when victory is achieved too easily, after all, and a certain amount of failure is expected by a player preferring Type 1 in order that their eventual victory seems to be a genuine triumph over adversity.

CONCLUSION

This chapter and the preceding chapter provide a general overview to the manner in which a game world abstraction can be constructed. The process is most effective when the choices of abstraction are in sync with both the vision for the game and the needs of the game's intended audience. One cannot simply construct an elegant game world abstraction without considering player needs except in a game which is motivated by artistic rather than commercial factors.

Game world abstractions are the beginning of game design, because in a complete design the abstractions need to be backed by game mechanics (which are usually numerical, logical, or algebraic in nature). Deciding upon the framework of the game world nonetheless serves to place the entire game design into a meaningful perspective, and understanding the process of abstraction can be the first step towards superior game designs.

ENDNOTES

[1] The battle at Chi Bi (which translates to "Red Cliff") in 208 A.D. is notable because it is a case where a superior strategy allowed a smaller force to overcome a much larger army.

[2] *Car Wars* was made into a video game named *Autoduel* (Origin, 1985). However, the strengths of the tabletop system related to its carefully balanced turn-based system, whereas *Autoduel* was worked in real time and was correspondingly less effective.

10 Game Structures

In This Chapter

- Pathfinding and Housekeeping
- Environmental Progression
- Mechanisms of Progress
- Playground Worlds
- Breadcrumbing and Funneling
- Replay Features
- Save Game Functionality
- Conclusion

All games are created from multiple elements that combine to create gameplay (or, in the case of toys, toyplay). Part of this gameplay involves the moment-to-moment actions of the player—the *core gameplay*. Another part of the gameplay involves the delivery of materials to the player through play. This aspect is the game's *structure*.

At the most basic level, structural design involves the game environment and how the player accesses new environments. Early arcade games and modern puzzle games use single-screen environments; when a screen is "cleared," it is replaced by an identical environment, often with increased challenge via extra speed or new game elements. Modern single-screen games are expected to provide multiple modes of play, which are accessed from the game's front end. The nature of the advance between discrete levels, or the access of modes from a menu, involves structural design.

Current video games have become much more complex in structure as well as core gameplay, to the extent that structural elements can make or break a game. A popular example would be the *Gran Turismo* series (Polyphony Digital, 1997 onwards) of car-racing games. Classic car-racing games used a linear progressive structure to introduce new tracks; *GT* and its sequels expand upon this greatly. By racing well, the player accumulates money with which to modify cars or buy new ones—and this aspect becomes the main focus of the game. This shift in gameplay, which extends the lifespan of the game greatly and provides a much-enhanced feeling of immersion, is almost entirely due to its structural design (though the popularity of the game might also be attributed to the realistic depiction of its vehicles, specifically of interest to the C1 and C2 market).

This chapter discusses the nature of video game structure and how it relates to different play styles. As with the majority of design elements, a game's structure can have an enormous effect on its ability to hit its target audience. Type 1 players (desiring agonistic play with scope for strategic optimization) are happy to play games that deliver their materials via a series of linearly unlocked levels. The tendency of this structure to create fail-repeat style gameplay can be a benefit to these players. Conversely, Type 3 players (seeking mimicry via direct experience of the virtual world) dislike fail-repeat gameplay; domain or contiguous world abstractions are preferable for these players, and the structure must take these needs into account.

PATHFINDING AND HOUSEKEEPING

The player's activities within a game might broadly be divided into two categories, here termed *pathfinding* and *housekeeping*.

Pathfinding activities involve the player actively attempting to locate the fastest method of game progression. FPS games favor pathfinding play (reflecting their roots as maze games)—the player typically moves from area to area, forging ahead, finding more powerful weapons and defeating more powerful foes. There is no sense of stability to a pathfinding-oriented game—the player is expected to play at the front edge of the game, ever pushing forward.

Housekeeping activities, meanwhile, involve the player exploring in a more circular manner, becoming familiar with an area and its contents. Collection gameplay is a housekeeping style, with the player effectively "tidying" the landscape, and domain-based platform games give a good indication of this style of play. By the time an area of a housekeeping game is fully complete, the player knows it back to front. Housekeeping gameplay tends to allow the player to push forward at their own pace and divide time as they want between breaking new ground and cleaning up familiar areas.

The vast majority of games feature both housekeeping and pathfinding activities. The balance tends to be generated by level design philosophy and structural design. *Resident Evil* (Capcom, 1996, 2002) provides a good example of balance between housekeeping and pathfinding play styles, with the player's preference of style determining the way the game is played (time-trialing of *Resident Evil* games is an acknowledged sport among H1 players, and is a pure-pathfinding mode of play delivering maximum scope for optimization through strategy, specifically regarding what to pick up and what to leave behind to save time).

Half-Life (Valve, 1998) is a great example of a primarily pathfinding game, and games such as *Splinter Cell* (Ubisoft, 2002) and *Hitman* (Io, 2000) present a form of pathfinding based around trail-and-error, satisfying the H1 enjoyment of strategic optimization. The Type 1 play style is associated with a desire for rapid progress and a tolerance for fail-repeat gameplay, and these are elements associated with games which are biased heavily towards pathfinding.

Animal Crossing (Nintendo, 2002) is one of few purely housekeeping games—the player is constrained to a small area that is filled with repeating activities and is allowed to generate their own goals in response to the activities presented. Most platform games, by comparison, are biased heavily towards housekeeping, but still have a clear pathfinding element—the player eventually chooses to move on to a new area, either simply because they can or because they have done everything they can in the current area.

Pathfinding and housekeeping play styles give the game designer what is possibly their most powerful tool for game pacing. *Pacing* is the art of delivering game material with timing, which is relatively easy within a non-interactive entertainment form such as a movie, but creates all sorts of challenges within an interactive video game. Short of forcing the pacing upon the player (that is, kill them if they don't keep up), it is hard to assess the player's interaction with a game's pacing at the design stage. By balancing pathfinding and housekeeping play, the designer can allow the player themselves to dictate pacing within the game space. This must be seen as a difficult but noble goal. *Resident Evil* displays a typical pacing model, with housekeeping activities (such as resource management, room searching, map-building, and burning zombie bodies) distracting from pathfinding progress (which is mediated by a kind of stylized scavenger hunt) should the player want them to, until the final section of the game in which narrative methods (the obligatory siren heralding total destruction of the play environment) support a more linear level design, forcing the pace into a higher gear.

In terms of structure, game environments do not need to be linked physically for these play activities to emerge—menu-based systems can be used in either manner. *Gran Turismo* can be invoked once more to illustrate this—though all game activities are initiated from a GUI map screen, players are allowed to indulge in housekeeping via menus and a central currency resource. The primary innovation of *GT* was to introduce housekeeping to the driving genre, which previously had concentrated on almost pure pathfinding style play (that is, beating each track in turn to win an overall championship). This technique is taken even further by *Road Trip/Choro-Q HG 2* (Takara, 2002), which uses a world abstraction to create what is probably the first true "CarPG."

Housekeeping and pathfinding provide a useful tool for considering aspects of structural design. One of the key questions that a designer should ask when approaching structural design is how they envision their players exploring the game space. A large part of this is balancing pathfinding and housekeeping elements in gameplay to the preferences of the game's intended audience.

Housekeeping, Pathfinding, and the Audience

There appears to be a broad bias among H1 and C1 players towards pathfinding play, and a general bias among H3 and C3 players towards housekeeping play; this might reflect the natural goal-orientation and desire for agon of the Type 1 play style, versus greater tendencies towards process-orientation and mimicry for Type 3 play. Type 2 play appears to be somewhere in between—the enjoyment of agonistic play provides the capacity to enjoy pathfinding for its own sake, but the tendency towards process-orientation means that players preferring Type 2 play are just as happy with the housekeeping activities found in games like *Civilization*. Domestic micromanagement of cities appears to be as pleasurable to the H2 as the measured destruction of their virtual enemies. Type 4 play appears to connect more strongly with housekeeping—especially housekeeping that is open to optimization through repeated actions.

In general, in pathfinding, play seems to relate to agon while housekeeping relates to mimicry, although you have the possibility of both agonistic and mimicry play in both pathfinding and housekeeping styles. For example, navigating a maze is a pathfinding activity, but can be approached both via agon (to escape as quickly as possible) or via mimicry (to enjoy being an escapee). Agonistic housekeeping takes the form of minmaxing in RPGs—the art of selecting the upgrades, equipment, and bonuses that give the avatar the best chance of domination within the world, something that appeals greatly to H1 players.

Players preferring the Type 1 play style, therefore, prefer pathfinding play not only because it gives greater scope for agon, but also because it meets other needs inherent to this style of play. It represents a direct form of goal-orientation—the reward of reaching a new area is in constant supply, meeting the Type 1 need for rapid progress—as well as provides great scope for strategizing through optimization.

Conversely, housekeeping activities place less stress on the player and allow players to form their own goals. This has obvious appeal to Type 3 players looking to maximize their sense of identity within the game world. Indeed, often the housekeeping activities presented have direct correlation with avatar definition, either through an RPG style system of leveling or via aesthetic choices on the part of the player.

Type 2 players, meanwhile, employ their skills for strategy and tactics in both pathfinding and housekeeping activities. Both approaches benefit from on-the-fly responses, so the Type 2 player shows no great preference, being able to enjoy both modes of play. In fact, combining these two play activities in one game seems to be of direct benefit towards supporting the needs of players preferring the Type 2 play style. Certainly, whereas Type 3 players spend large amounts of time pursuing entirely cosmetic housekeeping activities (such as painting their car a new color or choosing an outfit for their avatar—which are largely equivalent actions), Type 2 players are more geared to those housekeeping activities that still tie into game progress in some way, such as customizing a car in *GT* to improve its performance. This is a housekeeping activity, but it serves to further the player's overall progress in the game.

In summary, we see pathfinding as a goal-oriented, agonistic activity, and housekeeping as an activity that might be involved in process-oriented progress (as in customizing a car in *GT*) or in mimicry. Therefore, we associate pathfinding primarily with Type 1 play, and secondarily with Type 2 play, and housekeeping with all styles of play—but geared towards mimicry in Type 3 and 4 players, and agon in Type 1 and 2 players.

ENVIRONMENTAL PROGRESSION

The most basic aspect of structural design is the delivery of play environments to the player. Early arcade games used single-screen environments to host play. These were either constrained as in *Space Invaders* (Taito/Bally Midway, 1978) or "wrap around" as in *Asteroids* (Atari, 1979). The player could leave the environment only by completing the game goals set, and then typically arrived at another (identical) environment. But simultaneous to the development of arcade style games, text adventure games were providing complete (albeit abstract) worlds. These two styles still provide the limits of environmental progression in today's games, and a continuum exists between the two.

Game world abstraction and structural design are inseparable at this point. The four modes of regional game world abstraction—discrete level, continuous level, domain, and contiguous world—apply directly to structural environmental progression.

Discrete and Continuous Levels

The easiest and cheapest method of delivering gameplay progression, a linear sequence of discrete levels, has numerous advantages. The player's progress can be absolutely controlled, and all player choice is strictly limited. However, linear discrete levels provide pacing problems—difficulty bottlenecks might arise, destroying pacing and progress. Game variety can be used to provide pacing changes, but this suffers the same problem, especially if the game delivers one style of game more successfully than others (which is almost inevitable). Player taste is also compromised by use of varying play styles, as the more play styles implemented, the greater the chance of presenting the player with a style they do not like. If multiple routes are used to alleviate this problem, unseen material is being generated—a technique that undercuts the primary value of the discrete level progression, its low cost.

Linear level progression, therefore, is best used in low budget games with a single, strong core gameplay style. Game styles that thrive on single-note pacing work well, such as shooting and fighting games. Difficulty balance is of vital importance, so the intended audience for the product must be known—while Hardcore players (specifically H1) enjoy a single-minded bludgeon from one end of a linear game to another, all other players soon become frustrated and, with no other option given, stop playing.

A player's progress within a discrete level environment is almost always lost when a level is exited. Because of this, the discrete level system does not support housekeeping play as well as other structures. Housekeeping might still be maintained via a central game character (an inventory system with basic resource management of supplies, for example, or simple character-based resource distribution via a skills system). However, in general the discrete level abstraction best supports pathfinding play, and so is of most appeal to challenge- and progress-oriented H1 and C1 players.

Continuous level progression basically links discrete areas, disguising their discrete nature. As such it can be considered an "immersion-enhanced" version of the discrete level model, and is subject to similar pros and cons.

Domains and Contiguous Worlds

The primary difference between discrete level and domain abstractions lies in the empowerment of the player; while a linear level progression requires the player to forge ever onwards, the domain abstraction allows all game areas to exists simultaneously, once accessed. It is usual for domain abstraction games to access subsequent domains upon the player's completion of a subset of current domain goals. Once a new domain is accessible, the player can choose which they prefer to dip into.

The domain abstraction suits housekeeping play very well, though it is no barrier to pathfinding play styles. The domain structure fosters familiarity with game areas, which is vital to players who prefer to feel 'on top' of the game rather than pushing its edge (C3 and C4, for example). As such, domain structures make great "playground" games.

In general, it is a waste of a domain structure (and the extra time, effort, and money such an approach requires) to concentrate exclusively upon pathfinding play, so great attention must be paid to the nature of the housekeeping activities provided. *Ratchet & Clank* (Insomniac, 2001) is a good example of a domain-based game that concentrates upon a pathfinding style of exploration, but mediates this with housekeeping play in its weapons system.

Contiguous worlds also favor significant housekeeping components. By their contiguous nature, these worlds encourage the player to pass back and forth between the play areas, and a game design that does not make use of the expensive contiguity is wasting a great deal of effort. This is not to say that contiguous world games must ignore pathfinding—*Jak and Daxter* (Naughty Dog, 2001) and *Tak and The Power of Juju* (Avalanche, 2003) both include significant pathfinding elements in their contiguous worlds.

The *Legend of Zelda* games (Nintendo, 1987–present) provide a more traditional balance of pathfinding and housekeeping within a world structure, with "dungeon" challenge areas being exclusively pathfinding is style, while the "overworld" areas provide almost limitless optional housekeeping play for those who desire it.

If a game contains either a domain structure or a contiguous world, it is likely to be at least mid-budget in scope. A wide audience is therefore desired (narrowcasting being eliminated as a viable option due to cost). The world abstraction must therefore be exploited to please the widest possible audience. Housekeeping activities are the best way to do this; they please Type 3 (and potentially Type 4) players, do not put off Type 1 players, and add to the play window. The problem remaining is how to polarize a Type 1 evangelist cluster—a task impossible (in the West, at least) via housekeeping activities alone. Some pathfinding activity is required, which must seem essential enough to game completion to avoid alienating the H1s, but should be optional enough for Casual players to ignore.

MECHANISMS OF PROGRESS

The chosen game world abstraction dictates the delivery method of play environments, but the progress mechanism dictates when this occurs. A fully open game in which all environments are available simultaneously (the functional equivalent of a level select cheat) is rarely a good idea, because it limits the Type 1 player's motivation for progression while confusing the Type 3 by offering too many options. Indeed, even those players not prone to agon are still motivated to progress by the desire to see something new in the game.

A secondary factor involves game position—the deeper a player is in a game, the more satisfaction they feel at further accomplishment (this might be part of the reason that very long games are liked by H1 players). Without a sense of progress, as determined by the gradual release of game features to the player, this sense of achievement is impossible.

If players are to progress, there must be some kind of progress mechanism in the game they are playing. This in turn assumes *barriers*—features that retard the player's progress and must be overcome. The term barrier cannot be applied to retardants inherent to the core gameplay—for example, the space invaders in *Space Invaders*—as this eliminates any usefulness the term has. Rather, a barrier is a feature specifically designed to mediate player progress.

Barriers are of value for numerous reasons. To the Type 1 player, they give an objective, and suggest a challenge to overcome. Barriers can be presented in the form of puzzles, which appeal to Type 2 players. To the Type 3 player, barriers provide an excuse to explore and, by limiting progress, allow the player to define their boundaries (a step important to mimicry). No player enjoys drifting through a game heedlessly, unless that game has been created with toyplay in mind.

Barriers appear to be somewhat less important to Type 4 play, because this form of play is associated with emotional participation, and, as such, players preferring this play style are less concerned with strictly physical progress. They might, however, connect to barriers in the abstract sense of meeting the needs of NPCs. In this way, a player preferring Type 4 play might become involved in overcoming a particular barrier to progress simply because a character they have an emotional link to has asked for assistance.

Barriers

In games with progress mediated through core gameplay alone, no barriers exist. The example of *Space Invaders* given previously serves here. The only thing the player needs to do to progress (and progress in this case is in terms of score as much as in "level" or position within the game) is to destroy the invaders.

The most basic levels of *Gauntlet* (Midway, 1985) feature no barriers. The players can simply hack their way to the level exit and depart. In this, the level exit serves as a justification for the core gameplay—combat occurs to make the exit available. But the game very quickly introduces doors and keys. Doors cannot be opened unless the avatar approaches them while a key exists in their key register, at which point the key and the door both disappear. Players can carry more than one key, which also open locked treasure chests (here a choice between progression and score must be made). Doors act as simple barriers and require a key item to open, although key items need not be presented in the literal form of keys.

Barriers can also be bypassed remotely, which is to say from a distance. One of the most common forms of progress limitation seen in modern games (specifically action-oriented games in which temporary barriers are required to give a sense of progress, but are never required to actually retard the player) is the switch. The player is forced to locate a switch, which, when operated, opens a door (or dissolves a barrier by some other means—lowering water levels, rotating a room, causing an explosion, etc.).

The advantages of the switch are that it is an easy concept to grasp, it encourages exploration, and it requires no in-game inventory system. The primary disadvantage is that too many switches give a game section a mechanical feel—it becomes too apparent that the player is being led through the game, which might damage the feeling of immersion (and hence damage mimicry).

Most game analysts consider both keys and switches to be simple forms of puzzles. This is a convention of language, and need not suggest any actual brainwork in progression. However, genuine puzzles can be used as barriers—either by use of specific items in specific contexts (as in classic text and point-and-click adventures—use the oil to lubricate the nut, use the wrench to turn it); via positional puzzles using objects in the world (sliding blocks, example, or a whole series of related switches); or by more abstract puzzles presented as hermetic activities, as seen in games like *Myst* (Cyan, 1994). Type 2 players are actively drawn to puzzles, and they don't damage the enjoyment of Type 1 or 3 players unless they risk causing a bottleneck, freezing the player's progress completely. At this point, Type 1 players (specifically H1s) continue to butt heads with the puzzle until they solve it, and Type 3 players explore for a while and then give up, reaching for a FAQ or strategy guide, or a different game.

The final common form of progression mechanism is the token. Platform games generally present a number of identical tokens for collection, and this forms the goal of the game. When a set number of tokens have been collected (rarely are all available tokens required), new areas are accessed. A similar form of progress is apparent in extreme sports games, epitomized by the *Tony Hawk's Pro Skater* series (Neversoft, 1999 onwards). Here tokens are replaced by missions—the player must complete a set proportion of available missions to unlock new areas.

At the far end of the token spectrum, tokens become so numerous and easily acquired that they achieve the status of a currency, which might also be used as a progress mechanism (buying new cars in *Gran Turismo* allows more races to be run, for example). The primary difference between tokens and currency is that currency is open-ended, whereas a discrete, limited number of tokens are available in a game world. Games utilizing an internal currency challenge Hardcore players to buy everything, rather than collect everything.

Tokens are popular with Casual players, who like the simplicity of goal inherent in searching for many similar objects, and who enjoy the habit of token-progression games in allowing progress without all tokens being acquired. H1 players might enjoy tokens for a related reason—that collecting *all* the tokens is a challenge. The only significant problem with tokens (other than their inability to work in a non-domain structured game) is their apparent simplicity, which might alienate some players, specifically those preferring mimicry, although it should be noted that the clarity of purpose associated with collecting tokens is hard to replace in a more immersive form.

Imaginative use of barrier structuring can lead to fresh styles of progression. Though the preceding examples constitute the core of video game progress mechanisms, less obvious options also exist. Consider *Soul Blazer* (Quintet/Enix, 1992). Here a *Zelda*-esque overworld leads to dungeons, each of which contains switches. But rather than directly access barriers, these switches cause features to appear in the overworld—primarily characters in the form of people and animals—which in turn gift the player with the keys required to progress beyond the barriers. Unfamiliar progression mechanisms might not appeal to a specific demographic (though some Hardcore players actively seek out unfamiliar game styles and features), but can contribute to a game's unique identity—a factor that is useful for games of any budget.

Key Items

Key items require a little more discussion. You have three ways of designing key items—as *symbolic keys*, as *functional keys*, and as *tool keys*. The three types can be used in parallel (as they are in most of the *Zelda* games).

Symbolic Keys

A symbolic key does not actually do anything—it is rather a trophy that corresponds with a barrier being overcome. They are usually displayed graphically on a pause or inventory screen, but have no physical role in the game world, as is the case in many of the *Zelda* games—for example, the medallions in *The Legend of Zelda: The Ocarina of Time* (Nintendo, 1998), which do nothing except symbolize the completion of a dungeon, but trigger certain changes in the game world that allow progress.

A symbolic key does not require use in any way; the player merely has to have acquired it to pass through certain boundaries or to progress beyond a particular point. Its primary use is to help player awareness of the progress scheme, acting as a token of accomplishment, and often the only reason for the symbolic key to exist is because it is a narrative manifestation of the player's achievements.

In games where the player must collect a number of identical tokens to progress (as is the norm in platform games), the tokens can be seen to be symbolic keys. The player does not do anything with the items themselves per se, they merely have to collect a certain number of them to progress, and barriers are often clearly marked with the number of tokens required to bypass them.

Functional Keys

This must be actively used by the player avatar to pass a boundary. The various themed keys in the *Resident Evil* games, such as the Fire Key or the Shield Key, are an example. In some cases, the distinction between a functional key and a symbolic key can be slight, but in general, a functional key is used by the avatar in the game world, whereas a symbolic key is never used except collectively (as in platform games with a collectible item) or in a narrative sense (it might be given to an NPC in a cut scene, but the player's avatar never actually uses it for anything).

A functional key might not be a literal key, but might be an object required for a specific situation. We call this a *lock-and-key puzzle*: a barrier blocks progress and can be opened only with an appropriate object. The barrier might be a literal door, and the object a literal key, or they might be less obvious (a battery and an electric forklift) or borderline surreal (a model tank placed in a diorama moves a real tank to reveal a secret hatch). These examples are all from *Resident Evil: Code: Veronica* (Capcom, 2000), which like the other games in the *Resident Evil* series uses lock-and-key puzzles as the primary pacing mechanism.

This style of key enhances immersion, because it creates the illusion of the player interacting with the game environment. The primary use of this style of key is to dictate a player's exploration before a barrier is accessed; if the player is able to employ the functional key to counter the barrier, it is known that any information positioned on the route to that functional key has also been encountered.

Tool Keys

This style of key gives the player avatar some ability, which might also be used to bypass barriers, an approach that was pioneered in the *Zelda* games—the hookshot allows chasms to be crossed, the bow can be used to shoot certain active targets, and so forth.

Tool keys are a very powerful for immersion, because the interaction with the environment is "real"—the player has a tool that might be used in different ways to affect the game world. Good use of such keys is a difficult design challenge, however, as each tool must have significant enough uses to be relevant to the player, and the barriers in the world must be carefully positioned and tested to make sure the player cannot slip through without the appropriate tool (potentially getting stuck).

For something to be considered a tool key, it must be genuinely useful to the player in multiple situations, not just useful because it opens doors. If it is an item whose only ability is to bypass specific barriers, it is a functional key, but it is not truly a tool key, since tool keys by their very nature give the player new abilities that they can apply in different contexts.

In terms of game structure, tool style keys combined with a world region abstraction and basic puzzle and collection progress elements provide a very immersive, distinctive gameplay experience. This is the most expensive case, however. The more complex progress elements are rarely worth using in structurally simpler games—linear level games should concentrate upon delivering enjoyable core gameplay, including only enough progress mechanics to give a sense of achievement. Overworking a simply structured game is to miss the point of a simple structure.

One of the reasons that tool keys are so powerful is that they appeal strongly to practically all players. They engender a tremendous sense of progress, which appeals to Type 1 players (especially game literate Type 1s, who understand that tools generally provide access to whole new areas of a contiguous world). Type 2 players enjoy their use in puzzles, which can be extremely satisfying when two or three different tools are required to be used in concert. Type 3 and 4 players enjoy the scope for mimicry the tools allow—they represent new toys for the player to experiment with and enjoy.

PLAYGROUND WORLDS

So far, we have related structure primarily to gameplay. However, structure is also an element of toyplay as well. The twenty-first century has already seen an explosion in a new style of game, one designed around *playground worlds*. This trend has become so pervasive that major video game marketing is based around the concept, as with *Mercenaries* (Pandemic, 2005), which features the tagline "Playground of Destruction," and *Need For Speed: Underground 2* (EA Black Box, 2004), the tagline for which is "Welcome to the Ultimate Driving Playground."

The primary drives for this movement are technology (the ability to portray a large area in a contiguous fashion without undue draw distance issues) linked to a slow but progressive diversification of the games market, as new types of player become interested in games. In essence, the marrying of a playground world with a mission spine (both created from the same core gameplay systems) allows a wedding of agonistic and mimicry-oriented gameplay. The mission spine might be enjoyed by agonistic H1, H2, C1, and C2 players, while the playground provides ample expressibility for H3, H4, C3, and C4 players.

This diversity of play style might be understood in terms of pathfinding and housekeeping. Agonistic, Type 1 and 2 play is primarily focused in the mission spine, as players push further and further on into the game, attempting to be ahead of the difficulty curve. Pathfinding activities suit this style of play well—a mission spine presenting challenging activities meets this need, as does linear exploration into new territory. This suggests that some areas of the game environment should be left out of the player's hands until certain goals are met, though it is essential that the area available to the player from the start of the game is sufficiently large to support playground exploration and activities.

Mimicry, meanwhile, is uninterested in ideas of where the player "should" be within the game space. The point of this approach to play is to allow for involvement via the assumption of an alternative identity, something that works well in a playground filled with toys. Players preferring this type of play actively want to become familiar with their surroundings, something encouraged by housekeeping activities. It should be noted that housekeeping requires some optional goal to be apparent; collecting items is a good task to set, specifically without agonistic concerns such as time limits. A currency system allows housekeeping activities to remain flexible, because the player can always be rewarded in terms of the currency, no matter how small that reward. For players enjoying Type 3, process-oriented play, a simple pat on the head is often all that is required.

It is also easier to support process-oriented play (and by extension, Type 2 and Type 3 play) in a game that presents the whole environment to the player. If, when the first time the player encounters an environment, they are challenged to complete it, the player is likely to be forced to fail several times before they succeed (which is acceptable when Type 1 play is intended, but not when the audience is more diverse). Conversely, a playground world allows the player to build up familiarity through the natural osmosis of being in the world. In *Need for Speed Underground 2*, for example, players race in the same city that they travel around between races. Familiarity of routes is built up without the player being placed in a situation where failure is an option. This has the added benefit of smoothing both the learning curve and the difficulty curve of the game, which benefits Casual players immensely.

Ultimately, playground worlds are a product of structural expansion. The idea that a player must earn all their tools and rewards has been challenged; instead, players might be forced to work for tangible progression, but the majority of tools required in this are also available in other contexts, to be used however the player wants. Structure is concerned with the delivery of game materials to the player; five years ago, few people would have considered placing those materials in front of the player and letting them get on with it.

BREADCRUMBING AND FUNNELING

The term *breadcrumbing* describes the art of laying a distinct trail for the player to follow. This might be physical, as with a line of pick ups leading to an important environmental feature, or might take place in the narrative layer of the game, with NPCs within the game clearly directing the player along the spine of the game progression.

Funneling is of use in games with housekeeping or playground activities beyond the spine of progression. Funneling involves the player's being given clues and hints that, if followed, lead back to the game spine. This means that if players have spent a long time involved with nonprogression related activities, they can still find out what to do next and won't have to wander aimlessly until they stumble upon the next step in the progression spine.

Funneling can be performed in a direct fashion. For example, the player can be led to a checkpoint with an arrow, but then the player might feel obligated to follow the arrow, and so the game lacks the freedom to allow the player to involve themselves in other activities. Similarly, having the places where the next event on the game spine occurs clearly marked (as in the *GTA* series of games) is an example of a game world abstraction where the need for funneling has been minimized.

When funneling is absent, the result is that working out what to do next becomes a puzzle, and as such any game attempting to do this is likely to favor Type 2 play and specifically exclude Type 3 or 4 play, which is associated with a low tolerance for not knowing what to do next. This can be seen clearly with the *Fatal Frame* games (Tecmo, 2001 onwards), which feature a beautifully constructed breadcrumbing system that connects the game spine with both puzzles and atmospheric spot events, but which lacks the funneling to guide the player back to the path should they stray from it.

Examples of funneling failure takes place in *Legend of Zelda: The Wind Waker* (Nintendo, 2002) and is noticeable due to the otherwise extremely robust set of player aids in that game. Only one essential item, a map necessary to locate and board the mysterious ghost ship, has no game pointers toward it, relying instead on the player's remembering which islands they have fully explored. This oversight is uncharacteristic of a Nintendo game and is presumably due to the development contraction experienced by the *Wind Waker* team.

A specifically useful funneling technique for narrative games is to include one NPC within the game who always gives advice to the player. The player can be taught the function of this character in the early stages of the game, and can then return at any time if they get lost or stuck. It is essential that the help character always remains available to the player and that they are given sufficient dialogue to be useful. Player-solicited dialogue of this nature might give as many hints as possible, because players who do not need help need not access it, and so will not feel as though the game is being made too easy, as they might feel if the help is given by other means.

If a game has a structure complex enough to allow the player to get lost or stuck, or drift from the game spine for long periods of time (and a game doesn't have to be very complex for this to be possible), help is a required element. Breadcrumbing and funneling are powerful tools in the quest to negate player frustration.

REPLAY FEATURES

Game length is an issue provoking considerable debate in the games industry. Hardcore players, in part, judge a game by the amount of time they are allowed to be involved. Additionally, to achieve maximum propagation and sales to the Casual demographics, a game must have a significant enough play window to allow Hardcore players to evangelize games effectively. A short game, or one low on bonus content, does not absorb hardcore players for long enough for their Casual friends to become interested, but a long game is expensive to create and might not court a large enough audience to justify its costs.

In general, features that extend the play window of a game are termed replay features. This is a term common among Hardcore players, and user reviews regularly consider replay value of a game, though the exact meaning of the term does provide certain levels of confusion—can, for example, a game that you have not enjoyed playing still warrant replay? This chapter holds to the general definition that if a feature is intended to extend play window, then it is a "replay" feature, whether it has anything to do with actual replay or not.

Long games are more expensive. The majority of game styles do not support extensive play. Game narrative often cannot support itself when required to stay relevant for more than 8 to 10 hours of play. Additionally, many Casual players are happy to replay games that they have enjoyed many, many times, as long as those games do not deviate radically from an enjoyable core gameplay experience—and regularly stop playing games that do not present such core gameplay a long time before their natural end. These factors all suggest that increased play windows are best achieved via "bonus" features rather than extended game spines.

Traditional replay features, such as cheats, easter eggs, extra costumes, extra tools and toys (such as new cars in racing games), and unlockable modes tend to be presented upon game completion, or after specific tasks have been completed (such as a championship having been won in a sports or racing title). Though this style of replay feature is valuable, it relies upon significant player interest in the game to fuel replay. While H2 players might want to master their games, and therefore experiment with all possible features, H3 players are more likely to buy a new game than replay an old one. On the other hand, if goals relating to replay features can be set within gameplay, Hardcore players are highly likely to count these features as "essential" to achieving closure on a game, and so are more inclined to pursue them—extending the game's play window.

Perhaps the strongest way to present replay features as goals is as part of a playground world. Optional goals can be presented in a housekeeping fashion, and these goals might be pursued in-game, simultaneous to progress. These goals have the secondary value that players bored or confused by the game spine can stay within game, distract themselves with nonessential play, and then return to the spine when refreshed. It goes without saying, however, that such subgoals should utilize core gameplay systems, and not require new materials (as these imply considerable added expense).

The current acme for integration of replay features via a playground world is *GTA: San Andreas* (Rockstar North, 2004). Sub-missions based around being a vigilante, fire-fighting, taxis, ambulances, and even pimping all use core gameplay features, but have a feel that is distinct from the spine missions in the game. Exploration is also well used, with the game world featuring numerous unexpected features, such as base jumping, which is immediately suggested to the player when they discover a parachute set atop a particularly tall building. Rewards are generally quite modest, and do not seriously unbalance the game, but provide a sense of completion for the player.

The aesthetics of the game also contribute to extending the play window. The soundtrack and the beautiful scenery (enhanced by an often extremely orange day/night cycle) promote long-term cruising. The cars, though not significantly different (or always useful) from a gameplay point of view, provide enough variety to drive exploration, and challenge certain player types to drive them all at least once. Secret vehicles are also obviously a great help. But the key issue in *San Andreas* is that these replay features are accessed by the player during gameplay—they do not emerge between games, or in any fashion external to the game world.

Replay features of this kind do not require a contiguous world or domain abstraction. Games with a linear level structure can make use of this kind of approach when a hermetic level structure is used—if the player is free to access any level currently achieved for replay. *GoldenEye 007* (Rare, 1997) provides an excellent blueprint for this, with each level posing multiple tasks depending upon the difficulty level selected, and an unlockable cheat (often "toylike" in nature, such as paintball mode) also available as an additional challenge. Small visual flourishes like hidden cheese also help, as does the range of situations available from the toolset provided (using mines to blow up NPCs in cutscenes, for example).

The primary advantage of linear level structures is the amount of familiarity the player is allowed to gain in each level (for this reason, a greater number of small levels is preferable to fewer large levels). This can be exploited in many minor ways to encourage the player to mess around in their favorite levels again and again. It should be noted, however, that replay in linear level games is primarily a Hardcore tendency.

The hardest structure to exploit in this way is the continuous level structure. Players are expected to progress from one end of the game to the other, with little deviation. Play window in PC FPS games is extended primarily via multiplayer functionality, which suits an agonistic Type 1 and 2 audience, but has less appeal to Type 3 players. Type 4 players might play agonistic multiplayer games, but rarely online, because they lack the emotional context and immediacy that is generally required to feel a sense of participation.

SAVE GAME FUNCTIONALITY

Game saving has a great impact upon structural design. Many different styles of save systems are possible, and they all impact upon gameplay in a different manner. Additionally, certain systems are not suitable for certain audiences. A designer has to consider their save system at an early point in development.

One point of interest—rarely do you have a good reason to drop a player out of the game completely. Too many titles tend, upon player death, to revert to the title screen. This incurs loading times, puts a non-game barrier between the player and the play experience, and can alienate players. In games that do not provide in-game restarts (if they're attempting to appeal to H1 players, for example—no great reason exists to ever completely kill Casual players), a load option should be supplied at the point of game termination.

Save Anywhere

This save system is commonly used in PC games, especially FPS games. The player can save anywhere, and load at any time.

This save system is less common on consoles, primarily for technical reasons. The designer should be aware of technical issues when designing any save system, with the primary concern being the amount of data that is required to be saved. This impacts upon design—if the design requires objects to be dropped by the player and then retrieved, for example, the location data for each item must be saved, which expands the file (and also introduces testing issues).

You also face design issues with the "save anywhere" system. If the player can save anywhere, they might be tempted to save constantly. This breaks up the game flow and is generally unsatisfying (though it must be noted that H1 and H2 players generally don't mind this, and often actively prefer it to a designed save system, because it allows them to manipulate the save system for their own ends). If the game is difficult, short sections of fail/repeat gameplay are interspersed with save time. If the game is easy, the player might neglect to save and then be taken by surprise and be killed. This is generally irritating. A checkpoint save system can be implemented as an autosave to provide backup files for players for such circumstances, though this is something of an afterthought.

The other significant issue with a "save anywhere" system is that the player is required to judge whether or not it is "safe" for them to save. Less of a problem on PC, where multiple save files can be kept in parallel, this becomes quite significant upon console platforms, because it is possible that the player has only one save file (constantly rewriting it—especially if the file is big, as space on memory cards tends to be at a premium). If the player rewrites their one file just before an unforeseen accident happens, their game is over for good. Similarly, if the player saves without sufficient health or ammo (or similar resources) to progress, they might be forced to resort to a cheat to progress, which is never satisfying.

Games intended for anything other than an H1 or H2 audience should never incorporate a "save anywhere" system, as this system cedes all responsibility for game saving to the player—and many player types, including all Casuals (with the possible exception of C1), refuse to shoulder the responsibility inherent in being given the task of determining when to save the game.

Quicksave

The majority of "save anywhere" systems also incorporate a *quicksave*—hitting a control (or selecting a menu option on console) instantly saves the game to a dedicated quicksave file. The problems with this style of quicksave are therefore identical to that of the "save anywhere" system.

Other quicksave systems are possible. On console platforms, a quicksave usually takes the form of a RAM save, keeping progress in memory but not saving to memory card. If the machine is switched off (or crashes), progress is lost. This style of save is really justified only in very fail-repeat oriented games, such as *Abe's Exoddus* (Oddworld Inhabitants, 1998). These games are by definition of interest only to H1 players, so giving players responsibility for saving isn't such a big issue.

Quicksaves don't interrupt game flow as severely as full "save anywhere" systems, as save times are quicker. But they still alter the psychological flavor of games, giving a safety net feel that can damage certain games styles. Although empowering the player is a noble goal, quicksaves should be used cautiously, and as part of the game design, never to fix up difficulty balance issues or other design related problems.

Save Points

Save points are specific points within the game environment at which the player can choose to save. Saves can be limited (as seen in the *Resident Evil* series; see the section on "Limited Saves" later in the chapter).

This system allows good control of the data to be saved and allows for more controlled pacing of the game. However, save point systems usually dictate the replaying of game materials after a death, something that is unpopular with practically any type of player, especially those who prefer Type 3 play—their bias towards seeking experience through mimicry can be severely damaged by being forced to replay game sections. Save points also limit functional saving—for players with concerns other than video games, who might need to stop playing at a given moment, without having to work through the game to the next point.

Save points also generate a strange form of "scouting" play among certain players. After saving, the player quickly runs forward to see what comes next, scouts the area, and then reloads. This is not a problem per se, because only players who feel gain from such an activity will perform it. However, it might conflict with a designer's attempts to generate emotional content to their game, such as surprises and tension.

Save points provide a good, all-around save system appropriate for most games with linear or continuous level structures, and might be appropriate to some world abstraction games. It is usually better to have too many save points than too few, though pacing is an issue, because players are likely to save at each point, and so their emotional state alters depending on ease of save.

Some save points can be used only once. This is generally a poor system. Though it does generate tension, it also includes saving as part of the core gameplay of the product, and this form of "rationing" gameplay is generally unappealing to most players (H1s being the exception—rationed save points can be included in the strategic optimization process).

Checkpoint Saves

A *checkpoint save* is similar to a save point system, except that checkpoint saves automatically save game data. Upon death, the player character is returned to the last checkpoint they crossed. They usually have no choice in which checkpoint to use. Checkpoint saves do not save permanently (that is, they save only to RAM)— autosaves (see the next section) perform this function. As such, a permanent save system is also required (usually a hermetic save system; see the section on hermetic saves later in the chapter).

Checkpoint saves are easy on the player, and easy to understand. Their great advantage over save point systems is that the player might be allowed to retain all nonphysical progress data—that is, they can be allowed to keep objects picked up before death, changes to character setup, and so forth. This is highly recommended, because the only loss is in physical position—enough of a setback to satisfy H1 players (who require to be slapped on the wrist for failing or they question the challenge level of the game) but is not so much of a loss that Casual players can't absorb it.

Like save points, placing of checkpoints becomes an issue. They are highly functional for linear progression games, but less linear games (which might feature circuitous environments) can cause problems in logical checkpoint placing. Games of this nature often force the player to question why they were returned to a certain spot. Pacing issues are also important.

Checkpoints can be visible or invisible. Hardcore players seem to prefer visible checkpoints, while Casual players don't appear to care greatly, as long as visible checkpoints don't interfere with the perceived reality of the game.

Autosave

Like a checkpoint system, an *autosave* records data at specific points in play. However, autosave systems record permanent files—which might incur technical problems on console formats, because it is preferable not to hold up play, especially if saving is frequent.

Autosaves can be tied to physical location (acting like automatic save points), but more usually occur after specific events within the game world. Saving after a specific object is collected or task completed is sensible. Because saving is permanent, autosaves cannot retain game activities accomplished after saving, and so should be designed to retain all vital game events.

Autosaves have few problems when implemented correctly, but are more time consuming to get right. In addition, H1 players might be frustrated by a perceived lack of control in saving. For PC games, it might be wise to allow a secondary player-solicited save system as well as an autosave, as this accounts for most player biases.

Hermetic Saves

A *hermetic save* records only the player's progress data, but no world data—that is, the avatar's state is saved, but not the state of the game world. Because only progress data is saved, these saves tend to be small. In addition, this save system is perfect for Casual players (and the majority of platform games use this system)—all they need do is save before they switch off after a play session, with no need to juggle files or make qualitative decisions regarding the necessity of saving. The only down side is that some players complain when their save file doesn't restore their avatar to the position it was at when saving took place. This is strictly a minor quibble. Hermetic saves are not suitable for every game, but where suitable they are almost always a preferable option.

In a game structured with discrete levels, the hermetic save occurs once a level has been completed. Each level might have to be completed in one run, with failure necessitating a restart, or the save system might be implemented with a checkpoint system at work in-level. Either way, it is usual to force players to complete a level before switching off or lose their current level data. This system is perfectly adequate for the simple game structure it applies to. Its great advantage is that because no level data is required to be saved, saves can be small, a great boon on console, where memory card space is far from generous.

For domain and world region abstraction games you face the issue of where the avatar is to begin. It is usual to specify one domain of these games as the "hub" and replace the player in the hub upon loading.

Save Slots

Save slots are primarily related to hermetic saves and autosaves, but of relevance to all save types, specifically on consoles. If the game is to be saved by rewriting one file continually, it is vital to provide the player with more than one slot to save in, because more than one player might want to play using the same memory card. It is usual for players to create a save file upon starting a game, name it, then use it for the duration of the game.

Limited Saves

In theory, all of the previous systems can also use *limited saves*, but in practice this is most pertinent to save anywhere and save point systems. By limiting the number of saves available (either by providing items which grant limited saves, or by providing save points with limited saves) tension is maintained—the player can choose to save, but must treat saves as a resource, and so cannot save all the time.

This technique can work to a degree, if save numbers are high enough. *Resident Evil* games tend to provide plenty of saves, but use the number of saves as a scoring factor (thus bullying the Hardcore into saving less often). Casual players do not like these systems, however, as decisions regarding saving are never fun for them—to the Casual player, saving is a functional necessity, not part of the game.

The *Tomb Raider* series (Core et al, 1996 onwards) illustrates these issues. The original game used once-only save points, and the sequel used a save anywhere system. Advocates of the sweaty-palmed tension of the initial game claimed that the second game lacked tension due to the new system (in addition, difficulty was increased as an attempt at balance, which served only to create a massively fail-repeat experience). The third game in the series used pick-ups to provide limited saves, theoretically giving the player more choice over saving. In practice, save anywhere systems coupled with limited saves tend to encourage the player to keep one save in stock, but otherwise save when a new save object is found. The fourth *Tomb Raider* game reverted to the save anywhere system.

Halfway versions of limited saves have been attempted. *Extermination* (Deepspace, 2001) supplies the player with a battery, which is used in-game as a key object and to facilitate saving. The battery has limited charge, but can be recharged. If the player wants to do multiple actions with their battery and is nowhere near a recharge point, they might have to make decisions as to whether to progress or to save. In practice, this system doesn't work, because in order to remain fair, recharge points are quite easily found. All the system does is force players to recharge after every save or load, which is tedious (a similar situation to replacing one's ink cartridges back in the box after saving or loading in *Resident Evil*).

Bookmark

The *bookmark* save creates a single save file upon quitting the game. Upon loading, this file is destroyed. This means that the player can save anywhere, but cannot exploit this fact to act as a "safety net." A checkpoint system or similar is also necessary.

Hardcore players often don't like this system, but it suits Casual players well, and in fact makes a great deal of sense. Where hermetic saves and autosaves are not suitable, a bookmark save is well worth considering. It eliminates the stop-start play usually associated with save anywhere systems, allows players to stop play whenever they want, and provides few disadvantages. The timing of the destruction of the bookmark is an issue, however. Destroy upon loading, and crashes destroy entire games. But destroy upon saving, and hardcore players might be tempted to switch off the console and reload under certain circumstances. This latter is by far the lesser of two evils.

CONCLUSION

Structural design is as vital to a video game as mechanical design and is tied very closely to game world abstraction. Though enjoyable core gameplay is vital to any game, without a complementary structure, potential is lost.

While designing structure, the designer must be aware of their core gameplay and how best to complement it in structure. Simple gameplay can be improved and extended in lifespan by a supportive structure, based around player character enhancement or enjoyable progress mechanics. At the same time, the target audience must be considered when contemplating all aspects of the structure. If the audience is unlikely to play for more than an hour at a time, using a save point system is unlikely to be the best solution for the game save issues, for example.

When targeting the Hardcore audience, the structure of the game is dictated by the relevant play styles the game is intended to appeal to, and save mechanisms probably need to include at least some element that is mediated by the player. Conversely, a Casual audience is probably best served by a playground world structure and an automatic save system of some kind (autosave or hermetic save). The Casual player should also be able to stop playing at any time—either because of a hermetic save system or because a bookmark save is provided. Limited saves should be avoided for a Casual audience.

When players of Type 1 disposition are part of the game's audience, pathfinding play should be provided in some form. When targeting a Type 1 audience in isolation, a linear level structure is probably sufficient, and a quicksave system is probably advisable because it allows for victory to be won by optimization of saves—it might also be desirable to limit saves to increase tension and hence the payoff of fiero upon completing a challenge.

The Type 2 audience seems to thrive in an open environment, where many choices are available in parallel and the player need not be faced with a bottleneck when they face a specific problem they cannot overcome. Housekeeping and pathfinding activities are both enjoyed, barriers can be allowed to function as puzzles, and any save system is probably sufficient.

Type 3 players appear to thrive on housekeeping activities, and therefore a domain or contiguous world with a variety of activities supported must be considered a preferred approach. The mechanism by which a barrier is overcome should generally be explicitly made known to the player and should never be a puzzle. The save schema for an audience that is primarily Type 3 in preference should follow the guidelines for targeting a Casual audience—it should part of the background architecture of the game and not part of the gameplay.

Players preferring a Type 4 play style might benefit from a playground world, and like Type 3 players, seem to enjoy housekeeping activities, with little desire for barriers to be presented as puzzles. It is preferable for barriers to be presented to such players in the context of characters within the game world, rather than relying on the player's natural desire to overcome obstacles that are encountered.

By considering the structural needs of different players, you can determine the optimal structures for different games—you are able to use cheap-to-produce linear structures when the audience will not balk at such an approach and provide the diverse benefits of a playground world only when the game's audience is sufficiently large to justify the expense. In this way, consideration of structure contributes to the designer's aim of satisfying the needs of the participants of the design process, by respecting both the financial issues of the developer and publisher and the play needs of the audience itself.

11 Action Game Genres

It is in the nature of media that they become organically sorted into genres—categories or types of game. Movies, for example, are divided into genres such as action, comedy, romance, and musical; computer games have become similarly classified into broad genre categories, such as shooter, driving, adventure, and platform game.

International Hobo Ltd. uses a certain set of genre categories when it talks about games, and the definitions provided in this chapter draw from that background, which is based in part on historical factors. But the reader should bear in mind that another organization, Web site, magazine, or individual can quite validly have an entirely different way of defining what constitutes a particular genre—you find no right or wrong when it comes to language.

Given that, genre terms have two primary uses:

- To provide terminological shortcuts, allowing for the discussion of games without constantly describing the contents of each game
- To provide aid to game developers, publishers, and players—game creators can use the terms to analyze taste trends in players, while game-literate players can use genre terms while looking for suitable games to purchase

It is this second use that is of interest to this volume. Few game-literate players fail to recognize their own genre preferences. It is logical to expect that an analysis of game genre with relation to audience might tell us something about those audiences. But before such analysis can begin, we must establish the genre terms under discussion.

DESCRIBING GENRES

To accurately discuss genre from the perspective of market-oriented design, we must consider the meaning of the genre terms as applied to the games they describe. Why is a given game of a given genre? What do we mean when we use that genre term?

Genre Nucleation

Ultimately, like all words, genre categories are defined by their usage. We have no absolute way of saying which games belong to a genre, because genres are by necessity defined abstractly. An individual player can argue as much as they want about the definition of a genre, but other people might still tend to use the words in particular ways. Over the years the genres become defined solely in the way they are used. Genre terms might therefore change in meaning with time—as seen with the concept of "adventure" games. Older players who remember the heyday of text and point-and-click adventures tend to relate the genre term to those games, whereas younger gamers associate the term "adventure" with action/exploration games like *Legend of Zelda: Ocarina of Time* (Nintendo, 1998) or *Tomb Raider* (Core, 1996).

A genre term usually emerges when a sufficient number of games exist that are similar enough to require an umbrella term to describe them. The term itself might be coined in many ways, but traditionally the video game specialist press suggests terms, one of which then catches on with the rest of the gaming audience. Often video game companies attempt to suggest genre terms that suit them (by emphasizing the strengths or unique aspects of their games), though these terms might not catch on. *Resident Evil* (Capcom, 1996) successfully coined the genre term "survival horror" via text within the game itself. KOEI's desire to label their *Dynasty Warriors* games (Omega Force, 2000 onwards) as "battlefield combat" games has largely failed, at least in the West, perhaps due to the lack of similar product from other companies.

Games with elements comparable to those seen in the staple games of a genre might have existed before a genre term in coined. As a famous example, *Alone in the Dark* (Infogrames, 1992) existed before *Resident Evil* and shared a number of features, including prerendered backdrops, polygonal characters, a design oriented towards atmosphere, and a horror theme in narrative. But there can be no doubt that *Resident Evil* coined the genre term itself.

It is suggested, therefore, that rather than discuss which game was the first example of a given genre (an entertaining but fruitless task), the game that nucleates a given genre term is given conceptual precedence. The point of this rather abstract exercise is to create a yardstick by which to measure terminological slippage within genre terms. Like all language, genre terms are not fixed, and their meaning changes with time. By asserting that a single game (where possible) nucleates a genre, users of the term can monitor how changed the meaning of the term has become over time.

For example, in the case of the survival horror genre, the term has slowly stretched to encompass practically all games with horror-oriented narrative elements. Games such as *Silent Hill* (Konami, 1999) and *Fatal Frame* (Tecmo, 2001) share obvious similarities with *Resident Evil* (in their progress abstractions—the use of puzzles—and in their commitment to atmosphere via a specific visual projection), while other horror games such as *Clive Barker's Undying* (Dreamworks, 2001)—an FPS in style and sharing few design features with *Resident Evil*—are often considered to be "survival horror" games based upon their narrative content alone. More peculiarly, games featuring resemblances of form with establish survival horror games, such as *Disaster Report* (Irem, 2002)—a 3D third-person action adventure set in an earthquake-beset city—sometimes become included within that genre because no other genre term is more appropriate.

Genre Content

Once a genre-nucleating game is recognized, we can proceed to an analysis of game features. Analysis of aspects of design (both in terms of game world abstraction and in terms of structure) can shed much light on both the use of genres and their relative popularity with certain audiences.

Unlike movie genre terms, which are always based upon the expected narrative content of a product, game genre terms can refer to many different aspects of games. In brief, genre terms usually consist of one or more elements in the following categories:

- Input by control method (as in light-gun shooter or point-and-click adventure)
- Output by projection (first-person shooter, vert-scrolling shooter)
- Core activity (shooter, puzzle game)
- Narrative elements (survival horror, sports)
- Common game elements (platform game, maze game)

The genre term, then, gives a broad idea of game content. Further design elements must be analyzed on a case-by-case basis. Genres must exist because games demonstrate similar features to one another; it is these aspects of similarity that can be said to define that genre.

A note regarding "hybrids": genre discussion often uses hybrid genres—*Deus Ex* (Ion Storm, 2000) might represent a genre hybrid of FPS and RPG, for example. Hybrid genre terms are widely used and again help us understand what makes a genre. In the case of *Deus Ex*, the form of the game and its core activities are identical to a standard FPS. Its structure, however, (primarily its avatar modification layer) is more similar to an RPG structure than an FPS structure, giving it an unquestionable RPG "feel."

Use of Genre Terms

As mentioned previously, two primary advantages are granted by the use of genre terms; to allow for discussion (as considered by the definition concepts mentioned earlier) and to aid developers, publishers, and players as a tool for marketing or purchasing a game of specific content. This second point warrants some discussion.

Genre categories can be helpful because they help identify certain markets. An FPS has a certain audience of gamers, and an RPG has another, different audience. It helps game publishers to think in terms of genre, because by judging the size of the audience for a particular game, publishers can allocate appropriate development funds according to how much they hope to make from the sale of the game.

From the point of view of Hardcore gamers (and other game-literate players), genre categories help them identify the types of games they like. If a player played a certain game and enjoyed it, they want to find similar games to play in the future. Genres are a convenient shorthand to help players find the games they want to play.

The danger of thinking too rigidly in terms of game genres is that many games can be very difficult to associate with a specific genre. This can lead to certain games' struggling to get made or to sell, because of rigid thinking about genre categories. The limiting of creative features to better resemble genre norms is another danger.

In an ideal world, a great game would be a great game irrespective of its genre (although what a "great game" means without respect to audience is hard to say). Realistically, any game that attempts to push the limits of a genre category suffers some problems, and often those games that push too far from what has gone before suffer from a confused sense of identity, as disparate elements fail to integrate into a cohesive whole. However, those that succeed in the ambiguous middle ground often form new genres, and succeed beyond the extent of their peers.

Of course, it is in this area where audience analysis can be useful. How far can a game targeted at, for example, H1-only players (for example, a low budget game with a highly agonistic form) be pushed in terms of genre content? How "indefinable" can a game targeted at the widest possible market seem to be? It seems, for example, that C1 players require familiar game features to become enthusiastic about a game—or to be told by the Hardcore that it is absolutely unmissable.

On the other hand, logic suggests that the more intuitive Hardcore players do not need genre familiarity to be interested in a game. This might be considered true to an extent, but anecdotal evidence suggests that many Hardcore players buy games based upon the sort of game they feel like playing, usually described in genre terms—"I'd like to play an RPG." Similarly, many Hardcore players have favorite genres that become so highly prioritized that they have little time to explore new concepts in games, open though they might be to new content.

Perhaps the most curious observation on this subject relates to C3 and C4 players. These Casual players are generally considered to be less game-literate than others—in the case of C4 players, they might have enjoyed only isolated cases of video games in the past, such as dance mat games—and might not relate different styles of games at all. In this case, every new game approached is completely unfamiliar. The curious C4, then, is by definition almost totally open to games of genres completely indefinable (and therefore potentially off-putting) to more game-literate players.

Of course, as noted in previous chapters, current game sales to C3 and C4 players must either hit an evangelizing Hardcore demographic (to legitimize the game), have a huge marketing spend, or achieve direct exposure through some other mechanism (such as the placement of arcade cabinet dancing games in cinemas and malls). Games of indistinct genre might have trouble penetrating an evangelizing cluster, and publishers are unlikely to strongly market a game of a genre unfamiliar to them. As such, the open-mindedness of the Casual clusters cannot currently be exploited to drive innovation in games without some difficulty.

GENRE CLASSIFICATION

This chapter and the next present discussions regarding popularly used genre terms. These do not intend to present a complete, robust system of genre definitions. As discussed, genre terms are defined by their use. However, many genre terms have accreted so successfully (via use by the specialist press and via uptake by

Hardcore players discussing games on the Internet) that they can be considered to be universally accepted. These genres then provide a framework for the discussion of other, less easily defined games.

Traditional genre divisions begin, historically, with the division between action (or arcade) games and adventure games. The key difference between the two is in their attitude to time. *Action games* occur in real time; *adventure games* do not. In terms of early games, *Spacewar!* (S. Russell and Co., 1962) represents the emergence of action games while *Adventure* (W. Crowther and co., 1972 onwards) represents adventure games. Other early game genre separations emerged at this very early stage in game development—strategy and simulation. Strategy games were played in turn-based forms and resembled traditional table-top war games and board games. Simulation games (almost exclusively flight sims in the early days) presented real-time (but traditionally very slow) interfaces to present realistic mimicry.

When arcade games became ever-more popular with the introduction of *Pong* (Atari, 1976), *Space Invaders* (Taito, 1978), and *Pac-Man* (Namco, 1980), the length of time required to play games became their greatest separator in terms of genre; action games were played in arcades, as that form required short, adrenaline-fueled experiences to generate cash flow, while the slower game styles (adventure, strategy, and simulation) were played on computers (initially mainframes, later PCs and home computers). This created a schism between the video game and the computer game that remains to this day, though modern PCs host action games and some of the most popular game genres on console (such as RPGs) take a long time to play, and do not require fast reflexes.

Further divisions in genre terms became common as more games were created. Often, new terms were coined in response to narrative material in games (for example, racing games), in terms of core gameplay activity (shooters), or in terms of prominent game features (platform games, or platformers—presumably the term jumping games was too simplistic to be satisfying). Where game activities were identical in two different forms of game (for example, shooting takes place in both top-down vert-scrolling shooters and FPS games, but the two forms are very different and, importantly, have different audiences), more complex terms arose.

In modern games, the classic genres can be seen in many different forms and combined in many ways. This has necessitated even further genre divisions, and new terms continually spring up to describe game types made possible by the advance of technology (at the time of writing a solid term for *GTA*-style city-based driving games has not fully nucleated, but this genre has enough examples to solidify as soon as a suitable term is coined).

In discussion of genre terms, this chapter looks at broad ranging categories, such as "shooter" (itself an occupant of an even larger category term, action games) and then considers the various genres within these forms. In the case of shooters, this includes FPS, scroller, light-gun, and so forth. The term genre is applied in both cases, because we purposefully want to avoid suggesting a hierarchical taxonomy.

This chapter considers action games, those games played in real time, while the following chapter discusses adventure, strategy, and simulation games—traditionally played outside of real time, or at a significantly restricted pace. This division is largely artificial; it is designed for ease of use and once again should not be used to suggest any form of taxonomy.

ACTION GAMES

As has previously been noted in this volume, the genre of action games is not very descriptive, and so not very useful. However, it is still in common currency due to its value in separating reaction-based (or "twitch") games from other styles— having developed from arcade game content. In practice, the term *action game* usually denotes real-time control on the part of the player, and fast reactions might not be a prerequisite to play.

Because of the real-time bias of action games, Type 1 and 3 play styles might be better catered for than Type 2 (although many C2 players have similar abilities to C1 players and cross over into action games more readily). This is not to say that Type 2-oriented players cannot master fast action challenges; rather, the real-time elements necessitate simpler game styles that might fail to stimulate Type 2 players, especially H2s, as much as more broad-ranging, slower games.

Common genres with the action games category include the following: shooting games, platformers, fighting games, racing games, stealth games, and survival horror. Though many puzzle games such as *Tetris* (A. Pazhitnov, 1985) or *Bust a Move* (Taito, 1995) are played in real time and benefit from good reactions, they are conventionally included in the puzzle genre.

Shooters

Shooters are also known as shmups (short for shoot-em-ups), primarily in the U.K. where the term was coined by the shooter-happy editorial staff of seminal Commodore 64 magazine *Zzap 64*.

The shooter is one of the easiest genres to dissect in terms of content; if the player is shooting things, the game is likely to be a shooter. The exceptions to this primitive rule occur when a different genre content occludes the shooting portion. For example, most survival horror games include guns, but shooting is rarely the core game activity. Similarly, flight sims featuring war planes involve shooting, but their simulation element overrides the shooting from a genre point of view.

Due to the agonistic gameplay inherent to shooting, Type 1 play is well supported by this genre. It is clear that, while not all shooting play is biased towards a

Type 1 style, the popularity of this style of game among very Hardcore players has led to a general bias in shooting games towards Type 1 play, with much fail-repeat optimization, strategizing through prior knowledge, and a high level of challenge being widely demonstrated.

Classic Shooters

Nucleating game: *Space Invaders* (Taito, 1978)

A wholly invented term, *classic shooters* here is intended to denote the more basic shooting games in the history of the arcades—primarily *Space Invaders* and its offshoots, such as *Galaxians* (Namco, 1979), *Gorf* (Midway, 1981), *Phoenix* (Centuri, 1980), and *Tempest* (Atari, 1980), as well as other early shooting games such as *Asteroids* (Atari, 1979).

The key difference between the classic shooters and more complex forms of the genre lies in their structure. The early games are primarily progression-free (though *Phoenix* and *Gorf* feature a small number of different single-screen levels), and player skill lies in survival while generating scores. In terms of form, all of these games use a single screen to present the action; there is no scrolling or "off-screen territory."

These games are of little relevance today beyond their historical importance. The *Space Invaders* form evolved via scrolling into vert and horizontally scrolling shooters, while *Asteroids* (itself derived from *Spacewar!*) evolved into more complex vector thrust games such as *Oids* (FTL Games, 1987), and from there into the 3D domain in 3D space shooters.

Horizontally Scrolling Shooters

Nucleating games: *Nemesis/Gradius* (Konami, 1985)

Horizontally scrolling shooters present a 2D side-on third-person view to the player, typically involving movement from left to right. Though *Defender* (Williams, 1980) predates *Scramble* (Konami, 1981) and did nucleate a sub-genre of sorts that involved both left and right scrolling—including *Stargate* (Williams, 1981) and *Dropzone* (A. Maclean, 1985), both *Defender* clones—it had very little influence upon the development of the genre, which has been dominated by *Nemesis* (which was also released as *Gradius*, the name to which this sequence of games is now referred).

Scramble challenges the player to navigate multiple levels, signified by changing colors, terrain, and enemies. *Nemesis* ups the ante by including one of the first power-up systems seen in arcade games—collect glowing pods to advance a power-up ladder and choose when to select the highlighted bonus. The dynamic of collecting power ups and surviving multiple levels defines the genre even at the time of writing. Until the advent of 3D graphics, horizontal scrollers were one of the most popular game genres. It is likely that this style of game was appealing to H1 and C1 players until 3D graphics allowed for more identifiable scenarios in games. At the time of writing only H1 players care for this style of shooter, and then only rarely. Though 2D shooters aren't entirely lacking in interest to H3 players, vert shooters are more likely to appeal on account of fundamentally different biases in play, which we will discuss in the next section.

Later horizontal shooters include *R-Type* (Irem, 1987), which, like *Nemesis*, oriented its gameplay around a very identifiable power-up system—in this case the Force, possibly the most flexible game tool ever seen in a shooter. The legacy of this game theoretically came to a close with *R-Type Final* (Irem, 2004), which demonstrates both that the horizontal scroller is still a valid form today and that very little development has occurred within it since the 1980s. However, the *Gradius* series is still extant. *Nemesis* was followed by *Salamander* (Konami, 1986), which combined both horizontal and vertically scrolling shooting sections, and continued to produce sequels through to at least *Gradius V* (Treasure/Konami, 2004). Other noteworthy horizontally scrolling shooters include the *Thunder Force* series (Technosoft, 1990 onwards), the *Darius* series (Taito, 1986 onwards), and *Blazing Star* (Yumekobo, 1998). Various design differences also exist, such as the implementation of a four-way *Robotron*-esque (Williams, 1982) shooting system in *Vanguard* (Centuri, 1981).

Vertically Scrolling Shooters

Nucleating game: *Xevious* (Namco, 1982)

Vert scrollers demonstrate a direct development from the classic shooter style of *Space Invaders*. Three major factors have been added to the classic form: scrolling (allowing for progression within levels), 2D movement (up/down/left/right as opposed to *Space Invaders*' 1D of left/right), and power ups.

Vert scrollers are also obviously related to horizontally scrolling 2D shooters, but for reasons unknown, their disciplines remain highly specialized. Crack vert scroller developers Psikyo and Cave have both produced side scrollers—*Sol Divide* (Psikyo, 1997) and *Progear No Arashi* (Cave, 2001). Though both games are highly accomplished, they fail to match the highs reached by the vert scrollers created by the two companies.

Interestingly, though side-scrolling games have seen little development since their inception, vert scrollers have continued to evolve. This might be due to their suitability to arcade gaming. While side scrollers covert well to home formats, vert scrollers do not—arcade versions being presented on vertically mounted monitors, suitable to the screen dimensions (taller than they are wide). Home versions of vert scrollers include a "tate" option (rotating the screen display through 90 degrees, and requiring the player to turn their television upon its side), but this is obviously for the Hardcore only.

Whatever the reason for their continued evolution, vert scrollers demonstrate some of the most compelling old-school gameplay currently available. Early examples were restricted by hardware limitations. *Xevious, 1942* (Capcom, 1984), and *Raiden* (Toaplan, 1990) added design elements to the genre that can still be seen in modern versions, but were limited in their capacity for moving objects. Modern forms make use of newer technology to cover the screen with bullets. These bullet patterns, created from hundreds of sprites, change the primary play orientation of the modern vert-scrolling shooter from shooting to dodging—the term bullet maze has been used to describe these games. Tiny hit boxes (the portion of the player avatar that triggers death once hit) add to this specialization.

Though the modern form of the game is defined by *DonPachi* (Cave, 1995), a small but fervently keen market (specifically among Japanese Type 1 players) exists for this style of game, which has led to the existence of a large number of classic games in this genre. These include Cave's *DoDonPachi* (1997), *ESPra.de* (1998), *Guwange* (1999), and *ESPgaluda* (2003); Psikyo's *Strikers 1945* series (1995 onwards) and *Gunbird* 1 and 2 (1994, 1998); Raizing's *Battle Garegga* (1996); Capcom's *Gigawing* 1 and 2 (1999, 2000); and Treasure's console-based *Radiant Silvergun* (1998) and *Ikaruga* (2002).

As suggested, the primary audience for this genre of games is the H1, as the tremendous difficulty inspires fiero, and the fail-repeat nature of the gameplay encourages a high degree of strategy through optimization. However, the modern breed also appeals somewhat to H3 players through their use of very distinct scoring layers. *DonPachi* and its sequels use a combo system of scoring, *Gigawing* uses a bullet reflect system to provide strategy and score, and *ESPra.de* combines combos with a high number of pick ups. This trend is perhaps exemplified by *Psyvariar* (Success, 2000), which expands on the "scraping" dynamic first seen in *Radiant Silvergun* (the player can power up or score by scraping one's craft against bullets). *Psyvariar* concentrates its entire gameplay upon this scraping system (termed *buzz* within the game), leading to a curious inversion—the player is encouraged to desire being shot at. These scoring systems appear to appeal to the Type 3 enjoyment of finesse—in effect, the H3 player isn't achieving mimicry of a life situation, they are participating in mimicry of the game dynamic itself.

This genre, as stated, appeals to a very small but reliable core audience. That it still develops and evolves is fascinating and might suggest the mode of development of today's current genres. Scrolling shooters were a core part of the industry in the 80s and early 90s, similar in position to the FPS games of today. Their continued evolution through the support of the Hardcore (in part made possible by their low development overheads in terms of staff—the majority of the development is in play tweaking) suggests a potential model for comparison with today's key genres, which will also undoubtedly suffer a marginalization at some point in the future. As such, the vert scroller is perhaps the most fascinating of the retro genres.

First-Person Shooters

Nucleating game: *Wolfenstein 3D* (id Software, 1992)

Currently the most popular shooting genre, FPS games also demonstrate the most codified identity. Though in theory only a first-person perspective and some shooting are required for a game to qualify, the popularity of the early FPS contenders—*Wolfenstein 3D*, *Doom* (id Software, 1993), *Duke Nukem 3D* (3D Realms, 1996), and *Quake* (id Software, 1996)—ensured that the form quickly became standardized. The progression seen through these games—a gradual increase in three-dimensionality—demonstrates how clearly *Wolfenstein* and especially *Doom* defined the genre. You have very few developments in play, with the core structure (linear levels, key-and-door barriers) barely changing. Some aspects of the core gameplay can be seen to alter—primarily in a reduction of housekeeping elements (*Doom*'s secrets were important to its feel, but have been lost by *Doom 3* (id Software, 2004) in favor of a greater bias towards pathfinding). Power ups, too, become more controlled as the genre evolves.

The form, then, is as follows: The player, experiencing the world from a first-person perspective, usually from behind the bouncing barrel of one of multiple firearms, progresses through corridors (and the occasional open-air section) shooting enemies as they come. By locating keys, the player can progress through locked doors to eventually arrive at a goal.

It can be seen that this is a very agonistic Type 1 play style. In fact, the direction of the development (specifically in the area of pathfinding) can be attributed to the popularity that FPS games immediately found with the H1 audience, and more specifically with people demonstrating the character traits associated with programmers. The importance of multiplayer gameplay, specifically agonistic deathmatch play, to this genre also suggests that H1 players (and to some extent, H2 players) working with developers have biased the FPS genre to their own tastes.

The sales of FPS games tend to top out at the 1–2 million mark, with the exception of *Half-Life* (Valve, 1998) and *GoldenEye 007* (Rare, 1997), both of which sold around 8 million copies [GameState03], and *Halo* (Bungie, 2001), which has sold some 5 million copies [Thurrott04]. This supports to a certain degree the hypothesis that H1 players can support sales of up to a million, while C1 players can expand this further (with evangelization for the preceding titles bringing them ultimately to a much wider market).

The FPS genre is native to the PC platform and is the genre that made PCs a viable action game platform. Hardcore FPS players (H1 type) play on PC. However, a number of FPS games have been successful on console, including *Doom* (which worked very well on PlayStation); *Turok: Dinosaur Hunter* (Iguana, 1997), which brought 4 dimensions of control to the console FPS format; the previously mentioned *GoldenEye* and *Halo*; and *Metroid Prime* (Retro Studios, 2002).

GoldenEye and *Halo* demonstrate well the difference between PC FPS games and versions designed specifically for console. *GoldenEye* dispenses with quicksave functionality, replacing it with a well-designed hermetic level setup. It also removes the jump function and presents its simplest control scheme as default. *Halo*, meanwhile, skews the classic aim-oriented style of PC FPS games and makes avatar positioning more important to success than sharp aiming (which is made simpler due to a forgiving auto-aim). This re-orientation of core gameplay, in which tactical approach of large numbers of enemies is more important than control skills, makes the shooter more playable with the console controller, which is significantly less precise than a mouse. These changes almost certainly helped to extend the appeal of both games beyond the Type 1 audience to include some of the H3 and C2 audience clusters.

Unsurprisingly, conversions of PC FPS games to console, and of console FPS games to PC, sell significantly less well than they do on their native platforms and are also less well received critically. The two audiences are subtly different (though platform loyalty is also a factor).

While the majority of FPS games on all platforms are heavily biased towards pathfinding (with PC FPS games specifically oriented to optimization through repetition, via the quick-save option), *Metroid Prime* demonstrates an FPS style more Type 3 friendly. Gameplay is as oriented towards looking as shooting, controls are designed with low dimensionality of control in mind, and exploration is increased in importance. Only some extremely Type 1 pattern bosses damage this otherwise excellent revision of the basic FPS model. It might, however, be too late for this form of FPS to make inroads in player acceptance, because the public image of the FPS form is very fixed and Type 1 players are unlikely to evangelize Type 3-oriented FPS games particularly powerfully.

A more subscribed-to trend in FPS development is the real-world FPS, exemplified by such WWII shooters as *Medal of Honor* (Dreamworks/EA, 1999 onwards). These games appeal to the Casual demographic's Sensing bias by offering familiar, "realistic" settings, and as such can penetrate further into mainstream consciousness. Note that they primarily use movie paradigm reality as the basis for imagery. Squad-based shooters (now a genre in their own right) also prefer to use popular fictional realities—specifically Tom Clancy's vision of anti-terrorist action in games such as *Rainbow Six* (Red Storm, 1998) and its sequels. Squad-based shooters add a very strong strategic/tactical element to the genre, involving H2 players, and also provide excellent team based multiplay action (as in *Counter-Strike* (Valve, 2000), itself derived from Half-Life mods).

Third-Person Shooters

Nucleating game: *Max Payne* (Remedy, 2001)

Max Payne has been chosen to represent the nucleating game because it is the most recognizable game of this form. If a single game did initially inspire the category of third-person shooter, it is unknown.

Historically, these games are rooted in top-down scrolling shooters in which the player controls a soldier who can move in eight directions, while the playfield scrolls in one (usually upscreen). Examples include *Commando* (Capcom, 1983) and *Ikari Warriors* (SNK, 1986). This genre evolved via eight-directional scrolling into top-down maze shooters such as *Alien Syndrome* (Sega, 1987) by way of cross-pollination with *Gauntlet* (Atari, 1985).

However, the term *third-person shooter* has arisen only since the advent of 3D as a catch-all category. The term is a tricky one, because many games of a third-person perspective include shooting—for example, *Tomb Raider* (Core, 1996), *Metal Gear Solid* (Konami, 1998)—but apply more effectively to other genres. Correctly, it should be applied only to games in which shooting is the primary activity. It also tends to be used to describe human- or humanoid-avatar games, as space shooters (for example) are more usefully collated in a specific genre of their own.

One of the primary issues with this genre is the difficulty that lies in describing the various camera perspectives available. The term *third person* doesn't assume any specific camera position, and so side-on, top-down, or fixed camera perspectives are all theoretically eligible for inclusion. In practice, however, the "shoulder cam" (or "voyeur cam," or "heli cam") is standard for this genre—a camera mounted behind and just above the player avatar.

Modern third-person shooters include *Gungrave* (Red Entertainment, 2002), *Freedom Fighters* (Io Interactive, 2003), and *Armed and Dangerous* (Planet Moon, 2003). Note that these games are all notable in themselves, and no overwhelmingly dominant example of a third-person shooter exists in the same way you see in 3D platform games or racing sims. This is in part due to the catch-all nature of the category—this genre is made up of games that don't fit elsewhere, rather than games that fit the term well. As such, it is difficult to analyze this genre from an audience perspective, because few players actively seek out a third-person shooter.

The agonistic nature of the genre is obvious, so a Type 1 bias might be assumed, but the genre term has no connotation of structure, aesthetic, or core gameplay (beyond shooting), and so a more specific audience analysis is speculation. In that spirit, we can assume a pathfinding bias, a linear level structure, and a single gimmick per game (combos, bullet time, squad action)—all of which bias toward H1s, with some scope in gimmick to attract Type 3 players if the aesthetic features satisfy.

3D Space Shooters

Nucleating game: *Elite* (Acornsoft, 1984)

You find two basic types of space shooter—free range and on-rails. The latter are usually considered to form their own genre, leaving *3D space shooter* to describe any 3D shooting game in which the player has freedom of choice in their direction of travel. In some respects, vector graphics games such as *Space War* (Vectorbeam,

1977), *Tail Gunner* (Cinematronics, 1979), and *Battlezone* (Atari, 1980) are the spiritual ancestors of this genre.

Key space shooters include the *Wing Commander* series (Origin, 1992 onwards), *Star Wars: Tie Fighter* (LucasArts, 1994), *Descent: Freespace—The Great War* (Volition, 1998), *Star Wars: Starfighter* (LucasArts, 2001), and the seminal *Elite*, itself inspired by influential tabletop RPG *Traveller* (Game Designers' Workshop, 1977).

A related genre is the "dogfight" genre. Because airplane games are traditionally sims, and most non-sim video game dogfighting is done in space, this subgenre is underpopulated, but *Crimson Skies: High Road to Revenge* (FASA Studio, 2003) is a good example of an arcade-style 3D dogfighting shooter.

The primary problem with 3D space shooters is navigation in full 3D, a task that requires depth of control and good spatial awareness. Both these needs serve to alienate practically any form of casual play beyond C1, though modern versions usually incorporate sophisticated locking or enemy targeting systems. Even so, 3D space shooters are unlikely to appeal beyond Type 1 play, even though the structure and content of *Elite* itself appealed to Type 2 and Type 3 players as well, because combat was in essence an optional element of that game.

On-Rails Shooters

Nucleating game: *Star Wars* (Atari, 1983)

The term *on-rails* refers to restriction of movement—the controls do not allow a decision to be made regarding the direction of travel of their avatar (relating the genre to that of light-gun shooters). Control is usually by a targeting reticule, with shooting being more important than movement, though many games of this style make the avatar's movement follow that of the reticule, allowing the player limited maneuverability.

During play, on-rails shooters thrive upon the player's ability to become familiar with the level designs—reflecting their ancestry in side-scrolling shooters and allowing for styles of play based upon optimization. As such, they usually appeal to Type 1 players (specifically H1, because C1 players might find the perceived lack of control to be a barrier to enjoyment). Their other identifying feature is a tremendous concentration upon aesthetic elements—the predetermined nature of the play allowing for resources to be controlled and the environments to be as attractive as possible. This is made clear by *M.A.C.H. 3* (Mylstar, 1983) and *Firefox* (Atari, 1984), early on-rails shooters that both used laser-disc images to create backgrounds upon which sprites were superimposed. This visual aspect might interest H3 players, particularly with unique games such as *Rez* (UGA, 2001), which lacks the degree of challenge to involve purely Type 1-style players, but is tremendously appealing to Type 3 players due to its astonishing visuals and use of sound.

Key on-rails shooters include *Star Wars* (which attracted vast crowds in the arcades when first released largely due to the extent to which it captured the essence of the film in vector graphics), the *Starfox* series (Nintendo, 1993 onwards), the *Panzer Dragoon* series (Team Andromeda/Smilebit, 1995 onwards), and *Rez*. Also of significance is *Afterburner* (Sega, 1987), which presented a version of the on-rails shooter using sprite scaling technology; it first introduced a lock-on function to the genre, a development that became extremely important to later games.

Though *Rez* shows the possibilities inherent in this genre (due to the control simplicity) to create interactive audio-visual experiences that go beyond gameplay, it is sadly unlikely that this genre has any significant future in the modern video game market, except as a niche market.

Light-Gun Shooters

Nucleating game: *Duck Hunt* (Nintendo, 1984)

In this case, the example of *Duck Hunt* as a nucleating game is an approximation. Light-gun games were the first form of TV game designed, even before *Pong* (Atari, 1972) style games. Nintendo released laser-gun novelty games before branching into video games, and Ralph Baer (legendary designer of the Magnavox Odyssey and father of video games) had a working light gun before starting work on his version of the *Pong* game.

The obvious key factor with this genre is the use of a peripheral, the light gun. This can take numerous forms, including modern "sniper" versions. However, all games in this genre follow the same basic format; the player must shoot enemies on screen before they themselves are shot or otherwise damaged.

Key light-gun games include *Operation Wolf* (Taito, 1987), *Virtua Cop* (Sega, 1994), *Time Crisis* (Namco, 1996), and *House of the Dead* (Sega, 1997). *Time Crisis* adds a duck pedal to the format, but otherwise you have basically two styles of light-gun game; accuracy oriented (in which enemies fall easily, and reactions and accuracy are key—*Virtua Cop*, *Time Crisis*) and power oriented (in which enemies take multiple hits, often from close range, and speed of shot is more important than accuracy—*House of the Dead*).

Agonistic, skill-based, and requiring a peripheral, light-gun games appeal primarily to Type 1 players. However, the existence of the real gun makes mimicry very easy, so Type 3 players might also enjoy the games (this is presumably made more likely in games that reward finesse).

Platform Games

At their most basic level, platform games (or platformers) involve jumping—traditionally from platform to platform. However, it is interesting to note that though the original platform game, *Donkey Kong* (Nintendo, 1981), required no collecting activities of the player, the need to have the player explore the game world (vital in a game whose core gameplay involves acts of terrain navigation) quickly led to platform games showing a significant "collector" component. Previous collector games such as *Pac-Man* (Namco, 1980) used a maze to provide challenge; 2D platform games such as *Miner 2049er* (Big Five, 1982) used a similar style of gameplay, but with gravity supplying the primary dynamic (in the case of *Miner 2049er*, "collection" involved changing the color of every platform, but the similarity with *Pac-Man*'s collection aspect remains).

Two huge leaps have occurred in the life of the platformer genre, both supplied by *Mario*. *Super Mario Bros.* (Nintendo, 1985) defined the scrolling platformer (and the 2D platformer in general, although it was not the first), while *Super Mario 64* (Nintendo, 1996) defined the 3D platformer. Collection elements are core to each game, though other goals provide the primary motivation in each.

Since *Super Mario Bros.*, platform games have been enjoyed by Casual players, and for a time were (with racing and shooters) the most popular gaming genre—licensed products were quite likely to be platform games. The more open and explorable (that is, the greater the housekeeping bias), the greater platform games seem to appeal to Casual audiences. Players with a preference for Type 3 play seem to particularly enjoy platformers, because the flexible game worlds allow for mimicry via exploration. As Casual take-up of platform games increases, we see a reduction in game difficulty. As such, Type 1 players prefer other styles. Note, however, that evangelization does still occur, because Type 1 players are likely to recommend platform games to Casual friends as the most obvious choice for Casual gaming.

Classic Platform Games

Nucleating game: *Donkey Kong* (Nintendo, 1981)

As with classic shooters, this category is suggested to include old, arcade style single-screen games, since these have a specific place in gaming history. Games such as *Donkey Kong*, *Pitfall* (Activision, 1982), *Miner 2049er*, *Manic Miner* (M. Smith, 1983), and *Bubble Bobble* (Taito, 1986) provided staple gameplay for early gamers. The focus on less violent themes is a notable aspect of the platform game from the outset.

This style of game encounters an occasional resurgence—*Mario vs. Donkey Kong* (Nintendo, 2004), itself based upon *Donkey Kong '94* (Nintendo, 1994), shows that this format can still be compelling, and perfect for the handheld format as single-screen environments allow for easy start-stop play while traveling. Otherwise, this genre merely set the stage for what was to come.

2D Platform Games

Nucleating game: *Super Mario Bros.*

Though scrolling shooters had been around for some time, *Super Mario Bros.* provided the first explorable worlds that were greater than a single screen in size. Though its basic format was simple—move left to right in a 2D, side-on environment, avoiding or jumping upon enemies, and avoiding pits and hazards—the imagination on display in the game went far beyond this. Tiered collectables drove exploration (with a single coin being of minor value, but red and green mushrooms and fireflowers being significantly more worthwhile), while the structure used secret passages and areas to allow players to skip stages. This latter feature allowed expert players to advance in the game despite its having no save option.

The game inspired many other scrolling 2D platform games, and many classic series emerged, including *Castlevania* (Konami, 1986), which added weapon combat via a whip; *Wonder Boy* (Sega, 1986); and platform shooters *Metroid* (Nintendo, 1986) and *Mega Man* (Capcom, 1987). The PC platform also featured its own legacy of side-scrolling shareware platformers, including *Commander Keen* (Apogee, 1990) and *Duke Nukem* (Apogee, 1991).

One interesting aspect of the *Mario* legacy is his role as Nintendo's console mascot—something that led directly to the creation of *Sonic the Hedgehog* (Sonic Team, 1991), which, along with *Super Mario World* (Nintendo, 1990), heralded in a new era of platforming. In both these games, Type 3 gameplay is evident; the characters are extremely well defined and are supported by instantly identifiable worlds. Both games feature a high degree of exploration, and though play is oriented towards pathfinding, housekeeping elements do appear (Sonic's ring collection, Mario's search for secret areas). Sonic is the easier game, and arguably had greater appeal to the Western Casual market of this time, but both games helped expand the role of the platformer as a genre that anyone could play. Both games also serve H1 tastes well, of course, as the games market was dominated by this audience until the advent of the PlayStation in 1996.

During the PlayStation era, *Castlevania: Symphony of the Night* (Konami, 1997) demonstrated a possible future for the 2D platform game as a fully envisioned exploration adventure, bearing some similarity to *Super Metroid* (Nintendo, 1994) in terms of structure (both games draw heavily from *Zelda*'s system of tools and barriers) but retaining a feel of its own due to the inclusion of RPG elements of inventory and leveling. To H1 players, this combination should theoretically be irresistible, but the game failed to perform well commercially, perhaps because the 2D style failed to appeal to players now used to exploration in three dimensions. Sequels appeared on the Game Boy Advance (GBA), however—with handhelds becoming the modern home of 2D platformers.

One strain of 2D platformer to persist somewhat in the 3D-oriented market is the so-called "2.5D" (two and a half dimension) platform game. Here the game world architecture is presented in polygonal 3D, but the player can move only left or right through that world. Examples include *Spider* (Boss Game Studios, 1996), *Pandemonium* (Crystal Dynamics, 1996), and *Klonoa: Door to Phantomile* (Namco, 1997). A slightly different concept seen in *Tomba* (Whoopee Camp, 1997) presents a traditional 2D perspective but allows the player to move into and out of the screen via a series of layers of play.

2D platformers still hold great market potential, specifically due to low dimensionality of control and their extreme accessibility to Casual players. However, the 2D projection appears to be too removed from reality for a more sensing audience to buy into. It is possible we will see a resurgence of 2D games in the future, because we are fast reaching the point whereby improvements in 3D graphics are hard for the audience in general to identify. This might allow for a new generation of games using high-quality graphics but a 2D projection to take advantage of lower dimensionality of control in appealing to a wider audience.

Platform Shooters

Nucleating games: *Mega Man*, *Contra* (Konami, 1988)

Platform shooters are equally able to be cast as a subset of platform games or of shooters, because they combine the two game styles (shooting and jumping). The two nucleating games suggested here represent two different strains of platform shooter. *Mega Man* involves four-way scrolling and includes a bias toward pathfinding as the player attempts to navigate a series of discrete 2D side-on platform levels, their goal being a level exit or the defeat of a boss. *Contra* involves side-scrolling or vertical-scrolling shooting-oriented action, including gun power ups, simultaneous two-player action, and simple shooting-gallery levels presented in a 3D perspective. Pathfinding is no issue in the latter game, and though the presentation of the levels varies, shooting is always the core activity.

Platform shooters obviously derive from platform games, adding at minimum a shoot button to the jump function. As such, in their more platform-oriented form they appeal to a wider audience than pure shooters, though the mix of agon and mimicry is similar. The addition of an exploration aspect, initially in a pathfinding mode, but later including housekeeping elements (primarily through the addition of secret areas), creates a wide audience of H1, H2, and H3 players.

Important entries in the platform shooter genre include *Bionic Commando* (Capcom, 1987), which is notable for replacing a jump button with a grapple; *Shinobi* (Sega, 1987); *Turrican* (Factor 5, 1990); the *Metal Slug* series (Nazca/SNK, 1996 onwards); and the *Metroid* series (now evolved into FPS format). Both *Metroid* and *Turrican* are noticeable for including housekeeping aspects of play.

Modern examples of the 2D platform shooter include *Contra: Shattered Soldier* (Konami, 2002) and *Alien Hominid* (O-3 Entertainment, 2004) proving that, though unpopular, the form does remain tenable due to its low overhead requirements. In fact, both *Metal Slug* and *Alien Hominid* serve to demonstrate that 2D visuals create a video game aesthetic quite removed from that of 3D games; it is theoretically possible that this aesthetic will drive a minor resurgence of low tier 2D games on home consoles (with the target audience being specifically H1).

In a 3D form, both *Ratchet & Clank* (Insomniac, 2002) and *Jak II* (Naughty Dog, 2003) increase the emphasis on shooting in the 3D platform genre, mirroring the development of early 2D platform shooters. The addition of shooting increases the agonistic feel of a game significantly, especially when coupled with a pathfinding bias, suggesting an increase in Type 1 appreciation (while decreasing the potential for Type 3 uptake). Considering the importance in the modern market of games hitting both markets, it seems unlikely that a strong Type 1 bias applied to a traditionally wide-ranging genre can support many AAA products in the current market.

3D Platform Games

Nucleating game: *Super Mario 64* (Nintendo, 1996)

There appears to be a general consensus that no 3D platform game has managed to improve upon the structure, core gameplay, or aesthetical vision of *Super Mario 64*, despite its being released in 1996. Certainly, no game since has managed to appeal to so many different audiences simultaneously, with Type 1 players satisfied by its status and challenge and Type 3 players able to immerse themselves in its imaginative environments. Though relatively Casual-friendly, its time of release saw many more "realistic" (and less openly surreal) games launched on the PlayStation, perhaps making it seem rather old fashioned, and slightly irrelevant to modern Casual gamers. However, the vast wave of evangelization garnered from the Hardcore players, and the strength of the Nintendo brand image in the United States, must have pushed it into the hands of millions of Casual players.

3D platform games have been a staple of the video game world ever since. Their core dynamic is far less biased toward control accuracy than classic 2D platform games—something radically obvious when playing *Super Mario 64* in comparison with earlier *Mario* games. Because 3D navigation has its own challenges, accuracy in jumping and timing are generally made less important in 3D platformers. Of course, some exceptions exist, but these games tend towards platform adventures, which we will discuss shortly.

Mario provided not only a forgiving play experience, but also a far more user-friendly structure as well. Suddenly players weren't required to complete each level in order. The domain structure of *Mario 64* required players to complete only a fraction of the tasks available before moving on. We have referred to this at times as the "70% rule"—the idea that for a given game the player need complete only between two-thirds and three-quarters of the challenges offered to advance. As previously discussed, this structure is also echoed in extreme sports games, another Casual favorite (though C1 only).

Other platform games of note include *Banjo-Kazooie* (Rare, 1998), *Spyro the Dragon* (Insomniac, 1998), and *Crash Bandicoot* (Naughty Dog, 1996), which presented linear twitch platforming, with the player avatar running down fixed channels avoiding obstacles. Its simplicity, combined with its vibrant cartoon graphics, appealed greatly to early PlayStation Casuals.

At the time of writing, the 3D platform genre is in need of a new revolution. Since the core audience for platform games is the lucrative Casual market, specifically C3 players, it makes sense that the next great evolution in platform games comes in the form of completely non-agonistic games. By concentrating upon housekeeping and toyplay activities and presenting a virtual play park rather than a gauntlet of spiked pits and deathtraps, the only hurdle the platform genre would require to leap would be the Hardcore players themselves.

Platform Adventures

Nucleating game: *Tomb Raider* (Core, 1996)

The most noticeable 3D platform game of the PlayStation/N64 era, other than *Mario 64*, was surely *Tomb Raider*—a game so different in feel to Mario that many players prefer to consider it an adventure title rather than a platformer. Nevertheless, its core elements—jumping from platform to platform—are evidently evolved from classic platform games, and so the term "platform adventure," while not strictly in common usage, seems apt to describe this genre.

In many ways, *Tomb Raider* resembles classic platformers far more than Mario does. Rather than coax a Casual audience with ease of experience, *Tomb Raider* provides agonistic challenge after challenge, with fiero being the payoff of choice. In many ways, *Tomb Raider* represents a turning point in video game development—games were becoming big enough with a mass market to make Lara a superstar, but her game straddled the past and the future of games, providing the technological and aesthetic ability to attract new players, but primarily serving staunchly traditional Type 1 play. Although it is all but certain that some players played *Tomb Raider* for mimicry, it is likely they did not play it for long.

In every facet, *Tomb Raider* harks of the past. The controls are unfriendly, posing a challenge in themselves. Every move must be planned. Instant death situations abound. The structure is defiantly linear. It is not surprising that the moment that the Hardcore became disillusioned with Lara, the franchise began to sink, until, with *Tomb Raider: Angel of Darkness* (Core, 2003) the series was in such jeopardy that Eidos felt it necessary to take it from its creators and assign the next title in the series to another developer. Without staunch evangelization, *Tomb Raider*'s difficulty cannot be borne by anyone but the most Hardcore. Ironically, without the mass market interest in the early titles, Eidos might not have tried to release a franchise iteration every year, and this classic H1 series might still be thriving.

The platform adventure has an obvious precursor in *Prince of Persia* (Brøderbund, 1989), which combined platformer style environments with challenging sword fights and puzzles. Although in 2D, it has much in common with *Tomb Raider* in terms of the sense of high stakes action engendered and the combination of combat, exploration, platform jumping, and puzzles. Other games with platform adventure elements include *Duke Nukem: Time to Kill* (n-Space, 1998), *Deathtrap Dungeon* (Asylum, 1998), *O.D.T* (Psygnosis, 1998), and *Urban Chaos* (Mucky Foot, 1999). The physically beautiful *Ico* (SCEI, 2001), though not precisely a platform adventure, resembles the form greatly, specifically in its desire to strand the player high above solid ground with only their nerves to guide them. Its visuals and narrative subtlety suggest great Type 3 potential, but its gameplay is so unforgivingly Type 1 in nature that any tourist is likely to be quickly repelled.

In the twenty-first century, the "high stakes" 3D platform adventure has been re-envisioned by *Prince of Persia: The Sands of Time* (Ubisoft, 2003), which was greeted rapturously by Type 1 oriented players, specifically H1s, but sold in numbers suggesting lack of penetration into more Casual (and therefore more lucrative) markets [IGN04]. Although its beautiful environments could have served to produce mimicry play, the emphasis on challenge narrowed the audience considerably, and it is also possible that the setting was just not quite familiar enough for the Sensing-dominant Casual audience.

Platform Puzzlers

Nucleating game: *Out of this World* (Delphine, 1991)

Nominating a nucleating game for this minor genre is difficult; *Out of the World* has been chosen because it is the earliest game to represent the majority of the aspects of the form. The platform puzzler is defined by its de-emphasis on traditional twitch platforming skills and an emphasis upon positional puzzles. These puzzles are created by use of very tight game world abstractions, in which a small number of elements combine in predictable ways to create a great number of possible challenges. Other examples of the genre include *Flashback: The Quest For Identity* (Delphine, 1993), *Blackthorne* (Blizzard, 1994), *Oddworld: Abe's Oddysee* (Oddworld Inhabitants, 1997), and *Heart of Darkness* (Amazing Studio, 1998).

The genre appeals primarily to H1 and H2 players. Casual players are almost certainly put off by the incredible difficulty of this style of game, which requires pinpoint planning and execution on the part of the player—especially suited to Type 2 play with its Strategic/Tactical bias and inherent enjoyment of puzzles, although Type 1 play is also supported through the usual mechanisms of fail-repeat gameplay. These games are wonderful examples of tight game world abstraction, but their negative features often alienate a wider audience. The *Abe* games interested C3 players due to their charismatic presentation, despite the games being in 2D, but the difficulty caused the franchise to falter.

Nevertheless, the game world abstractions demonstrated might well suggest the basis for excellent toyplay style games based around the interaction of various game elements.

Fighting Games

Also known as beat-em-ups, the fighting game is typified by hand-to-hand or melee combat, with the player controlling a single avatar, and pitched against either a single or multiple enemies. In the case of one-on-one fighting, agonistic two-player combat is of high importance to fighting game players.

One-on-one Fighters

Nucleating game: *Street Fighter II* (Capcom, 1991)

Street Fighter II is not the first game of this nature—previous titles such as *Way of the Exploding Fist* (Melbourne House, 1985), *Yie Ar Kung Fu* (Konami, 1985), and *IK+* (A. Maclean, 1987) demonstrated the concept (head to head fighting using multiple moves triggered by control combinations), but *SFII* exploded the concept, defining the genre by introducing a recognizable cast of characters with different abilities, a whole host of moves triggered by new control methods (such as the quarter-circle forward), and combo and special moves.

The game was a massive hit in the arcades, primarily for its two player mode, the defining feature of every similar fighting game since. This illustrates the core attraction of the form: agon. Combined with the incredibly specialized control methods and the requirement for expert timing, this genre is almost purely a Type 1 genre, with the core audience being H1.

Nevertheless, the form flourished, possibly due to its ability to feature some of the most impressive graphics seen at the time (there being relatively low on-screen overheads, which allowed for an unprecedented quality of animation). Other key 2D fighting games include *Fatal Fury: King of Fighters* (SNK, 1991), *Mortal Kombat* (Midway, 1992), *Killer Instinct* (Rare, 1994), and *Guilty Gear X* (Arc System Works, 2000). Like the vertical shooter genre, the 2D fighting game has a keen but small following, which drives forward experimentation by small, highly specialized studios. Because each franchise has its own specialized fighting system, sequels are highly plausible, and many of the franchises (those of Capcom and SNK especially) have many iterations, some of which can be differentiated between only by experts.

Virtua Fighter (Sega, 1993) initiated the cycle of 3D fighting games, which played in the same manner as the 2D cousins, but demonstrated smooth animation via use of polygons. These games quickly overshadowed the 2D variety for the majority of players, though a keen hardcore continued the purity of fighting in-plane. Other 3D fighters of note include *Tekken* (Namco, 1994), *Dead or Alive* (Tecmo/Team Ninja, 1996), and *Soul Calibur* (Namco, 1998).

Though the 3D graphics increase the aesthetic appeal of these games to a broader market, their gameplay is still highly agonistic, and suitable only for Type 1 players, though H3 players might be attracted to the highly individualistic (and beautifully animated) casts of characters. For the most part, 3D fighting games draw upon the C1 market for their commercial success, but inevitably the H1 cluster is also required to evangelize.

Classic 3D fights allow little movement other than back and forwards and the occasional sidestep. A further sub-genre, exemplified by *Power Stone* (Capcom, 1999), allows for free roaming movement. This style of fighter is characterized by over-the-top power ups and is a little more friendly to a Casual audience, though not significantly. Other games in this sequence include *Kung Fu Chaos* (Just Add Monsters, 2003) and *Onimusha: Blade Warriors* (Capcom, 2004). Perhaps the most commercial example of this style of party-fighter is *Super Smash Brothers Melee* (Nintendo, 2001), presented in 2.5D and designed to be as user-friendly as is possible for the fighting genre. However, even this game has trouble penetrating far beyond H1 and C1 players.

Scrolling Fighters

Nucleating game: *Renegade* (Taito, 1986)

Kung-Fu Master (Nihon Bussan/AV Japan, 1985) predated *Renegade*, but only anticipated the genre, being more of a reaction test than a fighting game. This genre is typified by side-scrolling environments, melee-oriented enemies, and a smaller variety of player moves than one-on-one fighters. The player is expected to advance forward until the screen scroll locks, preventing forward movement, defeat the available enemies, and then move on when indicated.

Key examples include *Double Dragon* (Taito, 1987), *Golden Axe* (Sega, 1989), *Streets of Rage* (Sega, 1989), *Final Fight* (Capcom, 1989), *River City Ransom* (Technos, 1990), and *Guardian Heroes* (Treasure, 1996). More modern, 3D variants of the classic form include *Die Hard Arcade* (Sega, 1996) and *Zombie Revenge* (Sega, 1999).

While one-on-one fighters appeal to H1 players due to the strategic options granted by the wide move sets, scrolling fighting games appeal primarily to C1 players who enjoy the agonistic bias when coupled with simpler controls and a sense of domination.

In the twenty-first century, the scrolling beat-em-up has evolved in a number of ways. *The Lord of the Rings: The Two Towers* (Stormfront, 2002) and its sequel demonstrate a revision of the genre staples through production values and add mild avatar-upgrading to bolster a sense of progression. They are, however, extremely Type 1 in style and fail to appeal to a Type 3 audience who might otherwise be keen to mimic the characters of the *Lord of the Rings* license. Less linear environments, fewer control-oriented skill elements, and a lack of pattern bosses would have made the games more suitable for the wider market the license deserved.

More progressively, *Dynasty Warriors 2* (Omega Force, 2000) harnessed the concepts of fighting and moving and added a well-abstracted battle layer to the combats, allowing for great depth of play. As mentioned elsewhere, this series deserves its own genre, but other games that look similar in form such as *Chaos Legion* (Capcom, 2003) and *Drakengard* (Square-Enix, 2003), which also adds aerial combat by dragon, fail to reflect the strategic nature of the *Dynasty Warriors* games, instead presenting only the combat aspect.

Dynasty Warriors 2 demonstrates how the essence of a faded genre can be restored by clever design in both core gameplay and structure. While scrolling fighting games appeal only to Type 1 players, the battlefield elements of the *Dynasty Warriors* series attract Type 2 and 3 players as well. The appeal to the Type 3 player might seem out of place, but the historical Three Kingdoms setting of these games is as well-known in Japan, China, and Korea as the King Arthur legends are in the West, thus allowing for highly engaging mimicry. The games have been a huge commercial success for their publisher, KOEI, in Japan, but the unfamiliar setting means that when exported to the West, they are largely only of interest to the Hardcore markets.

Extreme Combat

Nucleating game: *Devil May Cry* (Capcom, 2001)

Not a generally accepted genre (for example, *Devil May Cry* is most usually associated with the survival horror genre, for apparently no reason other than its reputation as having once been intended as a *Resident Evil* game by creators Capcom), this term has been invented to apply to a number of similar games that belong in ancestry in part to 2D platform games and in part to fighting games. Their aesthetic is rooted in the anime tradition of Japan. Core gameplay involves melee combat, but controls are optimized to grant the player maximum stylistic expression during conflict.

As with the majority of games in this genre, H1 skills and patience are required to get the most from *Devil May Cry*. This may alienate Type 3 players who might otherwise be attracted by the sense of finesse these games could otherwise provide. For example, in *DMC*, Dante may launch himself into the air and then keep himself aloft by shooting rapidly at a foe beneath him. Key to this genre, attacks lock onto the enemies, making sure the stylish attacks do not go astray. Finally, combo attacks, or some method of chaining for points or style, provide reward for finesse.

Games such as the remake of *Shinobi* (Overworks, 2002) and its sequel *Nightshade* (WOW Entertainment, 2004), *Otogi: Myth of Demons* (From Software, 2003), and *Legacy of Kain: Defiance* (Crystal Dynamics, 2003) all feature aspects of style, auto-aimed attacks, and chain or combo potential. *Shinobi*, though presented as a traditional third-person action game, barely requires use of its camera, because once in the air its hero can target enemy after enemy remotely, with the skill based in the controls rather than in on-screen navigation. Platform elements are supported by chaining between enemies, killing as the player goes.

The form also includes ranged-combat games; though the combat style obviously differs, the key features remain the same: targeted attacks, style, and combos or chains for finesse. *Gungrave* and *P.N.03* (Capcom, 2003) are examples of ranged extreme combat games.

Though not yet commonly considered to represent a genre, these games demonstrate a modern evolution of old-school H1 games. Effectively emulating (with visual panache and progressive control schemes) how early video games felt to the player as a preteen, they are some of the first games to attempt to recycle old gaming conventions for a modern, adult audience who grew up with those classic games. Though this form is in its infancy, it warrants scrutiny. If it can manage to strike a better balance between the demands of Type 1 play and the potential for Type 3 style finesse, it could become a significant genre.

Racing

Early racing games were as simple as early sports games. Basic driving games such as *Night Driver* (Atari, 1976) seem based on even earlier mechanical novelty games, where model cars could be steered left and right before a projected image of a road. With *Pole Position* (Namco, 1982) the genre became a staple of the arcades, and a significant number of racing games have been key releases in every year of video game development, making them the most long-term popular style of game.

The key element of racing games is their simplicity. They demonstrate intuitive play (most people are familiar with cars and racing), they offer wish fulfillment (especially to agonistic C1 and C2 audiences), their controls are simple, and their goals are readily apparent. This level of immediacy naturally creates a wide audience appeal. In addition, racing games have been able to constantly develop, from 2D sprite-scaled racers such as *Out Run* (Sega, 1986) to the 3D polygonal representations of early nineties games, and beyond to today's titles, which often attempt to simulate realistic physics.

More advanced physics simulation is a key to the genre's progression—physical modeling of the behavior of cars on a racetrack is far easier than, say, modeling the physics of a human being jumping from platform to platform. While this means nothing to gameplay—realistic physics don't immediately lead to better play—it is important from the point of view of audience, with C1, C2, and C3 players particularly enjoying the illusion of realism.

It is likely that the racing genre will continue to be popular for as long as video games continue to develop, as long as new twists arise. The most modern development at the time of writing is the city-based driving game, which uses the intuitive racing game staples within a mimicry-oriented city environment to support both Type 1 and Type 3 gameplay and toyplay.

Driving Sim

Nucleating game: *Gran Turismo* (Polyphony Digital, 1997)

The key aim of the driving sim is to present a realistic driving experience. This does not necessarily translate directly to realistic physics—*Gran Turismo* doesn't allow players to crash, for example. Rather, these games force the player to drive in a similar manner to real-life expert drivers in order to win. For example, great emphasis is placed on braking, angle of approach, and racing line. They also emphasize real cars, either in form (if unlicensed) or in form and name (if licensed). Naturally, this appeals greatly to the many car buffs in the world.

Formula 1 games were the first to attempt simulation. *Revs* (G. Crammond, 1985), though it simulates F3 racing, led to the same programmer's involvement in the creation of *F1GP* (Microprose, 1990), also known as *World Circuit*. Further iterations followed, and this series is still renowned for being the apex of driving simulation in terms of realism. *Formula 1* (Bizarre Creations, 1997) is another notable F1 sim.

These early sim games are so realistic that they appeal only to a very small audience of Type 1 players, though Type 2 and Type 3 players might also have bought them. A similar situation applies to *Ferrari F355 Challenge* (Sega, 1999), which was designed to simulate its eponymous vehicle exactly and featured no external view options even when converted to console. The issue of first- versus third-person view in these games in worth some mention. Whereas many C1 players seem to consider the first-person view to be more immersive, Type 3 players appear to prefer an external view—perhaps because car chases in movies use a third-person view, perhaps because spatial awareness is dramatically increased in this view and perhaps because Type 3 players are mimicking being a car as much as being a driver.

Type 2 players might be drawn to serious car sims due to their strategic elements. Car settings provide a stiff challenge that can be tackled at one's own pace, and serious car sims often feature plenty of statistics, graphs, and charts to analyze, giving them an almost puzzling feel. In the case of the C2 cluster, the appeal is likely to mirror the C1 cluster—cars are common objects of identity and wish fulfillment, particularly among males. No obvious pattern of preference for first- or third-person view has been noted in players in this cluster; it is likely that C2 players, with access to Tactical skills that provide proficiency in a variety of situations, are comfortable with both approaches.

With *Gran Turismo*, a game emerged that managed to balance the feel of realism—with its need for accurate braking and an emphasis upon tactical racing—with playability and accessibility. Its groundbreaking structure, which incorporates RPG-esque elements, was also a significant draw, not least to Casual players who could immerse themselves in the progression experience and could make up for any lack of skill by upgrading their vehicles (though it must be noted that the "license" challenges in *GT*—intended to teach racing technique—can be incredibly difficult).

Since *GT*, this genre has flourished. Other key examples include *Metropolis Street Racing/Project Gotham Racing* (Bizarre Creations, 2000/2001), *Colin McRae Rally* (Codemasters, 1998), *TOCA Touring Car Championship* (Codemasters, 1997), *Tokyo Xtreme Racer* (Genki, 1999), and *Sega GT 2002* (Sega, 2002).

Arcade Racer

Nucleating game: *Pole Position* (Namco, 1982)

The defining feature of the arcade racer is that it does not encourage the player to drive as they would have to in real life—arcade racers make their own rules. This was necessary in the early days of arcade entertainment, because realistic simulation was technologically impossible. In the modern era, the bias towards realism in games (to help court the Casual market) has edged the arcade racer to the periphery of the racing genre, but its legacy is unmistakable.

In terms of audience, early arcade games delivered primarily Type 1 play, though H3 players could be attracted due to the impressive aesthetics of games such as *Out Run*—a game that provided Type 1 play through its time-based structure, but broader wish fulfillment via its representation of a Ferrari driving through beautiful landscapes. The majority of players could complete at least one section of the course, and most players seeking mimicry in the arcade did not expect their credits to last long, just to provide an entertaining experience.

As with *Out Run*, most arcade racers provided challenge via a timing mechanism; the player was challenged to reach a certain point before their timer ran down. Though this mechanism supported arcade play well, it has fallen out of favor even with H1 players in the modern era, due to its artificiality. Even so, it is still occasionally seen, as in *Out Run 2* (Sega, 2003) and *18 Wheeler: American Pro Trucker* (Sega, 2000).

Structurally, though *Out Run* introduced an interesting diverging level structure (at the end of each track section the player must choose whether to turn left or right; fifteen track sections are available, but only five may be driven in one game), arcade racers usually present a linear level structure. When polygonal 3D racers were introduced via *Virtua Racing* (Sega, 1992), the number of track sections available reduced due to the overheads involved in creating and tweaking them. It therefore became standard in games such as *Sega Rally Championship* (Sega, 1995) to allow the player to select the order in which they would run the tracks, but pitch the tracks at different levels of difficulty (this mirrors the structure of mid-period light-gun games such as *Virtua Cop*). This structure works well in the arcade and is friendly to both Hardcore and Casual players.

Linear level structures still dominate arcade racers today, as seen in the modern era's most popular arcade racer series, *Burnout* (Criterion, 2001 onwards). More creative structures would help arcade racers appeal to a wider audience, specifically C3 players, who should enjoy arcade racing due to its emphasis on fast fun rather than accuracy. With a suitably movie-oriented representation, such a game has the potential to be a big hit.

Another factor of potential importance to arcade racers, however, is gimmick. Classic arcade racers have usually presented a very specific identity to players. The most obvious example of this is the difference between *Daytona USA* (Sega, 1994) and *Ridge Racer* (Namco, 1993), two of the most loved arcade racers of the era. While the Sega game concentrated on tight handling, *Ridge Racer* introduced power-sliding to the arcade audience, and caused a sensation. Though the *Ridge Racer* handling system is far from realistic, it allows for exciting mimicry of TV fantasy car racing, with cars skidding sideways around corners. This also provides a very attractive challenge to Type 1 players, who enjoy the slow optimization of technique, lap upon lap, until the entire track is known and each distinctive corner can be taken perfectly.

Out Run 2 provides the apex of the power-sliding sub-genre, but its novelty might have worn off from a mass-market perspective. If the arcade racer is to survive, a new focus for core gameplay may be required. *Burnout 3: Takedown* (Criterion, 2004) identifies itself with crashes, becoming a significant critical success, while *Need For Speed Underground 2* (EA Black Box, 2004) presents a wish fulfillment fantasy of illegal street racing and is a significant commercial success.

Kart Racers

Nucleating game: *Super Mario Kart* (Nintendo, 1992)

By taking its premier cast of characters and attaching them to a friendly racing format, Nintendo created a much loved game in *Super Mario Kart* and launched the karting genre, characterized by low dimensionality of control and more forgiving physics. Interestingly, though the kart genre is conventionally considered to appeal to a wider market than realistic car racers (appealing to children and women as well as car-loving men), *Super Mario Kart* is notable for the level of challenge it poses at higher difficulty levels. Though the early cup is quite simple and winnable by a wide range of players, the third and fourth cups can be incredibly hard at the high end of the game. One might conclude that *Mario Kart* appeals to a C3 audience via its aesthetics, and a Hardcore audience via its difficulty weighting.

Nintendo used a progressive difficulty structure for numerous SNES games, including *Starfox* and *Super Punch-Out* (Nintendo, 1994). *Mario Kart* also pushes the structure of the racing games of its era by forcing players to progressively unlock new tracks and difficulty settings, meaning that the player is always posed with new challenges.

Since the original *Mario Kart*, the only kart racers to really enthuse players of any audience are other *Mario Kart* games, though an honorable mention must be granted to *Snowboard Kids* (Atlus, 1997), which successfully wed the philosophy of the kart racer with snowboarding, although its commercial success was limited. The genre remains a minor staple, however, and is specifically useful for promoting mascot-style characters beyond their native genre or for use with licenses, as shown by *Diddy Kong Racing* (Rare, 1997), *Crash Team Racing* (Naughty Dog, 1999), *Walt Disney World Magical Quest Racing Tour* (Crystal Dynamics, 2000), and *Wacky Races* (Infogames, 2000). Subsequent *Mario Kart* games include *Mario Kart Super Circuit* (Nintendo, 2001) on GBA and *Mario Kart: Double Dash!!* (Nintendo, 2003) on GameCube. The latter exhibits a style of chariot racing, providing the multiplayer that the series has always been famous for in the traditional agonistic format, and in a new co-operative mode which may appeal to Type 4-oriented players as well as Types 1, 2, and 3.

At the time of writing, the kart racing genre is flagging, as no company has managed to significantly innovate, leaving H1 players in particular with the feeling that the original is still the best. It is likely that this genre will remain a side-branch of racing games in general, as scope for development seems minimal. A key problem is that although kart racers are friendly to a Casual audience, being easier to learn and to play, the influential Hardcore, C1, and C2 players are having their play needs met by more realistic racing games, creating a schism in the market that undercuts the usefulness of the kart racers biggest asset—its accessibility.

Top-Down Racer

Nucleating game: *Micro Machines* (Supersonic, 1991)

The top-down racing genre first appeared on early computers, featuring vertically scrolling roads constructed of ASCII characters. The first top-down racer of historical significance is probably *Super Sprint* (Atari, 1986), a popular single-screen racer that inspired other games such as *Ironman Ivan Stewart's Super Off Road* (Leland, 1989). *Micro Machines*, however, changed the entire genre by including scrolling tracks, an imaginative representation featuring tiny vehicles in traditional settings (harking back to childhood play), and one of the tightest multiplayer modes ever seen. The key to *Micro Machines'* success in multiplayer gameplay is in keeping all the players on a single screen (no split-screens, which alienate non-game-literate players and anyone with eyesight problems). If a player falls behind, they must wait until a winner is decided; in the next point (which generally follows rapidly), everyone races again.

This genre reached its peak with *Micro Machines 2: Turbo Tournaments* (Supersonic, 1994), which used "J-cart" technology in its Sega Genesis incarnation (cartridges with controller ports built directly into them) to facilitate four-player games without the need for extra hardware (besides four controllers). The third iteration, *Micro Machines V3* (Codemasters, 1997) was released on PlayStation, which came with two controller ports as standard, meaning that extra hardware (a multi-tap) was required. This limited access to the multiplayer gameplay and, hence, retarded the success of the game. These games are at their best with four players sitting around the screen; they lack the participatory sense of friendly agon in one- or two-player modes, and it is this that is these games' real strength.

Comparison between *MM2* and *V3* is fruitful. The original format uses top-down views, while the polygonal evolution uses a dynamic camera that adjusts the viewpoint constantly to provide a view of the track ahead. The latter format causes the track to be occasionally obscured. Additionally, the leeway allowed for the players to risk shortcuts is reduced in *V3*, shifting the emphasis of the game somewhat—players are forced to be more accurate with their driving, and luck plays a lesser role. This factor is compounded by the addition of power ups to the PlayStation game. Ultimately, *V3* appeals more to purely agonistic Type 1 and 2 players who are willing to learn the intricacies of the tracks, while *MM2* appealed to a broader audience, because it was more instantly playable—C3 and C4 players could gain basic skills in a small amount of time, and expert play doesn't present an insurmountable advantage due to the ability to win by luck (something that appeals to Type 3 players, but something that Type 1 players dislike).

Despite some excellent further titles in the genre by Supersonic, including *Circuit Breakers* (1998) and *Mashed* (2004), both of which were critically acclaimed (and also solved the primary barrier to Casual play, that of relative control—some players find it hard to adjust to turning left and right with relative control with a fixed perspective), the genre failed to regain the commercial success of the *Micro Machines* heyday. The fact that the PS2 (like its predecessor) has only two control ports by default, but is far and away the most widely distributed console, probably factored into the failure of this form to regain ground.

Sports Racer

Nucleating game: *Wave Race 64* (Nintendo, 1996)

This is another catch-all genre, suggested for simplicity; the nucleating game in this case typifies the issues of the genre and is both an early and an exceptional example. This genre artificially includes all non-car racers, including water-based racers such as *Wave Race 64* and *Hydro Thunder* (Midway, 2000), snow-based racers such as *1080 Snowboarding* (Nintendo, 1998) and *SSX* (EA Canada, 2000), dirt-based racers such as *Freekstyle* (Page 44 Studios, 2002) and *Excitebike 64* (Left Field, 2000), and sky-based racers such as *N-GEN Racing* (Curly Monsters, 2000) and *Freaky Fliers* (Midway, 2003).

Though snowboard racers are close to mainstream, the preceding micro-genres all share a sense of gimmickry—if a type of race exists, chances are it will be used as inspiration for a video game. The key here is to accurately estimate potential audience and not fall into the trap of believing the game to be "the next big thing." Established sports such as snowboarding and motocross have researchable fan bases, which should suggest a potential audience size. Note that many of these games came into being in the wake of the success of extreme sports games such as *Tony Hawk's Pro Skater* (Neversoft, 1997), attempting to exploit the vogue for extreme armchair activities. *SSX* specifically typifies this "larger than life" attitude and spawned a whole brand ("EA Big") on the back of its considerable success. None of the other games promoted under the brand performed as well, though a few, such as arcade rally game *Shox* (EΛ, 2002), contained interesting features.

One of the primary characteristics of this form of bandwagon jumping is the overuse of existing formats. Few games in the genre make use of their subject matter to inspire gameplay, preferring to deliver standard racing action with a few twists. The great exception to this must be *Wave Race 64*, which uses its subject matter to its fullest, presenting water as a dynamic racing surface entirely dissimilar to tarmac. In terms of audience appeal, it was also very well judged, with appealing visuals and expressive control (not to mention friendly dolphins) fueling Type 3 interest and a nicely judged difficulty curve to provide challenge that supports both the Type 1 and Type 2 preferences.

Futuristic Racer

Nucleating game: *Wipeout* (Psygnosis, 1995)

In terms of audience analysis, probably no better example than the *Wipeout* series of games exists. In 1995, while Nintendo and Sega continued to court their traditional audiences, Sony released *Wipeout* with the PlayStation's Western launch and attracted a whole new generation of gamers, specifically via appeal to the club scene. Vibrant graphics, a licensed soundtrack of dance music, cutting-edge visual design by the Designers Republic, and cleverly chosen sponsors made *Wipeout* the perfect game to mount on gamepods in clubs.

Though the genre was already established by *F-Zero* (Nintendo, 1990), *Wipeout* launched at a time when polygonal 3D was still a relative novelty, and the swooping feel of its hovering futuristic vehicles made full use of the new medium. While the racing gameplay of the games appealed primarily to H1 players, the aesthetics appealed greatly to C1 and C3 types. It might have helped that *Wipeout* looked like a video game made real—nowadays such a visual impact is difficult to make. Interestingly, and in parallel with *Tomb Raider*, the representational features of the game (which were perfectly judged to appeal to a late teens/early twenties audience) weren't matched by the game design; in terms of core gameplay, *Wipeout* is very unforgiving. Its sequel, *Wipeout 2097* (Psygnosis, 1997) is better judged in this area, and many gamers whose first console was the PlayStation quote it as a favorite game.

As the PS2 era began, *Wipeout Fusion* (Sony Liverpool, 2002) launched. While perfectly comparable to its predecessors and by no means a creative failure, its lack of structural ingenuity made it feel (ironically) old and dated. The genre in general has had trouble keeping interest with modern gamers—though *F-Zero X* (Nintendo, 1998) was a welcome addition to the N64 lineup, games such as *F-Zero GX* (Nintendo, 2003) and *Quantum Redshift* (Curly Monsters, 2002) underperformed, despite excellent (albeit massively H1) design. It is likely that, because *Gran Turismo* introduced the same level of graphical excitement to real-world racers that *Wipeout* demonstrated in its futuristic scenes, the C1 and C3 audiences who were initially drawn to the future have become far happier to stay in a familiar present.

A special mention must go to *San Francisco Rush 2049* (Midway, 2000), which included cars with wings. Though wholly unsuited to practically any audience, specifically reality-sensitive Casual players, its highly entertaining car-hurling mode has yet to be reproduced and might end up being one of the lost gems of gaming, for future data-archaeologists to discover.

City-Based Driving Game

Nucleating game: *Driver* (Reflections, 1999)

Examples of this genre can be seen as far back as *Turbo Esprit* (Durrel, 1986) on the ZX Spectrum and C64, which presented the player a city in which to drive. More recently this genre has become hugely popular due to the success of *Driver* and the *Grand Theft Auto* (DMA Designs/Rockstar North, 1997 onwards) games. The games preserve the racing genres simplicity of control, while increasing the scope for wish fulfillment—crucially, these games allow the player to cause traffic carnage on the streets. Had they been presented as realistic sims, in which crashing was actively discouraged, their popularity would not be so great.

One of the key advantages city-based drivers have over other racing games is the potential for variety. Not only do many of these games allow the player to leave their car (though this is an expensive option, principally viable in AAA titles only), but also the city structure allows for the efficient reuse of materials in mini-games, extra modes, and exploration goals. This adds a significant Type 3 bias to play already appealing to H1, C1, and C2 players.

Though *GTA* dominates this genre, numerous notable entries exist, including the arcade slant of *Crazy Taxi* (Sega, 1999), the highly Type 1-oriented *The Getaway* (Team Soho, 2002), the C1 and C2-oriented *Need For Speed Underground 2* (EA

Black Box, 2004), multiplayer *Midtown Madness* (Angel Studios, 1999), obscure Japanese fun-racer *Runabout* (Climax, 1997), and the light gun/driving hybrid *Starsky and Hutch* (Mind's Eye, 2003).

Though expensive to make due to the overheads implied by the creation of a city, this genre is so popular that its expansion is inevitable. What is surprising is that this expansion is likely to be driven as much by the creation of toyplay as agonistic gameplay—a comparison between *GTA III* and *GTA: San Andreas* (Rockstar North, 2004) shows a significant reduction in difficulty and a considerably increased emphasis on toyplay-style activities over agonistic missions (though a mission spine still provides for the necessary Type 1 audience).

Survival Horror

Nucleating game: *Resident Evil* (Capcom, 1996)

Though a relatively small genre when compared to categories such as shooter or racing game, the survival horror genre is distinct enough to be considered separately. In many ways, it marks the development of one of the first modern genres—being a blend of so many aspects of previous games, we have no choice but to consider it on its own terms. Where a control mechanism or play perspective doesn't suggest a genre (as in racing or FPS), we can expect to see more genres of this style emerge as games continue to develop.

The survival horror genre is characterized primarily by its commitment to atmosphere. This is not to say that these games are light on design expertise or gameplay; merely that atmosphere is inseparable from gameplay. *Resident Evil*, for example, is a very easy game to play if one ignores its atmospheric effects; if the player allows themselves to be immersed in its world, however, it feels tremendously dangerous. Crucially, this suspension of disbelief is made very easy, if not compulsory, by excellent atmospheric design.

Resident Evil demonstrates other factors key to the genre, though due to the need for this genre to expand to include other atmospheric horror games, not all need to be present for a game to qualify for inclusion. The fixed-camera perspectives (initially of value in creating an identifiable real-world environment via pre-rendered backgrounds at a time when the available poly counts were unsuitable for the task) were once staple to the genre. A narrative aspect is as important to survival horror as it is to adventure or RPG, though the stories can be quite simple in scope. Structurally, the traditional survival horror progression mechanisms—barriers dissolved by use of extremely simple puzzle items, employed not to provide challenging puzzles but to require environmental exploration—are still highly observable in practically all examples of the genre. Finally, simple resource management is an identifiable ingredient (the limited bullets of *Resident Evil* put the survival into the horror), but doesn't seem to be necessary to the form.

In terms of audience, the strong bias towards atmosphere and narrative are obvious draws for Type 3 players. Type 1 players happily play the games for challenge and, as mentioned previously, play the games as quickly as possible, effectively time-trialing them. This activity makes full use of Type 1 style strategic optimization and, crucially, reduces the atmospheric and narrative factors of the game to zero. The puzzle elements are, however, too simplistic to attract serious Type 2 interest, though C2 players might enjoy this style of game if the resource element is not too restrictive—that is, if tactics beyond "conserve everything" are possible.

One aspect worthy of note with regard to *Resident Evil* is its pacing. By use of circular level design in its early stages (the classic mansion contains two primary loops, and the player can choose to switch between them at the central atrium and approach them in either direction), the game retains a strong housekeeping feel in its early hours. As the game progresses, it becomes gradually more pathfinding-oriented, until the final sections are a linear rush to the end. This pacing mirrors that of a horror movie (with tense early reels and a knock-down, drag-em-out final reel) and also means that the point of widest accessibility is at the start of the game.

Finally, the real-world environments and strong movie-paradigm recognition in representation help the genre appeal more widely. Case studies show that even when Casual (specifically C3) players do not enjoy playing these games, they can enjoy watching them being played. In some cases, players might even enjoy controlling the avatar at times of low stress, only to pass the controller to a more experienced player when the situation becomes too tense—the video game equivalent of covering your eyes in the scary parts of a movie.

Three primary factors restrict the accessibility of the classic form of survival horror, however. The first is control. Fixed camera angles initially created the need for relative control, but the sharp switches between camera angles often cause confusion. More seriously, some players simply cannot mentally process relative control very easily—this function might be akin to rolling your tongue, either possible or not, with no relation to player ability. This problem, when applied to extremely tense action situations, causes frustration. Many players throw down the pad before they even reach such a situation.

The second issue is that of conservation. The player of a classic survival horror game must be aware that their supplies must last the entire game. Many players report starting a *Resident Evil* game and playing quite happily until a "biting point" (a position of temporarily increased difficulty, such as a boss) made them realize that they'd been too frivolous in their use of resources (in the case of *Resident Evil*, healing herbs and bullets of various kinds). Restarting a game after hours of play is generally too great a barrier to enjoyment.

The final problem is that of save points. Type 3 players especially dislike repeating sections of games, as this interferes with their sense of mimicked reality—in very few areas of life do we get to repeat actions and reverse our mistakes (interestingly, repetitive activities such as racing laps of a track do allow this). If a survival horror game becomes too difficult and a section requires to be replayed once too often, the Type 3-oriented player is likely to reach for a different game.

It is also interesting to note that the tense atmosphere might itself alienate casual players. Though these players might happily watch a horror movie, crucially they are passive in that activity, enjoying what amounts to a harmless thrill ride. In a horror game, the player might find the tension (related as it is to their own competence in play) to be too stressful to enjoy.

Because of these reasons, survival horror games sell primarily to an H1/H3 market, with some C1/C3 take-up with especially popular entries in the genre. This audience is more than adequate for mid-sized developments. Developments of significant AAA scope, such as the expensive *Resident Evil 4* (Capcom, 2005), require a larger audience, however. Capcom is required to invest in their premier franchise, but whether it can find a sizable enough audience (especially as the design concentrates upon more pathfinding, Type 1-oriented play than the traditional balance of pathfinding and housekeeping seen in previous *Resident Evil*s) remains to be seen.

Notable survival horror games, besides the *Resident Evil* series (all of which are of interest, with 2 being the most Casual-friendly and 3 being most Type 1-oriented of the classic format), include the *Silent Hill* series (Konami, 1999 onwards), the *Fatal Frame* series (Tecmo, 2001 onwards), the *Alone in the Dark* series (Infogrames/Darkworks, 1992 onwards), and the *Clock Tower* series (Human/Capcom, 1995 onwards).

Interesting variations on the core elements of the genre are demonstrated by *Hellnight* (Atlus, 1999) and *The Note* (Sunsoft, 1997), which both use a first-person perspective (as do parts of *Silent Hill 4* and the *Fatal Frame* games); *Sweet Home* (Capcom, 1989), which combines horror and RPG elements to startling effect considering its native platform of the NES; *Galerians* (Polygon Magic, 2000), which combines survival horror with anime-inspired psychic teenagers and drugs; *Siren* (SCEE, 2003), which combines horror, stealth, and difficulty; and *Eternal Darkness: Sanity's Requiem* (Silicon Knights, 2002).

This last game attempts to solve the key problems facing a Casual player in the context of survival horror games. While it succeeds in its mechanical aims (control is simplified, resources do not need conserving, the camera rarely causes problems, and it doesn't provide the intensity of fear associated with other survival horror games), and while its aesthetics are unarguably pleasing, it fails in key areas.

Its use of a Lovecraft-inspired narrative is difficult for a Casual market to digest (Lovecraft-inspired movies have also failed to penetrate the mainstream, perhaps because the mainstream isn't quite paranoid enough to enjoy the bleakness of cosmic horror, although a few have enjoyed cult success). Its use of pattern bosses, though limited, poses a barrier. Perhaps most seriously, in terms of structure and core gameplay, the game feels very repetitive, possibly the biggest barrier to the significant C3 take-up it required and, arguably, deserved. Nevertheless, it is a brave attempt to envision a form of survival horror that doesn't rely on constant play tension to drive it, and as such *Eternal Darkness* is worth studying by designers who intend to follow this path in the future.

Stealth

Nucleating game: *Metal Gear Solid* (Konami, 2000)

The stealth genre is a very diverse genre, but the different forms visible within it usually reflect other, more established game genres (such as FPS or platform game). As such, no sub-genres to the stealth genre exist—a stealth FPS is conventionally considered an FPS game first and foremost and stealth game second. Stealth has become one of the staple core gameplay styles and as such is included as an element in many games of many genres. The reason for including stealth as a genre in its own right is as a forum to discuss the style of play, rather than to correctly catalog its position among other games.

Stealth play initially seems to have developed from classic "avoidance" gameplay. In shooting games we see a balance of offense and avoidance; in *Pac-Man* we see a greater emphasis on the avoidance of danger. Add discernable senses to the ghosts in *Pac-Man* (so they could accurately react to the hero's presence), and it would be stealth game.

Indeed, the use of radar in the popular *Metal Gear Solid* (a top-down display at the corner of the screen presenting a simplified image of the surrounding area—crucially including the "cones of vision" of patrolling guards and surveillance cameras) is reminiscent of classic avoidance play. This is relatively unsurprising, as the original *Metal Gear* (Konami, 1987) also presented a simplified version of stealth play, and is very avoidance-oriented.

As the term suggests, stealth play involves avoiding being detected by enemies. You have two basic styles of play; the first is pure avoidance, in which the player attempts to completely evade enemies, and the second is stealth-by-murder, involving the player sneaking up behind enemies and killing them (or knocking them out) before they are detected. The majority of games take the second form, or blend the two.

Unlike other genres, perspective, structure, and elements of core gameplay beyond the stealth aspects are unimportant to the stealth classification. Within the genre we see first-person stealth games, such as the *Thief* series (Looking Glass et al, 1998 onwards); many third-person games, such as *Metal Gear*; stealth games that involve a purely linear level structure, such as *Tom Clancy's Splinter Cell* (Ubisoft, 2002); games that involve other aspects of core gameplay such as melee combat, as in *The Mark of Kri* (Sony San Diego, 2002), or platforming, as in the *Tenchu* series (Acquire, 1998); and so forth. Many games include stealth elements because adding basic senses to enemies is not difficult, resulting in games where stealth is a theoretical option, but is not expected, such as *Legacy of Kain: Soul Reaver* (Crystal Dynamics, 1999). Because it is one of few very fundamental core gameplay styles, it is often seen in ambitious hybrids like *Deus Ex* (Ion Storm, 2002), a game that covers the majority of gameplay bases, from shooting through puzzles to RPG.

You face two key design issues with any game involving stealth, however. The first is in representation. For the player to believe in the scenario presented, they must be discoverable. However, games in which stealth is the primary core gameplay do not really want the player to be discovered, as this breaks the gameplay. Modern games must be sufficiently forgiving if they are not to alienate the Casual audience, so it is no longer sufficient to end the game there and then. The most common solution is the one defined by *Metal Gear*; that an alert is raised, but will be cancelled if the player manages to hide for long enough. This sometimes raises issues of suspension of disbelief—the sixth time Snake is detected while locating the Metal Gear Rex, you would expect the guards to be a little more suspicious. Games set in the past, where radio technology didn't connect every guard in the area, have an advantage here.

The second design issue inherent to stealth games is intelligence. How does the player know where their enemies are before they stumble upon them? Here, many ingenious solutions have been seen. *Metal Gear* uses its radar, which is functional, anti-immersive, and has been dropped with *Metal Gear Solid 3: Snake Eater* (Konami, 2004). *Tenchu* presents the player with a "chi meter," which includes visual data on the enemy's state of awareness (unconcerned, suspicious, alert) and a number representing the distance to the nearest enemy. This allows the player to estimate the positions of enemies from some distance away, but can be confused by the appearance of multiple foes. The system works well, but creates a very slow game, for which patience is a prerequisite to enjoy.

Mark of Kri, meanwhile, allows the player to direct an avian familiar from predefined perch to perch; looking through the eyes of this bird allows barbarian hero Rau to assess the odds beforehand. This solution is immersive; sadly, the game fails to gel its well-designed stealth elements with its less-favorable melee combat.

The most interesting stealth game from the point of view of intelligence has to be *Siren*, a survival horror/stealth hybrid that involves largely defenseless avatars attempting to evade *shibito*, the walking dead, in a rural Japanese location. As part of the scenario, the player characters are gifted with the ability to "sight jack"—to look through the eyes of others. By tuning into the surrounding *shibito*, the player can estimate their position, and so time their movements to remain unseen. This solution is certainly innovative, and surprisingly immersive, but is tremendously unfriendly to most types of player, as detailed knowledge of the game environments is required to survive, and this knowledge can be gathered only in a trial-and-error manner. This can appeal only to Type 1 players (and even then, C1s are unlikely to be attracted to the slow, psychological bias of the game).

An alternative solution to intelligence is to present the player not with data regarding their enemies, but with data regarding their own status. Both *Thief* and *Splinter Cell* provide a light meter that tells the player how visible they are. Intelligence is otherwise supplied by visual and audio cues.

Of these methods, only the *Metal Gear* radar is simple and intuitive enough to avoid a serious learning curve at the start of the game, a factor it is preferable to avoid if a Casual audience is to be courted. A more significant advantage of the radar is its ability to maintain pace in the game. The slower forms of stealth game intelligence (and the more elaborate the system, the slower the play seems to become) hinder Casual players. C3 players might enjoy the mimicry inherent to stealth (with its resonance of childhood hide and seek) except that as a gameplay style, it refuses to let them dictate the pace of their play. This problem is compounded further if failure leads to repeated gameplay.

One interesting possibility of the stealth genre is to appeal to players seeking Type 2 play. Both *Oddworld: Abe's Oddysee* and *Beyond Good &Evil* (Ubisoft, 2002) use stealth play to provide puzzles, presenting the player tight game world abstractions that depend upon the interrelation of predictable elements. In the latter game, for example, the player's heroine can confuse enemy guards temporarily by hitting a switch on their backs, which vents their breathing equipment. Doing this causes other guards in the area to run and help their comrade. The heroine can also hide in certain areas based upon line of sight. Each stealth situation has a specific solution (though players might choose to fail and fight their way onward).

This style of puzzle element retains the basic "hide and seek" bias of stealth gameplay, but the puzzle overtones give it a more cerebral feel than Solid Snake's espionage antics, perhaps more suitable to a Type 2 audience. Additionally, the addition of the second route makes the system suitable for C3 style players as well. (It is worth noting, however, that *Beyond Good and Evil* included many core gameplay styles in addition to this minor stealth aspect and, as such, is not the most suitable product for a wide audience, despite its production values and charm.)

Taken as a whole, it is likely that the problems of representation, intelligence, and pacing will not be overcome to a degree that pure stealth games can ever appeal to the lucrative Casual markets as well as other games. Stealth games using conventional approaches, therefore, should probably be designed for purely Type 1 play, although it might be possible to loosen the essential elements of this style of play to broaden the appeal. The stealth element might be used as a contributory form for core gameplay, but in this the designer should preferably ensure that the player can either tackle the stealth aspects at their own pace or bypass the stealth requirements entirely.

CONCLUSION

This chapter has looked at the major genres that are often grouped under the umbrella term of action games. It is clear that while some action genres have a narrow appeal (often to just those with a tolerance for Type 1 play), a wider audience can be courted, including the Type 3-oriented player, who can be supported through a lowering of difficulty and atmospheric or narrative elements, and the C2 player, who has much overlap with the C1 player's tastes where there is a realistic setting and a smoother difficulty curve. Additionally, an atmosphere of friendly agon can be used to include those preferring Type 4 play.

If we consider the schism between console and PC-based gameplay, we see that console games—primarily action titles—generally sell in greater quantities than PC titles (though certain breakaway hits can sell in considerable quantities on either platform). This likely reflects ease of hardware use, and the key issue that many players use PCs for work and so prefer to spend their leisure time away from their computers. It also inevitably reflects the content of the games, with PCs hosting many genres that do not have a significant foothold on console formats, specifically non-action games.

In the next chapter, we consider the wide variety of games that demonstrate less of an action-oriented bias.

12   Genres: Quest, Strategy, and Simulation

In This Chapter

- Quest
- Strategy
- Simulation
- Miscellaneous
- Conclusion

The last chapter discussed game genres suited to action-oriented play. This chapter investigates the less action-based game styles—quest games, strategy game, and simulations. Again, the genre categories used have been created to allow sensible arrangement of information and are not intended to represent taxonomies.

Video game audiences have become very diverse. The traditional split between arcade gamers and adventure or strategy gamers (symbolized before the rise of the FPS by the split between console and computer gamers) no longer holds much weight. Considering all games by play type gives a much more accurate picture of why different players prefer different games, allowing game features to be optimized to a target audience. This is specifically of interest to such niche genres as the classic adventure game—while you can cheaply make games of this genre (since their core audience prioritize a specific form of gameplay over expensive aesthetic polish), it is vital that the product produced accurately represents the true needs of the audience if narrowcasting sales methods are to be successful.

QUEST

The term *quest game* is here used as an umbrella term, simply to avoid multiple use of the term *adventure*, which is taken to have a specific meaning. One advantage of this term is that the RPG genre can usefully be grouped beneath it, resembling as it does the adventure style more than action games.

A second advantage is that the term quest accurately describes the core value of the games grouped here. All tell stories, and, due to the nature of the medium, these stories tend towards the epic (with more intimate stories better suiting action games). Players expect their quest games to last for many hours of play, so stories are often wide in scope.

Whatever the specific mechanics of the quest game, then, one thing relates them all—that the player is cast as a protagonist within a story setting and is expected to discover or contribute to the resolution of the story through play. Being so narratively oriented, this genre has great appeal to wide audiences, with games grouped under the category collectively being able to support all four types of play. Which genres supply which style is down to the specifics of structure and core gameplay.

As a general guideline, H1 players might be drawn to any genre, while all of the quest types can supply Type 2 and Type 3 play. RPGs and adventures with accessible control mechanisms can supply Type 4 play, with RPG games in particular being associated with the H4 cluster.

Adventure

The earliest genre schism in video games took place between action (or arcade) games, which required real-time reaction, and adventures, which didn't. Action games generally took the form of dedicated, coin-operated arcade hardware, while adventures were traditionally played upon mainframe computers.

A certain cerebral nature defines adventure games. While success in action games is often a matter of reflexes, adventures typically allow time to think. Whatever the control method used, the form usually involves the player exploring a virtual environment and interacting with features within it. This interaction then leads to further exploration, as access to new areas is gained. Interactions usually take the form of logical puzzles involving objects or characters. The core gameplay can be said to comprise of exploration and puzzle solving; structure is defined by the progress mechanisms and barriers used, but is usually presented to the player in the form of a contiguous world. It is worth noting that, in the early days of video games, adventure games were the only games able to present this sense of scope in their environments. Much of their appeal might have been due to this.

Adventures typically provide Type 2 play because of their focus on puzzle solving. Depending on their mode of representation, they might also appeal to Type 3 players. H1 players might become involved with the challenge of completing adventures, because their strategic skill sets are suitable for this task. C1 players, however, seem to grow bored unless stimulation is supplied constantly. If the games involve significant interaction with NPCs, H4 players might become interested.

Text Adventure

Nucleating game: *Adventure/Colossal Cave* (W. Crowther and co., 1968 onwards)

As suggested by the name, text adventures present descriptions of a game world environment in text, on a location by location basis. The player can interact with the environment via typed input, which is processed into a predefined set of commands by software known as a parser. The degree of interaction is limited primarily by the sophistication of the parser (how many words are known, and how complex word structures can be and still be understood by the machine). With no animations to limit player actions, and so, in theory, anything is possible (or, more accurately, all actions have the same "cost" to the programmer). Some text adventures used static or even crudely animated images to brighten up the games, but these functioned much as illustrations in books do and had no influence on the primary input and output mechanisms.

The focus of puzzles in text adventures was strongly related to an inventory, as is clearly indicated by the shorthand *inv* (or even just *i*), which could be typed to display the collection of objects the player had acquired. Typical challenges involved finding items and then using them in the correct ways while in the correct locations. Sometimes objects could be combined or used upon one another.

The split between action and adventure games in the early computer era bore no similarity to the modern split between Hardcore and Casual-suitable games. All games, including adventures, were made and played by Hardcore players. This is to say, adventures exhibited H1 and H2 play; the puzzles were devious and difficult, and players could easily die if they made a wrong decision.

The advent of microcomputers allowed text adventures to reach a new audience. During the home computer era, text adventures enjoyed a status equal if not greater than that of the most popular action games, as proved by the excitement that surrounded the launch of *The Hobbit* (Beam, 1982) on the ZX Spectrum.

Certain companies had the reputation for being specialists in the text adventure genre; the most important of these were Infocom and Magnetic Scrolls. Infocom pioneered the text adventure format; their first game, based upon *Adventure,* was *Zork: The Great Underground Empire* (1980), which still remains their most famous title. Others include *A Mind Forever Voyaging* (1985), *Trinity* (1986), *Leather Goddesses of Phobos* (1986), and *The Lurking Horror* (1987).

Magnetic Scrolls formed in 1983 and created text adventures until 1992. Two elements characterized their games—first, the inclusion of a considerable number of beautifully drawn still images to provide some visual stimulation (although these could be turned off) and second, a parser of unparalleled complexity for its time, which could handle instructions for stacking objects in and on each other at a level of detail beyond any logical necessity. So proud of the parser was the Magnetic Scrolls team that they even gave it to an expert in AI to assess. He started by typing: "I think therefore I am." To which the parser replied: "Oh you do, do you?"

Their more noteworthy titles include *The Pawn* (1986), *Guild of Thieves* (1987), *Jinxter* (1987), and *Fish!* (1988). In terms of design, Magnetic Scrolls attempted to avoid placing excessive demands of completeness on the player and were artful at avoiding some of the usual exactness of the form—*Guild of Thieves* could be completed without all the treasures being collected, for example, and *Jinxter* experimented with a game design in which the player could not die.

Text adventures still have a small but very loyal following. Referred to as "Interactive Fiction" (IF) by their fans, modern versions of these games often provide less Hardcore experiences, focusing instead upon the artistic potential of the form. Nevertheless, accessibility to a wide audience is limited. That the games require too much reading is less of an issue than the fact that wrestling with the parser is half the challenge of this style of game and can quickly tire Casual players.

Point and Click Adventure

Nucleating game: *Maniac Mansion* (LucasArts, 1987)

The defining feature of point and click games is their interface—using a mouse, the player can interact with the adventure game world by clicking upon objects and commands. Initiated by LucasArts via their SCUMM engine, and first seen in *Maniac Mansion*, the point and click interface was never standardized, instead evolving through multiple generations of adventure game. The approach had grown out of the increasing formalism of text adventures; most games shared a set of common commands such as *inv* and *x* for examine, and it was becoming increasingly apparent that the potential expressiveness of the parser was actually a barrier to enjoyment from a wider audience.

Usually presented in a side-on 2D projection, a standard interface would allow the player to click on the screen to move their character, and click on objects to examine them, pick them up, combine them, and use them. Like the text adventures they developed from, point and click games were typically very inventory-oriented, with challenges involving finding items, then using them in the correct places. Story is also very important to this style of game.

For some time, point and click adventures held a great degree of prestige, initially on home computers such as the Atari ST and Commodore Amiga, and later on PCs (where the genre can still be seen today). *The Secret of Monkey Island* (LucasArts, 1990) was the one of the most important games of its era and is still considered to be the classic example of the point and click form. Other games of note include the *King's Quest* series (Sierra, 1984 onwards, point and click from *KQ5*, 1990), *Sam and Max Hit the Road* (LucasArts, 1993), the *Broken Sword* series (Revolution, 1996 onwards) and the *Discworld* series (Perfect Entertainment, 1995 onwards). Like text adventures, this genre of game has a huge and distinguished history that is beyond the scope of this chapter.

The point and click style of game has fallen out of favor. *Broken Sword: The Sleeping Dragon* (Revolution, 2003) dispensed with the classic point and click interface of its predecessors (which is less suitable to console games) and replaced it with fully 3D navigation, while retaining the adventure puzzle style of gameplay. That the game failed to resurrect the genre suggests that it is not the interface that puts modern players off, but the style of game itself. The slow, thoughtful puzzling style is now acceptable only to H2 players, though a recognizable hardcore of adventure players play practically any adventure released—creating a possible niche market for low-budget games that use creativity rather than polish as their selling point.

Action Adventure

Nucleating game: *The Legend of Zelda* (Nintendo, 1986)

In this case, *Zelda* provides more of a figurehead for this style of game. As one of the most lauded game world abstractions in video game history, the *Zelda* games demonstrate an excellent combination of Type 1 action, Type 2 puzzles, and Type 3 mimicry. However, this form of game existed before *Zelda*, notably on the ZX Spectrum in the form of games like *Avalon* (Graftgold, 1984) and *Tir Na Nog* (Gargoyle, 1984) and on the Commodore 64 in the form of games like *The Staff of Karnath* (Ultimate, 1984) and *Entombed* (Ultimate, 1985). Indeed, the popularity of this style of game on home computers caused U.K. specialist press magazine *Zzap 64* to dub them aardvarks for simplicity, the term based around the double a alliteration of arcade adventure.

The defining feature of action adventures is the ability to explore a contiguous world environment while solving adventure-like puzzles using real-time control of an avatar or agents. Of specific interest is game structure. Because action adventures present whole worlds to explore (of whatever scale), they challenged designers working with technologically limited platforms to simulate the feeling of congruity. Structural variations help create the feeling of sizable, explorable worlds. Progress mechanisms such as barrier puzzles enhance the feel of world exploration, allowing the designer to force the player to criss-cross the landscape, leading them to become familiar with it and reinforcing a sense of scale.

Zelda uses a key/barrier progress structure; the player uses tools to gain progress beyond recognizable barriers. This structure is of specific interest to Type 3 players as it allows for a certain degree of expressibility. The use of recognizable barriers is key because it encourages the player to remember places previously in the game where new tools might be of use. This gives the games a far greater feeling of existing within a world (as opposed to a set of flick-screen environments).

Alundra (Matrix Software, 1997) apes the classic *Zelda* style and introduces interesting structural aspects by representing some of its areas as conceptual dream worlds. *The Battle for Olympus* (Broderbund, 1989) chooses *Zelda 2: The Adventure of Link* (Nintendo, 1987) to provide its game world abstraction—a top-down scrolling map screen gives access to side-on 2D platform levels, which include classic lock-and-key and tool-based progress puzzles. *Demon's Crest* (Capcom, 1994) and *Actraiser* (Quintet, 1990) also trigger side-scrolling levels from overmaps, the latter including a simple god-game mode as well, to excellent effect.

Both the NES version of *Rygar* (Tecmo, 1987) and *Blaster Master* (Sunsoft, 1988) use a twin-abstraction structure to present their worlds. Both games alternate their environments between a side-on 2D perspective facilitating platform gameplay and a top-down 2D perspective allowing for more *Zelda*-style exploration. The change of perspective increases the sense of scale of the games, increasing in turn the sense of exploration (though both games are primarily pathfinding in nature). Type 3 play is aided, and C2 players might also find themselves drawn to this mix of typical action and adventure elements.

Another interesting structural variation is seen in *SoulBlazer* (Quintet, 1992), which features very *Zelda*-esque core gameplay linked to a game environment created of domain overworlds, each with their own dungeon. As the player progresses with their dungeoneering, parts of the overworld (such as characters) are restored, allowing for further progress. Slight variations on this theme are seen in *Illusion of Gaia* (Quintet, 1994) and *Terranigma* (Quintet, 1996), and the three games form an unofficial trilogy. Similar in some respects is *Dark Cloud* (Level 5, 2000), which strays into RPG territory.

A mention must also be made of *Ecco the Dolphin* (Novotrade, 1993), a maze game set underwater. The aesthetics of this game (including the atmospheric music) add greatly to an otherwise punishing Type 1 experience. Nevertheless, it deserves mention due to its beauty and originality of form.

These games all encourage Type 3 play through a sense of place. C2 players are also likely to be attracted to action adventures. H1s, meanwhile, are becoming less interested in the genre as its difficulty level drops dramatically—compare the challenge presented by early *Zelda* games with the considerably easier *The Legend of Zelda: The Minish Cap* (Capcom, 2004) for example—though all *Zelda* games include strong H2 puzzling challenge in some form.

Role-Playing Games

Computer role-playing games evolved from pen-and-paper RPGs, which are played through conversations between players, each taking the role of a single character, and a games master (GM), who "referees" the game, providing the game world and the results of all player actions. In replacing the GM with a computer, much of the ability for players to actually "role play" was lost, creating games that focus upon the gradual improvement of character abilities instead. This improvement is usually fuelled by advantages gained from combat, most commonly in the form of experience points.

This character advancement layer defines the cRPG game structure. Without such a layer, the game reverts to an adventure form. Progression is achieved via pathfinding in the game world supported by housekeeping activities (usually taking the form of talking to NPCs and shopping for character improvements). Core gameplay usually consists of exploration and combat.

RPGs differ in terms of their mix of elements. Western cRPGs usually provide more open progression structures, sometimes based on character advancement alone. Their combat tends to be simplistic, with the emphasis being placed upon character generation and optimization. These games are most popular with players who enjoy a minmaxing style of play (acquisition of advantage through detailed optimization, which is highly Type 1 in nature) or with players who enjoy balancing disparate game elements (Type 2). Hardcore players are significantly more likely to play RPGs than Casual players, because of the fantastical representations typical of the genre and because of the often significant amount of numbers and stat-balancing that is vital to success.

Japanese cRPGs, meanwhile, tend to limit the amount of balancing through optimization, preferring to use robust progression structures and highly controlled character advancement schemes. Their game worlds are usually very tightly designed and less "free range" than those of Western games. Emphasis is placed upon story (something that is often all but ignored by Western RPGs). One key difference between Japanese and Western RPGs is in player identification with the game characters. Western RPGs usually allow players to create their own characters, while Japanese games usually offer the player preset characters, who come complete with back stories and personality traits—this is the previously identified split between character expression and playing in character. Noticeably, you find very few first-person Japanese RPGs.

This impacts significantly upon the audience that can be reached. Japanese RPGs are enjoyed by H1 players (especially if they provide a significant challenge), but are also played by H4 players, who enjoy the sense of participation they achieve with the game characters. The relative simplicity of the game systems allows the H4 player to enjoy the development of their characters without having to make too many value judgments or study for too long. Conversely, Western RPGs appeal to H1 players but less so to H4 players, because the openness of these games often limits the narrative and emotional development possible within the story.

Other play types are also interested in RPGs. The Japanese strategy RPG ("strat RPG") has a distinct design bias toward Type 2 play, and H3 players enjoy all kinds of RPGs if a good story is in place. As a crude generalization, however, if they don't like the story, the H3 player won't like the game.

First-Person RPG

Nucleating game: *Dungeon Master* (FTL, 1987)

The first person RPG genre was well catered for before *Dungeon Master*'s release—via releases such as *Wizardry: Proving Grounds of the Mad Overlord* (Sir-Tech,

1981), *The Bard's Tale* (Interplay, 1985), and *Might and Magic* (New World, 1986). However, *Dungeon Master* sums up the essence of this genre very well.

The core gameplay of these early games involves exploring twisting labyrinths via a flick-screen, tile based system (mapping along the way using squared paper); fighting monsters in random encounters; gaining treasure and experience points; and so improving character abilities. In general, no barriers to progress existed besides difficulty—parties were allowed to wander anywhere they could reach. *Dungeon Master* adds sophistication to this by providing a scheme of keys and doors, but the progress mechanism is still shallow.

It is also notable that none of these early RPGs were very strong in terms of story, usually providing a framing narrative, then leaving the player to battle their way to their goal with minimal plot, character interaction, or character development.

More narrative-oriented first-person RPGs were pioneered by SSI with their Gold Box range of licensed *D&D* games, which initiated with *Pools of Radiance* (SSI, 1988). These games included conversations with NPCs, plot developments, and even interparty affairs and relationships. Though exploration proceeds in a small, flick-screen first-person window, combat takes place in a turn-based tactical style, using a top-down view of the terrain populated by character and monster graphics as viewed from the side.

One key element of all these games is the ability to create one's own party of adventurers with various classes and abilities at the start of the game (though *Dungeon Master* forces players to select up to four characters from a range of 16 preset possibilities). This feature has been key to the Western strain of cRPG since their inception, inspired as they are by pen-and-paper RPGs.

Other notable flick-screen first person RPGs include the *Eye of the Beholder* games (Westwood, 1990 onwards), *Lands of Lore* (Westwood, 1993), and *Bloodwyche* (Mirrorsoft, 1989), which offered two-player simultaneous cooperative play.

With the advent of polygonal 3D, the genre gained its most notable games in *Ultima Underworld: The Stygian Abyss* (Blue Sky, 1992) and *Ultima Underworld 2: The Labyrinth of Worlds* (Looking Glass, 1992). These games provided early texture-mapped 3D exploration, and though they contained strong RPG elements, they incarnated the player as a single character of fixed (though undefined) identity, breaking with tradition. These games led to the creation of the *Elder Scrolls* series (Bethesda, 1993 onwards), which provided the modern acme of the genre, *Morrowind* (Bethesda, 2002).

The classic form of first-person RPG is absolutely dead, unable to survive even in a handheld form. Even the 3D form is unpopular when compared with third-person RPGs and, especially, console-based Japanese RPGs. Nevertheless, the form is open to interpretation, so a resurgence might occur. Though the core audience for the *Elder Scrolls* style of detailed RPG is primarily H2 and H3, simpler iterations exploiting the epic nature of the form could conceivably be of interest to C3 players. A less fantastical representation might be required, however.

Western-Style RPG

Nucleating game: The *Ultima* series (Origin, 1981 onwards)

The *Ultima* series dominates the development of the Western third-person RPG. Though early games were extremely simple, from the fourth iteration onwards, the storylines of the games would break new ground in RPGs, and in video games of any kind. The focus was upon moral development, a fascinating re-imagining of the RPG staple of character improvement. Players took the role of the Avatar, brought to the world of Britannia to save it from times of peril. The series reached its zenith with *Ultima VII: The Black Gate* (Origin, 1992).

The form of the third-person Western RPG—almost exclusively a PC-based genre—took some time to settle, with each new iteration of *Ultima* presenting new features and interface. With *Baldur's Gate* (BioWare, 1998), however, the genre crystallized. The basic format involves a point and click interface, a set of player characters, possibly with a single narrative lead (though all can be controlled), real-time combat (with a pause key to allow for strategizing), and the requirement to save a world by leveling up and gaining treasure. Structurally, a central narrative spine leads through areas in which interaction with NPCs might develop subquests, each with their own treasure and experience bonus.

Similar games in this sequence include *Fallout* (Interplay, 1997), *Planescape: Torment* (Black Isle, 1999)—often quoted for excellence of story in such discussions, *Icewind Dale* (Black Isle, 2000), and *Arcanum: Of Steamworks and Magick Obscura* (Troika Games, 2001). It is noticeable that the D&D license dominates this genre (as it has tended to dominate the commercial side of tabletop RPG games). Fantasy settings dominate RPGs in general, and within that milieu D&D dominates as one of a very few viable licenses. *Neverwinter Nights* (BioWare, 2003) pushed the genre a little further by including fully modable online elements, allowing players to use the software as a "*D&D* adventure creator" for use with their friends.

The Western RPG's native platform is the PC, but console equivalents do exist. Games of this style usually feature real-time gameplay and might be more action adventure in feel than RPG, though the core elements of structure remain. Examples include the SNES *Shadowrun* (Beam, 1993) and the PS2 *Baldur's Gate* games (Snowblind/Black Isle, 2001 onwards), the latter of which resemble *Gauntlet* (Atari, 1985) as much as traditional RPGs.

One sub-genre worth mentioning is the "Euro-RPG." Examples include *Divine Divinity* (Larian Studios, 2002), *Sacred* (Ascaron, 2004), and *Kult: Heretic Kingdoms* (3D People, 2004). These low-tier games feature game designs focused specifically upon meeting the needs of Hardcore (H1, H2) RPG players and add very little in the way of unnecessary bells and whistles. These games show that you can make a successful product for a fraction of AAA cost if narrowcasting to the target audience can be carried out effectively. Games of this nature will never hit big, but usually generate more revenue than their development costs, which is a sufficient goal for small teams making games for love, not fame, and a perfectly reasonable commercial goal for small publishers.

Hardcore Western RPG players appear to be looking for certain specific elements, in particular strong character generation systems that give them plenty of choice, skill and magic systems with plenty of depth and scope for minmaxing, lots of varied side quests, plenty of choice of equipment, and an unforgiving difficulty curve with multiple "biting points" to provide fiero. Aesthetic qualities are far less important than strategic factors and challenge (H1), although the audience for such games can take in the H2 cluster (with suitable game mechanics) or H3 cluster (with a strong narrative drive).

Japanese-Style RPG

Nucleating game: *Final Fantasy* (Squaresoft, 1987)

Compared to its Western cousin, the third-person RPG is a far more stabilized form in Japan, where it is immensely popular. It is typified by a simple, robust structure that uses repetitive random combats to generate play time during exploration sections, which take place in top-down environments loosely maze-like in nature. The player usually controls a predefined avatar personality, but is given access to the abilities of other characters in combat via a party system (usually only three characters are allowed in combat together at once). Exploration phases alternate with housekeeping phases, in which the player explores villages, talks to people, buys equipment, and occasionally plays mini-games.

The dynamic of the core gameplay—combat—is also usually highly codified, traditionally using a turn-based format in which characters are allowed a single action per round of combat, either an attack, a special move of some description, magic (including healing, which provides the basic resource dynamic of this style of combat), or the use of an item. Modern Japanese cRPGs often use a real-time variant of this style of system, and a game's combat system is often its second most defining characteristic (after narrative material).

This basic format—exploration, combat, housekeeping—can be seen throughout the genre. It can also be seen beneath the surface in Western-style RPGs, but those games prefer to disguise their abstractions and accentuate their extensiveness, while the Japanese breed tends towards the opposite approach. Equipment systems in Western games, for example, often offer many different weapons of similar quality to account for player choice; Japanese games rarely include more than a single weapons-chain of progressively improving weapons for each character.

Important Japanese RPGs include the *Final Fantasy* series—specifically *Final Fantasy VII* (Square, 1997), historically the best selling cRPG with 7.8 million copies sold worldwide [Gamestate03]—the *Dragon Quest/Dragon Warrior* series (Enix, 1986 onwards)—of which, *Dragon Warrior VII* is a notable high seller at 6 million copies [Gamestate03]—the *Star Ocean* series (Enix, 1996 onwards), *Chrono*

Trigger (Square, 1995), *Xenogears* (Square, 1998), *Grandia II* (Game Arts, 2000), and *Skies of Arcadia* (Overworks, 2000).

One aspect that is telling regarding the Japanese RPG format is the importance of character design, especially to Japanese audiences. Popular artists are often hired to design the key characters in these games, and paintings or CGI renders are used as promotional materials, for calendars and in other spin-offs such as "making of" art books. This emphasis upon character gives a clue as to a key part of the target audience of these games—H4 players, who enjoy the sense of participation with the game cast, although it is certain that H1 and H2 players are also part of the audience.

H4 players do not find this element in Western RPGs, where characters are often player-defined and have no personality in a narrative sense. Japanese games, however, put great emphasis on story with direct relation to character development. (H3 players also play RPGs if the stories are sufficiently engaging to their tastes, though it should be noted that H3 players happily achieve mimicry in either Western or Japanese RPGs and might prefer the former due to the ability to define their own characters.)

The sales of Japanese RPGs (which at their highest might be four or five times greater than sales of Western RPGs) [Gamestate03] demonstrate the benefit of hitting both Type 1 and Type 4 audiences together. It should be noted, however, that Western RPGs can be made much more cheaply than the Japanese style, which require high aesthetic values, so niche audiences might be cultivated.

Strat RPG

Nucleating game: *Final Fantasy Tactics* (Square, 1997)

The strategy RPG has been popular in Japan for years, first emerging in *Fire Emblem* (Nintendo/Intelligent Systems, 1990) before accreting in form with the *Shining Force* series (Sega, 1992 onwards). Originally viewed from a top-down perspective, the genre acquired its now-standard isometric perspective with *Ogre Battle* (Quest, 1994). After the success of *Tactics Ogre* (Quest, 1995), Squaresoft enlisted Quest to create *Final Fantasy Tactics*, the game that brought the genre to the notice of Western players (though *Ogre Battle* had been popular). Other notable games in the genre include the *Front Mission* series (Square, 1995 onwards); *The Arc the Lad* series (G-Craft/Cattle Call, 1995 onwards); *Ring of Red* (Konami, 2001), which adds a live-action combat-engagement sequence to the genre; *Disgaea: Hour of Darkness* (Nippon Ichi, 2003), based around a dungeon hack RPG structure (which we will discuss shortly); and a rare Western-developed strat RPG, *Gladius* (LucasArts, 2003).

The defining feature of the strat RPG is the melding of a simple strategic engine (resembling the Western squad-based tactics genre, utilizing a grid-based environment upon which to move a small number of individualistic characters in turn-based combat) with an RPG structure focusing upon character development via experience systems. You see usually less overworld exploration than other Japanese RPGs, due to the length of combat. Story is also important, but delivered in chapter structure, with both story and character-housekeeping sequences occurring between often linearly structured battles.

Control is usually simple, and units generally are able to make one move (of varying distance) per turn, and take one action (attack, defend, use item, etc.). The relative simplicity of the combat sequences is offset by often hugely complex character modification, with housekeeping often taking as much time as the battles themselves. As such, this style of game appeals to Hardcore players only, especially Type 2 players who can use their Strategic-Tactical skill sets without having to worry about quick response times.

Dungeon Hack

Nucleating game: *Rogue* (Arnold, Toy, and Wichman, 1980 onwards)

Though *Diablo* (Blizzard, 1996) is the most commercially important game of the dungeon hack (or hack) genre, it doesn't accurately represent all core features of the genre. Games of the hack genre are often referred to as *Rogue*-like games. Other games in the sequence include *Hack/NetHack* (J. Fenlason and co., 1987 onwards), *Moria* (R. A. Koeneke, 1983 onwards), and *Valhalla* (Norsehelm Production, 1993).

The key element of hack games involves randomized environments ("dungeons" created of rooms and passages) and treasure and monsters generated from tables and lists. The player is assigned a single character, which is usually definable in terms of various aspects including class, and moves through the dungeon levels, fights monsters, and gains treasure and power via experience and equipment. You find very little story content to these games. The term *hack* comes from the sensation of wading through dungeons killing anything that appears.

Traditionally, these games were created on mainframes and distributed via the fledgling Internet. *Rogue* used ASCII graphics to present its locations (and was the first graphical quest game). The major hack games are still free to download, and many different programmers work on them, adding new features and updating regularly. The commercial strain of the genre uses the random elements of location, monster, and treasure to present open-ended dungeoneering to a specific form of RPG audience. Though the lack of story and character causes these games to lack Type 3 or 4 appeal, H1 and H2 players enjoy the sense of power gain, and play is driven by a desire to find new and better equipment. Because this equipment is delivered pseudo-randomly, you can find a great strategic element in the application of equipment to a character—items might combine positively with one another, for example.

This style of play cannot realistically be promoted to a wider audience, though it can be used to bolster longevity of games in other genres, as seen in Japanese games such as *Disgaea: Hour of Darkness* and *Azure Dreams* (Konami, 1997). The former uses hack elements to provide an open-ended strat RPG, while the latter uses a dual structure involving town building funded by the spoils of a hack. In the spirit of hybridizing genres, it would be fascinating to see if the hack genre concepts could be applied to a racing game, for example.

Creature-Raising Game

Nucleating game: *Pokémon Red/Blue* (Game Freak, 1996)

Though not sold as an RPG, *Pokémon* exhibits many design features inherent to the Japanese RPGs, including exploration punctuated by turn-based combat and the gradual increase in power of the characters (in this case, fantasy beasts that fight at the behest of the player's avatar). The game initiated a worldwide *Pokémon* craze among children, partly due to its cleverly created virtual world, which kids loved to learn about, and partly due to the collecting element (which was boosted by the option to trade beasts between cartridges), selling some 8 million units [Gamestate03].

The other appealing feature of *Pokémon* is the element of creature raising. Players catch Pokémon, use them in their own teams, and watch as the creatures slowly become more powerful, sometimes gaining new powers and, in certain cases, evolving into different types of monsters altogether. Perhaps inspired by the earlier *Tamagotchi* craze (LED creature-raising egg toys first created by Bandai in 1996), players form a bond with their creatures via the experience of watching them grow. This aspect of *Pokémon* spawned a sub-genre of its own.

The appeal of creature-raising games comes from identification with the creatures—something that appeals to both H4 and C4 players (though the latter find complex RPG elements off-putting). Other play types might be catered for by creature raising games, depending on the other gameplay aspects they include. For example, *Pokémon* appeals to H1 players, who enjoy attempting to learn everything about suitably detailed game worlds. *Azure Dreams* (Konami, 1997), a blend of dungeon hack and creature-raiser, appeals to H1 and H2 players as it provides a very stiff challenge, incorporating multiple disparate elements. *Black & White* (Lionhead, 2001) combines creature raising with a technologically advanced god game, appealing primarily to H2 players.

Monster Rancher (Tecmo, 1997) allows the player to generate monsters using data from any CD and pit them against other monsters in combat, appealing to a Type 3 sensibility and encouraging H1 players to find the "perfect creature." *Jade Cocoon: Story of the Tamamayu* (Genki, 1998) introduces creature blending—creatures can be combined and change in shape accordingly. This RPG is relatively Hardcore in nature, featuring little character interaction or story elements, but the creature aspects expand its appeal beyond the H1 audience to H3 and H4.

RPG Hybrid

Because the RPG structure embeds a repetitive core gameplay element into a complex structure of character development and exploration, it has great scope for hybridization. Indeed, many games during review are described as having "RPG elements"—

usually meaning upgradeable avatar abilities. *Gran Turismo* (Polyphony, 1997) demonstrates this by allowing a significant amount of car upgrading within a "game world" of different races accessed via a menu (which is represented as a map).

Road Trip (Takara, 2002) takes this hybridization of racing core gameplay and RPG structure even further, presenting a contiguous world for the player to drive around, featuring embedded races. The player's car can be upgraded in multiple ways, and other cars can be talked to, brought items, raced, etc. *Road Trip* is the first full-fledged "CarPG," and though its low budget and representation (cute anthropomorphized cars that talk to each other and live in neatly decorated houses) might put off players who prefer their racing games to be realistic, it does offer an excellent model of a genre with plenty of room for expansion. The game was created as merchandising for Takara's *Choro Q* toy line in Japan, reinforcing the point that licensed games need not be unoriginal.

Other forms of play might be substituted for RPG combat. *Deus Ex* (Ion Storm, 2000), often considered to be an RPG in its own right, exhibits every indication of being an FPS, but also includes character modification and NPC interaction. Because the first-person RPG is an accepted genre, the combination isn't revolutionary, but it does demonstrate how the expanding of structure can completely alter the feel of the game. An early FPS/RPG hybrid is *Strife* (Rogue Entertainment, 1996), which used the *Doom* (id Software, 1992) engine, and indeed plays like a *Doom* RPG.

Squaresoft's *The Bouncer* (Dream Factory, 2000) adds character modification to the scrolling beat-em-up, while *Legaia 2: Duel Saga* (SCEI, 2001) is an RPG that triggers special moves in turn-based combat via fighting game style button combinations; *Armada* (Metro 3D, 1999) adds RPG leveling to the scrolling shooter genre, *Koudelka* (Sacnoth, 1999) presents an RPG with the representation of survival horror, and *Castlevania: Symphony of the Night* (Konami, 1997) combines platform leaping with leveling and use of equipment.

Of course, once you have a significant number of hybrid games of a given type, a new genre nucleates, as seen with strat RPGs.

One final RPG hybrid is worth noting. After *Magic: The Gathering* (Garfield Games/Wizards of the Coast, 1993) had achieved phenomenal (and practically overnight) success, and founded the commercially significant trading card game (or collectible card game), a computer version inevitably followed (Microprose, 1997). Trading card games became extremely popular and many variants emerged, including a *Pokémon* collectible card game (Tsunekaz Ishihara, Kouichi Ooyama, and Takumi Akabane, 1996), which was also converted to a video game—*Pokémon Trading Card Game* (Game Freak, 2000). Further trading card game elements appeared in video games, including licensed products such as the *Yu-Gi-Oh* series (Konami, 1999 onwards) and original RPG products such as *SNK vs. Capcom: Card Fighter's Clash* (SNK, 1999), *Lost Kingdoms* (From Software, 2002), and *Baten Kaitos: Eternal Wings and the Lost Ocean* (Monolith Software Inc., 2004). These games feature both direct conversions of card games, and action elements using cards as a central theme.

The crossover between the tabletop trading card games and video games serves to underline the point that video game design isn't a discipline separate from that of traditional game design and also serves as a caution to game designers to be aware of gaming trends in all formats.

Massively Multiplayer RPGs

Developed from the early MUDs (multi-user dungeon or domains), text-based games based around an online community, with the environment being database mediated), Massively Multiplayer Online RPGs (MMORPGs) present many players with a single world to explore. Though these games offer gameplay similar to that of single player RPGs, including quests, leveling, and treasure, the multiplayer nature of the games means that social dynamics are more important to the success of the games.

Players might play MMORPGs for many reasons, including community and financial issues (as some people play to make money). As such, the form requires specific attention and research and cannot be fully considered in terms of the DGD1 model. However, the research that has been conducted seems to indicate that the audience for such games spans all four Hardcore clusters (H1, H2, H3, and H4) but does not penetrate significantly into the Casual market.

STRATEGY

The roots of the strategy game predate video games by decades. In the late fifties, Charles Roberts founded Avalon Hill and published *Tactics II* (1958) and *Gettysburg* (1958), which were the first table-top war games. Although an extremely niche market in modern terms, in this pre-video game, pre-role-playing game, and pre-collectible card game era, war games founded the hobby games industry, and their influence on the development of games is not to be underestimated. *Chainmail* (Guidon Games, 1971), which was a stepping stone towards the first role-playing game, *Dungeons & Dragons* (TSR, 1974), was inspired by these games, and the core of mechanics that are used in turn-based strategy games of all kinds owe their genesis to games published by Avalon Hill.

In their time, Avalon Hill was the major force in war game publishing, rivaled only briefly during the 1970s by SPI, and their catalog of games contains many of the most influential war games and board games ever published. This includes *Panzerblitz* (1971), *The Russian Campaign* (1976), *Squad Leader* (1977), and *The Civil War* (1983) [Costikyan98]. They also published the most widely distributed edition of *Diplomacy* (Allan Calhammer, 1954; first commercial release 1959), which is considered by some to be the most significant board game of the twentieth century, although its complexity greatly limits its commercial value. Additionally, they were responsible for bringing to the United States (and the attention of a wider public in general) some of the most influential board games, of which the most notable is *Civilisation* (Francis Tresham, 1980), which directly inspired Sid Meier to create his own game with the same title. Indeed, early editions of *Sid Meier's Civilization* (Microprose, 1991) contained a flyer promoting the board game [Rudnik05].

Turn-based strategy games (and by extension all strategy games) have their roots in these early Avalon Hill games. Notions such as turn sequences, hex-based maps, dice for resolution of conflict, comparative matrices, and almost all the other elements that underpin strategy game design date back to this era. Although we can only speculate, it seems certain that the audience for these games was primarily agonistic H1 and H2 players (especially the latter), and certainly where war games are still played today, it is mostly by players fitting the profile for the H2 cluster.

The earliest strategy games on computers, such as early *Star Trek* games (D. Matuszek and co., circa 1970), were written in universities on mainframe computers and displayed events in text or ASCII formats (there was also an Atari 2600 version). As soon as computers grew powerful enough and were more widely available, board game and tabletop war game conversions became popular, and many of the deep, complex games by Avalon Hill were converted into video games during the transitional period of the 1980s. It was natural to convert these games to a computerized form, because it took the time-consuming bookkeeping out of the hands of the players and automated it.

The basic form of strategy games involves a set of discrete rules that are transparent (i.e., the player is aware of them) and must be exploited to full advantage by the player, who seeks to attain whatever victory conditions the rules state. Strategy games are not generally played intuitively, by mimicking reality, as other game styles might be. Instead, players must experiment within the framework of the rules until they discover a strategy that will maximize their advantages and minimize their weaknesses. If the games rules are well balanced and interact in interesting ways, continued play can reveal the subtleties and allow mastery of the rules system.

Later development of strategy games began to concentrate upon different elements of the games, so different genres became available, as popular features were reused and game styles accreted in the usual ways into recognizable forms. Though the strategy genre is too wide to fully encompass, this section investigates some of the most popular forms.

Turn-Based Strategy

Nucleating game: *Sid Meier's Civilization* (Microprose, 1991)

The turn-based strategy game genre existed before computer games did, and as such the nucleating game has been chosen as a representative of the genre in general. *Civilization* contains many of the elements of strategy games, though the genre is so diverse that no game can contain every element; as has already been noted, *Civilization* traces its descent directly from strategic board games.

Turn-based strategy games inherited the general form of board games, primarily with grid or hex maps to mediate movement of units, and a turn-based time abstraction (board games are fundamentally incompatible with a real-time approach), which was initially necessary because computer hardware simply wasn't powerful enough to run such games in real time. It is worth commenting, however, that H2 players appear to genuinely prefer the time to think offered by the turn-based approach, favoring as it does strategic problem solving over instinctive quick thinking.

Actions are also simulated in the same way, via stats and randomized numbers. The primary advantage of computer strategy games is that the computer bookkeeps the game—although when playing a board game, players can modify poorly considered or broken mechanics, an act impossible with a computer game.

Turn-based strategy games are most beloved by the H2 player, for whom they represent perhaps the embodiment of Strategic Type 2 play, and case studies of H2 players repeatedly feature games of this type, especially those of the *Civilization* series. Some appeal exists to H1 players (as these games can be an excellent source of fiero), and C2 players with the willingness to tackle a complex rules system (often with a high learning curve) might also play turn-based strategy games, although generally only if they are based in a somewhat familiar setting (classic fantasy included).

This genre is exceptionally diverse, but some titles of note include *Computer Diplomacy* (Avalon Hill, 1984), *Panzer General* (Strategic Simulations, 1994), *Master of Magic* (Simtex, 1993), *Master of Orion* (Simtex, 1994), *Fantasy General* (SSI, 1996), and of course the *Civilization* series itself, and by extension *Sid Meier's Alpha Centauri* (Firaxis, 1999).

Squad-Based Tactics

Nucleating game: *X-Com: UFO Defense* (Mythos Games, 1994)

Tactical squad-level turn-based skirmish games require the player to move a small number of troops around small-scale battlefields, locating and defeating enemies, and occasionally performing other tasks. The games usually intersperse tactical gameplay with some degree of resource management, via a secondary engine.

The *X-Com* series of games is the preferred squad-based tactics game. Casting the player as director of international anti-alien taskforce X-Com, soldiers must be hired and equipped, then sent on missions to locate and eliminate alien threats. Resource management involves building bases around the world, balancing budgets, and researching alien technology to develop new weapons and equipment with which to fight. The turn-based tactical sections are therefore tightly bound to the resource systems; the player might want to capture a new alien type alive for research, for example, adding new challenge to a mission.

RPG elements are also included, as each squad member has stats that rise as they use their skills. This feature highlights the similarity between squad-based tactics games and strat RPGs, the major difference being the level of complexity of the turn-based combat itself. While strat RPGs simplify combat by allowing one move and one action per unit per turn, *X-Com* and other squad-based tactics games use an action point system to mediate unit actions. Every action (moving a given distance, firing, crouching, picking something up, etc.) costs a discrete number of points, deducted from the units stock. Once the points are drained, the unit can do nothing more. Points are replenished at the start of each turn.

This system, coupled with fog of war (enemy units can be seen only when in line of sight of a friendly unit), adds greatly to the tension of this style of game (as does the depth of character development, which makes losing a unit very painful). It is common for blithely deployed units to run out of action points at precisely the wrong time, leaving them exposed during the enemy turn. Because units are moved one by one, it is not unusual for the player to spend a turn trying to "rescue" a badly positioned unit with other units. This gives the games a feeling of urgency, as well-laid plans start to slip into chaos.

The primary difference between squad-based tactics games and classic turn-based strategy games is in scale; squad-based games rarely allow units to be generated during combat and usually limit the number of units available in a single encounter. Where classic strategy games create depth via numerous units, squad-based tactics games create depth via the degree of action available to each unit.

Squad-based tactics games deliver primarily Type 2 play, but might encourage H1 play if sufficiently challenging. They tend not to work very well on console format, due to their relative complexity. As noted, their console equivalent is the strat RPG.

X-Com: UFO Defense was designed by Julian Gollop, whose earlier games, including *Chaos* (1984), *Rebelstar* (1986), and *Laser Squad* (1989), are worthy of note, as is *Laser Squad Nemesis* (Codo Games, 2003). Other squad-based tactics games include *Jagged Alliance* (Madlab Software, 1994), *Battle Isle 4: Incubation* (Blue Byte, 1997), *S2: Silent Storm* (Nival Interactive, 2003), *Fallout Tactics: Brotherhood of Steel* (Micro Forté, 2001), and *Shadow Watch* (Red Storm, 2000).

Real-Time Strategy

Nucleating game: *Command & Conquer* (Westwood, 1995)

The two-player Sega Genesis game *Herzog Zwei* (Techno Soft, 1990) reputedly inspired the development of *Dune II: The Building of a Dynasty* (Westwood, 1992), which defined the RTS form and led to the production of *Command & Conquer*, which in turn exploded the genre.

The core features of the classic RTS style are a production aspect, in which the player must build facilities, harvest resources, and generate units, and a combat element, requiring troops to be moved into position and given targets. While these forms of play had been seen before, RTS games force the player to pursue both aspects simultaneously, in real time. This creates a level of frantic action completely at odds with traditional strategy games.

RTS games reward logistical skills, as the player must balance attack and defense with steady, measured production, based upon resource estimates. It is the production aspect that secures victory rather than the tactical deployment of forces, so it follows that those with Strategic/Logistical skills enjoy the games the most—Type 1 play is well catered for, especially C1 play, although H1 players do enjoy these games and H2 players might enjoy the strategy and agonistic elements even though turn-based approaches generally represent a better fit to H2 play needs.

This explains the relative popularity of the RTS genre; the C1 demographic is significantly larger than the traditional audience for strategy games, the H2 demographic. The genre fails to provide any Type 3 or 4 appeal, however—the lack of mimicry inherent to the core gameplay leads some Type 3 players to compare the games to spreadsheets.

Very few RTS games exclude the production mechanic, and the decision to do so results in a fundamental shift in the bias of the game. The *MechCommander* series (FASA Studio, 1998 onwards) gives the player a team of units to which the only housekeeping is in salvaging and upgrading equipment. This, in part, was a purposeful step to reflect the kind of play in the *BattleTech* table-top war game (FASA, 1984) that these games are based upon. The result is a game that H2 players (and some H1 players) tend to greatly prefer to conventional production-driven RTS, but the core target audience of C1s is lost because Logistical skills have been made irrelevant and Strategic and Tactical skills have increased in importance.

For a time, RTS games matched FPS titles for popularity on the PC platform, but their strength has waned, and the number of new RTS titles being produced has fallen. Nevertheless, the genre continues to sell extremely well in its more popular forms, primarily the *Warcraft* series (Blizzard, 1994), of which *Warcraft III* (Blizzard, 2002) adds quest game elements; the *Age of Empires* series (Ensemble Studios, 1997 onwards), which adds a dash of *Civilization* to the mix; and the *Total War* series (The Creative Assembly, 2000), which harks back to the strategy genre's roots with increased complexity.

Other popular RTS games include *Total Annihilation* (Cavedog, 1997), *StarCraft* (Blizzard, 1998), and *Homeworld* (Relic, 1999), which introduces the fully 3D battlefield of open space.

Strategic Quest

Nucleating game: *Heroes of Might and Magic* (New World Computing, 1995)

The original strategic quest game is *King's Bounty* (New World Computing, 1990), from which *Heroes of Might and Magic* directly evolved. In *King's Bounty*, the player moves a single avatar around a large scrolling map, which is formed like a maze. The primary concern is to collect gold and raise an army with which to subjugate neighboring castles, some of which are occupied by a series of villains and their armies. The ultimate goal is to find a treasure, the position of which is slowly revealed by the acquisition of a treasure map, a piece of which is gained upon the defeat of each of the villains.

As the player moves from continent to continent, the villains become tougher, but money becomes more plentiful, allowing for the recruitment of more and better troops. Troop numbers are limited by a leadership stat, which can be raised by numerous means and forms the main source of RPG-like character improvement. Combat initiates a turn-based tactical mode, in which the player can move each of their armies (represented by a single unit), attack, shoot ranged weapons, and cast spells. The game was remade for PS2 as *Heroes of Might and Magic: Quest for the Dragon Bone Staff* (3DO, 2001).

The strategic quest genre, then, is defined by the combination of strategy game and RPG elements. The player has specific characters to use, with their own statistics, equipment, and potential to increase in power, but these characters are used in a strategic manner. A quest is pursued, but via strategic and logistical means rather than by narrative methods.

As already mentioned, *Heroes of Might and Magic* is derived directly from *King's Bounty*, with some tweaks. It replaces direct avatar control with a point and click system and adds multiple agents at the player's control. Villains are replaced by fewer enemies, who do not merely wait at their castles to be beaten, but send heroes of their own to fight the player and each other. The changes introduce more strategy, as castles must be supplied with garrison troops. The core of the game is still resource management, exploration, and combat, but the elements blend better.

Other games that provide a similar form of gameplay include the *Warlords* series (Strategic Studies Group, 1990 onwards), which has no tactical combat system but retains a similar focus in gameplay to *HOMM* (specifically in balancing armies and garrisoning captured castles), the *Age of Wonders* series (Triumph Studio, 1999 onwards), and *Master of Magic* (Simtex, 1995), which is closer to a fantasy *Civilization* than *HOMM*, but still retains much of the quest strategy feel.

Quest strategy games can be played in a Type 2 manner, but also invite a looser style of play that might appeal to Type 3 players who like the idea of strategy games, but don't want to spend too much time learning. The combination of Strategic and Logistical elements also suggests an appeal to Type 1 players. These games are very immediate, though they have enough depth to please H2 players, and they have generated a cult following. Their application to a wider audience is unlikely, however, due to repetitive micro-management supply mechanics that are fundamental to the form. Although they have a fit to the skill set of the commercially important C1 player, the immediacy of the RTS genre is always likely to be preferred.

SIMULATION

When we talk about games of simulation, we are specifically referring to those games where mimicry is of paramount importance. These are games that are concerned with the reproduction of reality in some way, as is obviously seen in the genre of vehicle simulators, the most obvious example of which is the classic flight simulator form. Some games of simulation—such as pure flight sims, sim games, and life sims—are concerned only with mimicry, while others—such as sports games and god games—contain highly agonistic elements while still being dependent upon successful mimicry for their success.

Vehicle Simulation

Nucleating game: *Microsoft Flight Simulator* (subLOGIC, 1982)

Vehicle simulations are brought together in a single section for convenience. Realistic car sims have been discussed in the previous chapter, in the section on racing games. Though car games are the most popular vehicle sims, many other vehicles have been simulated in the history of games. Most of these appeal to the same type of person: those who prioritize realism, enjoy learning new things, and have patience in the face of adversity. It is likely that the players of such games tend towards Type 1 tendencies simply because of the patience required to master them, although the Type 2 player's desire for mastery might be apposite. Although we associate Type 3 and 4 play with mimicry, no desire for technical accuracy exists with these play styles, and it is accuracy that vehicle simulations are concerned with.

Flight sims were the first games to attempt to genuinely simulate a vehicle, possibly because they could be created with very simple graphics—a line for a horizon, two more for a runway. These early games gave the player little to do other than take off and land again, but they were so difficult that just reaching level flight was a triumph. Microsoft's version has been chosen as the nucleating example, because it has the longest legacy, now dominating the niche market it commands to the point by which few other flight sims are made.

Flight sims can be broadly divided into three categories, commercial aviation, combat, and arcade. The third category represents flight games like the *PilotWings* games (Nintendo/Paradigm, 1990, 1996), which use realistic physics but simplify the controls to allow a wider variety of players to enjoy the flights—Type 3 players might enjoy the physical beauty of this style of game. However, beauty is expensive, so games of this type are a gamble (and relatively rare).

Many other vehicles have been simulated in video game form. In general, these games are similar to flight sims in that their attention to detail makes them harder to learn than arcade-biased games, restricting their audience to H1 and H2 audiences who also have an interest in those vehicles. These games are best developed by small teams who have a genuine interest in the vehicle in question, because they are not routes to fast profit.

Notable vehicles simulated include trains via *Microsoft Train Simulator* (Kuju, 2001), submarines via *Jane's Combat Simulations - 688(I) Hunter/Killer* (Jane's Combat Simulations, 1997), tanks via *Armored Fist* (Novalogic, 1994), warships via *Naval Ops: Warship Gunner* (Micro Cabin, 2003), trucks via *Hard Truck: 18 Wheels of Steel* (Sunstorm Interactive, 2002), and spaceships via *Microsoft Space Simulator* (The Bruce Artwick Organization Ltd, 1994).

Steel Battalion (Capcom, 2003) is an honorable mention; though mechs do not exist, *Steel Battalion* manages to simulate their piloting, being played with a custom controller that emulates all the functions of a "real" mech control panel, including an eject button—the player must press this before death to prevent their player data being erased permanently.

Sports

Nucleating game: *Dr. J and Larry Bird Go One on One* (Electronic Arts, 1983)

Sports are one of the earliest identifiable game genres. The Magnavox Odyssey games system was supplied with colored overlays to be attached to the player's television, allowing the basic pong-style games to be played as "hockey," "football," and "tennis." The name *Pong* (Atari, 1972) itself is resonant of sports. *Atari Football* (Atari, 1979) was immensely popular, though basic.

Dr. J and Larry Bird Go One on One is especially notable because it featured the first sports license, a realistic and identifiable representation, and provided Electronic Arts with a business strategy that has led them to become the world's biggest independent publisher. By attaching two huge sports stars to their basketball game, EA managed to appeal to people who didn't necessarily play video games, but were invested in the cultural landscape of their time.

Since then, sports games have become one of the most lucrative genres, with yearly franchise entries by numerous series. EA dominates and has premier franchises in most sports, most notably *Madden NFL* football (1988 onwards), *FIFA* soccer (1993 onwards), *Tiger Woods PGA Tour* golf (1998 onwards), *NBA Live* basketball (1994 onwards), and *NHL* hockey (1991 onwards).

Other notable sports games include top-down soccer games *Kick Off* (Anco, 1989) and *Sensible Soccer* (Sensible Software, 1992), *International Superstar Soccer/Pro Evolution Soccer* series (Konami, 1995 onwards), multiplayer-friendly *Virtua Tennis* (Sega, 1999), highly abstracted boxing game *Punch-Out!!* (Nintendo, 1984), and the *All-Star Baseball* series (Acclaim, 1999 onwards).

Action-based real-world sports games are required to appeal to the widest possible audience, but generally target C1 and C2 players. A trade-off must usually be made between accuracy and ease of play. It is usual to allow play with two or three buttons only (pass and shoot in soccer, for example), but to load subtlety onto other controls. This allows players to play immediately, but to grow in experience as they play.

Another strain of sports game is represented by the management sim. Here the player uses screens of statistics to make decisions designed to lead their team to victory. The most notable entry in this genre is the *Championship Manager* series (Sports Interactive, 1992 onwards). This style of game delivers primarily Type 2 play, but sports-literate Type 1 players might also enjoy it.

A final category of sports game is the future sports sub-genre, which presents real-time live action gameplay based upon wholly invented sports set in the future. The only notably successful entry into this genre is *Speedball 2: Brutal Deluxe* (Bitmap Brothers, 1991); the Casual audiences who enjoy real-world sports do not want fictional sports that have no cultural significance, while Hardcore audiences who might be tolerant of fictional sports might be put off by the relative simplicity of the games presented, when compared to real sports.

Extreme Sports

Nucleating game: *Tony Hawk's Pro Skater* (Neversoft, 1999)

Though not strictly simulations, extreme sports games are obviously related to sports games and require an element of reality to appeal to their primary audience of C1 and C2 players, as indicated by the need to identify a cult sporting personality to act as a titular figurehead in most games of this style. Agonistic in nature, they nonetheless depend upon a high degree of mimicry in order to succeed.

Tony Hawk's Pro Skater is one of the most important games of the PlayStation era, as it demonstrates genre nucleation exceptionally clearly. In attempting to produce a game emulating the excitement and philosophy of skateboarding, Neversoft blended various game elements to create something that looked and felt completely fresh. Within 2 years it had established such a strong genre (as rival companies attempted to exploit its popularity with a key market) that new extreme sports games often seemed tired and derivative. By the release of *Tony Hawk's Pro Skater 4* (Neversoft, 2002) the genre was established enough to spawn bizarre novelty extreme sports games such as *BMX XXX* (Z-Axis, 2002), *Toxic Grind* (Blue Shift, 2002), and *Sky Surfer* (Toka, 2001).

When considering the value of innovation in video game development, it should be remembered that a new form can nucleate a genre that, within 3 years, might become almost passé. Other concepts, those that don't catch on, become identified as oddities. Innovation, then, becomes trapped between mainstream normalcy and the distrust of the strange.

The core gameplay of the extreme sports genre involves the player's avatar riding a suitable piece of extreme sporting equipment and interacting with environment scenery to pull tricks, score points, and achieve task goals. Tricks are usually triggered by button combinations, often fighting-game style. Tasks, meanwhile, often resemble platform gameplay with added momentum. One feature of the extreme sports genre to cross back into other games is grinding. Grinding involves the player avatar "riding" a rail; directional control on the part of the player is removed, possibly to be replaced by a "balance meter." Minus balancing issues, grinding can be seen in *Sonic Adventure 2* (Sonic Team, 2001) and *Kirby Air Ride* (HAL Labs, 2003).

Extreme sports games resemble 3D platform games in terms of structure as well. Players unlock new domains by completing a proportion of goals in other levels (by the "70% rule"), which might include scoring challenges, locating collectibles, or pulling specific stunts. Character improvement is also usually included (stats might be upgraded by finding tokens or merely as a result of playing), which echoes the RPG structure a little.

One significant structural change has occurred since the inception of the genre. The *Tony Hawk* games initially presented time-limited gameplay, with players attempting to do as much as possible in two minutes. This style mimicked skateboarding competition rules. *Aggressive Inline* (Z-Axis, 2002) dropped this convention, allowing the player as much time as they wanted (and shifted timed tasks to internal events triggered from NPCs). This style more resembles street sports, in which the participants practice their skills upon everyday features of the landscape. *Tony Hawk's Pro Skater 4* (Neversoft, 2002) was the first of its series to feature no time restriction, thus "legitimizing" it as a genre element.

Other than skateboarding, a number of real-world extreme sports have been mimicked by games, including BMX with *Dave Mirra Freestyle BMX* (Z-Axis, 2000) and *Mat Hoffman Pro BMX* (Runecraft, 2001), inline skating with *Aggressive Inline*, surfing with *Kelly Slater's Pro Surfer* (Treyarch, 2002) and *Surfing H3O* (ASCII, 2000), wakeboarding with *Wakeboarding Unleashed featuring Shaun Murray* (Shaba Games, 2003), motocross with *Freestyle Metal X* (Deibus, 2003), and snowboarding with *Shaun Palmer's Pro Snowboard* (Dearsoft, 2001) and *Amped: Freestyle Snowboarding* (Microsoft, 2001). Note that snowboarding games tend to be focused either upon tricks (using an extreme sports structure) or racing. Motocross games usually include both in equal measure, split into different modes, as with *Big Air Freestyle* (Paradigm, 2002) and *MX Superfly* (Pacific Coast Power & Light, 2002)

The extreme sports genre is a Western-originated genre, and Japanese designers do not create games in this style. *Jet Set Radio* (Smilebit, 2000) features in-line skating, but the core gameplay and structure of the game are completely different to those of the extreme sports genre. Grinding is automatic (with no balance element), graffiti spraying "collection" replaces task completion as a progress mechanism, and a linear level structure replaces the platform game structure of extreme sports. *Jet Set Radio Future* (Smilebit, 2002), its sequel, is a 3D platform game in all but representation.

Extreme sports games are popular with C1 and C2 players. Their structures allow players of all abilities to play, and their resemblance to real-life activities also appeals to a Casual audience, especially young males. H1 players might also enjoy completing every task for challenge and learning every move and trick and probably provided the evangelism required to propagate awareness to a wider audience.

Sim Game

Nucleating game: *Sim City* (Maxis, 1985)

Sim and management games are related in many functional and historical ways to strategy games. However, they are characterized in general by the lack of combat and a general focus instead upon production or construction. Despite their relationship to strategy games, the play of sim games is squarely focused upon mimicry and not agon, and often toyplay is more prevalent than strict gameplay.

Sim City, the game that defines the genre, allows the player to create and maintain an entire city. Subsequent games of the format followed the same basic model, in allowing the player to build and maintain *something*. That something might be an ant colony, a farm, a tower block, or a golf course, as in *Sim Ant* (Maxis, 1991), *Sim Farm* (Maxis, 1993), *Sim Tower* (Maxis, 1995), and *Sim Golf* (Maxis, 1996), a theme park or hospital as in *Theme Park* (Bullfrog, 1994) and *Theme Hospital* (Bullfrog, 1997), or a transport network or another theme park, as in *Transport Tycoon* (Microprose, 1994) and *Rollercoaster Tycoon* (Chris Sawyer Productions, 1999). In *The Sims* (Maxis, 2000), the most popular sim game of all time and the best-selling PC game of all time [Gamestate03], the player gets to build and maintain actual *lives*. We discuss this particular title in a separate section, however, as slightly different issues apply.

Sim games resemble childhood activities, such as building forts out of cardboard boxes or castles in the sand—or, in the case of *The Sims*, a dollhouse. Certain players gain a great deal of satisfaction not just in the creation, but the management of things. The smooth running of *Sim City* provides excellent H2 play, offering strategic play rooted in mimicry. C2 players, meanwhile, enjoy reacting to crises in their virtual worlds.

Traditionally, the games were too remote to fully appeal to Type 3 or 4-oriented players, although H3 players appear to have enjoyed the toyplay experiences presented by many of the games cited earlier as examples of the form. With the creation of *The Sims*, faces, names, and personalities were put to the sim entities, adding the key emotional element to allow C3 and C4 players to relate to the play experience. C4 players especially are well suited to a more emotional sim game, enjoying participation but also having access to Logistical skills.

Sim games are almost always toyplay friendly. The majority of sim games feature sandbox modes in which players face no challenge, just the opportunity to play with the game elements. In many ways, *Sim City* developed toyplay in 1985, though only recently has a significant audience for toyplay contributed their entertainment money to the cause of game development, allowing the industry to experiment with the form.

The games industry must experiment with these elements, but it is likely that we will see sim-like elements of building and maintenance bleed further into other styles of game, to mesh with narrative elements and create extremely lucrative games that span multiple play types, taking in the needs of Type 3 and 4 play as well as the more traditional demands of agon.

God Game

Nucleating game: *Populous* (Bullfrog, 1989)

The defining quality of god games is that the player is given the powers and role of a god or supernatural entity. In the case of *Populous*, this is directly the case; the player raises and lowers land to allow the inhabitants of a world to build houses and prosper. Enemy gods generally also exist, as do their followers, and they compete for space. The player has many godlike powers with which to blast the heretics, however, including lightning, fire, and earthquakes.

God games are associated with this feeling of nurturing or terrifying a population, rather than any specific commonality of core gameplay. The raising and lowering of land in *Populous*, for example, did not nucleate a genre of its own; rather, it was the role of the player, and the reactions of the virtual entities in the game world to the player, that defined this type of game.

It is this interaction between player and the inhabitants of the world that we assert as the defining feature of a god game. Many sim games resemble god games in that the player has influence upon virtual lives, but, crucially, in sim games the virtual entities do not acknowledge the existence of the player. Additionally the player rarely has powers that could be considered supernatural. This means, for example, that *Dungeon Keeper* (Bullfrog, 1997) could be considered as a god game rather than "sim dungeon." *Civilization* is often related to the god game genre, and this positioning is a matter of personal taste; though entities in the world do react to the player (by building monuments and so forth), the player does nothing that is specifically god-like and might prefer to cast themselves in the role of a powerful leader (much as powerful leaders historically cast themselves in the role of a god).

That said, the audience for god games is practically identical to that for sim games (primarily Type 2), because the core play tends to be similar. The acknowledgement of the player by virtual entities does give god games a warmer tone than the majority of sim games (at least where the relationship between the player and the game entities is positive), so Type 3 and 4 players might find them rewarding, too. However, the bias of god games has tended towards agonistic play—we have yet to see a completely toyplay-oriented god game (unless one considers *The Sims* to meet this description), and indeed a gap in the market might exist for such a product.

The god game genre includes titles such as *Afterlife* (LucasArts, 1996), *Black & White*, and *Ghost Master* (Sick Puppies, 2003), which is unusual in that the player's role is that of a ghostly civil servant rather than a strict god. The relationship between the player and the virtual entities in this case is solely that of inducing terror (or on occasion, madness), which the player does by use of a team of quasi-autonomous entities who also interact with the player in certain ways, and indeed the goal of most of the challenges presented is to scare away all of the mortals living in a particular location. The player's presence is acknowledged in general only when ghostbreakers and exorcists attempt to eliminate the unseen force that is manipulating the haunting.

Doshin the Giant (Param, 2002) represents a rare console-specific god game; here, the player is actually manifested as a god-like avatar in a world of virtual entities and can raise and lower land to please or punish them (harking back to *Populous*), as well as move trees and otherwise adjust the environment either to win the love or fear of the people. It is oddly schizophrenic, in that the player can switch between a good and bad avatar form essentially at will—using one to repair the world and elicit love and the other to wreak destruction and elicit fear.

Both *Ghost Master* and *Doshin* represent an attempt to combine Type 2 puzzle-oriented play with Type 3 toyplay. The former succeeds for the most part in appealing to these audiences, and indeed received excellent reviews, but because it downplayed agonistic elements, it struggled to acquire the necessary degree of evangelism required for commercial success (although presumably greater marketing presence could, in principle, have offset this). *Doshin* offered quite satisfying toyplay, puzzles in the sense of ascertaining how the game world functioned, and some goal-oriented gameplay in the building of monuments to Doshin by the people. Unfortunately, it was far too slow for most players to enjoy and also possessed a surreal quality not uncommon in Japanese games, which probably did not connect well with a Western audience.

Life Sim

Nucleating game (Western-style): *The Sims* (Maxis, 2000)
Nucleating game (Japanese-style): *Tokimeki Memorial* (Konami, 1994)

Though *The Sims* is clearly evolved from the sim game and god game genres, its billing as the "real-life simulator" makes its appeal clear. Comparable to a dollhouse for teenagers and adults, *The Sims* allows players to assume a god-like overview of life, presenting virtual human beings as toys to be manipulated. This is a very Western version of the life sim concept, casting the player as a neutral force not fully invested in a smaller world that they can control. Parallels can be made with Western RPGs, which present parties of player-created characters who are personality-neutral in narrative terms and who obey the player's wishes during the quest.

The Sims delivers extremely strong Type 4 play, as the player is asked to participate with their Sims in a very non-goal-oriented manner. The primary audience for the game is C4, whose Logistical skill set is compatible with the repetitive mechanical substructure of the game, although it is likely that this could be considerably downplayed without hurting the appeal of the game, as the sequel *The Sims 2* (Maxis, 2004) appears to have attempted. Type 3 players also might have enjoyed *The Sims* for its toyplay, but were probably less influential in its success.

The Japanese market has produced several games that are closely related to *The Sims*, in terms of the focus of their play, but follow a very different approach, in which a specific narrative situation is in place. Parallels exist with the Japanese RPG, which tends to identify the player with a single central character whose personality is extremely defined in narrative terms, usually including a backstory featuring relationships with other in-game characters (as in *Final Fantasy VII*, for example, where hero Cloud is the player's primary focus, but who has a personality of his own and relationships, including bonds with both Tifa and Sephiroth).

This immersive attitude to role-play is inherent to the Japanese "life-sim" genre, most famously exemplified by the "dating sim" also often known as *bishoujo* games, a Japanese word that can be translated as "pretty girl"—used to describe all games featuring graphics of young anime girls, including many *hentai* (pornographic anime) games. *Bishoujo*, however, can be used to describe any game with this content, not just dating sims.

The most famous dating sim is *Tokimeki Memorial*, in which the player takes the role of a young man in a Japanese high school, who must attract and date one of a number of girls, each of whom has a distinctive personality with likes and dislikes. Two forms of core gameplay are found; on the one hand, players must choose appropriate conversational options from multiple choice lists when talking to girls, and on the other, they must balance their life activities, all of which add or detract from a series of stats that document the character's being. At the end of the game, the player discovers which girl their character most appeals to (if any).

Though initially thought to be targeted at male players, upon release it became apparent that female players were enjoying *Tomimeki Memorial* [Yukino01]. It is noticeable that unlike previous dating sim games, *TokiMemo* contains no sleaze or sex and is presented as a very innocent romantic story. While the romantic elements no doubt appeal to female players, it is also likely that Type 4 participation experiences result from *TokiMemo*'s play.

The statistical aspects of the genre reflect RPGs, and often RPG-style exploration elements are incorporated—because H4 players enjoy Japanese RPGs, this is a natural connection. It is a key point, however, that rather than reflecting physical prowess like the majority of RPG stats, dating sim stats reflect all aspects of personality. This sense of growing a personality (rather that creating a warrior) is vital to the genre.

The game was a huge hit in Japan and kick-started a small industry of spin-offs, both within and outside of the gaming sphere. It was never released in the West, however, and the dating sim game (though championed by a small number of players able to read Japanese text) has a bad reputation in the west as a "loser" activity, perhaps due to the impression that the games are aimed at males who cannot happily talk to girls in real life. If this prejudice can be overcome—perhaps by repositioning the genre as life sims rather than dating sims, as seen with the *Princess Maker* series (Gainax, 1991 onwards), which places the player in the role of a father bringing up a young woman in a fantasy land—then this genre has worldwide potential with Type 4-oriented audiences.

The popularity of this style of game in Japan, plus the style of RPG popular there, suggests that Japan has a significantly more developed Type 4 video game audience than the West.

MISCELLANEOUS

Not all genres of game fit cleanly into neat categories. For example, some classic games such as *NiGHTS: Into Dreams* (Sonic Team, 1996) have no real genre to call their own at all (*NiGHTS* is a critical and cult favourite game, but its form is difficult to emulate without directly copying it, and its sales figures suggest that such an effort might not be worthwhile). Because this discussion of genre is not concerned with taxonomy, the inclusion of a miscellaneous category does not present any serious issues.

Puzzle

The majority, if not all, of traditional play forms have been converted to computer at one time or another. Puzzles, a traditionally popular form of entertainment defined by their appeal to thoughtful experimentation in search of an abstract solution (taking apart, putting together, filling in, completing), are no exception. Even the *Rubik's Cube* was converted to a video game form with *Rubik's Cube* (Atari, 1983) on the Atari 2600, despite costing significantly more than the original piece of plastic and being much less easy to use. It did not sell well.

Due to the simplicity of puzzles, and their enduring popularity in all forms, puzzle games are some of the most accessible video games, and are often played by a wide audience.

Action Puzzle Games

Nucleating game: *Tetris* (A. Pajitnov, 1985)

Tetris dominates the puzzle genre. It exemplifies a certain breed of action-puzzler, in which the player is expected to manipulate game pieces into a certain order under pressure from time or an opponent. In the case of *Tetris*, falling blocks must be juggled into space; *Puzzle Bobble/Bust a Move* (Taito, 1994) features the matching of similarly colored bubbles via a shooting mechanism, *Columns* (Sega, 1990) involves more matching of colors, this time with falling blocks, as does *Puyo Puyo* (Compile, 1991), and *Wetrix* (Zed Two, 1998) challenges the player to catch water by dropping walls onto a flat, isometric plane to build reservoirs. It is usual to see multiple versions and variants of each style of game, each featuring slightly tweaked features—*The New Tetris* (H2O Entertainment, 1999), for example, actually improves upon the classic formula by adding a "spare piece slot" for the player's use and introducing the act of building silver and gold blocks from multiple types of the same piece for extra points.

Puzzle games are inherently accessible, as the dimensionality of their control is extremely low. Though abstract, puzzle games still appeal to a wide audience through their simplicity; it is also possible that *Tetris*, for example, harks back both to classic puzzles and to building-block games that players recall from childhood. For whatever reason, most players seem able and willing to play these games; Type 1 players can play for challenge or competition, Type 2 for strategy and forward planning, Type 3 for altered states experiences (the games become extremely hypnotic after a short time of playing, perhaps a consequence of flow being generated by the simple, persistent "tidying" tasks presented), and Type 4 for friendly agon.

Of these play types, it is the C3 players who seem to play for longest, and in fact many players play only *Tetris* and play no other video games at all.

Tetris must be considered to be one of the most successful (due to its cultural significance) and elegant video games of all time; if a single game were to be placed in a space pod for the interest of aliens, to represent all game-kind, *Tetris* would be it.

Adventure Puzzle

Nucleating game: *Myst* (Cyan, 1994)

Though all adventures feature puzzles, *Myst* represents a genre in which gameplay consists only of puzzling. Presenting a game world via static, prerendered screens, the player can click upon parts of the screen to move about the world and to access puzzles. Unlike traditional adventures, which attempt to use lock-and-key barriers that are woven into the game world, *Myst*-style games present abstract puzzles simply for the sake of it. The flow of these games involves exploration (which, due to the beauty of the worlds—a hugely important factor to these games—emulates a form of "virtual tourism" on the part of the player), which is punctuated by progress-retarding puzzles, such as the need to fix an alien machine by considering its underlying logical principles, for example.

Some games take the abstract nature of the fantasy worlds they provide to a higher level. While *The 7ᵗʰ Guest* (Trilobyte, 1993) presents a recognizable spooky mansion setting, games such as *Blue Ice* (Psygnosis, 1995) create their own abstract worlds, in which puzzles can bear little relation to real world logic at all. This style of game more resembles an abstract form of technological art than traditional games. It is notable that these games feature less formal narrative than traditional adventure styles, though games like *Zork Nemesis: The Forbidden Lands* (Zombie, Inc., 1996) present FMV-based NPCs with which players can interact to a limited degree.

In part, sales of these games were driven by the introduction of CD-ROM drives to PCs in the early nineties. The CD format's ability to hold many times the data of a floppy disc allowed for much more lavish, prerendered visuals and FMV, and the initial instances of the genre were impressive due to this technology. Once the technology was established, however, the popularity of the genre faded. This pattern directly mirrors the introduction of laser disc technology into arcades by games such as *Dragon's Lair* (Cinematronics, 1983)—initial excitement slowly fading as the form became familiar and the degree to which gameplay was hampered by the technology became obvious.

These games appeal to both Type 2 and Type 3 players, the former enjoying the puzzles and the latter enjoying the attractively presented virtual worlds. The puzzles often become very frustrating to the Type 3 players, however, who really just want to explore and don't achieve satisfaction from hard-won solutions. Now that real-time 3D worlds can be produced, Type 3 players have considerably less interest in this type of game. It is worth noting that the point and click interface of this genre is extremely accessible, and the lack of fast action and instant deaths makes the games somewhat friendly to Casual players.

Desktop Puzzle Games

Nucleating game: *Minesweeper* (Microsoft, 1991)

Minesweeper is one of the most widely played games in the world, in part because it is a de facto component of several popular operating systems. Other desktop staples such as *Hearts* and *Solitaire* (both traditional card games) also entertain audiences of a size that most video game developers can only dream about. These games are all accessible, easy to understand, and provide entertainment in potentially tiny play sessions, making them ideal for extremely casual lunch-time play. The fact that they are distributed without any specific cost is another factor in their success that cannot be ignored.

Some traditional video game manufacturers have attempted to enter this market of 'micro-games"—with *Indiana Jones and His Desktop Adventures* (LucasArts, 1996) and *Star Wars: Yoda Stories* (LucasArts, 1997), LucasArts attempted to broker their key licenses into a potentially huge Casual market, without significant success. It is possible that the games failed to catch the attention of Hardcore players and hence weren't sufficiently evangelized to reach their target audience or that the target players were unwilling to pay money to replace perfectly serviceable games that were free. Nevertheless, with high Internet connectivity, the potential for this sort of game as freebies and promotional items might generate new entries into the genre.

Rhythm Action

Nucleating game: *PaRappa the Rapper* (NaNaOn-Sha, 1996)

The most accreted form of rhythm action game works in a similar fashion to the classic *Simon* (MB Games, 1978) device; the player is told what to do, and they do it. This usually takes the form of arrow or button commands appearing on screen, scrolling toward an "action" signifier to provide timing. The twist is provided by the rhythm element—the player must press the correct controls in time with music, which might alter in quality if the player does badly at the game. It is this sense of interaction with the music that provides the appeal of these games.

While the game is being played, a player can do little but stare at the command instruction display. To provide a sense of connection, however, and for the benefit of onlookers, brightly colored animations play behind the commands, often quite surreal in their nature, as in *PaRappa the Rapper* in which a dog is taught to rap by an onion in order to impress a sunflower, or *Space Channel 5* (Sega, 1999) in which ace space reporter Ulala defeats an alien invasion through dance and retro psychedelics.

Other variations on the genre include *Frequency* and *Amplitude* (Harmonix, 2001, 2003), which combine a music mixing element with button-pressing rhythm action; *Mad Maestro* (Desert Planning, 2002), a classical music conduction game; and *Bust-a-Groove* (Metro Graphics, 1998), which features agonistic dance-offs.

The most important form of this style of game is represented by *Dance Dance Revolution* (Konami, 1999), which scrolls arrows vertically upon the screen that correspond to four pressure-sensitive footplates upon which players stand. By stepping upon the appropriate plate at the correct time, players dance their way through music tracks. The intuitive gameplay coupled with infectious music and the potential for two-player party fun, specifically in public, appeals greatly to C4 and also to C3 players, something that has led to a minor boom in dance mat sales throughout the world.

Other hardware-oriented rhythm games include *Beatmania* (Konami, 1998), initiating the "Bemani" series of games and played with a keyboard/turntable combination; *Samba De Amigo* (Sonic Team, 2000), played with maracas; *EyeToy: Groove* (SCEE Studio Soho, 2003), played with Sony's EyeToy; and *Donkey Konga* (Namco, 2003), which uses custom bongo controllers.

Traditional Games

Nucleating game: *Monopoly* (multiple versions, 1985 onwards)

Non-strategical, more family-oriented board games are often translated directly to a video game format. *Monopoly* (Charles B. Darrow, 1934) is a classic example of this trend. They are commercially significant if only because their low development costs mean that few copies need to be sold to make back costs, but the video game versions rarely add anything useful to the games, except computer opponents should a player want to play alone.

This is true of early conversions such as *The Computer Edition of Scrabble® Brand Crossword Game* (Turcan Research Systems, 1989) and *Risk* (Panther Programs, 1986). Later versions attempted to add additional gameplay, as seen in *Risk: The Game of Global Domination* (BlueSky Software, 1997), which adds a fully blown strategic mode to the classic game and *Monopoly Tycoon* (Deep Red Games, 2001), which adds Sim elements to the board game license.

Any specific tweaks given to the games apply to different audiences—deeper strategy and more options are usually added, appealing primarily to Type 2. In terms of licensing, the brand names are familiar and unthreatening, but Type 4-oriented players would generally prefer to play the original board games with friends, and the most commercially successful board game brands such as *Trivial Pursuit* (Horn Abbot, 1982) and *Jenga* (Leslie Scott, circa 1970) are largely kept in circulation by Type 4 players.

Electronic trivia games such as the *You Don't Know Jack* series (Berkeley Systems/Jellyvision, 1995 onwards) are a rare case of traditional games achieving greater appeal and market success. Trivia games are particularly enjoyed by people with the Logistical skill set (C1 and C4 audiences) and can appeal to both Type 1 and 2 audiences in terms of agon and Type 4 audiences in general because of the sense of participation. It should be noted, however, that these games have not sold anything close to the 70 million copies that the traditional board game version of *Trivial Pursuit* has achieved worldwide [Trivial05].

Another case of unusual market success for electronic adaptations of traditional games occurs periodically with adaptations of TV game shows, such as with *Who Wants To Be A Millionaire?* (Jellyvision/Hothouse Creations et al, 1999). The form has been around for some time with licensed adaptations of shows such as *Wheel of Fortune* (Softie, 1987; Artech Studios, 1998) and *Jeopardy!* (ShareData, 1987; Artech Studios, 1998). In many cases, these adaptations provide very satisfying play experiences (in part through the mimicry engendered), and recently more effort has gone into thinking about what play experiences should be supported, as with *American Idol* (Hothouse Creations, 2003), which draws from the rhythm action genre to support its core gameplay.

The appeal of such games is focused upon the Casual audience, because they lack the complexity and expressiveness that Hardcore players seek and also draw upon brand recognition for their sales appeal. The fact that they have almost universally a low or trivial dimensionality of control is a great help in this.

Party Game

Nucleating game: *Mario Party* (Hudson Soft, 1998)

The point of party games is to allow multiple people to play together without there being any need for them to learn complicated rules or control systems. *Mario Party* takes the form of a board game in which landing upon certain squares triggers mini-games, which are played by one to four players. Each mini-game takes a very short amount of time to play.

Mini-games define the party-game format; the combining structure is really just a scoring system to provide an eventual winner, as a way to bring the game to an end. The mini-games are typically balanced in terms of luck and skill, allowing agonistic players to enjoy competition, but meaning that players who just want to participate need not suffer undue stress.

Bishi Bashi Championship Mini Game Senshuken (Konami, 1996) brought party games to the arcade, with later home versions. Other notable party games include *Wario Ware: Mega Party Games* (Nintendo, 2003); *EyeToy: Play* (SCEE London, 2003); *Sega Superstars* (Sonic Team, 2004), which also uses the EyeToy; and *Super Monkey Ball* (Amusement Vision, 2001). Although *Super Monkey Ball*'s primary game mode is a very Type 1 control challenge style game, it includes six mini-games that among them appeal to all play types and provide excellent party play.

While the mini-games themselves might appeal to any play type, this form of game is a good match to Type 4, because of its capacity to provide participation with a backdrop of friendly agon. Additionally, it has an appeal to Type 3 players—at least for as long as the mini-games presented are new and entertaining. Agonistic Type 1 and 2 players might engage in this style of game as a social convenience, but would generally prefer more complex games.

CONCLUSION

Games of strategy largely support Type 1 and Type 2 play, depending upon whether real-time logistics (Type 1) or turn-based strategy (Type 2) is preferred, while games of simulation are largely concerned with mimicry and court a more diverse audience. Sports games reflect typical Type 1 and 2 tendencies, sim games tend to be skewed more to Type 2 and 3 play styles, and life sims are largely of interest to people preferring Type 4 play. Type 4 play is also supported by traditional, rhythm action, and party games, the latter two of which also support Type 3 play.

Arguably, the widest appeal comes with the simplest games, as puzzle games seem able to satisfy the needs of all four play types. However, design of a puzzle game is non-trivial, and few puzzle games have achieved the success of *Tetris,* which has sold 33 million units worldwide [Gamestate03], making it the second highest selling game of all time. We will likely not see another puzzle game achieve such success, but it would be inadvisable to rule this out as a possibility.

Designing a game for an audience is not a process of picking an audience and then making a game in a genre that appeals to that audience. Rather, we need to understand which elements of games appeal to audiences. Because genres relate games via commonality of elements, they can be a useful tool with which to explore audience taste. Once this information is distilled, games can be designed that take into account audience needs without being constricted in their vision by narrow genre definitions.

Ultimately, change is inevitable. Whether change is gradual, as with RPGs, or rapid, as in the nucleation of a genre like extreme sports, the video games world adapts largely in response to the buying habits of the audience. By considering the ultimate purpose of games—to be enjoyed by players, to make money for developers and publishers—and biasing their design towards these goals, designers might exert a little more control over the gradual shifts in genre, pushing games in desirable directions and maximizing their potential.

13 The Evolution of Games: Originality and Chreodes

In This Chapter

- Chreodes
- The Creative Explosion
- The Underground
- Extinction
- Conservatism versus Originality
- Conclusion

W hy are we not inundated with new and original games? Developers, publishers, and reviewers alike are crying out for originality, yet rather than being washed away in a flood of creativity, the games we see appear to be predominately clones of one another. In an industry that seems to be dominated by sequels, it is easy to see why such accusations could be leveled, but the question of the alleged absence of creativity warrants a closer examination.

Games are frequently accused of being derivative, but is this conservative approach to games development actually a problem? When a developer has a hit new game, sequels are an inevitable next step. Of the top fifteen best-selling titles on PS2 in Europe in 2003, only two represented new IP [Parker03], and this is a typical situation in regard to game sales. Furthermore, it is believed that while movie sequels tend to gross 75% of the original, a game sequel grosses about 125% of the previous title [Rouse99]. In a competitive market, companies whose existence depends on regular income cannot be expected to abandon the brands that have achieved proven market success, and definite issues surround the question of whether or not sequels have any obligation to tread new ground.

To explore the possible factors behind the apparent contradiction of a market apparently craving originality but delivering largely similar product, we need a mechanism to consider the market as a whole. To enable us to build a mental image of the shape of the market, we need a metaphor. Starting with an idea proposed in the 1950s, we will use the concept of *chreodes* to travel back almost 600 million years to begin our search for fresh perspectives on the question of originality in games.

CHREODES

The notion of a chreode, or a pathway of probability, was created by the biologist C.H. Waddington in the 1950s as part of his attempt to find descriptive language to describe the way organisms develop [Waddington57]. He was largely concerned with the process of embryonic development, but the idea applies to any field of probability. The term is not in wide use in the modern scientific community, but this does not reduce its value as a metaphorical concept.

An easy way to picture chreodes is to consider a commonly encountered example, for example, the flow of water over a surface that can be eroded. Initially this surface is flat, but as water flows across the plane of the material, it gradually begins to erode a canal. If no random factors were involved, this canal would be an even trench in the surface, but because the flow of water is a chaotic process, the canals that result spread out unevenly. The deepest parts of the pathways occur where most erosion take place, with shallower channels spreading out around it.

If you imagine a ball placed at the top of the canals, it rolls down and ends up at the lowest point of one of the pathways. It is most likely to end up at the bottom of the deepest and widest channel, but has a chance of ending up at the end of any of the pathways. The waterways that result are a physical representation of the fields of probability that could be used to mathematically express the shape of the canals.

Figure 13.1 (taken from Waddington's book on the subject of chreodes in genetics) demonstrates the notion of a chreode graphically.

With respect to the development of organisms, the whole sphere of organic life can be pictured as a probability field, with chreodes representing the different kingdoms of life and within those pathways, smaller chreodes representing orders, genus, and species. These chreodes channel the possible developmental options for evolving life; a shallow channel represents an instance of life that can easily evolve into new forms. A deeper chasm is representative of a species or set of species that

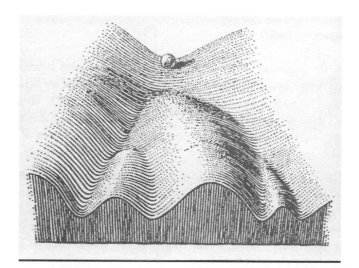

FIGURE 13.1   Illustration of a ball at the top of a chreode set; an "epigenetic landscape," taken from *The Strategy of Genes*, C.H. Waddington; George Allen and Unwin Ltd, 1957.

have painted themselves into an evolutionary corner (generally implying that they are both highly specialized and highly successful).

Polychete worms, for example, are an abundant, simplistic life-form that has evolved into and taken over a particular niche. So engrained is their position in this niche, that they are effectively doomed to remain in their current form, barring an improbable series of events, and have remained effectively unchanged for millions of years. This does not blunt their success at exploiting this niche, however. Mammals, by comparison, are complex entities with considerable room to maneuver in an evolutionary sense and have taken over many different niches—herbivores, carnivores, and omnivores of all manner of sizes on the land; bats in the air; and cetaceans in the sea—and remain one of the orders of life with the greatest mobility of form (when looked at in geological time, at least).

Similarly, the entirety of games can be looked at as a series of chreodes, with the channels corresponding to the genres of games. This landscape would include all types of games, with a ubiquitous and simple game like *I Spy* (with little room for innovation or mutation) being much like the polychete worms, and computer and video games more like our friends the mammals in their potential for diversity. For our purposes, we will focus on just the landscape represented by the different forms of computer games.

THE CREATIVE EXPLOSION

By mentally rendering the sphere of organic life and the games market in terms of a landscape of chreodes, we create a metaphorical model allowing us to make comparisons between the evolution of life and the evolution of computer games. From a certain perspective, the evolution of life has been about an ever-changing, diverse set of creatures discovering, adapting to, and exploiting a number of evolutionary niches. Games, similarly, have been a varied set of genres exploring a set of market niches. Food to an animal is much like money to a game because if the game does not prove profitable fewer and fewer people are willing to make more games in that genre.

In both cases, early examples were simple, and without any existing chreodes to limit and channel the next stages, an explosion of originality resulted. Games were unconstrained by preconceptions, and so explored all manner of directions, only learning the hard way what would prove profitable and what wouldn't. Life, too, started with no competition for resources, allowing an unprecedented era of biological creativity with all manner of strangeness resulting.

This early period of developmental simplicity for organisms was the Cambrian (570–505 million years ago). The huge diversity of multicellular life that came into existence in the early Paleozoic has been termed "The Cambrian Explosion." With only very basic life to compete with, and essentially no competition for organisms that could move and search for food, diversity was unparalleled. Fossils show creatures like opabina, which appears to have five eyes at the base of a head stalk, and hallucigenia, which apparently supports a trunk and globular head on seven pairs of rigid spines. These species have no known descendents—rather, they are experimental oddities, forced out of the evolutionary game by luckier and more successful species [Gould86].

The "explosion" for computer games took place in the 1970s and 1980s. This period contains a number of game oddities with few or no modern descendents. In the arcade, we find games such as *Circus* (Exidy, 1977), which featured clowns bouncing off a seesaw to pop balloons, or *Sundance* (Cinematronic, 1979), in which players score points by opening hatches to catch suns that are bouncing between two grids [Klov93]. Like opabina and hallucigenia, these games are early experiments that just didn't pan out (although not necessarily because they were deficient for some reason).

What happened next also parallels between the two metaphorical realms. The Cambrian was followed by the Ordovician, which brought along the first fishes, and by the time of the Devonian (sometimes called "The Age of Fish") just a hundred million years later, fish had essentially completely exploited their niche. Compare the success of the genre exemplified by Taito's 1978 *Space Invaders* (albeit not the first shooter), which by the 1990s had evolved into the first-person shooter and had codified the genre into a streamlined, simplistic game structure making it the fish of the games world.

Returning to the concept of chreodes, the pathway of probability defined by fish constrains certain aspects of what a fish can be. In general, any fish is going to be a vertebrate that lives in water and acquires oxygen for respiration through gills. Many differences can be found between any two fish species (saltwater or freshwater, large or small, tropical or arctic), but almost all fit the basic general description.

The mudskipper—which spends part of its life out of the water—represents a tiny side chreode in the canal of fish, showing a little biological creativity. It's quite possible that similar species that shared that chreode in the past were the ancestors of all land vertebrates, including the versatile mammals, but first they had to overcome the substantial energy barrier of living outside of water, a barrier represented by the steep sides of the fish chreode. That putative evolutionary breakthrough would have been made considerably easier by the lack of any significant competition for land at the time.

In our comparison of metaphors, we have made first-person shooters the equivalent of fish (admittedly a largely arbitrary conflation). In principle, at least, the mudskipper of first-person shooters could appear at any moment, opening up a new chreode and new possibilities. The question is, "What is the equivalent energy barrier to the fishes' life in water problem in respect of first-person shooters?"

That the chreode metaphor holds any water for game genres at all suggests that something is constraining their evolution. Barring the existence of other inheritance mechanisms, the nature of genetics (and specifically DNA-based genetics) serves to provide the framework limiting the rate of mutation and change in organisms. However, the reason evolution takes place primarily on the scale of millions of years is that biological evolution appears to be largely driven by essentially random processes, which are very slow indeed. Games are designed—why should they show the same slow rate of change (albeit on the faster scale of decades)?

We have already observed that market competition for revenue can be seen to parallel competition for energy (food) in organic life. Nebulous "market forces" might also be seen to be the constraining force that prevents originality, or at least restrains it. The companies that underwrite games development (an increasingly expensive business) are unwilling to invest millions of dollars on games projects without knowing that they will get a correspondingly large return on their investment. That the right project might create new genre territory (found a new genre chreode) and be worth a fortune is offset by the general difficulty of assessing the market prospects of anything that deviates from previous product. The market knows only what has sold in the past—it has no way of accurately assessing what will sell in the future.

This situation might be the reason that many games designers choose to blame the publishers for the state of the industry. Nonetheless, when you are aware of a problem, the first barrier to progress has already been removed. Additionally, it is not that the publishers are not interested in originality, just that changes are constrained to a gradual process. By working within the existing chreodes, we have a mechanism for introducing elements of originality with some confidence that they will still appeal to a significant proportion of the market.

THE UNDERGROUND

We have seen the codification of form in other media where the cost of production or the size of the audience has risen significantly; witness the chreodes of mass market literature or the channels of Hollywood. Creative and original films and books come from a vibrant underground (where the cost of creation is fractional compared to the mass market end of the spectrum). Gradually, changes in the underground filter through the whole of the media landscape. The same is broadly true of games.

Wolfenstein 3D (id Software, 1992) was not a major release for any publisher, but rather a small shareware title that caught the imagination of a large audience. In doing so, it expanded and deepened the chreode of first-person shooters and as such caused it to "break away" from the shoot 'em up chreode that went before it. Until this point, the major commercial titles were 2D scrolling shooters—and while *Wolfenstein 3D* was not the first FPS, it was the game that began the process of 2D shooters being forced out of the games ecosystem and largely replaced with the first-person shooter (and other 3D shooter games).

In this case, the breakthrough was technological in nature. Improvements in hardware allowed for fast rendering of simple full 3D environments with the illusion of solidity (earlier 3D games being largely vector graphics and basic polygonal structures). The creation of other games chreodes have been founded by other factors.

The Sims (Maxis, 2000), while making use of improved technology to power its AI, could have easily occurred several years earlier because the breakthrough here was primarily design-level. Graphically simplistic, the game hooked into the same fly-on-the-wall instincts that made reality TV popular. It expanded the chreode begun earlier by simple "virtual pets" and *The Activision Little Computer People Discovery Kit* (Activision, 1985), which was also a big hit in its day, relative to the size of the market at the time. *The Sims* has yet to manifest its possible influence on games within its genre (and hence its chreode), but it is clear that the sim game genre has never experienced such commercial domination by a single game before.

These examples show two different ways in which new game chreodes (or new paths within existing chreodes, depending on your perspective) can come into existence: one through the small but significant computer game underground, the other in a high-profile, abundantly funded project. In both cases, however, the changes have come from within existing chreodes. Except for the earliest years of the games industry (and with the possible exception of the Japanese games industry), the freedom to be relentlessly innovative must be constrained by the financial needs of the companies that create games.

EXTINCTION

As well as acquiring new chreodes, a landscape of probability can lose canals and pathways. This does not happen with our original example of water eroding a plain (not without some contrivance), but it happens biologically in the form of mass extinctions. Accepting the plausible but still debatable Alvarez Hypothesis, the dinosaurs were wiped out at the end of the Cretaceous by the impact of a giant meteor, and whole chreodes representing dinosaur and other species were wiped out from the probability landscape of organic life [Alvarez80]. These mass extinctions extend to games, too.

The arrival of the Sony PlayStation (and to a lesser extent, the Nintendo 64) with architecture specifically geared to rendering in 3D marked a mass extinction of 2D games, with no 2D genre being unaffected. The 2D games, like the dinosaurs, were driven to occupy new niches in order to survive. For the dinosaurs, they appear to have taken to the skies and survived in the form of birds [Ackerman98]. For 2D games, the handheld market has kept them alive.

A theory that is gaining ground in the paleontological field is based upon the observation that the fossil record is not a continuous record of change. Rather, mass extinctions mark boundaries between geological ages, and the fossils that can be found in one era vary significantly from the fossils found in another. Rather than seeing continuous change between species in the fossil record, it seems as if species reach a state of relative stasis—with very similar fossils being found across tens or hundreds of millions of years of rocks—with change occurring largely in the wake of a mass extinction. This is the theory of punctuated equilibrium [Gould93].

Why should it be that change occurs most rapidly in the wake of an extinction? One way to picture this is to consider the situation in light of our chreode models. When a system is left to its own devices long enough, the set of chreodes becomes a series of deep, distinct channels. New options are constrained because most entities (games or organisms) are canalized into the most successful forms. When a mass extinction occurs, large areas of the landscape of probability are wiped out (or at least, temporarily ignored). It is exactly equivalent to new niches opening up to exploitation, and sudden and significant changes are free to occur. The explosion of variety in the Cambrian Explosion can be seen as a result of unfettered freedom to explore new niches, and the wake of a mass extinction can be seen the same way.

We have likened the arrival of an easy-to-program 3D architecture to the extinction of the dinosaurs, but not all games extinctions originate from advances in hardware. Prior to 1985, the arcade game market was characterized by games in which you paid for a single game and then played for as long as you could on one credit. *Pac-Man* (Namco/Bally Midway, 1980) typified the arrangement, with a series of ever-more challenging mazes facing the player, and the reward coming for getting as deep into the game as possible, and from getting high scores. Games typically used lives as a mechanic to determine game length, so that a good player could last more or less indefinitely, while a poor player had a short play experience.

The arrival of *Gauntlet* (Atari, 1985) heralded a mass extinction in the arcades and the start of the "pump and play" era. The notion of a "continue" had been around before, but games were not designed with this method of playing in mind. The design principle was generally that players would put more money into the game in order to get better at it.

Gauntlet threw the old design principle away and replaced it with a life-resource that ticked down as the players progressed through the game. Now, players with a lack of skill could remain in the game by adding more money for more credits. Progress through the game was dominated not by the player's skill (although it remained a factor) but by the amount of money the player was willing to commit to the game. The fact that *Gauntlet* combined this financial masterstroke with an ambiguous multiplayer mechanic that offered both cooperation and competition in the same environment served only to heighten its appeal.

The mass extinction that resulted lead to an era in which any player could see the end of any game—if they were prepared to pay to see it. This also led to more games being designed with an end point in mind because no one would be compelled to pay more money if the game simply repeated. Whereas before the expert players were the people returning to the games repeatedly, but were spending less and less money to play as their skills improved, now the arcade was opened up to the masses. All you needed was cash, and you could see as much of a game as you wanted.

The chreodes representing the simple repetitive structure that had driven games design prior to 1985 were wiped out almost completely, and although this structure is still used in many simple games (e.g., those on mobile phones), its commercial significance has fallen away to almost nothing. This extinction was not driven by hardware, but by design issues. It is similar to situations in biology where the arrival of new species with certain competitive advantages results in the sudden extinction of previously successful species.

Applying the concept of punctuated equilibrium to games suggests that metaphorical mass extinctions are a potential mechanism for originality to flourish—albeit briefly—but predicting how and when such an extinction will take place is an inexact science. For example, it is easy to predict that breakthroughs in interactive storytelling will create a mass extinction at some point, but much harder to anticipate exactly which breakthroughs will cause this and which genres of games will be hit hardest by the transition. Similarly, cheap availability of virtual reality equipment will doubtless have characteristics of a mass extinction, but how and when this will occur is impossible to elucidate.

The failure of one game does not cause an extinction; only the market collapse of an entire genre can be reasonably considered a "game extinction." Whereas in usual circumstances the chreodes of the games industry act like an eroding river, carving out the shape of the landscape of possible games and reinforcing the pathways of the successful products, an extinction marks a period of upheaval. The old chreodes collapse and become filled in, and the flow of the canals of probability take a new course—or in some cases they collapse completely and cease to exist. This hints at the extent to which originality can impact on the landscape of the games market.

CONSERVATISM VERSUS ORIGINALITY

Evolution is frequently imagined as a constant and gradual progression of advancement—in life, from single-celled creatures to multi-cellular life to comparatively "advanced" organisms like mammals and birds. The metaphor of the "ladder of progress" that has become synonymous with evolution is actually highly misleading. The most successful life forms in terms of the total biomass sustained are still the single-celled organisms; the greatest variety of species and maximal adaptability lies with the insects. Mammals, with some 4,000 species, are a very small part of life as a whole [Gould95]. Complex life has exploited certain niches, but left to their own devices the larger organisms hit periods of comparative stasis.

Dinosaurs were the prevailing multicellular form for almost two hundred million years; only their extinction at the end of the Cretaceous provided the opportunity for mammals to take their place. During the Mesozoic, when the dinosaurs "ruled the Earth," they refined their biological "designs" gradually, but these changes were very gradual. After an extinction, the rate of change accelerated as the landscape of life went through a period of dynamism, before settling down into a new, comparatively stable state. If it were not for the periods of conservatism in biological evolution, however, it would be difficult for any progress to be made. If mass extinctions occurred every million years, and not every fifty million years or so, no stable ecosystems could arise.

The same lesson appears to apply to games. Periodic outbreaks of originality, and the corresponding extinction of certain game genres, are useful to drive the form forward, but the conservative intervals between these events are what serve to sustain the market. Refinement of design is as valuable a process as raw originality.

Sequels serve an important role in the development of games and one quite separate from the occasional ground-breaking games that reconfigure the chreodes in a part of the landscape of games.

The value of sequels is well known by publishers and developers alike, although they sometimes feel the need to publicly play down this conservatism and make claims to originality where no such claims are warranted or needed. Capcom completely recognizes this pattern and freely identifies their market strategy as founding new chreodes with original products (or exploiting existing chreodes with new games) and then refining and exploiting that chreode with a series of sequels that expand upon and polish the original game play. (Capcom does not use the term chreode, but the comparison is valid.)

Even the gaming press recognizes the value of sequels, albeit reluctantly. *Edge* magazine's review of *Warcraft III: Reign of Chaos* (Blizzard, 2002) takes an almost apologetic tack. It is apparent that they enjoy and think highly of the game, yet the author seems to feel the need to make excuses for the game's lack of originality [Edge02]. There is no need to apologize for games that fulfill the role of sequels perfectly; *Warcraft III* refines the gameplay from earlier installments in the series, adding polish and clarifying the core gameplay. The market success of the game serves only to underline the point that the audience was looking for more of the same, and Blizzard's conservatism is in line with the needs of the market. They know which chreode they are exploiting, and have no need (with this particular product) to attempt to define new pathways.

By comparison, games such as *Legacy of Kain: Soul Reaver 2* (Crystal Dynamics, 2001) and *Shadow Man: 2econd Coming* (Acclaim Studios Teesside, 2002) have been criticized for not capitalizing on the strengths of earlier games in their sequences. By striking out in new directions, they have expended much of their development resources trying to break out of their current chreode, rather than refining the strengths of the originals. (In these particular cases, technical issues relating to the architecture of the PlayStation 2 are likely to have been key factors, showing once again the impact new hardware can have on the shape of the games landscape, though it is notable that *Legacy of Kain: Defiance* (Crystal Dynamics, 2003) on Xbox once again redefines the focus of the *Kain* series.)

The value of sequels to the market is that their chreodes are clearly defined: original thinking might be required to fix apparent flaws in the initial outings, but refinement of the game design is a sufficient goal for any sequel. Originality should not be allowed to detract from the strengths of the previous game designs in the series. Considerable effort (and money) is sometimes spent fighting against the shape of the chreodes of the market, when it is rarely the sequels that are in a position to affect significant change.

CONCLUSION

Throughout this chapter we have compared evolutionary biology to the games industry with a somewhat cavalier attitude, and before closing it is worth pointing out a few critical points. First, this comparison is not rooted in science, but rather in an artistic viewpoint. We cannot claim to have proved anything by conflating organisms with games, merely to have explored the area of games more fully by virtue of a metaphorical construct (in this case chreodes).

The value of thinking in terms of chreodes is that it provides us a physical correlate for an otherwise ephemeral concept; we cannot see the shape of the games market, but imagining it mapped out by chreodes that represent the probability of a game following a particular design "canal" enables us to think about that market in new and interesting ways.

By using this perspective, we have been able to suggest that originality, if it is to flourish in a financially driven art form, should take advantage of new opportunities presented by breakthroughs in design and technology, but not stray too far from the commercially viable probabilistic real estate at the center of the market's chreodes. A place for rampant, uncontrolled originality exists (as the Japanese market demonstrates most clearly) but only on cheaper projects that can afford to gamble on their appeal.

We have also suggested that the shape of the market can be massively impacted by periodic "mass extinctions," when previously viable genres lose their sales appeal, or old design methods become invalidated by new approaches to core issues. Each mass extinction in the games market represents an opportunity for new and original games to flourish, and as suggested by the theory of punctuated equilibrium, between these periods of rapid change the shape of the landscape of games remains relatively static.

By using this perspective we can suggest that originality can totally reconfigure large areas of the chreodes describing the games market—but that anticipating how and when these changes occur is largely a black art. It is easy to make predictions as to the nature of the changes, but not to the specifics of the games that will make the changes. The lesson here, perhaps, is that publishers looking to be at the forefront of change in the industry should occasionally step outside of their existing brand chreodes and gamble on new design or technology, because the potential rewards for founding a whole new chreode branch has the capacity to exceed the value of mining out existing chreodes.

The obvious candidates for such originality (from a publisher's perspective) are licensed games, ironically the traditional reserve of the most conservative of designs. Because these games already have a certain expectation of audience from the appeal of the license itself, they are great opportunities to pursue originality. However, this is only the case when the license materials suggest a new form of game play. Forcing innovation on a license that would be better served by a more conservative approach is more likely to result in developmental resources being wasted trying to break out of a chreode that would serve the licensed game more than adequately.

Despite the continual call for originality, it remains the case that the whole of the landscape of games remains valid territory (at least until an extinction radically alters the shape of the terrain). Conservative approaches to design—the decision to work within an existing chreode rather than attempt to create a new one—are populating viable niches in the market, and all such niches are viable for occupation. The refinement of an existing chreode is as valuable a contribution to the evolution of games as the foundation of new pathways.

Computer games have been driven by originality, but sustained by conservatism. Looking at this process through the metaphor of chreodes, and specifically through parallels with the journey of life, provides tools for thinking about how and why this might be, some advice for sustaining the market's viability, and perhaps some scant clues to the future evolution of the art form.

Glossary

70% rule: The idea that for a certain game the player need only complete between two-thirds and three-quarters of the challenges on offer in order to advance. This is a design rubric intended to help the appeal of a game with a *Casual* (q.v.) audience.

AAA game: Any game that has been developed with sufficient budget and emphasis on quality to be considered to be of the highest quality in comparison to other games developed at the same time.

Action depth: The number of actions (or subactions) required to execute an outcome in a particular menu system.

Action space: A projection of all the possible activities that can be carried out within the game world, in terms of the actions a player can take and the contexts to which those actions apply.

Advocate: In terms of the game design process, a person who attempts to represent the needs of a particular *participant* (q.v.) in a game project, often a participant who otherwise has no direct voice in the game design process, such as a member of the audience.

Agent: Any autonomous or quasi-autonomous entity in the game world, such as a unit in an RTS game.

Agon: Games of competition. The class of games identified by Roger Caillois that are focused around competition and the desire to prove oneself in direct contest with others [Caillois58].

Alea: Games of chance. The class of games identified by Roger Caillois that, in their purest form, are focused around surrendering to chance or destiny so that one's own abilities are irrelevant in the outcome [Caillois58].

Artisan: One of the four patterns of behavior in temperament theory. The Artisan temperament is associated with a desire for freedom to act and the ability to make an impact.

Avatar: Another name for the player's character or game world representative.

Barrier: A feature specifically designed to mediate player progress, usually by blocking egress until the player acquires the mechanism to nullify or bypass the barrier.

Bennallack demographics: A set of demographic groups identified by Owain Bennallack [Bennallack02]. The categories are informal and based upon observation rather than data analysis.

Bipartite health: A health abstraction consisting of two separate components, such as health and armor, that are subject to different game rules.

Breadcrumbing: Laying a trail that the player can follow in order to complete the game. It can be a trail of items or a narrative trail.

Capricious logic: Any logical system that does not remain consistent.

Casual gamers: A hypothetical audience segment that is believed to buy and play fewer video games than the *Hardcore* (q.v.) audience.

Character expression: Allowing the player to express their own needs and personality through the capacity to define or alter the appearance or nature of the central character.

Chreode: A pathway of probability or channel in a particular landscape of probability. In terms of the game market, commercially successful genres represent chreodes.

Concept model: A framework taught to the player that assigns a single conceptual role to each control (e.g., "Action" or "Attack").

Conqueror: The archetype of the Type 1 play style, focused on challenge and fiero.

Contiguous world: A set of *domains* (q.v.) that are seamlessly joined together from the player's perspective, also referred to as a world.

Continuous environment: A set of *levels* (q.v.) that are seamlessly joined together from the player's perspective.

Contractile elasticity: A type of *elasticity* (q.v.) characterized by the freedom to throw out game design components.

Demographic game design: An approach to designing games whereby the design is tailored to meet the needs of target demographic groups.

Design-integrated narrative: Developing a game design and narrative design in parallel, such that both story and design issues are treated as separate aspects of the same process.

Dimensionality of control: A measure of the degree of complexity inherent in a control mechanism. It is expressed as a numerical figure, relating to the number of binary states or linear axes affected by controls.

Diplomatic: The skills associated with the *Idealist* temperament (q.v.), focused around empathy and abstracting in order to resolve differences.

Domain: A section of a game environment that is arranged as a hermetic "mini-world," usually with a thematic base, and containing a variety of different play activities.

Elasticity: The amount of freedom a game design has to alter during the expansion and contraction phases, that is, how flexible the game design is to unexpected changes during the development process.

Enfolded dimensions: In the context of *dimensionality of control* (q.v.), enfolded dimensions are those that have discrete states but do not represent a continuous dimension, for example, the discrete rotation of a piece in a puzzle game.

Expansile elasticity: A type of *elasticity* (q.v.) characterized by the freedom to incorporate new game design components.

Expressibility: Of an interface, referring to the degree of options and choices of action that the player has in the game world.

Extensive design: The inclusion of an exhaustive collection of features in a game design.

Fiero: The emotional feeling of triumph over adversity. It is often expressed in body language by raising your arms above your head.

Flow: The experience of devoting total concentration effortlessly upon a task, also known as "optimal experience" [Csikzentmihalyi90].

Functional key: An object in a game that is used to unlock a specific barrier to progress. A functional key need not literally be a key; it can be an item that "solves" a puzzle when it is used.

Funneling: Providing assistance to a player (especially through dialogue and narrative) in order to lead them back to the spine of the game.

Game world abstraction: The process of producing a description of the functionality of a game world, or the description resulting thereof.

Guardian: One of the four patterns of behavior in temperament theory. The Guardian temperament is associated with the need to belong and a sense of duty.

Hardcore gamers: A hypothetical audience segment that is associated with buying and playing a considerable volume of games. Also known as "Core gamers."

Hotspot: A point in the game world where the avatar can interact with the world in a meaningful way.

Housekeeping: A type of play activity concerned with repeated actions and either unconnected or tangentially connected to progress, such as collecting items in a platform game or customizing the player's avatar. It is primarily a process-oriented activity.

Idealist: One of the four patterns of behavior in temperament theory. The Idealist temperament is associated with a desire for unique identity and a search for meaning and significance.

Ilinx: Games of vertigo. The class of games identified by Roger Caillois that are focused around temporary annihilation of consciousness by surrendering to acceleration, dizziness, or any other tendency which is contrary to self-awareness [Caillois58].

Immersive menu: A selection mechanism equivalent to a menu that is imbedded into the game world and seamlessly integrated with it.

IP: Acronym for "intellectual property," which in the context of games usually refers to the characters, setting, and other details associated with a particular brand.

Learning curve: A conceptual measure of how hard it is to learn to control or use a game.

Levels: In the context of this book the term *level* is used to refer to discrete areas for play, as opposed to *continuous environments*, *domains*, and *contiguous worlds* (q.q.v.).

Lock-and-key puzzle: A basic puzzle that has only one solution—the addition or application of a particular object. This is a type of *functional key* (q.v.).

Logistical: The skills associated with the *Guardian* (q.v.) temperament, focused around optimization and standardization.

Ludus: Tending towards play regulated by rules. Roger Caillois considered games to vary between ludus at the most regulated extreme and *paidia* (q.v.).

Manager: The archetype of the Type 2 play style, focused on mastery and problem solving.

Market-oriented game design: A type of *demographic game design* (q.v.) in which the target demographics are chosen to maximize sales for a given game project.

Meta-rule (1):   In game design, a guideline that governs the construction of game rules, e.g., "the player's avatar cannot die" dictates that no rule can exist that would cause the player's avatar to die. Similarly, "greater risk should lead to greater reward" is a meta-rule suggesting a theme to be expressed in the game rules.

Meta-rule (2):   A game rule that applies in a separate sphere of application to the core game rules, such as a house rule employed by people playing a board or card game, especially where that rule expands beyond the usual scope of the game rules.

Mimicry: Games of simulation. The class of games identified by Roger Caillois that are focused around emulation—a make-believe experience in which the participant steps outside of conventional reality and pretends to be something else [Caillois58].

Overloading: Controls are considered to be overloaded when one key or button can be used to produce multiple different actions that do not share a common conceptual basis.

Paidia: Tending towards spontaneously creative play, unfettered by rules (as termed by Roger Caillois). Its polar opposite is *ludus* (q.v.). It is similar in some respects to *toyplay* (q.v.).

Participant (1): In terms of the game design process, a person involved in a particular game project, either during the development phase or as part of the audience for the game once it is released.

Participant (2): The archetype of the Type 4 play style, focused on enjoyment in a social context or emotional context.

Pathfinding: A type of play activity concerned with direct progress, especially finding the route to advance within the game. It is considered to be primarily an agonistic, goal-oriented activity.

Playground world: A game world in which the player is given immediate access to a large environment containing many different elements with which they can experiment at their leisure.

Playing in character: To take upon the specifically presented identity of a game character as a role and to play the game as if the player were this particular character. This approach is in some respects in opposition to *character expression* (q.v.).

"Pump and play": Of a coin-operated arcade game, characterized by allowing the player to keep playing the game provided they keep adding coins.

Rational: One of the four patterns of behavior in temperament theory. The Rational temperament is associated with a desire for knowledge and competence.

Resetting: Of a game world, referring to the tendency of the contents of the game world to return to their neutral state, usually when the player's avatar is not present.

Simplicity: Of an interface, supporting the required degree of actions in a minimal form.

Spine: A sequence of actions that allows a player to progress through the core game materials and reach the end of the game. It is of particular relevance to narrative-driven games, and not all types of game have a functional spine.

Strategic: The skills associated with the *Rational* temperament (q.v.), focused around the capacity to anticipate problems and to determine how to reach an imagined future state.

Symbolic keys: Trophies within a game that are awarded at the same time as the player acquires access to new areas.

Tactical: The skills associated with the *Artisan* temperament (q.v.), focused around the capacity to swiftly read context and react appropriately.

Tight design: The situation whereby all of the features in a game design support the core concept.

Tool key: An item in a game that gives the player's avatar new abilities, which can in turn be used to overcome barriers in the game world.

Toyplay: Unstructured play within a game; play that does not consist of set goals or objectives (except those that the player sets for themselves).

Wanderer: The archetype of the Type 3 play style, focused on seeking a unique experience and having fun without being hindered by difficulty.

World: See *contiguous world* (q.v.).

References

A condensed version of the Chapter 1 material appeared as "My Karma Ran Over Your Dogma," first published in *Develop*, issue 27 (April 2003).

Chapter 4 is based upon "Demographic Game Design: How to Make Game Design as Important as Marketing," a brochure published by International Hobo Ltd. in 2004.

Chapter 7 based upon "Golden Rules of Interface Design," first published in *Develop*, issue 11 (October 2001) and issue 12 (November–December 2001).

[Ackerman98] Ackerman, J., "Dinosaurs Take Wing: New fossil finds from China provide clues to the origin of birds." *National Geographic* 194 (1998): pp. 74–99.

[Adams01] Adams, Ernest. "Dogma 2001." Available online at *http://www.gamasutra.com/features/20010129/adams_01.htm*, February 2, 2001.

[Alvarez80] Alvarez, L.W., Alvarez, W., Asaro, F., and Michel, H.V., "Extraterrestrial cause for the Cretaceous-Tertiary extinction." *Science* 208 (1980): pp. 1095–1108.

[Bennallack02] Bennallack, Owain, "Post-Tribal Punters." *The Market for Computer & Videogames* (Issue 186, May 17, 2002): pp. 53–55.

[Berens00] Berens, Linda V., *Understanding Yourself and Others: An Introduction to Temperament*. Telos Publications, 2000.

[Burgess91] Burgess, G.H., *Shark Attack and the International Shark Attack File*. ISAF, 1991.

[Caillois58] Caillois, Roger, *Les Jeux et Les Hommes*. Gallimard, 1958.

[CAPT02] *Estimated Frequencies of the Types in the United States Population*. Center for Applications of Psychological Type, 2002.

[Costikyan98] Costikyan, Greg, "A Requiem for the Hill or I Dreamt I Saw Charles Roberts Last Night." Available online at *http://www.costik.com/arequiemfo-ed-1.html*, January 27, 2005.

[Craig03] "The Myers-Briggs Personality Types (according to Craig)." Available online at *http://209.15.29.56/myersbriggs/personhome.htm*, November 24, 2003.

[Csikzentmihalyi90] Csikzentmihalyi, Mihaly, *Flow: The Psychology of Optimal Experience*. HarperPerennial, 1990.

[Donovan03] Donovan, Tristan, "Game Developer Reports: Top 20 Publishers." *Game Developer* (September 2003).

[Edge02] Author uncredited, "Warcraft III: Reign of Chaos (Review)." *Edge* 114 (2002): p. 91.

[Ekman03] Ekman, P., *Emotions Revealed*. Times Books Henry Hold and Company, 2003.

[Falstein01] Falstein, Noah. "The 400 Project." Available online at *http://www.theinspiracy.com/400_project.htm*, January 12, 2005.

[GameState03] "Focus: The Best Games Ever vs. The Biggest Selling Games Ever." *Game State* (issue 2, 2003).

[Gamewire04] Thornquist, Rick, "Klaus Teuber Interview." Available online at *http://www. gamefest.com/news/feature_detail/1375_0_3_0_C/*, August 2004.

[Gould86] Gould, Stephen Jay, "Play it again, life." *Natural History* (February 1986): pp. 18–26.

[Gould93] Gould, Stephen Jay and Eldredge, Niles, "Punctuated equilibrium comes of age." *Nature* 366 (1993): pp. 223–227.

[Gould95] Gould, Stephen Jay, "Ladders and Cones: Constraining evolution by canonical icons." Taken from *Hidden Histories of Science*, Granta Publications Ltd, 1995.

[Guinness05] *Guinness World Records 2005*. Guinness, 2005.

[HireGolden03] "A Brief History of Myers-Briggs Typology." Accessed online at *http://www.hiregolden.com/preemploymentservices/typology.htm*, November 24, 2003.

[History05] The History Channel, "The History of Toys and Games: Inventors." Available online at *http://www.historychannel.com/exhibits/toys/index.html*, January 14, 2004.

[Hoyle46] Morehead, Albert H. and Mott-Smith, Geoffrey, *Hoyle's Rules of Games*. Plume, 1946.

[IGN04] "Graphs: Prince of Persia. Ubisoft's would-be blockbuster sells worse than expected." *IGN*, February 2, 2004. Available online at *http://ps2.ign.com/articles/488/488969p1.html*, January 25, 2005.

[Keirsey78] Bates, M. and Keirsey, D., *Please Understand Me: Character & Temperament Types*. Prometheus Nemesis, 1978.

[Klov93] Originally by Mike Hughey with contributions by Jeff Hansen, revised 1993 by Jonathon Deitch, revised 1998–1999 by Brian L. Johnson, *The Killer List of Videogames*. 1993, 1998–1999, 2000. Available online at *www.klov.com*, June 2003.

[KYT03] "Know Your Type: Personality Testing for Groups and Individuals." Available online at *http://www.knowyourtype.com/careers.html*, November 24, 2003.

[Lazzaro04] Lazzaro, Nicole, "Why We Play Games: 4 Keys to Emotion without Story." Presentation at GDC 2004.

[Leinfellner03] Leinfellner, Richard, "Globalisation: Friend or Foe?" Presentation at GPDC, October 8, 2003.

[Megagames03] "Who is a Hardcore Gamer?" Available online at *http://www.megagames.com/hardcoregamer.html*, November 24, 2003.

[Parker03] Parker, Nick, "New Platforms, Niche Markets." Presentation at GPDC, October 8, 2003.

[Pathways03a] Personality Pathways, "Introduction to Myers-Briggs Personality Type & the MBTI." Available online at *http://www.personalitypathways.com/MBTI_intro.html*, November 24, 2003.

[Pathways03b] Personality Pathways, "What is your Myers-Briggs Personality Type?" Available online at *http://www.personalitypathways.com/type_inventory.html*, November 24, 2003.

[Pelley00] Pelley, John W. (Ph.D.), *Implications of Personality Type for Teaching and Learning*, Texas Tech University Health Sciences Center, 2000.

[Penguin79] Parlett, David, *The Penguin Book of Card Games*. Penguin, 1979.

[Rouse99] Rouse, Richard (III), "Everything Old is New Again: Remaking Computer Games." *Computer Graphics* Volume 33, Number 2 (May 1999). Available online at *http://www.paranoidproductions.com/gamingandgraphics/fourth.html*, January 24, 2005.

[Rudnik05] "Civilization." Available online at *http://nudnik.ru/entry/3042*, January 27, 2005.

[Schick91] Schick, Lawrence, *Heroic Worlds*. Prometheus Books, 1991.

[Thurrott04] Thurrott, Paul, "Halo 2 Poised for Record Sales." *Windows IT Pro*. Available online at *http://www.winnetmag.com/Windows/Article/ArticleID/44453/44453.html*, November 8, 2004.

[Trivial05] "Trivial Pursuit: The Most Popular Trivia Game in the World." Available online at *http://www.trivialpursuit.com/trivialpursuit/news_pr031403.html*, January 12, 2005.

[USDI00] *Connecting Personality Types with Careers and Jobs*. U.S. Department of the Interior, 2000.

[Waddington57] Waddington, C.H., *The Strategy of Genes*. George Allen and Unwin Ltd, 1957.

[Watt03] Watt, Keith, Untitled essay. Available online at *http://www.public.asu.edu/~pythagor/Keith502%5B1%5D.doc*, November 24, 2003.

[Wellspring03] Wellspring Consulting, "Insights." Available online at *http://www.wellspring-consulting.com/insights.htm*, November 24, 2003.

[Wikipedia04] "Species." *Wikipedia*. Available online at *http://en.wikipedia.org/wiki/Species*, January 12, 2005.

[Yoshimura97] Yoshimura, Noboru and Anderson, Phillip, *Inside the Kaisha: Demystifying Japanese Business Behavior*. Harvard Business School Press, 1997.

[Yukino01] Yukino, Yoshi, "My Sweet Valentine." Available online at *http://www.freetype.net/features/games/tokimemo/index.html*, February 13, 2001.

Index